UA
646.85
.N37   NATO's northern
1985   allies

$42.50

DATE			

NATO'S NORTHERN ALLIES

Other Research Volumes from
The Atlantic Institute for International Affairs

*BANKS AND THE BALANCE OF PAYMENTS: PRIVATE LENDING
IN THE INTERNATIONAL ADJUSTMENT PROCESS*
  Benjamin J. Cohen, in collaboration with Fabio Basagni

*NEW LIMITS ON EUROPEAN AGRICULTURE:
POLITICS AND THE COMMON AGRICULTURAL POLICY*
  François Duchêne, Edward Szczpanik, and Wilfrid Legg

THE INTERNAL FABRIC OF WESTERN SECURITY
  Gregory Flynn and Josef Joffe, Yves Laulan, Laurence Martin,
  and Stefano Silvestri

THE PUBLIC AND ATLANTIC DEFENSE
  edited by Gregory Flynn and Hans Rattinger

THE FUTURE OF BERLIN
  edited by Martin J. Hillenbrand

*NATIONAL INDUSTRIAL STRATEGIES AND THE WORLD
ECONOMY*
  edited by John Pinder

*TOWARDS INDUSTRIAL DEMOCRACY: EUROPE, JAPAN AND
THE UNITED STATES*
  edited by Benjamin C. Roberts

JAPANESE DIRECT FOREIGN INVESTMENT
  Sueo Sekiguchi

NATO'S NORTHERN ALLIES

The National Security Policies of
Belgium, Denmark, the
Netherlands, and Norway

Edited by

Gregory Flynn

An Atlantic Institute for International Affairs
Research Volume

ROWMAN & ALLANHELD
PUBLISHERS

CROOM HELM
LONDON & SYDNEY

ROWMAN & ALLANHELD

Published in the United States of America in 1985
by Rowman & Allanheld, Publishers
(a division of Littlefield, Adams & Company)
81 Adams Drive, Totowa, New Jersey 07512

Copyright © 1985 by the Atlantic Institute for International Affairs

Library of Congress Cataloging-in-Publication Data
Main entry under title:

NATO's northern allies.

(An Atlantic Institute for International Affairs
research volume)
    1. Europe, Northern—National security—Addresses,
essays, lectures.   2. North Atlantic Treaty Organization
—Addresses, essays, lectures.   I. Flynn, Gregory.
II. Series.
UA646.85.N37   1985   355'.03304   85-14510
ISBN 0-8476-7444-4

British Library Cataloguing in Publication Data

NATO's northern allies: the national security policies of
Belgium, Denmark, the Netherlands and Norway.—(An
Atlantic Institute for International Affairs research
volume)

    1. Europe—National security
    I. Flynn, Gregory II. Series
    327'.094   UA646
ISBN 0-7099-1051-7

85 86 87 / 10 9 8 7 6 5 4 3 2 1

Printed in the United States of America

Contents

Tables and Figures

Figure

Preface

Over the last decade, the countries on the northern periphery of NATO have conducted intense debate on Alliance policy and membership. Belgium, Denmark, the Netherlands, and Norway—all founder members of the Alliance—have experienced high levels of domestic dissent in recent years, in contrast to the high levels of consensus characterized by the earlier postwar period. The study on which this book is based examines this change in public opinion and its implications for the Alliance.

This is the second book by the Atlantic Institute for International Affairs on the internal fabric of the Atlantic Alliance. It focuses on the interaction between domestic considerations and security policy priorities in Alliance countries in order to understand better the factors producing conflict or agreement about Alliance policy. This approach was particularly appropriate in examining the evolution of opinion during recent years in the four countries studied.

The Institute collaborated with each of the following national institutions: the Danish Institute for International Studies in Copenhagen, the Netherlands Institute for International Relations "Clingendael" in The Hague, the Norwegian Institute for International Affairs in Oslo, and the Center for Strategic Studies at the University of Leuven. The authors are or have been affiliated with each of these institutions and twice collaborated with outside experts to evaluate the manuscripts. The first meeting was held in November 1982 outside Copenhagen with individuals representing major political tendencies in the four countries and included several experts on Alliance policy. The second meeting with academic and policy specialists from the four countries took place in March 1983 outside Oslo. The study was thus exposed to maximum useful criticism and interchange prior to its emergence in final form.

This book deserves careful reading by all those who are convinced they have understood what has been transpiring in the countries under discussion or in the Atlantic Alliance in recent years. It demonstrates that the conventional wisdom generated by increased public debate has in fact dramatically oversimplified causes and effects. While important changes have taken place, the evolution of events in these four differs little from countries like Germany. Understanding how much of the phenomenon was structural and how much issue specific, how much secular and how much cyclical, is critical to assessing prospects for the future. This book provides the basis for that understanding.

I want to thank the Ford Foundation for the generous grant that made this project possible.

Richard D. Vine

Introduction

GREGORY FLYNN

For most observers of the Atlantic Alliance, the period since 1979 has been one of the most critical in its existence. Having decided to modernize its medium-range nuclear arsenal in response to the arrival of strategic parity and the SS-20, and simultaneously to negotiate with the Soviet Union in an attempt to obviate the need for the modernization, the Allies entered a period of seemingly unparalleled acrimony, both at home and between one another. The Alliance had known difficult periods before, but this time it was not the capacity of individual countries to make policy that was being called into question; it was their ability to execute collective decisions. The domestic consensus so critical to the conduct of consistent foreign and defense policy in modern democracies appeared to be crumbling. The Alliance suffered because policy consultations were reduced to discussions about what was domestically acceptable.

Analysts and government officials alike have asked themselves whether the phenomenon of the past few years represents a popular revolution that requires a change in some of the fundamental assumptions on which NATO strategy is based. The nuclear protest that spilled into the streets during the early 1980s was indeed greater than anything previously seen. For many, this indicated a long-overdue democratization of defense policy within member countries of the Alliance. Since nuclear risk is shared by all, was it not natural, even inevitable, that those whose lives are at stake have a more direct say as to how they are to be protected? The only response to the phenomenon could be more open decision making and a sharp reduction in the role played by nuclear weapons in Western deterrent strategy. There were others who did not believe the phenomenon represented a secular change in the popular predisposition to leave security questions to political leaders. Even this group, however, never denied that something of significance had changed; they were simply unconvinced about the precise nature of the phenomenon and, above all, about the antidotes being offered.

In addition to the questions about public opinion and nuclear strategy, there was a second debate arising from events following NATO's double-track decision of December 1979. The two debates naturally interacted, but there were indeed two separate issues involved. The second debate focused on what it meant for the Allies to take a collective decision and then to discover, to borrow a phrase from Stanley Hoffman, that the balance did not balance at home. To what extent did participation in a unanimous Alliance policy decision bind an ally to its faithful execution, and to what extent could domestic difficulties associated with the execution of such a decision justify postponement of the day of reckoning or a reversal of policy? For many, particularly in Washington, willingness to execute a decision jointly arrived at was a test of loyalty to the Alliance. Political leaders were elected not only to make themselves popular but also to take difficult decisions in the larger interests of their nations and the alliances in which they were engaged. Those who failed to do so were undermining the very foundations of mutual trust on which an alliance is built and providing an opening for the Soviet Union to manipulate the relationship between Europe and America. There were others, and not only in Europe, who considered that the issues involved in the nuclear debate were so important that, unanimous decision or not, to make deployment a test case of Alliance solidarity was to risk turning revolt against a specific Alliance policy into revolt against the Alliance as a whole. Moreover, no government could be expected to sign its own death warrant by blindly executing a decision "known" to be opposed by a majority of its population, no matter how great the importance of Allied unity.

Each of these debates had the effect of focusing attention on the four countries under study in this book—Belgium, Denmark, the Netherlands, and Norway. Not exclusively, of course, and not even primarily, since concern was above all directed toward the Federal Republic of Germany. But the nuclear allergy that registered all over Western Europe, with the exception of France, seemed to be particularly acute in these four countries, perhaps because here the effect of the allergy on government policy was most marked. The Netherlands even bequeathed its name to a new dreaded disease: Hollanditis, supposedly the worst form of nuclear pacifism. Denmark was chosen for a similar honor, as Denmarkization came to connote chronic underpayment of one's share of the collective defense burden, the most pernicious form of freeloading. At least as interesting, however, is the fact that these four countries were not only the object of increased attention by others, but were themselves taking a serious look at what it meant to be an ally, and they were beginning to exert more influence on Allied decision-making processes than ever before.

So there is good reason to examine these four countries, for they have been key actors in an Alliance trauma from which lessons must be learned. Moreover, there exists a critical gap in the manifold studies that have appeared on the Atlantic Alliance and its perennial fight for survival against the odds of history. For, plowed as that terrain is, there is no serious study of these four countries as allies, let alone of the ways in which they are evolving as polities, or of the factors that will condition their security-policy priorities during the coming years. They have been studied individually, but usually in the form of longer historical analyses of their foreign policies or of shorter treatments of current security-policy problems as seen from Oslo or The Hague. And there have been studies of regional security problems relevant to one or more countries as in those on the northern flank, or on Nordic security questions, but there has been no work that provides an adequate backdrop for understanding the positions of these countries over the past few years or a good analysis of those positions and their meaning for these countries' future profiles as allies.

The project that resulted in this book has had two main objectives. The first was to analyze the particular choices made by these four countries during the recent period of Alliance difficulties and the factors that produce these choices. This would help us to determine whether there has been some pattern common to the four and to explore whether certain characteristics tend to distinguish these countries from others in the Alliance that have experienced similar levels of acrimony, or whether, in fact, they have simply been part of a larger phenomenon in Western Europe. The second objective was to examine the increased impact these countries have had on Alliance policy over the past few years—whether this is likely to continue, and whether there is need for the Alliance to balance its general interests with those of these particular allies.

To this end, we have conducted an in-depth study of each of the countries and two comparative analyses of all four: one on the dynamics of acrimony and one on the dynamics of Alliance policy making. To obtain the maximum basis for comparative analysis, the country studies are presented according to a common outline that seeks to highlight factors relevant to their common experiences as allies and allow sufficient latitude to bring out particular national characteristics. Each investigates the historical roots of the decision to align, the existence of certain enduring security preferences, and the ways in which these two have been reconciled in policy. The studies then examine the basic patterns of policy priorities during the period in which defense policy was not contentious at home. The bulk of each chapter then looks at the factors responsible for promoting change in the way each country has formulated security priorities and at the ways in which disputes have been played out in domestic political life. Finally, the studies analyze the broad outline of future priorities, the extent to which these are likely to be in harmony with Alliance requirements, and the extent to which they are likely to be a continuing source of contention at home.

The basic underlying thesis of the work presented in this book is one that is unlikely to confirm most peoples' preconceptions. The analyses popularized by those seeking to make a political impact have almost always oversimplified a set of processes frequently long in gestation and complex in cause and effect. Those who seek the proof of a revolution and a description of its origins will not find it here. Nor will those people be vindicated who have been convinced that nothing at all has changed and that no adjustments need be made in the way we go about formulating defense policy. There has been no public upheaval and yet there have been changes that must be acknowledged and to which we should adapt. The failure to do so will mean strengthening the phenomenon present during the past few years.

What has that phenomenon been if not a groundswell of popular revolt against nuclear risk? The studies presented in this book confirm work that has been done elsewhere on public opinion and defense.[1] As Josef Joffe demonstrates, what we have been witnessing over the past few years has much more to do with the functioning of our political systems than with publics at large. Acrimony there has been, but, above all, political acrimony and politically driven dissent. This is not to argue that publics have not been participants in the process, but that they have been the followers, not the leaders, the byproducts and not the catalysts. The phenomenon has above all been a repoliticization of defense.

Each country study illustrates well the roots of controversy that are to be found in a combination of certain structural changes in the way political systems deal with security issues and of several changes in the international environment. Each of the countries has distinct particularities, but the pattern is relatively clear, and it is the same as that found elsewhere in Western Europe. The structural political changes all have affected the way which political consensus is managed. In Denmark and Belgium there has been a new political dynamic at work since the early 1970s, created by the fragmentation of political parties and coalition governments with ambiguous governing mandates. This has heightened the bargaining power of minority opinion and made for weak governments incapable of decisive action on a widening range of controversial issues, including defense. In the Netherlands, and Norway as well, parliaments and parties have asserted a role in a domain previously reserved for a much smaller group of political elites. As Jan Siccama has described for the Dutch case, one finds a fundamental change in the bargaining mechanisms among political elites from different parties and in their relationship with their respective bases as the result of the "depillarization" of Dutch society. In the Norwegian case, a similar breakdown of party discipline seems clear, above all in the relationship between the center and the periphery of the Labour Party after a long period in government. The consequence in all cases has been that the management of consensus has become more difficult because of a reluctance to compromise in the name of national interest. In fact, the very nature of that national interest has become the subject of political debate.

These structural political changes coincided with the fact that changes in the international context increased the natural division of political elites over security policy. The global economic downturn and the decline

---

1. Gregory Flynn and Hans Rattinger, eds., *The Public and Atlantic Defense* (Totowa, N.J.: Rowman and Allanheld, 1985).

of détente at the end of the 1970s, as well as the need to take decisions about the strategic consequences of parity and the arrival of several new technologies all contributed to this new international context. The problems were particularly acute in the countries under study in this book, above all for the Social Democratic and Labour parties, which had dominated a great deal of recent political life in all four. As Joffe points out, the combination of economic stringency and an unclear vision of the future East-West relationship meant that too many basic principles underlying too many strands of Social Democratic policy were being challenged at once. Moreover, populations clearly were in no mood to continue to support Social Democratic governments incapable of bringing budget deficits and spending priorities under control. They were turned out of office in all four countries between September 1981 and October 1982. The clear popular predisposition against nuclear weapons became a tempting target in the battle for electoral survival.

This was the phenomenon and the factors that produced it, the source of the dissensus within the four countries studied in this book. There was nothing unique about the four, however, since both the structural/political, and the environmental factors were operative in countries other than those considered here, particularly in the Federal Republic of Germany. The four are nevertheless good case studies that demonstrate the more general rule.

More unique was the impact these countries have had on the conduct of Alliance policy over the past few years. The four must be distinguished from their larger allies, such as the Federal Republic, if only because their larger brethren, and especially the Germans, are always central to the debate on every major Alliance issue (some would even argue the cause in the case of Germany). It is more unusual for the debate in these countries to play such a central role in Alliance deliberations. Much of this stemmed from the circular impact that debates in these countries had on the one within the Federal Republic, and vice versa, through mechanisms such as Scandilux—the Social Democratic caucus initiated among the parties of these four countries, which has links to sister parties in Germany and Britain. But two of the four countries, the Netherlands and Belgium, were slated for deployment of the new NATO missiles and the interaction of the political debates between these two countries and their Scandilux partners was alone adequate to heighten the importance of national choices for Alliance outcomes.

In discussion about the problems of decision making and influence within the Alliance, most people have chosen to focus on the issue of participation in an actual decision, and the modalities thereof, as the key to generating a sense of involvement in a process where the smaller allies normally feel marginal. This is one of the reasons why many attached such importance to the fact that the NATO double-track decision was a collective one that imposed responsibilities on those who participated in its original drafting. The possibility for influencing deliberations toward a different outcome had existed within the councils when the policy was being developed, and it had not been used. Each of the Social Democratic parties in question in this book had been in government during the period in which the double-track decision was being elaborated.

But this direction of analysis misses an important point. Influence, at least the constraining influence we are concerned with here, does not stem from participation in a decision but from participation in the execution of the decision. In the case of NATO's nuclear-force modernization, had several of the nondeploying countries decided to work against the double-track decision prior to December 1979, the Alliance would surely have made such a decision among the group of concerned countries—those scheduled to deploy if deployment became necessary. The group of concerned countries' approach was that which had been used to decide the initial deployment of tactical nuclear weapons in Europe in the late 1950s. Yet even if this approach had been used in 1979, it is certain that the problems experienced thereafter would not have been much different. Difficulties would have existed in at least Belgium, the Netherlands, and the Federal Republic. Even the Scandilux caucus would probably have existed, since its formulation was an initiative of the Dutch Labour party in search of support.

There is, of course, a case to be made that once a country has participated in a joint decision there must be an overwhelming reason not to execute it. This would indeed be especially true for parties in office when a decision is made, who later find it convenient in opposition to complicate the execution of the very decision to which they had earlier agreed. The argument gains additional force when the grounds for nonexecution stem more from party political considerations than from any fundamental change in factors that produced the decision in the first place. But this debate is beside our main issue, which concerns the relationship of these countries to the formulation of Alliance policy. The keys to that influence were their centrality to the execution of the deployment side of the decision, and the feeling of the opposition that it could gain electorally *and* make a difference in the final outcome.

How repeatable is this convergence of circumstances? The studies in this book clearly show that the acrimony was issue-specific. There was no breakdown in the broader security-policy consensus in these four countries. The Alliance retains strong public and political support, as does the need to maintain a balance of power with the East and a strong defense. The issue concerned only the particular double-track decision and NATO's nuclear strategy. There is little reason to believe that any policy issue other than a nuclear one could ever produce the same level of emotional dissent.

The only other two potentially controversial policy areas would be out-of-area questions and new conventional strategies, based on the premise of striking deep into enemy territory. Discussion of the latter runs into a strong predisposition that NATO strategy must be visibly defensive, and discussion of the former runs into an equally strong predisposition that these are questions for individual allies, not for the Alliance. However, these are not issues of domestic controversy in the countries studied; the strong predispositions are multipartisan. Thus, there is little possibility of them participating in an Alliance decision and becoming key to its execution; dissent would be registered earlier on. To begin with, therefore, the potential for another negative tug-of-war between these four countries (and some others) and Alliance councils will be intimately linked to the future need to take decisions on nuclear issues.

Two additional sets of factors that provide clues to the future possibilities for acrimony and influence—and for the types of adjustment within the Alliance that could minimize those possibilities—can be drawn from the studies in this book. The first concerns the structural political fallout from recent debates. As pointed out above, one of the reasons why these debates were possible was the fact that defense decision making, at least for major policy decisions, had become more open as a result of the breakdown of traditional bargaining mechanisms among political elites. A second reason has been the fragile nature of the coalitions governing these countries for roughly the past decade. Both of these factors will remain present for the foreseeable future. These factors alone do not promote dissent, but they do provide a context in which minority voices can more easily exert an influence on government policy.

Minority protest is likely to be minimal if the nuclear issue is not on the agenda, and unless major political figures decide to use the issue for their own political purposes. In other words, minority dissent alone will make more noise than difference. But there is one additional element that will also play an important role here: The need to make a decision and defend it serves to crystallize opinion and dissent. To the extent that governments must defend policy decisions before parliaments, the chances for mobilizing opposition increase. There is a question, for instance, as to whether events in Norway and Denmark would have taken the path they did had the two countries not been dealing with issues of formal national policy, as opposed to simply a decision by others eventually to deploy new nuclear systems in several Allied countries. In the absence of a serious shakedown of the political systems in these countries leading to more stable governing majorities, there may be a case, as Johan Holst argues, for avoiding to the extent possible the need to turn Alliance issues into issues of national policy in these countries.

The second set of factors concerns the relationship between arms control and defense in Alliance policy. It is clear that one of the reasons why the NATO double-track decision created so much controversy was the very linkage between arms control and nuclear modernization. The initial logic was clear enough, but it was predictable that the Alliance would end up by placing a reverse leverage on itself, with its conduct at the Geneva negotiations coming under greater scrutiny than that of the Soviet Union. The NATO decision placed arms control and nuclear modernization as tradeoffs for one another, and this is a tradeoff where inevitably popular and political sentiment will always be on the same side of the issue. Arms control will always be preferred to more, or modernized, nuclear weapons if the question is posed in these terms. The reality, however, is frequently that one may need both changes in force structure and arms control, not one *or* the other, because each accomplishes a different objective.

The specific lesson of formal double-tracking has surely been learned, but the risk is that the crucial underlying lesson will be overlooked. Weapons never make sense in the absence of a context, and the objective of linking modernization and arms control was in fact to provide the necessary context, to hold out the possibility that this decision did not simply mean an acceleration to the arms race. The objective was correct even if the means were incorrect, and the danger is that the two will be confused.

As is pointed out throughout all of the studies in this book, there is an overwhelming commitment on the part of the populations in these countries (which is widely the case elsewhere as well) to minimize the East-West confrontation and diminish the role of military force in providing security. Nuclear weapons become tolerable only to the extent that political leaders are convincing in their efforts to reduce the likelihood of nuclear war. The solution is not to reject the realities of the nuclear world, but to have a strategy to transcend those realities. When an adjustment to the West's nuclear posture becomes necessary—and this is inevitable—the only way to avoid such debilitating controversy as occurred in the past few years is to make sure this adjustment forms part of a long-run vision of the East-West relationship that promises more than perpetual confrontation.

The work in this book thus leads to the conclusion that the end of the 1970s and early 1980s represents a very particular convergence of circumstances, both in terms of what produced political dissent in the four countries and in terms of what produced the special influence on Alliance deliberations. At the level of political systems and Alliance policy, we witnessed what Josef Joffe calls the "cyclical burst," rather than the "secular break." The preconditions obviously could once again unite to provoke a replay, but the lessons from the recent episodes indicate clearly how to minimize that possibility. The key will be whether Allied leaders are capable of developing a strategy for coping with Soviet power that tempers confrontation with cooperation. Security requirements must not be allowed to become a pseudonym for reinforcement of a dangerous status quo.

To the extent that this is understood, the relationship between the smaller northern European members of NATO and the Alliance is likely to be no more or less tumultuous than in the past. The four will continue to seek more influence in Alliance councils and will often refuse to accept the levels of responsibility this implies. They will always want their own particular security needs guaranteed by the Alliance but will avoid uncomfortable involvement in wider issues. The Alliance, for its part, will always want these countries to bear a greater share of the overall burden of collective Western defense. The larger allies will be loath to relinquish the control that a greater input from these countries would inevitably mean. Such are the relations between uneven allies.

NATO'S NORTHERN ALLIES

1

The Passive Constrained: Belgian Security Policy in the 1980s

LUC REYCHLER

Introduction

The complexities of Belgium as a country are not always easy to grasp. A small, businesslike state located at the center of Europe, it has only 10 million inhabitants. It is an important center in international, diplomatic, economic, and strategic networks. For many, Belgium connotes Flanders fields, or the Battle of the Bulge; for others, the headquarters of the European Community and NATO, the Concours Queen Elisabeth, or the strife between the francophone Walloons and Dutch-speaking Flemings. It is a country whose national self-definition also finds itself the object of perpetual revision.

Overall, Belgium is one of the most economically sensitive and vulnerable countries in the world. In 1981 the Gross National Product was 3,607 billion Belgian francs. The export of goods and services amounted to 2,685 billion, or 74 percent of the GNP; 2838 billion was paid for imports, or 79.1 percent of the GNP.[1] Belgium is dependent on other countries for 84 percent of its energy supplies. It is not surprising, therefore, that economics play a very significant role in the Belgian threat perception.

The provision of external security has been entrusted in the postwar period to two organizations: the European Community and the Atlantic Alliance. The European Community is instrumental in defending

Without the fine research work of Mr. Jorg Leenaards and the diligent typing of Ms. Magda Verboomen, this chapter could not have been delivered on time. I am also grateful to Marc Riga, Annick Boeykens, Rudy Vranckx, Lieven De Winter, and Johan Ackaert for their assistance.

Belgian economic and political interests in the East-West, North-South, and West-West contexts; the Atlantic Alliance looks after Belgium's defensive interests in the East-West military conflict.

This chapter will deal primarily with Belgium's position in the Atlantic Alliance. To understand this relationship, it is critical to recognize the importance Belgium attaches to the nonmilitary aspects of its security and the framework chosen for providing this security. The two form an interdependent whole.

In 1949 membership in NATO was considered the best possible course for Belgian postwar policy. Today, in spite of the existence of a considerable range of criticism, NATO has retained this support. The Atlantic Alliance is generally considered a sine qua non for the realization of national security in Belgium. Nonetheless, there is no longer the unquestioning support of the Alliance that there once was. Many changes have reshaped the way that Belgium looks at its national defense.

To gain a better understanding of the evolution of Belgium's attitudes toward its security and the Alliance, it is useful to look first at the country's pre-NATO history. An examination of the past reveals that the road toward alignment was long and painful. Bitterly learned lessons about the fallacies of neutrality and appeasement encouraged a close association with other countries of the Western world, to ensure "security and prosperity."

From the time of the creation of the North Atlantic Alliance until the mid-1970s, support for Alliance policies was based on a broad national consensus. The nature of this consensus will be described in the second part of this chapter by examining three key events during the 1950s and 1960s: Germany's entrance into the Alliance, the installation of nuclear weapons on Belgian territory, and the transfer of NATO headquarters. The country's defense efforts and public attitudes toward NATO will also be discussed.

The third part of this chapter will look at present security-policy difficulties that are attributed to a confluence of several factors. Most involve changes that have taken place in the political process, in the economic condition of the country, or in the perception of the security scene. To understand best the interaction of these three as cause and effect in the evolution of the Belgian security policy, the section looks first at those changes that have taken place in the domestic political and economic context. Some ways in which these changes have been reflected in actual policy debates are then discussed.

In conclusion, the chapter profiles Belgium's future as an ally in the 1980s. It seeks to pinpoint those factors that will have greatest influence and to indicate the general orientations Belgian policies can be expected to follow in the coming years.

The Road Toward Alignment

Traditionally, Belgium has been the centerpiece of Europe and among the most attractive spoils of war. Its protected harbors, its central location vis à vis other European countries, and the presence of well-trained and enterprising inhabitants has made it a power asset. The strategic location of Belgium frequently made it a pathway for foreign armies and an ideal bridgehead for military forces coming from England or, as is now the case, from the United States.

As demonstrated in two world wars, Belgium is vulnerable to attack from all sides. It has some natural obstacles, such as a short coast on the North Sea and the rough wooded areas of the Ardennes in the southeast. Although some additional defense capacity is provided by the Maas and Schelde rivers, several canals, and the possibility of flooding extended areas in the western part of the country, these obstacles would not significantly slow down a powerful adversary.[2]

How have the Belgian decision makers coped with these strategic challenges? It was the generally favorable attitude of the British toward Belgium that allowed it to challenge the existing order and break into the European system.[3] After the revolt of 1830 had destroyed the main barrier constructed in 1815 against future French attempts at expansionism, disagreements arose among the European powers as to what Belgium's future role should be in the European balance of power.

At the London Conference of 1839, a compromise was achieved: Belgium would continue to play its role as a buffer state (against the French), and its foreign policy would be checked by the creation of *enforced neutrality*. During the rest of the 19th century, different interpretations of the implications of the internationally recognized "neutrality status" provided a long struggle between those in Belgium who considered a national defense effort necessary and those who considered that Belgian security was guaranteed by the major powers. There was great resistance in the Belgian Parliament to planned defense expenditures, but the king relentlessly insisted on military strength. The king's recognition of the importance for a small power of adequate military strength was a key influence in Belgium's foreign policy. It was a belief that was to be upheld by his heirs against many parliamentary attacks.

The German invasion of 1914 brought the status of enforced neutrality to an end. One of Belgium's main war aims called for a revision of Point IV of the Treaties of 1839, in order to allow Belgium to be neutral by its own accord; that is, it desired its independence to be guaranteed, but only in a manner compatible with full Belgian sovereignty. The Treaty of Versailles provided Belgium with the control it sought over its status. During the ensuing period the country adopted a security policy based not only on its membership in the League of Nations but also on a search for equally close relations with England and France. Belgium thus tried to combine a *universal* and a *regional* approach to security.

In 1919 the Belgian Government approached France and Britain. Although it failed to obtain a bilateral pact with England, its negotiations with France achieved some success. In 1920 the two countries signed a military accord. This agreement did not imply a military defensive alliance, but rather technical agreements to set up a concerted defense to counter any unprovoked German aggression against either country.

Announcement of this military accord brought instantaneous and strong reaction. It was praised by the majority of Walloons and greeted by the militant Liberals and those Catholics who admired France for her loyalty during the war and who disliked the growing impact of the Flemish views in national politics. Many Flemings disapproved of the accord, fearing that it increased Walloon influence and adversely affected the campaign for Flemish rights. Each group suspected that this agreement might lead to a strengthening of defense measures for Wallonia at the expense of Flanders.[4]

The existence of an antimilitaristic attitude, a consequence of the degrading and grueling war experience, influenced the Flemish response. A radical expression of this antimilitaristic mood came from the Association of Flemish Veterans (Verbond van Vlaamse Oudstrijders). It considered Belgium safer disarmed than armed and consequently pleaded for a nonmilitary defense.[5] The extreme peace stands, however, never carried the day. Radical Socialists also voiced strong opposition to the accord, but experienced leaders such as Emil Vandervelde demonstrated more flexibility in their attitudes. In contrast to the prewar period, where most Socialists entertained radical antimilitaristic attitudes, much of the leadership had become more realistic. The shattered myth of Socialist internationalism, the rise of Communism and later of Fascism and Nazism, and the assumption of governmental responsibility all contributed to this change.

In 1924 Belgium became a party to the Locarno agreements, which brought about the strongly sought-after British guarantee of Belgium's eastern border. This agreement strengthened the guarantee provided by the League of Nations and rectified the "imbalance" exhibited by the accords with France. Subsequently, the military accord with France was perceived as redundant and inconvenient.[6]

Twelve years later, in 1936, the scene changed drastically. The League of Nations and the Locarno agreements, the two pillars of Belgian security, collapsed. Germany remilitarized the Rhineland while France and Britain did not interfere. Equally important, the League of Nations failed to sanction Italy for her attack against Ethiopia. The growing insecurity on the European scene made the Belgian Government aware of the necessity of speedy and massive rearmament. To achieve this the government had to convince the Flemish public and the Walloon Socialists that the Belgian army would be used exclusively for defensive and national purposes. To satisfy those wishes, the Minister of Foreign Affairs, Paul-Henri Spaak, advocated a "free-hand policy." This policy was fully supported by King Leopold III, by a great majority of the public, and by most members of Parliament.[7] But no crash armament program was begun. A combination of factors contributed to the delay in the military buildup: domestic turmoil, the Belgian aversion to military affairs, the fear of enhancing the likelihood of invasion because of the existence of desirable munition factories, and the country's predilection to invest in commerce, finance, and manufacturing.[8] This new policy of armed neutrality did not succeed in keeping war from the Belgian territory.

From the dramatic experience of the German invasion in May 1940, Belgium learned two important lessons. First, neutrality and military independence do not guarantee security. Second, to secure peace, more efficient international arrangements were needed. Although Belgian policy makers spoke positively about a universal organization for peace and security, immediate political considerations predominated. Consequently, they preferred a regional solution.[9]

At the end of 1947, Western Europe seemed to be most receptive to a regional-security approach. The first concrete steps were made by Britain, who proposed to France and the Benelux countries that they should create a multilateral defense organization. Belgium responded favorably and, along with the Dutch, promptly began to draft a reply. Brussels and The Hague were in general agreement, but enough difference of opinion existed to delay the answer being sent until the very day the French and the British delivered their proposals. Even though there was some debate between the Belgians and the Dutch about how close they should allow themselves to be drawn into the Franco-British camp, they were firm in their insistence that what was needed was a regional agreement. They preferred the establishment of a security community rather than the creation of a traditional alliance based on bilateral agreements. Paul-Henri Spaak fervently promoted this idea.

In the end, the vision of the Benelux countries prevailed. On 17 March 1948, the Treaty of Brussels was signed, providing for strong multilateral and regional cooperation. The treaty was ratified by the Belgian Parliament with little difficulty; only the Communists voted against it. This widespread support was not only based on the recognition of the failure of neutralism and appeasement but also on the conviction that in the postwar world only an organized Europe could again play a role. Europe had to unite or sink in decadence.[10] The treaty represented a step toward a further integration of Europe. Military and political pacts were to be reinforced by economic agreements. Moreover, there existed the perception that a de facto Eastern bloc had been established by the many political, military, and economic accords between the USSR and the Eastern European countries. A regional organization including Eastern Europe was thus considered undesirable because of a lack of enough common interests to create a durable alliance. The organization of Europe was also seen as a precondition to receive the needed American economic and military aid.

During the parliamentary debates the political parties stressed that the treaty should not preclude a détente policy or lead to the creation of perpetual power blocs.[11] The Liberal spokesman R. Gillon applauded the treaty but at the same time stressed the need to curb prejudices and misunderstandings through the development of cultural relations between Eastern and Western Europe. The Socialist representative H. Vos, while supporting the treaty, pleaded for a continuation of the economic negotiations and relations with the Soviet Union and the other Eastern European countries.

The logical consequences of the Brussels Pact were fulfilled thirteen months later with Belgium's entrance into the North Atlantic Treaty Organization. The United Nations had failed to achieve what had been expected of it. NATO was now considered a basic security necessity. The organization was meant to protect basic democratic principles and, together with the Marshall Plan, prevent Communist subversion. It was also frequently argued that Belgium, as a member of the Atlantic Alliance, would receive more aid from the United States to rekindle her economy.[12]

These arguments were used in the Belgian Parliament to defend the formation of the Alliance. The parliamentary debate revealed a strong fear of Soviet expansionism and the importance of the defensive character of the Alliance. In addition, all major political parties reiterated that an effective military defense should not exclude an active détente policy or further polarize the world into two power blocs. In May 1949 the Belgian Parliament ratified the NATO pact by a large majority.[13] Only the Communists objected, since they considered it not only an aggressive agreement but also inconsistent with the U.N. Charter. The Belgian choice rested on historical experience—neutrality had failed twice, and a universal organization did not provide a reliable basis for security.

Belgian foreign policy in the postwar period thus represented a historical discontinuity, since it was the first time that Belgium belonged to a military alliance. At the same time, alignment can be seen as the continuation of a policy that Belgium had tried to put into effect since World War I. When Belgium's enforced neutrality status ended, the country tried to organize a security policy on a global and regional level, first by becoming a member of the League of Nations and then by trying to establish some kind of defense cooperation with Britain and France. At the end of World War II, Belgium still tried to pursue the same objectives; namely, a global and regional organization of her security policy. The latter, however, was considered to be much more effective. Thus, Belgian membership in NATO represented the result of a security-policy evolution that had begun in 1918.

The Nature of Consensus

The Framework

From the time of the creation of the North Atlantic Alliance until the mid-1970s, Belgium essentially strove to maintain a defense policy consistent with the will of the Alliance as a whole, or more specifically, with its most powerful ally, the United States. It did so within the framework of a permissive domestic political context; controversy over Alliance policy was minimal and essentially confined to peripheral groups that exercised little influence. For nearly thirty years, the Belgian role in the Atlantic Alliance enjoyed a broad national consensus.

Several basic principles that characterized Belgian policy during this period provided the foundation for this consensus. First, loyalty as an ally was always considered to be a paramount consideration, not only in terms of verbal commitments but also in terms of equitable material contributions. Even when disagreements resulted on specific issues, Belgium sought to play a positive role in the Alliance. Second, there was constant concern for providing the necessary security, although *at the lowest possible level*.[14] This principle was reflected in Belgian defense efforts, but it also influenced the Belgian role in the arms control and reduction talks that emerged during the 1960s.

Third, solidarity in the Alliance was a major Belgian priority. Consequently, it adopted the role of intermediary in times of international tension in order to reduce the possibility of conflict within the Alliance.[15] As former Belgian Foreign Minister Henri Simonet observed, "If you reviewed the relations between the major countries within the Alliance, and even in the most recent history, you would find a considerable number of misunderstandings, tense situations, and frequent ruptures, which would have been redressed and limited if the small countries had played a more positive role."[16] Belgium especially stressed the importance of maintaining solidarity with the United States.

Fourth, in accordance with the principle of equality among partners, Belgium attempted to ensure that the small powers continue to play an influential role in the analysis and decision-making processes. In particular, it tenaciously sought to prevent one single power, or the combined major powers, from monopolizing the policy-making process. Paul-Henri Spaak conveyed this concern in a discussion with Khrushchev when he reportedly said, "Great powers don't like the representatives of small powers to show too much independence. They are wrong."[17] Simonet warned about the passivity of his country: "Because of our passivity, we are creating a grave situation . . . we are giving an alibi to the great countries to become what they think they already are, that is to say, the real hard core of the Alliance."[18]

Fifth, Belgium's conception of its role favored a strengthening of the European voice in the Alliance, an idea that was pursued actively. It felt that the appearance of Europe as one entity "would strengthen the Alliance, because it would provide more political equilibrium in East-West relations. One can easily see how natural the Alliance could rest on those two main pillars. And in some cases, a United Europe could even play the role of motor."[19] In addition, Belgium felt that Europe could contribute to a more nuanced approach to international political problems, and consequently to more harmonious solutions.

Finally, Belgium saw itself as the bridge builder between East and West. The chief political actors in this area were Paul-Henri Spaak and Pierre Harmel.[20] Belgium's active engagement in the politics of détente, dialogue, and arms control was initially bilateral, but when this approach revealed less than hopeful prospects, Belgium opted for a more multilateral approach.[21] NATO was considered not only as a military alliance but also as an instrument to promote détente. This policy was evoked by Foreign Minister Harmel: "As long as one doesn't succeed in reaching real disarmament, and as long as the level of armament doesn't change, the Belgian Government will not give up the security provided for by NATO. But we are convinced that the efforts with respect to détente and peace are more important than the defense efforts."[22] This attitude laid the basis for Belgian détente efforts both within the Alliance and in the multilateral forums that developed in the 1970s.

These principles characterized the conduct of Belgian security policy during most of the postwar period. Although there were some disagreements as to actual programs along the way, security policy was, as noted, generally marked by a firm commitment to NATO and limited domestic controversy. By examining some of the major NATO issues that confronted Belgium during this period, it can be seen how these general preferences were reflected in several key policy decisions and where differing perspectives did exist.

Germany's Entrance into the Alliance

There was little resistance in Belgian Government circles to the idea of German rearmament. The main concern was to control the rearmament process. As early as 1950, NATO recognized the need for a number of German divisions for the defense of Europe. Although all participants concurred in principle, no agreement was reached toward advancing its realization. Nevertheless, the member-states declared on 18 December 1950 that it would be the duty and the right of the Federal Republic of Germany to associate itself with the defense of Europe.

The history of the period is well known. Winston Churchill supported the idea of a European army in which the German divisions would be incorporated. At first, Belgium supported this idea. France, however, resisted and presented instead its own version of a European army. The French Pleven plan for a European Defense Community (EDC) proposed creating a fully integrated European army and thereby prevent the creation of separate German divisions. On 27 May 1952 this plan was accepted and signed by six European countries.

The Belgian Government, headed by Minister J. van Houtte, declared its enthusiastic support for EDC membership, saying that it helped achieve several fundamental policy objectives: the creation of a more effective military force, the integration of Germany into the Western community, and a unification of Western Europe that respected the proper character of each nation.[23] Belgium also supported the EDC because it strongly disapproved of Germany's direct entry into NATO. The Belgian Minister of Foreign Affairs, Paul van Zeeland, characterized the latter option as a policy of adventurism and confusion.[24]

On 26 November 1953 the Belgian Parliament ratified the EDC treaty, eighteen months after it was signed. There was an obvious conflict between the government's determination to have the treaty ratified and the slowness with which the Parliament handled the ratification. The

House of Representatives simply ignored the government's request for quick action, acting only after considerable delay. This was "the result of the confusion in public opinion. The idea of rearming Germany, in whatever way, was far from meeting general support. In both the parties of the Governmental coalition, as well as those of the opposition . . . the hesitators and the adversaries were numerous."[25] Ultimately, the Belgian House of Representatives ratified the treaty by a vote of 148 to 49, with 3 abstentions, and the Senate did so with a vote of 125 to 40, with 2 abstentions.

The greatest opposition came from the Communist Party, which considered the EDC as a source of great danger to Belgian security. It argued that "Germany is still a threat for her neighbors. The only thing her ambitions still lack is a military force, and this will be provided by the EDC."[26] Although dissenting voices in other parties were rare, nonetheless some did exist. For example, the Christian Democrats J. de Vleeshauwer and M. Brasseur were opposed because of the implied limitations on national sovereignty. There were also a number of representatives who considered the treaty as inconsistent with the constitution. Finally, there was a group of critics, such as the Socialist Hendrik Fayat, who made their approval contingent upon the creation of a European political community in order to ensure the democratic nature of the defense policy-making process.

Not much is known about the public's attitude toward the EDC, since several parliamentary efforts to introduce a referendum were unsuccessful. One public-opinion poll held in 1953 and conducted in 33 firms showed that 73 percent of the working class was opposed to the EDC; however, the limited external validity of this poll makes any generalization of Belgian public opinion impossible. When the EDC failed in 1954 and British Foreign Minister Anthony Eden proposed the establishment of the Western European Union (WEU), there was practically no resistance within the Belgian Parliament. In 1955 the House gave its approval with 181 in favor, 9 against, and 2 abstentions. Many of the opponents of the EDC considered the WEU as less radical and thus a more acceptable way of incorporating Germany in NATO. In addition, the WEU was considered to be less humiliating to Germany. The WEU opened the way for Germany's entrance into NATO, and when this happened on 5 May 1955, there was virtually no opposition in Belgium.

The Installation of Nuclear Weapons on Belgian Territory

In the 1980s questions concerning nuclear weapons and their installation on Belgian territory became the focal point of numerous peace-group activities. This level of activity contrasted sharply with the relatively low level of public initiative during the 1950s and the early 1960s. This fact may seem surprising, since Belgium has had nuclear weapons on its territory since 1963, but it does reveal the domestic security consensus that existed in the earlier period.

The installation of nuclear weapons on Belgian territory was a consequence of the 1957 NATO decision to equip the European Allies with tactical nuclear weapons. There was practically no debate in Parliament, and the Minister of Defense responded openly to the few questions raised. In June 1962 Christian Democrat P. W. Segers informed the House of Representatives that the Belgian army had possessed dual-purpose delivery systems for several years. In February 1963 he further specified that they consisted of eight-inch Howitzers, "Honest-John" and "Nike" missiles, as well as two fighter squadrons that could be equipped with tactical nuclear weapons. He indicated that the nuclear munition was still not on Belgian territory, but it was expected sometime in 1963. In addition, he stressed that the plurality of the nuclear stock would be stationed on German territory close to the army units. The Belgian Government considered the installation of tactical nuclear weapons as a necessary response to counter the Soviet threat.[27]

The reactions of political parties differed greatly. The Communist parties fervently objected to the decision. In the Socialist Party, a great majority was opposed to the creation of stocks or delivery systems on Belgian territory,[28] although a minority, headed by Paul-Henri Spaak, considered nuclear weapons to be essential for a modern army and that defense without such arms was unthinkable.[29] The Christian Democrats also considered atomic weapons as indispensable for Belgian defense. On 5 February 1963 Christian Democrat A. de Boodt declared that equipping the Belgian army with tactical nuclear weapons was both acceptable and necessary.[30] The Liberals shared the view of the Christian Democrats. In the end the nuclear weapons were installed with little publicity or parliamentary debate.

It was not until 1972 that the matter again emerged, when a question was raised in the Defense Committee about the possession of nuclear weapons by Belgium. Minister of Defense Paul van den Boeynants confirmed the existence of nuclear weapons on Belgian territory but denied that Belgium possessed nuclear weapons.[31]

The Belgian Government and Parliament expressed much greater concern over the intermediate-range nuclear weapons that were implied in the Multilateral Nuclear Force (MLF) plan of President Kennedy. Initially, Foreign Minister Spaak had a positive attitude, since he thought that such a multilateral force would obviate the need for national nuclear forces and consequently prevent nuclear proliferation. It was also assumed that the plan would provide the allies with a voice in the decision-making process concerning the use of these weapons. Nevertheless, he felt that the American proposal had come too late and that the harm had already been done.[32] When France responded negatively to the American proposal, Spaak stated that while a feasibility study would be interesting, Belgium would not participate in financing a Multilateral Nuclear Force.

Parliamentary resistance to the MLF plan was also greater than resistance to the initial installation of nuclear weapons on Belgian territory. Not only Communists and Socialists opposed the plan, but people like the Christian Democrat De Boodt also rejected it. Although he considered the installation of tactical nuclear weapons on Belgian territory to be necessary, De Boodt opposed the storage of strategic nuclear weapons on Belgian territory because of the unacceptable dangers to which the population would be exposed.[33]

The resistance against the installation of *strategic* nuclear weapons on Belgian territory was also felt within the government. Minister of Defense Segers reiterated his preference for a maritime solution; that is, the installation of the MLF on ships and submarines. In December 1962 he declared that the government would not approve the installation of such weapons on Belgian territory. In the end, many experts agreed that a multilateral force, in which every participating country had a veto power, could never function efficiently.

How did public opinion respond to the issue of the installation of nuclear weapons on Belgian territory? It is difficult to answer this question, since no appropriate public-opinion polls are available; an assessment can be made, however, on the basis of the demonstrations concerning the nuclear issue.[34] The first "antiatom march" took place on 10 April 1960. Approximately 4,000 people, mostly from the left of the Belgian political spectrum, marched from Mol to Antwerp under the banner "No to Nuclear Killing." This march was inspired by identical marches organized in England under the auspices of the Campaign for Nuclear Disarmament (CND).

The success of the first demonstration stimulated the organizers to plan another. On 24 March 1963 a march was held in Brussels with estimated participation ranging from 4,000 to 10,000. The following year the march expanded to approximately 15,000 participants. The demonstrators now came from a much wider political spectrum and with quite varied motivations. These included opposition to atomic weapons and delivery systems on Belgian territory if possessed by the Belgian army; opposition to nuclear proliferation; support for an immediate stop to all atomic tests, for a destruction of all nuclear weapons, and for a general, mutual, and controlled disarmament process; support for a reduction and reconversion of military expenditures to the social and cultural sector, and to aid for the Third World; and demand for a nonaggression pact between NATO and the Warsaw Pact Nations. The antinuclear marches reached a peak on 28 March 1965, when some reports estimated participation as high as 20,000.

In the same period there was also a growth of what was known as the 8th May Movement. This movement wanted Belgium to play the role of initiator and mediator in the fight for peace and against the danger of a nuclear war. Its demands were generally in line with the other antinuclear marches, except that the other protests were not aimed specifically at the issue of nuclear weapons on Belgian territory. On 8 May 1962 the movement held is first protest march under the motto "8 May 1945, a token of hope, an expression of will." Subsequently, the movement made a great effort to diversify its action to several cities. (In 1963 marches were held in thirteen cities; in 1964 they expanded action to fifty cities.)

The movement was pluralistic and included sixty-one organizations, including the two main labor unions. In parliament Socialist I. van Acker expressed his implicit support for the movement. Many religious leaders such as Cardinal Suenens and the bishops of Liège and Tournay were equally supportive.

Also worth mentioning is a demonstration "for peace" organized by the Socialist International on 6 September 1964, with estimated participation varying between 23,000 and 70,000. This certainly indicated a growing concern in Belgium about the danger associated with nuclear weapons. After 1965, however, there was a decline in antinuclear protest activities, with only a slight flare-up in March 1969.

The size of demonstrations in the 1960s was significantly smaller than those that occurred nearly two decades later. Nevertheless, public opinion was not indifferent to the issues of nuclear weapons, particularly their installation on Belgian territory. Moreover, it is interesting to note a certain discrepancy between the attitudes of the parliament and public opinion. While public opinion was at least aware of the nuclear issue, the parliament never held a serious debate on the subject. One of the factors that helps to explain this is the long-held assumption in the Belgian system that defense and security issues should be predominantly dealt with by the government and only in the second instance at parliamentary level. This was not to be challenged seriously until 1979.

Defense Efforts

Two important indicators of the Belgian commitment to the Alliance are its defense expenditures and its military manpower. By looking at the fluctuations that have occurred in these areas, it can be seen that Belgium generally responded to needs as stipulated by the Alliance. (See Table 1.1). During periods of international tension, both defense spending and military manpower were substantially increased. During the periods when no such explicit Alliance requirements existed, however, the tendency was to move in the opposite direction. The country lowered the level of defense spending and reduced the strength of the armed forces, often by shortening the length of required military service.

The Korean War provided the occasion for the first major change in Alliance requirements. NATO adopted a forward defense strategy in response to the attack on South Korea that demanded much greater Western military capabilities and thus a considerable increase in Belgian defense efforts. The Korean War made a strong impact on the public. Fear of communist aggression against Europe made acceptance and support of the rearmament program easier to obtain.[35] With the help of military and economic aid provided by the United States under the Mutual Defense Assistance Program (MDAP), defense expenditures were increased considerably. Belgian defense expenditures more than doubled as a percentage of the Gross Domestic Product (GDP) between 1950 and 1952.

Table 1.1 Evolution of Defense Expenditures in Market Prices and as a Percentage of the GNP

Year	Defense Expenditures (millions BF)	% GNP	Year	Defense Expenditures (millions BF)	% GNP
1953	20,589	5	1969	33,754	2.9
1954	20,707	4.8	1970	37,388	2.9
1955	17,857	3.9	1971	40,654	2.9
1956	17,887	3.7	1972	45,183	2.85
1957	19,232	3.7	1973	50,533	2.8
1958	19,254	3.7	1974	57,739	2.75
1959	19,658	3.7	1975	70,899	3
1960	20,209	3.5	1976	81,444	3.1
1961	20,641	3.4	1977	89,480	3.1
1962	22,341	3.4	1978	99,726	3.25
1963	23,596	3.4	1979	106,472	3.3
1964	26,241	3.4	1980	115,754	3.3
1965	26,606	3.1	1981	125,689	3.5
1966	28,169	3.1	1982	131,817	3.4
1967	30,336	3.1	1983	137,163	3.3
1968	32,319	3.1	1984	147,496	3.4[a]

[a] Estimates from *Jane's Defense Weekly* (12 January 1985): 54; and from *NATO Review,* 6 (1984).

Source: P. Manigarf, "L'évolution des dépenses militaires en Belgique dupuis 1900," *CRISP, Courrier Hebdomadaires* (30 January 1983): 7.

Beginning in 1954, however, Belgian military efforts gradually waned. In terms of percentage of the GDP, defense expenditures fell from 5.3 percent in 1954 to 3.8 percent in 1964. Several factors accounted for this downward trend.[36] First, the 1954 Geneva agreements on Indochina, temporary détente in East-West relations, and the inauguration of the peaceful coexistence policy of the Soviet Union all helped to lessen Belgium's threat perception. Second, Germany's inclusion in NATO and its resulting rearmament lightened the defense burden on Belgium. Third, the growing internal demands for more welfare-state policies (at the same time that American military aid was reduced) forced the Belgian Government to divert funds that might have otherwise been assigned to defense programs. There was not, however, a strong decrease in defense expenditures, but rather modernization and reorganization became "the magic terms for a gradual reduction of defense efforts. The tone was: let us create a well-trained and well-equipped force that will cost us as little as possible and still be acceptable to our allies."[37] Concurrently, as shown in Table 1.2, there was clearly an emphasis from 1960 to 1978 on reducing operational costs where possible in favor of the reorganization and modernization of equipment.

Table 1.2   Distribution of Military Expenditures: Manpower, Operations, and Military Equipment

Year	Manpower	Operations	Military Equipment
	%	%	%
1966	51.8	32.0	16.2
1967	54.0	31.7	14.2
1968	49.0	34.2	16.8
1969	48.4	29.6	22.0
1970	49.9	28.8	21.3
1971	50.1	30.1	19.8
1972	51.6	27.9	20.5
1973	53.5	28.4	18.1
1974	52.5	28.0	19.5
1975	49.8	28.9	21.3
1976	52.1	26.7	21.2
1977	51.4	26.3	22.3
1978	50.2	25.1	24.7
1979	51.0	25.5	23.5
1980	49.1	25.5	25.4
1981	49.7	26.8	23.5
1982	50.1	26.7	23.2

Source: Parlementaire Dokumenten Kamer, 4-IX (1981–82) no. 2.

Although defense expenditures increased in absolute terms with a yearly average of just over 4 percent, it decreased as a percentage of both total government spending and of GDP. At the end of the period in question, however, the annual defense budget actually grew both in absolute and real terms; in addition, there was also a rise of defense spending as a percentage of the GDP between 1974 and 1978. Despite the fluctuations, Belgium's share of NATO's defense expenditure (including U.S. and French spending) increased from 0.73 percent in 1954 to 1.64 percent in 1975 (see Table 1.3). Thus, from a financial-burden-sharing standpoint, Belgium continued to be a loyal ally.

The changing strength of the Belgian army did not necessarily correspond to the fluctuations in defense expenditures. The size of the Belgian army has actually followed its own pattern over the years, in accordance with changes in NATO's needs and strategy. As shown in Table 1.4, the strength of the Belgian army peaked at about 145,000 at the end of the Korean War (1954). Henceforth, there was a general decline in the number of Belgian troops.

The reasons for the decline generally are the same factors that affected military spending from 1954 to 1978. One way of controlling the strength of the army was by changing the length of required military

Table 1.3   Evolution of the Belgian Share in NATO Defense Expenditures

1954	0.73%	1968	0.75%
1955	0.64%	1969	0.78%
1956	0.61%	1970	0.89%
1957	0.62%	1971	0.94%
1958	0.82%	1972	1.23%
1959	0.81%	1973	1.32%
1960	0.83%	1974	1.33%
1961	0.81%	1975	1.47%
1962	0.79%	1976	1.58%
1963	0.82%	1977	1.57%
1964	0.89%	1978	1.64%
1965	0.87%	1979	1.66%
1966	0.79%	1980	1.64%
1967	0.73%	1981	1.58%

Sources: 1954–57: *World Armaments and Disarmaments SIPRI Yearbook 1976 (London: Taylor & Francis, 1976); 1958–71: SIPRI Yearbook 1979 (London: Taylor & Francis, 1979); 1972–81: SIPRI Yearbook 1982 (London: Taylor & Francis, 1982).*

service. As shown in Figure 1.1, there has been a steady decline in the required length of service, which roughly corresponds to the decline in the number of men in the Belgian armed forces.

The maximum length of required service came during the Korean war in the early 1950s. In March 1951 the Christian Democrats, who were then the leading party in the government, found it necessary to extend the period of military service from twelve to twenty-four months. This decision was fiercely attacked by the Communists, Socialists, and Liberals (although the latter objected for different reasons than the leftist parties). Eventually, leftist agitation aroused public opinion, and after demonstrations and riots, which occurred even on military bases, the requirement was reduced to twenty-one months in August 1952. By 1954 the period of required military service had been shortened to eighteen months, then to fifteen months in 1957, and finally to twelve months in 1959. Since then, the period has been steadily reduced.

Rising manpower costs after 1965 increased pressure on the government to find more efficient ways to operate the military. In 1968 the government coalition of Christian Democrats and Socialists announced the continuation of a reorganization and efficiency program in accordance with a five-year plan scheduled from 1968 to 1973 and approved by NATO. The plan foresaw qualitative and structural improvements that would compensate for a reduction of the number of men under arms. During the period of this program, the Belgian army was reduced from approximately 110,000 to 98,000 soldiers.[38]

On 10 November 1972 the government presented a reform program

Table 1.4   Evolution of the Strength of the Belgian Army

Year		Year		b
1949	67.056	1968	98.681	
1950	81.622	1969	93.701	
1951	127.640	1970	95.307	
1952	136.129	1971	94.651	(107.000)[b]
1953	148.495	1972	94.861	(107.000)[b]
1954	143.524	1973	91.537	
1955	140.274	1974	87.383	
1956	127.591	1975	87.619	(103.000)[b]
1957	113.571	1976	87.393	(107.000)[b]
1958	115.884	1977	88.918	(107.000)[b]
1959	110.085	1978	92.629	(109.000)[b]
1960	108.360	1979	93.951	(107.000)[b]
1961	107.029	1980	92.209	(108.000)[b]
1962	105.597	1981	93.708	(109.000)[b]
1963	105.398	1982	93.619	(110.000)[b]
1964	104.050	1983	95.160	(109.000)[b]
1965	102.956	1984	92.400	(108.000)[b]
1966	103.610			
1967	103.533			

Sources: —P. Manigart, *Les forces armées belges en transition: Une étude sur le concept de déclin de l'armée de masse* (Thèse de doctorat, University of Leuven, 1983), 751.
—N.I.S., Annuaires Statistiques de la Belgique.
—*NATO Review* 1 (1977, 1978, 1979, 1980) and 6 (1983, 1984).
[b]These are NATO figures, based on different calculations.

that provided for the further shortening of the required period of military service and a limiting of recruitment to one conscript per family. The plan also foresaw the gradual cancellation of deferments for students, the organization of a general civil conscription, and a solidarity tax for those freed from military service. The final reforms under the professionalization plan took place in 1974. These reforms provided for a gradual reduction of military service to six months (to be achieved in 1978) and a recruitment of professional soldiers to compensate for the lowered intake of conscripts. However, lack of money impeded the full implementation of this plan. Not much more has been done beyond the reduction of the conscription period to ten months when stationed in Belgium, or eight months when stationed in Germany. The latest government agreements seem to be in favor of a status quo, the objective remaining a reduction of military service to six months, but only if budgetary conditions become favorable.

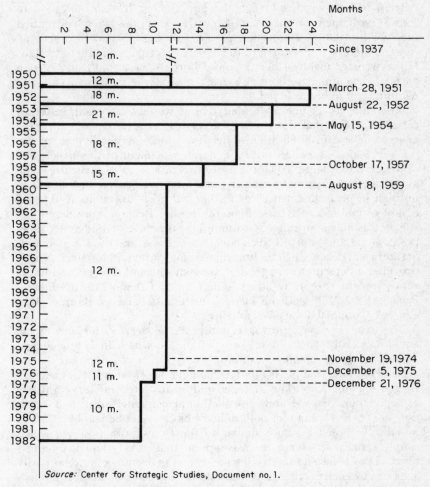

Source: Center for Strategic Studies, Document no. 1.

Figure 1.1 : Evolution of the length of military service.

Transfer of NATO Headquarters to Belgium

The transfer of NATO headquarters to Belgium was one of the few issues to incite debate about Belgian policy during the first thirty years of alignment. At the outset, Foreign Minister Pierre Harmel told the parliament that it would be the first to be informed about any decision concerning the relocation so that it could discuss the issue "in such a way that each can assume his part of the responsibility. It was the Government that would have the burden of the responsibility to decide, and the Parliament that would approve or disapprove."[39] But relations between parliament and government became strained when Harmel told a

Belgian newspaper that in fact the government felt no obligation to consult parliament on the issue of transfer, since the latter had ratified the North Atlantic Treaty and as a result was obliged to accept all consequences of it. President of the Senate P. Struye responded strongly. If the transfer involved new financial burdens or would cause certain parts of the country to become extraterritorial, the parliament, he said, had the right to be consulted.[40]

When the government decided that it would accept a transfer of certain NATO installations to Belgian territory, the parliament opened a general debate in June 1966. The discussion was not limited to the transfer issue but evolved into a general assessment of the actual relevance of the Atlantic Alliance, its future task, and its structure. The government argued that a collective and integrated defense could still be justified in peacetime as well as in times of crisis. In addition to being firmly committed to Article 3 of the treaty, Belgium considered the Alliance as an important way to minimize the defense budget. A small power alone could not afford an adequate defense, and the area demanding sufficient defense had become increasingly larger.[41] Moreover, NATO provided a deterrent to aggression by guaranteeing direct Allied intervention in the case of an attack. The Christian Democrats, the Liberal Parties (PVV-PLP), and the Flemish Federalist Party (Volksunie—VU) generally supported the government.

The issue, however, provoked a rupture between Paul-Henri Spaak and his Socialist Party. A majority of the Socialists, including Spaak, supported the government, although they put more emphasis on the necessity of adapting NATO to the changing environment. They wanted Belgian membership to be characterized by an active pursuit of a policy of negotiation, détente, and controlled disarmament, leading to a condition where the abolition of both military blocs would be feasible.[42] Other Socialists adopted a stance similar to the Communist position, which simply refused to accept the assumption that NATO had maintained peace. They believed that stability had been the product of nuclear parity achieved by an arms race, which should be stopped and all military blocs dissolved. Moreover, they accused Germany of using NATO to promote revanchist policies. Similar opposition came from the smaller Brussels and Walloon parties—the Front Démocratique des Bruxellois Francophones (FDF) and the Parti Wallon—both of which proposed realigning Alliance policy with the prevailing circumstances. The Brussels Party recommended the parallel reduction of forces and the dissolution of both blocs; the Walloon Party went so far as to demand an immediate dissolution of NATO.[43]

With respect to the future tasks of the Alliance, the government stated that "as long as one doesn't succeed in reaching real disarmament, and as long as the level of armament doesn't change, the Belgian Government will not give up the security provided for by NATO. But we are convinced that the efforts with respect to détente and peace are more important than the defense efforts."[44] This approach would become the basis of

Belgium's détente policy, and it also contributed to the Belgian initiative that led to the so-called Harmel Exercise. Nearly everyone concurred. Although differences did arise as to the best way to achieve détente, all political parties generally supported the government's position.

Parliament finally discussed restructuring NATO and the pros and cons of transferring NATO installations to Belgium. In both the House of Representatives and the Senate, the discussion resulted in motions being submitted by the governing parties (the Christian Democrats and the Liberals) that basically reflected the government's position on NATO, détente, and the consequences of the transfer for Belgium.

The motion in the House stressed Belgium's continuing loyalty to the Alliance and its commitment to a policy of détente and international cooperation. It also indicated that the transfer would not create additional expenses for Belgium, since all partners would help to meet the cost. Finally, it portrayed the move as an illustration of Belgium's solidarity with the Alliance. The issue came to a vote on 21 June 1966 and was passed with a margin of 118 to 61, with 16 abstentions.[45]

The motion submitted to the Senate resembled the House motion, although it was a little more detached and it requested a new investigation into the means whereby Belgian troops were stationed in Germany. The special preliminary vote on the Senate motion's last paragraph, concerning the compatibility of the transfer with Belgian détente policy, illustrates the import placed on this policy. Of the 151 senators present, 140 approved the motion, 5 did not, and 6 abstained. The final vote on the transfer issue resulted with 96 in favor, 33 against, and 22 abstentions.[46]

Thus, in the middle of the 1960s most parties continued to believe that NATO was vital to Belgian security. Nevertheless, all speakers also stressed the need for cooperation with Eastern Europe. As to the question of housing the NATO installation, opinion divided between those who were willing to commit themselves to new responsibilities within NATO and those who were reluctant to do so. This demarcation was to grow in importance, as will be seen later.

The Emergence of Détente and Arms Control

To complete the picture of Belgian security policy during the period of national consensus, it is necessary to consider in more detail the importance attached to détente and to reducing East-West tension. This desire was expressed at the time Belgium joined the Alliance. As a small power and export-oriented country, Belgium has traditionally considered international cooperation vital to its existence. The debate on the transfer of NATO institutions to Belgian territory catalyzed discussions over détente and cooperation with the Eastern European countries, which grew in prominence during the ensuing period. Some of the more cynical observers asserted that there was a special connection between Belgium's new found interest in détente and the transfer of NATO installations to Brussels. In particular, they claimed that Foreign Minister Harmel's détente policy was initiated to placate internal opposition to the transfer. Those assertions, however, were inaccurate. Belgium's overtures to the East had begun as early as 1965, and since then officials have enjoyed numerous contacts with the USSR, Poland, and Yugoslavia.[47] Harmel himself elegantly countered such accusations during a speech to the Belgian Senate on 16 March 1971. He said:

> In a recent work by an American diplomat who has been living with us for a long time, I have read that Belgium . . . has pursued this policy [of détente] as a sort of psychological counterweight of our loyalty to the Alliance since NATO located its general secretariat and SHAPE in Belgium. In my opinion, this is a wanton evaluation. Rather, we thought that for the sake of peace, at least as many diplomatic as military risks should be taken.[48]

Harmel followed his détente policy cautiously and persistently. He was careful to make a distinction between the three areas—military, economic, and political—in which détente could bring about substantial changes.[49] In Belgian politics, the widening of cultural, technological, commercial, and economic contacts was given first priority. Frans Govaerts cites several reasons why Belgium was, at that time, in the best position to play an important role in the field of détente: (1) it had traditional links with Eastern Europe; (2) it was one of the members of the U.N. Group of Nine established on 21 December 1965 to further contacts between East and West; (3) it was a small NATO partner with a very low defense effort; and (4) it expressed an unquestionable loyalty to the Alliance.[50]

Belgium was also convinced that détente could succeed only through the cooperation of all the member-states of the Atlantic Alliance. In the initial stages of détente, Belgium played a very active role in the general process. For example, it was the first NATO country that made official contacts with the Soviet Union after the Czechoslovakian crisis of 1968. It was also the first NATO country to recognize officially the German Democratic Republic. Belgium also supported the initiatives taken by GATT (General Agreement on Trade and Tariffs), the Council of Europe, and the OECD toward more open relations with the East.

In the first part of the 1970s, Belgium continued to participate actively in détente and disarmament forums such as the Conference on Security and Cooperation in Europe (CSCE), the negotiations on Mutual and Balanced Force Reductions (MBFR), and the United Nations. Under the auspices of the U.N., Belgium chaired a group studying a regional approach to disarmament.[51] However, beginning in the mid-1970s, Belgium's promotion of détente became much less pronounced as the general consensus on how best to encourage détente collapsed.

Public Attitudes Toward NATO

The Belgian public's attitude toward NATO, and more generally toward security and defense issues, has not been the subject of serious and systematic research effort. It is therefore difficult to provide an accurate picture of the evolution of Belgian public opinion toward NATO membership. Nevertheless, by examining the available data, it is possible to ascertain a general idea of how the Belgian public has perceived the Alliance during most of the postwar period.

In 1957, the Institut Universitaire d'Informations Sociales et Économiques de l'Université Libre de Bruxelles (INSOC) published the results of an opinion poll in which those interviewed were asked what they thought of the idea of integrating the Belgian army into an international organization.[52] Fifty-five percent of the interviewees believed it better for Belgian security and defense to be integrated, while 29 percent opted for an army with a strictly national character. Another question measured, although indirectly, was public appreciation of NATO membership. Forty-three percent of the Belgians interviewed thought that Belgian membership helped to prevent a war on their territory, while 29 percent thought that it did not. While these data show less than overwhelming confidence in NATO membership, they are too sparse to do more than hint at the possibility of underlying concern in some parts of the Belgian population.

Another opinion poll, held ten years later, tried to assess the attitudes toward relocation of Supreme Headquarters Allied Powers Europe (SHAPE) to Belgium.[53] Quite remarkably, most Belgians did not know much about NATO or SHAPE: 66 percent of the respondents were not able to give a definition of NATO or SHAPE. Yet on the whole, the balance of responses about NATO was positive. With respect to the issue of the transfer of NATO installations, the Belgian public's responses were also positive, although tempered with disinterest: 31 percent were in favor, 14 percent were opposed, and 53 percent had no opinion or gave no answer. The number of those in favor of the transfer was much smaller than those who supported NATO in general.

In the same poll, the Belgian public was asked to express its preference for measures that might possibly contribute to a better understanding between non-Communist and Communist countries. The suggested measures were: (1) try to conclude political and economic agreements with the Communist countries without dissolving NATO; (2) organize a common defense in a new organization containing only non-Communist European states; (3) immediately reduce the military potential of the non-Communist countries without waiting for a similar move by the Communists; or (4) dissolve NATO. An overwhelming 62 percent opted for the first solution; the second was favored by 10 percent and the third by 11 percent. Only 5 percent opted for the dissolution of NATO. The rest (13 percent) had no answer. The figures from 1967 clearly show that by the end of the 1960s the Belgian population was still strongly in favor of continuing membership in NATO.

The same was true almost ten years later, judging by a poll held in 1976.[54] At that time, 38 percent of those interviewed considered the cost-benefit balance of Belgian membership in NATO as positive. Yet it is again remarkable that 43 percent of those questioned had no opinion.

The poll also allowed for a breakdown by age and geographical location. When one looks at age as a source of variation, it is interesting that the younger generation expressed a more positive attitude than the older generation. There was also a palpable difference between the three Belgian regions. The Flemings were more positive (41 percent) than the Francophones (32 percent), but less positive than the inhabitants of Brussels (45 percent).

Polls conducted in recent years offer additional insights into Belgian attitudes toward NATO. Asked in 1980 which defense framework is preferable, 28 percent of the Belgians queried replied NATO, 23 percent Western Europe in NATO, 16 percent Western Europe alone, and 7 percent a national defense.[55] In 1982 a similar question was repeated: 25 percent of those polled wanted to continue NATO; 18 percent preferred a Western European defense structure within NATO; 8 percent desired to withdraw the Belgian forces but stay in NATO for certain issues; 7 percent chose an independent European defense, and 5 percent chose a purely national one; only 2 percent wanted to rely more on cooperation with the Soviet Union.[56] In the 1980 poll some other interesting figures emerged: 36 percent of Belgians believed that their country had more advantages than disadvantages as a member in NATO, while 26 percent believed the opposite, whereas in the 1976 poll the figures were 38 percent and 19 percent, respectively. And the most recent poll undertaken, in September 1983, asked directly for the public's attitude toward NATO. In this poll 51 percent responded favorably, 24 percent negatively, and 33 percent either did not know or had no opinion. Of the 24 percent who opposed NATO, 13 percent wanted a European organization, 7 percent desired the elimination of NATO, and 4 percent advocated a Belgian withdrawal from NATO.[57]

Overall, several general patterns emerged in the evolution of public opinion toward security issues. First, positive responses have always dominated. Even though unanimous support for NATO never existed, neither did substantial opposition. Second, the number of no-opinion or no-answer responses decreased with time—from 53 percent in 1967, to 43 percent in 1977, and to 20 to 30 percent by the early 1980s. This tendency must be treated with due caution, however, since the questions asked were not exactly the same. This trend would nevertheless coincide with the otherwise observable growing interest in security questions that has taken place in Belgian politics. Finally, there also seems to be a rise in the percentage of negative responses to NATO-related questions as political parties and the public have become more interested in Belgian security policy. But this judgment is again subject to the same methodological reservations.

What all of the above adds up to is that for thirty years after World War II, Belgian defense policy was characterized by a widespread consensus. This consensus was expressed at three levels. At the level of governing elites, the consensus with respect to Alliance policy remained virtually complete. Since 1950, all governments strived to fulfill their NATO commitments. There was less consensus in Parliament, but since it generally played a rather passive and secondary role in the defense decision-making process, its influence did not lead to much variation in policy. At the level of public opinion, positive responses in favor of NATO were more numerous than negative. By the end of the period, however, the groundwork had been laid for things to come.

The political and economic environment in Belgium had begun to change, as had the world outside. Consensus was widespread during the existence of a Cold War climate, but by the beginning of the 1970s, decision makers had to deal with rising expectations of détente. With the exception of Gaullist France, there had existed a great cohesion among the external reference groups of the Belgian decision makers. By the mid-1970s, however, this consistency no longer prevailed. On the domestic scene decisions had been taken in a unitary state ruled by a coalition government consisting of national parties. The 1970s witnessed a regionalization of Belgian politics and concomitantly a fractionalization of the national parties. In contrast to what lay in store, in the latter period the economy was characterized by growth, which helped to ease most defense-budget disputes. Defense decisions were also taken by a small elite group who shared a similar view of the world, based on lessons drawn from the experiences of neutrality and appeasement. Practically no important public discussion about security and defense issues occurred, and no significant single issue groups of counterelites with competing world views existed. The army played her traditional role of "la grande muette."

Of all the decisions made during the first thirty years of alignment, only two represented "salient new commitments": the MLF decision and the transfer of the NATO headquarters in 1966. Feelings in Parliament and in the political parties ran high when the country was confronted with decisions that were considered to increase risks or to involve major budget increases or allocations. At those moments the political process became polarized between those who were willing to commit themselves to new responsibilities within NATO and those who were opposed. Under the new conditions prevailing in the 1970s, it was only a matter of time until similar issues arose that would strain consensus much more fundamentally and call the whole process of legitimizing Belgian security policy into question.

Legitimization of Security Policy

Belgian consensus on security policy began gradually but visibly to erode around the middle of the 1970s. Until then, the government had been able to limit discussion of defense issues to a restricted group of elites. The Parliament and the public were rarely thoroughly informed. The decisions were legitimized by referring to them as responsibilities derived from NATO commitments. In addition, the Belgian Government conveyed the impression that it was making a contribution to the NATO decision-making process.

Several events signaled a change in the "politics-as-usual" approach toward security. In 1973 high-school students went on strike to protest against the Van den Boeynants plan, which would have abolished their possibility to defer military service. In 1975 political parties and public opinion were again aroused by a discussion about the purchase of new fighter planes. The press depicted it as the "purchase of the century." The decision contrasted significantly with the more familiar piecemeal decisions. The high price of the planes, coupled with the deteriorating economic situation, fueled much debate. Soon afterward, public awareness was further aroused by President Carter's announcement of U.S. intentions to deploy Enhanced Radiation-Reduced Blast (ERW) bombs in Europe. It became obvious that the Belgian Government was no longer the "cavalier seul" in the security field. Under pressure of action groups and public opinion, the government for the first time moderated its security policy. The situation then came to a head with the 1979 NATO INF (Intermediate-Range Nuclear Force) decision, with Parliament asserting new demands for a voice in decision making. Until that time, there had been overall consensus that matters on the foreign-policy agenda were exclusively the concern of government.

One of the main causes of the changing attitude toward security policy was an altered perception of the Atlantic Alliance and the United States. During the postwar period many politicians endeavored to enhance their careers as either proponents or opponents of the Alliance. Initially, only the proponents reaped reward. Eventually, however, the situation changed. Opponents, such as Socialist representative Henri Rolin, were able to achieve comparable status with such leaders as Paul-Henri Spaak.

Several factors account for this shift. First, the international situation in the 1950s stifled opposition to Alliance Policy; the Cold War made criticism of Alliance policy unpopular. Furthermore, critics were not able to present a constructive alternative to existing arrangements. Both of these conditions, however, had changed by the mid-1970s. In Belgium, as in other European countries, the generation of the 1960s made a great impact on the public, with a closely related increase of antimilitarism and a stronger appeal of the left. Opponents of the Atlantic Alliance thus enjoyed a more favorable setting for their ideas. Also, their criticism became more constructive than it had been previously. They stressed, for example, the importance of a European pillar, the necessity for greater European security cooperation, and the greater independence of Europe within the Alliance. Their influence was further reinforced by East-West détente.

Another important reason for this change stemmed from the United States' involvement in Vietnam. The American image suffered considerably from the war in Vietnam and its graceless ending. Traditional bonds eroded, not only because of America's conduct of the war but also because the United States lost the war. Seeing the eagle deeply entangled in political and military turmoil reduced the feeling of reassurance that Europe and Belgium always had derived from their greatest ally.

This feeling was later reinforced when SALT II certified the existence of strategic parity between the two superpowers. The feeling of uneasiness became even more manifest in the late 1970s because of the frequent oscillations in U.S. foreign policy. A lessening in U.S. attraction accompanied America's decline in military power. The sometimes ill-timed and imprudent American references in the early 1980s to contingencies such as limited nuclear war were illustrative of this. Western Europe believed that the new focus on nuclear war-fighting and war-surviving capabilities would make nuclear war more likely. People were frightened by the specter of a third world war fought in Europe while the homelands of both superpowers would remain unharmed.[58]

By the early 1980s the commitment of American power to the defense of Western Europe thus no longer provided the political reassurance it once had for an appreciable number of Belgians.[59] Moreover, the feeling of reassurance has not been reestablished by the proposed improvements in the mechanism of deterrence. In the calculus of nuclear deterrence, the installation of Pershing IIs and cruise missiles and the U.S. development of a capacity to carry on and "prevail" in a nuclear exchange may appear appropriate, but such calculus does not translate easily into the language of political reassurance, certainly not in Europe, where any kind of nuclear exchange spells almost inconceivable disaster.[60]

The present security-legitimation difficulties are thus the consequence of a confluence of several factors. They involve changes that have taken place in the political process and in perceptions of the international environment. Both have reshaped the way that Belgium looks at defense. In order to best understand the interaction of these two as cause and effect in the evolution of Belgian security policy, we will look first at those changes that took place in the domestic political context, and then at some of the ways that they have been reflected in actual policy debates.

Changes in the Political Process

A first impression of the Belgian defense scene reveals a stark contrast between its serious defense efforts and the shallowness of its security-policy community. With few exceptions, the Belgian contribution to thinking about security and strategy has been sparse. The evolution of interest in this area was inhibited by several factors. On the domestic level, for example, it was constrained by several aspects of Belgian intellectual tradition, by unsatisfactory research opportunities, and by a lack of attention by government and the political parties. In the academic world there was not only an overly slow emancipation of the study of international relations from history, law, and economics departments but also a certain indifference to, and even a lack of esteem for, the field of strategic studies. In the past, the analysis of defense and security problems was predominantly left to the government, the army, and the Ministry of Foreign Affairs.

Two other explanations for the neglect of strategic affairs in Belgium are to a great extent also valid for most other West European members of NATO. First has been the long-term subordinate position of the European member-states within the Alliance—not only in military terms, but also in terms of financial burden sharing. This dependency relationship relegated Western Europe to play a more or less passive role in the formulation of NATO's defense policy. Second, this passivity was reinforced by the long absence of European political cooperation. Such a situation implied a virtual taboo on any official discussion about a European profile in defense policy.

Several factors became apparent at the end of the 1970s and began to alter this state of affairs. The net result was the development of a considerably more complex domestic context for defense decision makers than had existed in the 1950s or 1960s. The most significant of these was simply the increasing public attention to defense and security issues and a proliferation of channels via which attitudes could be expressed (political parties, press, and action groups). There was the exponential growth of the number of books and articles concerning security and defense written by Belgian authors, and the birth of a number of Belgian periodicals concerned chiefly with security problems; for example, *Tijdschrift voor Diplomatie, Veiligheid en Strategie,* and several periodicals of the peace movement. In addition, there was considerable growth in the peace movement. Of the sixteen existing Belgian peace organizations, two-thirds were created after 1975. Several political parties established study groups that were concerned with defense issues. Finally, there was the establishment at the end of the 1970s of two new research centers: In 1978 the Royal Higher Institute for Defense created a Center for Defense Studies, and in 1979 the University of Leuven established a Center for Strategic Studies.

In addition, as a consequence of the greater degree of schooling and public information, public opinion adopted more of an "elite-challenging" than "elite-following" attitude. The public seems to have become increasingly opinionated in the last few years, as is suggested by the decrease of the no-opinion/no-answer responses in polls. Also, there has been a definite increase in the number of critics of the Alliance, who as a rule have been better prepared to present their arguments more effectively. This has had a major impact on the ability of the public to influence the decision-making process, and thus it has become more politically effective.

It is also clear that the security debate has been affected by the advent of a whole new generation who share none of their parents' experiences from the period immediately after World War II. They do not recall the time when Americans and Europeans worked closely to form a military alliance and to reconstruct Europe's shattered economy. They also have no adult memory of the Cold War. Instead, their perceptions have been shaped by the American involvement in Vietnam and by American domestic crises such as Watergate. Consequently, the "successor generation" tends to be somewhat more antimilitaristic and holds a less positive image of the United States. As shown in Table 1.5, the under-25 group is markedly less accepting of government decisions than the older generations.

The new-found Belgian interest in defense issues was significantly fueled by the discussion concerning the production and installation in Europe of new nuclear weapons and by the deteriorating economic situation. The discussion has been monopolized by two themes: (1) the chances of Europe being involved in a nuclear war and (2) the development of a more cost-effective defense policy. The opposition complained about the too high risk load and too low cost-effectiveness of the existing defense policy. The opposition was much more effectively organized at the end of the 1970s than in earlier periods.

While the 1950s could be considered as the trial period of the postwar Belgian peace movement, peace organizations began in the 1960s to have some effect on the policy-making process. By the 1970s, especially in the latter half, they became a not-insignificant actor. Their increasing importance was linked above all to the frequently inadequate governmental responsiveness to public concern with respect to security and defense-related issues. The improved debating skills of the peace-movement elite, combined with their much more efficient national and international organization, added greatly to their credibility in the political process.

Nevertheless, the success of the peace movement has been complicated

Table 1.5   Analysis of Belgian Public Opinion

Question: Do you accept the installation of American missiles in Belgium?

	Yes	No	No opinion/ No answer
Level of education			
—Primary School	19%	44%	37%
—Lower Secondary School	23%	42%	36%
—Higher Secondary School	30%	41%	29%
—Technical College	33%	43%	24%
—University	39%	39%	22%
—Other	29%	42%	29%
Age			
below 25	17%	49%	34%
25–35	26%	43%	31%
35–45	31%	42%	27%
45–55	28%	43%	30%
55–65	27%	43%	30%
over 65	23%	37%	40%

Source: L'Evénement, no. 35, 1980.

by regional variations. Pacifist tendencies seem to be stronger in Dutch-speaking Flanders than in French-oriented Wallonia, in spite of the fact that Wallonia is a Socialist stronghold. Some explanations cite Wallonia's greater dependence on military-related business, the larger exposure in Flanders to political ideas and actions coming from the Netherlands, or the greater impact of the Church on Flemish people. Another explanation is the different historical experiences of both regions. In the years following World War I, the Flemish soldiers, who had made up 80 percent of the Belgian army and had waged a brave resistance, were not rewarded by the ruling Francophone elite. The grueling war experience and the subsequent contemptuous treatment by their French-speaking commanders contributed to the growth of Flemish antiwar and antimilitaristic attitudes. When, during World War II, King Leopold III signed the Belgian capitulation, he was praised by a great number of Flemish people. They believed that in doing so, he had saved Flanders from disaster, and thus they supported his ultraneutralist stance vis-à-vis the exiled Belgian cabinet in London, which regarded itself as an ally of England and France. After the war the antiwar sentiments remained surprisingly strong in Flanders. Having been latent during the Cold War period, they reappeared as East-West tensions diminished and fear of the Soviet forces faded. In the course of the 1960s and 1970s, more Flemish citizens—directing their political commitment more exclusively to Flanders itself—began to reject the Belgian unitary state and its defense policy.[61]

Although less strong than in the Netherlands, the Catholic church does play a considerable legitimizing role in the peace campaign. It usually does this indirectly, mostly through the grass-roots policy of the most influential Catholic peace organization, Pax Christi Flanders, which has been able to rely on the support of the highest advisory council of the Catholic church, the Interdiocesan Pastoral Council (IPB). The IPB has, however, occasionally taken direct action. On 17 October 1981 the council pronounced itself against any further armament and in favor of a nuclear freeze. The council stated that a limited unilateral step would enhance the chances of real negotiations and of mutual disarmament. The risks of the noninstallation of the cruise missiles and the Pershing IIs were considered to be lower than the risks associated with a further weapon escalation.[62]

In addition, the Belgian peace movement has been strengthened by the growing trend of transnational cooperation. In April 1982 a multinational meeting took place in Brussels in which Belgium was represented by groups such as the "Comité National d'Action pour la Paix et le Développement" (CNAPD). During the debates, an agreement was reached concerning the need for global action and cooperation. This was considered not only the best way, but the only way to apply pressure adequately.[63] In September 1982 there was a meeting of the International Center for Peace Movement Communication and Coordination (IPCC).

This meeting was attended not only by representatives of peace movements from thirteen Western European countries but also for the first time by representatives from the United States and Canada. At this meeting national and international actions were planned against the installation of new nuclear weapons.[64] Other examples of the increased transnational consultation and coordination were the efforts of Pax Christi and representatives from the American Freeze movement in Antwerp in January 1983.

Another factor that significantly changed defense policy making has been the regionalization of the country and fractionalization of the parties. This development made any governmental decision making more difficult; instead of negotiating an agreement among two or three parties, the coalition governments had now to deal with four or six. Decision making was further complicated by the fact that practically every allocation of the defense budget became part and parcel of the ongoing regional disputes. Issues of a strategic and military-technical nature tended to become quickly issues of a politico-economic nature, such as who would get how much economic compensation. The long and tedious discussion about the replacement of the 116 Starfighters by 102 American F-16 fighters can only be understood in this context.

The regionalization contributed also to the polarization of the defense debate, more particularly as a consequence of the breakdown of the Belgian Socialist Party in the mid-1970s into a Flemish (SP) and Francophone (PS) Party. The PS entertains a more moderate platform with respect to defense than her Flemish counterpart; for example, whereas the SP absolutely opposed the installation of cruise missiles, the PS developed a position much more in tune with that of the government. Explanatory variables are the existence of a larger military industry in Wallonia and the existence of different external reference groups. The SP gets cues from the Dutch, German, and Scandinavian sister-parties, while the PS is not insensitive to what happens in France.

To understand fully the Flemish Party, it is also necessary to look at some changes that have taken place within the party. At about the same time of their split into a separate party, the older leadership of the SP was replaced by a younger generation, made up of such people as Karl van Miert, Louis Tobback, and A. van den Bossche. In need of refurbishing a somewhat tainted party image, they opted for a more populist and New Left look. To achieve this, special attention was given to foreign policy issues, such as Zaïre and defense and to the growing peace movement. When in opposition, the pursuit of policies linked to this new identity became more vigorous.

All of the above changes exposed defense decision making to more internal and external pressures and made it a more open process. The result was a sharp reduction in the permissiveness of the political context for defense policy. The political parties began an attempt to exploit the emerging concerns by including in their platforms more attention to defense and security problems. The strongly felt need for more expertise stimulated a number of parties to create special defense study groups. Defense policy became an important issue in the parliamentary elections of November 1981. According to certain analysts, the election outcome, especially that of the CVP (Christian Democratic Party) and the PS, was partially influenced by the parties' stances on nuclear missiles.[65] Even though all the parties had known since 1977 that a NATO missile decision was impending, the Flemish Socialist Party was the only party who prepared its "missile dossier" seriously. Thus, it is not surprising that its influence on the government became considerable.

Those critical of NATO defense policy have not only become more organized, penetrating the political process, but also have been successful in shaping the debate.[66] Although the peace movement contains persons supporting approaches to peace, the nuclear pacifists have set the tone. They share a strong contempt for the two superpowers, and thus their political outlook has a strong nonaligned bias. The action of the antinuclear movement feeds also on a moral-idealistic approach to international relations. Its members believe in the virtue of fair intentions, trust, and unilateral gestures of goodwill. Some of their proposed disarmament measures are inspired by the work of Charles Osgood.[67]

Despite their reiterated disapproval of both superpowers and defense blocs, most of the criticism has been reserved for the United States and NATO. The United States is usually portrayed as the main culprit in the nuclear arms race. Even when confronted with conflicting information, the peace movements easily explain it away: In the arms race action-reaction model, the Soviet Union is usually depicted as the reactor. The military crackdown against the independent Solidarity trade-union movement was rationalized away by contending that the Soviets had hardened their position as a consequence of the deterioration in East-West relations and President Reagan's allegedly warlike policy. This type of closed-minded analysis gives any freeze or unilateral disarmament proposal an aura of rationality. Thus, it cannot be expected that the role of the peace and antinuclear movements will automatically diminish in the post-INF period. A further growth, however, would not necessarily imply more influence; any expansion of the movement might increase the battle over the operational definition of peace and thus weaken their present cohesion.

The more open security debate did not come without some banalization. The present discussion suffers a great deal from emotional oratory, selective perception or presentation of facts, reductionist arguments, linear thinking, and inadequate moral analysis. Also, several alternative defense proposals are long on prescription but short on analysis.[68] But the change has been real, and even if the emotional pitch does not remain, it is certain that the formation of security policy will never again be as closed as it was during the first two-and-a-half decades of Belgian alignment.

One of the major causes of the present state of affairs is the fact that Belgium's political leaders have allowed the defense debate to be dominated by those who oppose most defense efforts. As a result, the supporters of NATO programs have been on the defensive, and public opinion has become increasingly sympathetic to the arguments rejecting NATO programs. Belgian political leaders have not made a major political effort to gain the initiative in the public debate.

Initially, the government had an attitude of disdain toward the growing domestic defense debate, and thus it largely tried to ignore such a development. Some decision makers expressed surprise or lacked the training to cope with or understand fundamental criticisms. They frequently dealt with the criticism by labeling it as too emotional or uninformed. Nevertheless, the growing public involvement in Belgian defense-policy questions required the decision makers to make a much greater effort to legitimize their policy.

In recent years, it is evident that there have been changes in the attitude of the government, including the development of an acute awareness of the necessity of providing the public with better information. Defense Minister Freddy Vreven has treated defense as a matter of concern for all citizens. He has argued that the defense-policy-making process should become more transparent and develop what he called a "preventive information policy."[69] Without any doubt, there is a strong need for a better informed public. The problem, however, is not only a lack of information, but a lack of credible information. It would also be immeasurably beneficial to stimulate the growth of a greater mass of independent defense- and security-related expertise.

The requirements for conducting a consistent and reasonably effective long-term security policy have changed. The Belgian Government faces a completely new task in legitimizing security policy. It will succeed only by convincing a considerable number of members of Parliament, the administration, and the public that it has a reasonable, adequately conceived security policy. This presupposes two things. First, the government must convince these groups that the objectives are desirable and worthwhile, and that its policy conforms to the dominant national values and contributes to their achievement, thus establishing the *normative legitimacy* of its security policy. Second, the government has to convince the population that it knows how to realize those long-term objectives, and that it has adequate means and sufficient insight into the behavior of other states and the changing world situation, thus creating *cognitive legitimacy* for its security policy.

The popular and political legitimacy of defense policy rests on both components being satisfied. The present discussion about security and defense in Belgium is mainly focused on the cognitive component. The majority of Parliament and the public identifies itself with the national interest to be defended, but it is no longer willing to accept that specific government decisions are necessarily the best way to secure those interests. Critics thus focus on the effectiveness and efficiency of defense policy. The basic challenge to the government is to restore a more broad-based cognitive legitimacy to its security policy.

Changing Perceptions of the Security Scene

The changes that have taken place in the political process have been crucial factors in the decline of the Belgian security consensus. Equally important, however, are the changes that have taken place in the way that Belgium perceives its security scene. In one sense the evolution of the political process has influenced the development of these new perceptions, yet in another sense these new perceptions have been instrumental in promoting the changes in the political process. It is especially interesting to examine some of these perceptions that provide a clear demarcation from the period of unquestioned consensus.

THE DEFENSE BUDGET: THE ECONOMY AND THE SECURITY CONNECTION. The deterioration of economic conditions in Belgium in the 1970s was one of the two factors that fueled the country's new debate about defense policy. In the 1950s and 1960s Belgium's defense effort had fluctuated, but once targets were established there were few problems in achieving those goals. By the end of the 1970s this was no longer the case. An increased financial burden of defense, serious economic difficulties, and the increased politicization of defense questions more generally combined to make Belgian defense policy a major casualty of the economic recession. This has of course been more or less true of all European Allies, but the Belgian case is particularly interesting because it has been one of the most acute. Two elements are important to understanding this situation.

First, Belgium was one of the countries hardest hit by the world recession (see Table 1.6). The economy's vulnerability, combined with the cumulative impact of a weakening industrial base, years of underinvestment, a generous welfare state, and consequently a huge budget deficit, forced Belgian governments to implement increasingly far-reaching countermeasures.

The general story is not unfamiliar. Since the early 1970s, unemployment has risen steadily. In contrast to the period from 1964 to 1973, when the jobless rate was 2.3 percent, the number out of work from 1974 to 1983 averaged 8.7 percent (see Table 1.7), reaching over 14 percent by the end of the period. The problem would have been less intractable if Belgium had been alone in its economic plight, but the openness of the Belgian economy (see Table 1.8), combined with the global recession, made it impossible to use exports to ameliorate domestic economic conditions. Moreover, imports were less easy to reduce than exports, and this produced a sharp deterioration in the Belgian balance of trade (see Table 1.9). The effect of stagnating trade on the Belgian economy was dramatic, since exports of goods and services account for two-thirds of the GDP. (The corresponding figure for the U.S. economy is 10 percent.)

Table 1.6   Gross Domestic Product

	1974	1976	1978	1980	1981	1982
Belgium	4.5	5.5	3.2	3.2	−1.1	1.1
EEC (average)	1.6	5.0	3.3	1.0	−0.3	0.5

Source: OECD Historical Statistics, July 1984.

Table 1.7   Unemployment Rate

	1974	1976	1978	1980	1982
Belgium	3.1	6.6	8.1	9.0	13.1
EEC (average)	3.1	5.2	5.5	6.0	9.2

Source: OECD Historical Statistics, July 1984.

Table 1.8   Exports and Imports of Goods and Services

Exports

	1975	1977	1979	1981
Belgium	53.7	55.9	59.5	68.7
EEC (average)	26.7	28.7	28.9	30.9

Imports

	1975	1977	1979	1981
Belgium	53.3	56.7	61.2	70.9
EEC (average)	25.9	28.0	28.8	30.7

Source: OECD Historical Statistics, July 1984.

Table 1.9   Trade Balance as a Percentage of GDP

	1973	1975	1977	1979	1980	1981
Belgium	2.2	0.4	−0.8	−1.7	−2.7	−2.2
EEC (average)	0.4	0.7	0.8	0	−0.8	0.2

Source: OECD Historical Statistics, July 1984.

The negative trade balance, which began in 1977, thus placed additional pressure on an already-strained economy.

The generous Belgian welfare state with its substantial unemployment benefits further exacerbated the country's financial predicament during the 1970s. As the jobless rate continued to rise, umemployment benefits increasingly drained the government's financial resources and helped produce a growing budget deficit. An increasingly pressing priority of the Belgian Government thus became to regain control of the deficit (see Table 1.10). In view of the high tax burden on Belgian citizens, the reduction could only be realized by cutting public expenditures. At the same time, the government was obliged to try to raise substantial international loans and to negotiate for wage moderation with the unions. Belgium's traditionally sacrosanct automatic wage-indexation system had to be replaced by lump-sum increases. This made it all the more difficult for the authorities to reduce public expenditures and consequently the budget deficit. Despite severe pruning and a series of stern measures, the deficit for the proposed 1984 budget still represented 11.5 percent of the GNP.

If the government had not been able to bring the fiscal difficulties of the Belgian state under control by the early 1980s, it had nevertheless succeeded in implementing austerity policies unprecedented in Belgium since the earliest postwar years. While the adjustment measures were all aimed at strengthening the future economic potential of the country, they also seriously strained the social fabric of the country, a fabric already severely stretched by the renewed tensions between the linguistic communities. By the end of the 1970s, visions of the future were of prolonged difficulties, and the environment had become one where people were looking for scapegoats.

Second, and surely not unrelated to the first, the Belgian public believes that the most important threats to the country are economic. When asked to indicate whether threats to security were predominantly of a political, military, or economic nature, 50 percent thought they were economic, 40 percent military, and the rest classified them as political.[70] Moreover, Belgium strongly feels the economic influence of Japan and the United States, and occasionally it considers this influence to be threatening. Even though the economic decline has largely been caused by structural problems, excessive welfare-state burdens, and a pessimistic

---

Table 1.10   Belgian Budget Deficits as a Percentage of GNP

1972	1973	1974	1975	1976	1977	1978	1979	1980
5.8	5.3	4.3	6.8	7.6	7.7	8.1	9.4	11.8

Source: Nationale Bank: Verslagen, 1980.

business psychology, U.S. economic policy has unquestionably accentuated the downturn. Multinational corporations also play an important role in the Belgian perception of economic threats. These corporations, because of their share in the Belgian economy, exercise considerable influence. Belgian policy makers, however, see them as much less of a danger than does the public, which considers them as the second major factor of economic insecurity. (Both policy makers and the public consider their dependence on energy and raw materials as the main economic threat to Belgian security.)[71] It is also interesting to note that 68 percent of the public has believed that the energy policy of the United States is an economic threat, and that the threats emanating from the economic, financial, and technical power of the United States and the Soviet Union are equal.

For our purposes here, the consequences of these perceptions were two. The first was that by the end of the 1970s the overwhelming majority of the population was concerned primarily with resolving the country's economic difficulties and was little interested in the requirements of defense; the military was dealing with only a secondary threat to security. Second, the perception that the Allies, principally the United States, were contributing to Belgium's economic vulnerability made Belgians less willing to follow the rigid defense guidelines determined by Alliance policy.

The consequence of these two conditions, along with the general politicization of defense, was to make the Belgian defense budget a more contentious item by the end of the 1970s. Because the military sector does not enjoy a powerful, widely based constituency, as do other segments of the state budget, defense expenditures have a higher propensity to become the focus of attention when economizing is necessary. Thus, as the economic situation worsened in the late 1970s, the government had an increasingly difficult time in merely maintaining levels of defense expenditure, let alone raising military allocations, as was urged by NATO.

Defending defense expenditures in Belgium was no longer a politically or economically attractive option. In 1980, 40 percent of those asked considered Belgium's military efforts useless, while only 31 percent thought they were useful; 29 percent expressed no opinion.[72] A plurality of those who considered the efforts as useful, however, also judged them to be unsatisfactory (20 percent); and the plurality of those who responded negatively toward Belgium's defense admitted nonetheless that these military efforts were necessary (24 percent). Despite the low appreciation of the army's capability, only 33 percent of the public believed that this inadequacy should be redressed by an increase in the defense budget, and, in fact, 53 percent were opposed to such a move.[73] Younger members of the Belgian population registered the most outspoken opinions. In July 1980 the Le Soir–RTBF poll indicated that 55 percent of the younger citizens believed that if the country needed to economize it should begin with defense.[74]

By 1979 the economic crisis had hit the Ministry of Defense, with the budget showing an annual decrease in spending of one percent. The Belgian Government took the position that all ministries had to join in the economization measures. In 1980 the government approved an across-the-board budget cut of all ministerial departments, including a 2.2 percent cut for defense. Minister of Defense Charles Poswick objected, demanding instead a ten percent increase. He even threatened to resign if this demand was not satisfied. In the end, the government and the Minister reached a compromise. In 1981 and 1982 the government again economized. In 1983 the increase of the defense budget was set equal to the inflation rate; in real terms this meant a cut of 5 billion Belgian francs from original targets.

The effects of the stringent defense budget have been felt in the military posture, but they have been felt even more severely in the modernization process and the operational capacity of the Belgian forces. Moreover, the lasting economic depression has created a climate of frustration, which the opposition and the peace movements have effectively exploited. They have made a great effort to link defense policy with the crises of unemployment, recession, inflation, and the persistent North-South gap. Consequently, defense has become a scapegoat for many and reducing defense efforts a panacea for curing many ills. This linkage policy not only enhanced the popular support of the peace movements but also relieved them of the more difficult task of evaluating defense and security policy on its own terms. The linkage strategy has also made it more difficult for the government to legitimize its security and defense policy.

While Belgian security policy is still determined by a strong NATO commitment, social and economic factors have sharply curtailed the government's freedom. The imperative of reducing the budget deficit meant that the 3 percent real-growth target would have to be financed by either shifts from social-security provisions or by higher taxes. The latter was economically inadvisable and the former was politically unthinkable. The only mitigating factor has been the government's desire to prevent a further decline in the domestic arms industry, but this has been a minor consideration compared to the overwhelming pressure for spending cuts.

THE CRUISE MISSILE: AN IMPROVED DETERRENT—A NEW COMMITMENT?
Unlike the original deployment of nuclear weapons on Belgian territory, the cruise-missile issue became a main stumbling block in Belgian defense policy. The issue catalyzed a considerable latent concern about such problems as the risks of nuclear war, the decoupling of Europe and the United States, and low cost-effectiveness of present international security policies. One reason was that the discussion about cruise missiles increased the fear among a greater number of Belgians that Europe might become a battlefield for settling a conflict between the two superpowers. For Louis Tobback, a spokesman of the opposition, the installation of the INF on European territory implied a division of the NATO zone into a sanctuary (the United States) and a less-sacred zone (Europe).[75] A second reason was that INF was seen as further decoupling the United States and

Europe by increasing the transfer of responsibility for Alliance security to the European Allies. The destabilizing impact of the installation and its nefarious effect on the nuclear escalation process was also feared. In addition, the INF issue became, from a political point of view, even more pungent when it acquired a symbolic meaning as peace movements started to use the cruise-missile stand as a shibboleth for distinguishing peace-minded from nonpeace-minded citizens.

Originally the INF issue didn't seem to be a problem; the government had even planned to decide the question autonomously. In reply to a parliamentary question raised by Tobback, the leader of the Socialist faction, Foreign Minister Henri Simonet answered that it was not the duty of the government to organize a parliamentary debate before the INF decision was made. In its declaration of 17 October 1979, the government indicated its intention to determine policy and then convey the decision to the Parliament. Again, no parliamentary debate was promised. It was only during the last few weeks before the NATO meeting on the deployment decision that most political parties started to consider the issue seriously. When the results emerged, the Communists (KPB), the Socialists (SP and PS), and a coalition of the Flemish National- ists (VU) and the Walloon Rally (RW) were against; the other parties were, though sometimes with nuances of differences, for the installation, with or without the negotiation linkage.

Within some parties, the discussions were also a source of tension. The Flemish Liberal Party (PVV) was for deployment, but the youth branch of the party, which was against it, protested the decision of the party bureau. The French-speaking Socialist Party (PS) was equally divided. Simonet had to defend his position (installation and negotiation) before a majority of the party, who were opposed. Eventually, the party decided to insist on postponing the decision for a period of six months.

The Flemish Christian Democratic Party (CVP) came out in favor of the installation, despite some opposition from its youth branch and the union side. The Brussels French-speaking Democratic Front (FDF) agreed in principle to the deployment, but it demanded a six-month postponement of the decision. The French-speaking Christian Demo- crats (PSC) waited longest to take a position. Their final decision was a synthesis of what the SP, the PS, the CVP, and the FDF had agreed upon—that is, to start INF production and negotiations and to stop the production when the talks produced results.

Evidently, there was no definitive consensus among the parties. More important, however, was the lack of agreement within the coalition government (CVP, PSC, SP, PS, and FDF).[76] Among the coalition parties, there were proponents and opponents of various options,[77] which in- cluded rejection of Alliance policy and of the installation of the cruise missiles on Belgian territory; acceptance of Alliance policy and rejection of cruise missiles; acceptance of NATO policy and of the stationing of cruise missiles; and acceptance of NATO policy and of a partial installa- tion of cruise missiles.

In spite of the government's opposition, a measure of parliamentary debate did develop. A joint commission of the Foreign Affairs and Defense Committees from the Senate and the House of Representatives gathered to hear the government's arguments. In addition, five members of Parliament, from the CVP, the SP, and the VU, introduced a resolution wherein a governmental statement, followed by a parliamentary debate, was demanded.[78] The government was reluctant, but through an introduction of nine interpellations from different political parties, Parliament succeeded in forcing a debate.[79] Although the parties could not agree on how the issue should be resolved, all of them were displeased with the lack of adequate information and the disrespectful, negative attitude of the government toward a parliamentary debate. Finally, because of a lack of consensus within its own ranks as well as parliamentary pressure, the government was forced to assume a more accommodating position.[80]

On 12 December 1979 a compromise was reached among the coalition parties. They decided to support production, but to postpone the installation decision for six months in order to allow the government time to assess the existence of signs of Soviet moderation. This agreement was presented to the Parliament, and the Prime Minister requested a vote of confidence. The decision was endorsed with 130 for, 48 against, and 8 abstentions.

This decision, however, did not mean the end of the cruise-missile debate. In April 1980 the second Martens Government fell over a state reform issue. The new government declaration, agreed upon by the six coalition parties (CVP, PSC, SP, PS, PRL—the French-speaking Liberal Reform Party, and PVV), stipulated that the negotiation efforts should be continued and that a new installation moratorium be set for the end of 1980. At the occasion of the North Atlantic Council meeting in Ankara in June 1980, Belgian Minister of Foreign Affairs Charles Nothomb stated that domestic problems inhibited his country from providing a definitive answer about the installation of the INF weapons.

After the Soviet decision to start negotiations, the reactions in Belgium were divergent. Some, like Minister Nothomb (PSC) and Minister Poswick and his party (PRL), thought that the time had come for Brussels to speak out in favor of the installation in order to prevent Belgium from becoming "le membre malade de l'OTAN."[81] Others expressed the opinion that there was no need for haste in reaching a decision. The Flemish Socialist Party insisted on respecting the governmental accord, and consequently the moratorium was maintained until the end of 1980. André Cools, chairman of the French-speaking Socialist Party, expressed his uneasiness over "those who feel that they are authorized to validate a policy that is based solely on military pressures."[82]

A quick decision was further hindered by the fact that the House of Representatives postponed a debate about the INF weapons that was originally planned for July until October because of an overflowing socioeconomic agenda. Pressured by Germany and the United States,[83] Nothomb pressed once more for approval, but mainly because of Socialist resistance, a decision could not be reached. After the summer recess of 1980, the debate again became animated. The French-speaking Socialist Party thought that it should wait for the results of the U.S. and German elections and the start of the CSCE Review Conference in Madrid; the French-speaking Christian Democrats were of the opinion that they should take a positive stand as soon as possible. The Flemish Liberal Party and the Flemish Christian Democrats defended similar positions. Among the coalition parties once again a certain tension developed with respect to the INF issue.

On 19 September 1980 another compromise was reached. The compromise implied that the government, after six months, would survey the status of the negotiations between the United States and the USSR and then reach the necessary conclusions as to whether or not to install some or all of the cruise missiles. The coalition parties seemed to be satisfied; however, their contentment seemed to be based on different interpretations. For some (for example, the PS), the compromise implied that if no results were attained after six months a decision would have to be made about the installation of the missiles. For others (the PVV), it meant that if no results were reached it would automatically lead to the installation of the GLCMs (ground-launched cruise missiles).

Eventually, the September 1980 accord was extended indefinitely. In the revised governmental declaration, however, the decision was to install the missiles when a semiannual evaluation indicated that no results could be expected from the negotiations. After more than a year of the fifth Martens Government, no evaluation seemed to have taken place. But in June 1982 the Flemish Christian Democratic Party declared that in view of the first semiannual evaluation and the developments at Geneva, it considered the installation unnecessary for the time being. The positions of most of the other political parties remained the same, with the exception of the Flemish Socialist Party, which became more radical, stating that under no conditions was it willing to accept the installation of cruise missiles on Belgian territory. It even went as far as to make the acceptance of its position a sine qua non for its participation in government.

The debate over the cruise missiles catalyzed the coordination of many action and pressure groups. This phenomenon expressed itself more sharply in Flanders than in Wallonia and Brussels, chiefly because of the better organization of the peace movement in Flanders and the differing interests of both the other regions. Because of its relatively strong military industry, Wallonia has always benefited from weapons production and is still an important supplier to NATO.[84]

The opposition to the INF modernization plans came not only from peace organizations, such as Pax Christi, Justicia et Pax, Mouvement Chrétien pour la Paix, and Ikove, but also from the union side. The Bureau of the Belgian Socialist Union (ABVV) explicitly denounced the stationing of both the Soviet SS-20s and the American missiles. On 7 December 1979 the Christian Union denounced the absence of a parliamentary debate and requested a postponement of six months before implementing the NATO decision in order to give negotiations a chance. Their general position was reiterated in May 1983, when the Christian Union demanded that the NATO countries, as a gesture of goodwill, support a no-first-use policy and suspend the installation.

In December 1979 a protest rally of 40,000 to 50,000 persons was held in Brussels. The demonstration was organized by the National Committee for Peace and Development (CNAPD) and the Flemish Action Committee Against Nuclear Weapons (VAKA). Participating were representatives of the SP, the PS, the VU, the KPB (Communist Party of Belgium), and some parliamentarians from the CVP and the FDF, who attended as individuals rather than as party representatives.

The same peace groups also organized the "200,000 Protest March" of October 1981. A number of parties subscribed to the march committee's platform, but for various reasons the PVV, the CVP, the PSC, the PRL, and the UDRT (Respect for Labor and Democracy party) refused to be associated. The Flemish Liberals (PVV) decided that they could not sign the platform because of their conviction that negotiations could succeed only on the basis of a strong position; they considered the platform of the demonstrators therefore to be counterproductive. The Christian Democrats (CVP and PSC) expressed an understanding of the ideals that stimulated the demonstration but didn't subscribe to the platform, since its biased character was not in line with the party's more positive appreciation of Atlantic solidarity. The UDRT considered all discussions on disarmament as demagogic, and, in addition, they were convinced that the demonstration was manipulated: "The UDRT is fundamentally in favor of peace, but refuses to participate in biased and foreign controlled demonstrations."[85] Nonetheless, the massive attendance indicated that the influence of the pressure groups could not be underestimated. The impact of the protest march on the November election results in still an open question. According to some analysts, the CVP lost partially because of its somewhat aloof attitude toward the demonstration, even in spite of the participation of the Christian Unions.[86]

The VAKA and CNAPD were also active at the municipal level. Their purpose was to get as many municipalities as possible to come out against the installation of the nuclear missiles on their territory. By the end of 1983 more than 200 municipalities had made such a decision. In Flanders approximately 60 percent of the municipalities decided against the installation.

The Belgian public generally sides with the opposition with regard to the INF modernization. In 1980, 41 percent of those interviewed expressed themselves against the installation, 26 percent were in favor, and 33 percent expressed no opinion.[87] A year later, the number "against" had increased to 50 percent.[88] Since the question was phrased in categorical terms, it is difficult to interpret the answers. A less-loaded question—for instance, in more conditional terms—would without any doubt provide a different distribution of responses and considerably facilitate the interpretation. For example, a 1982 poll showed that 25 percent of the Belgians interviewed believed that their security would be enhanced by the installation. Approximately as many (22 percent) thought that their security would be weakened, and 27 percent were convinced that it would make no difference whatsoever.[89]

A subsequent opinion poll indicated that 79 percent of the Belgians were against the installation. The question, however, was again worded in categorical terms.[90] A differently phrased question gave a totally different distribution of responses; it indicated that 62 percent of the Belgian population were proinstallation.[91]

There are also contradictions in public opinion, such as the attitudes of the 15–24-year-old age group, that further hinder definitive interpretations. This age group is the most negative toward the cruise missiles, yet at the same time it expects the least negative impact of the installation; 34 percent would feel safer, and 26 percent think it would make no difference.[92] These findings suggest that the attitudes toward the installation on Belgian soil are not solely based on rational "security considerations."

Contours of Belgian Policy Toward NATO in the 1980s

Belgium's future role in the Alliance will depend on many factors. First, two groups that exercise opposing influences on the security debate seriously constrain the freedom of political authorities. While not structured in the same way as those that exist in the Netherlands, they nevertheless function essentially as two main veto groups. On the one hand, there is a pro-NATO elite, which can be found mainly in the Foreign Affairs and Defense department bureaucracies and in political parties like the PVV-PRL (Liberals) and the CVP-PSC (Christian Democrats). This elite tends to see most NATO decisions as synonymous with Belgian security interests. On the other hand, there is an antinuclear group involving the peace movements and represented heavily in the SP and the PS (Socialists), the VU (Flemish Regionalist), the Ecolo-Agalev (Environmentalists), the KPB—PCB (Communists), and the Wallon Regionalists. To this group one can also add a few dissenting voices within the Christian Democratic parties. Nuclear weapons present the main issue of cleavage between these two factions, but they also have a general difference of approach to defense and foreign policy.

Second, under these circumstances much will be determined by the composition of ruling coalitions. No government will have the freedom of maneuver previously enjoyed by political leaders from the 1950s to the mid-1970s. Governments formed largely on the basis of economic-policy considerations will inevitably find their flexibility to deal with issues on the Alliance agenda limited by differing approaches to security policy. The highly fractionalized Belgian political scene makes it likely that the presence of these conflicts will be the rule, not the exception. During the period of the Center–Christian Democrat–Socialist coalition led by Wilfried Martens, the INF issue was extremely delicate for the government to handle, whereas the fall of the government and the departure of the Socialists slightly improved the flexibility of the ministers to deal with preparations for deployment. Although the new government had to proceed cautiously, preliminary steps were taken to enable work to begin on a site for the cruise missiles.

Third, the shape in which new issues emerge will have a significant impact on the way the political system handles them. Until now, most governments have tried to avoid confronting difficult issues directly and thus confronting their constituents with clear political choices. On INF, for instance, they have postponed making decisions while continuing to reiterate their belief in arms control negotiations. Above all, the Belgian Government has failed to take the initiative in the public debate over security policy. The future shape of the debate will depend on whether this situation is allowed to continue or whether governments will begin to play a more active role in defining the terms of the debate. If governments fail to respond convincingly to the many pertinent criticisms of their policies, the existing credibility gap will widen. It seems this fact has been understood. The government and the ruling political parties now realize that the nuclear issues will not quietly slide into obscurity, and that if they do not make a major effort to regain the initiative in the public debate, political consequences may be profound. The distribution of INF information folders, the Tindemans initiative, and the visit of the chairman of the Flemish Christian Democratic Party to the Soviet Union indicate a change in the governmental approach from an aloof, reactive disposition toward a more responsive, leading role.

Fourth, the nature of the issues with which the government will be confronted will themselves determine whether the intensity of recent controversies persist. The nuclear issue lent itself to mobilizing discontent more easily than most other defense questions; traditional budgetary questions will divide the two veto groups, but major political debate will not be as sustainable as with questions of nuclear strategy. Thus, some issues will be dealt with more in a business-as-usual fashion. The key factor will be whether new issues arise that eventually will be perceived as requiring significant new commitments.

A fifth trend that could change significantly the dynamics of the defense debate is the growing politization of the peace movement. The major political parties made great efforts to encapsulate and dominate a part of this movement. As a consequence of the politization process and of the conceptual demystification of the term "peace," one may well find that a considerable number of the followers of the peace movements may leave the alternative circuit to engage in a more broad-minded and politically traditional peace and security-policy debate. In this context the government can be expected to make a serious effort to improve Belgian education in strategic and international studies. This is considered as a means to enhance a more decisive policy and to back up a Belgian role as initiator in the field of arms control while refurbishing influence in the decision-making process of the Alliance. The latter will be necessary to diminish a widespread feeling of frustration stemming from a sense of political inefficacy in the NATO decision-making process, or, in other words, to lessen a prevailing national self-image of being a loyal but mainly a dependent variable.

Finally, Belgium's role in the Alliance will depend greatly on the behavior and priorities of its major external reference groups: the United States, West Germany, France, England, and the Netherlands. These countries will not only provide cues for Belgian defense policy but also will set the limits for domestic political conflict. Debate over security policy in Belgium will not take place in a vacuum; its intensity will grow and diminish at least partially as a function of pressures from those partners that it traditionally uses as reference points, as well as being influenced by the nature and intensity of domestic debate in those countries. The perception for instance, that the U.S. Government was pursuing a policy of brinkmanship or was striving toward nuclear superiority would inevitably provoke a continuation of controversy in Belgium and raise further skepticism about Alliance policies. In addition, these countries will determine the parameters of Belgian influence on Alliance policy, which in turn will influence the domestic debate. Belgium will probably try to reassert its former role as initiator within the Alliance, both for reasons of domestic politics and international prestige.

With respect to the specific issues, Belgian policies during the rest of the decade can be expected to follow several general orientations that collectively symbolize an adherence to continuity. The first of these will be a concerted attempt to *avoid significant new commitments* in defense policy. Belgian governments do not like to stumble over defense and security issues. Since World War II, many governments have been threatened by regional and economic problems, but not until 1979 was a government endangered by a security issue—namely, the installation of INF weapons on Belgian territory.

Reluctance to accept new commitments will stem from consideration of finances and risks. But above all, hesitation will come from the fact that such new commitments tend to polarize the traditional multipartisan security consensus, and consequently they disrupt the smooth functioning of government that is necessary for coping with the economic security concerns. Coalition parties are loath to dissolve the government over controversial matters. The fact that the Socialists compromised on the INF question, accepting production while installation was postponed, illustrates this inclination. The Socialist Party shared the opinion that dissolving the government in a critical economic period would be irresponsible. As a result, governments will probably direct policy away from moves to increase the cost of defense (for example, the Rogers 4 percent plan), and even more so, away from commitments that are perceived to raise the risks for Belgium (for example, cruise missiles).

Most Belgium officials will also continue to oppose moves to extend the NATO intervention zone as stipulated in the NATO charter; that is, beyond Europe, North America, Turkey and the islands falling under the jurisdiction of the member-states and lying to the north of the Tropic of Cancer. The potential of this issue to catalyze political controversy was illustrated by a short debate in 1981 about the American Rapid Deployment Force (RDF). Some feared that the government had committed itself to help this force by permitting the construction on Belgian territory of American depots that would be used to support the RDF in times of crisis. The Flemish Socialist Party considered such a deployment not only as contradictory to existing Belgian law, which states that Belgium cannot engage in commitments that are not limited to the NATO zone, but also as a dangerous policy, since Belgium could unwillingly be held hostage to the Reagan Administration's actions concerning Western "vital interests" outside the NATO zone. The government responded by stressing that it had no depots planned for the RDF and that any extension of the NATO zone was out of the question. This position, however, was qualified by stipulating that bilateral accords exclusive of NATO business could be concluded with the United States.

The second basic orientation of Belgian security policy will undoubtedly be toward finding *a more cost-effective security policy*. Belgium will seek to provide the necessary security at the lowest possible level of effort. Part of the commitment to achieve a more cost-effective security policy involves the question of resources and budgets. Each government since 1980 has declared that defense expenditures cannot be granted an exclusive status when it is time to economize. This policy has provoked little or no criticism from political parties. There appears to be a general agreement about the principle of linearity when it concerns budget cuts. With the exception of the PSC, the CVP, and the VU, all political parties have explicitly emphasized the necessity of economizing on the defense budget, and this includes even the PVV, which has demanded a 5 percent cut in investment expenditures through a more rigorous application of contract procedures. The PSC has not specifically opposed the recent defense cuts, but it has demanded that the Belgian army—despite budgetary difficulties—should stay fully operational. The CVP has argued that Belgium ought at least to strive to maintain defense expenditures at the same percentage of the GNP. Thus, there is a constant financial push to find ways to get more for each franc spent and to spend less for the same degree of defense. Making Western defense more cost-effective is likely to be a predominant theme in Belgian policy during the coming period, despite the fact that Belgian political leaders cannot currently agree on exactly how these goals should be pursued.

At the same time, increasing attention will continue to be given to conventional defense, mainly because of the growing belief that measures to correct the existing conventional imbalance are a prerequisite for progress in nuclear arms control. This concern, however, will not result in a massive transfer of resources to conventional capabilities, but rather it is likely to stimulate initiatives aimed at a further Europeanization of defense and, above all, of weapons production, and at finding ways to break the impasse threatening the MBFR negotiations. The Belgians will hope to bring about a corrected balance at a lower level.

The third orientation of Belgian security policy will be *the long-standing dedication to arms control.* Although the desire to create a more cost-effective security program will inspire the government to pursue arms-control negotiations, this commitment stems from much more than just this financial concern. Public support for defense efforts will depend strongly on the ability of the government to convince its public that NATO is actively and seriously negotiating at the various armament levels. To enhance its credibility, the Belgian Government will almost certainly reassert its traditional initiative role in this area.

Thus, Belgian demand for a less offensive military posture in the East and West and for more viable arms-control arrangements and confidence-building measures is likely to grow. At the nuclear level, Belgium will probably continue to support NATO's flexible response doctrine. There will be pressures, however, not only from the antinuclear lobby but also from other sectors to reduce and finally eliminate destabilizing nuclear weapons. The chief targets are likely to be the most vulnerable weapons (land-based), first-strike weapons (SS-20, 21, 22, and 23, and Pershing I and II), and self-deterring weapons (battlefield nuclear weapons). All of these measures will be aimed at obtaining more security with less cost and less risk. There has been a great deal of public and political frustration regarding arms control and disarmament negotiations. As observed by peace organizations and parties opposing current security policy, growing arsenals have not delivered more security, but rather less security, or, euphemistically stated, equal security at a greater price. The rising mutual overkill capacity further contributes to these fears. Some people also wonder why NATO continually cries wolf, despite the fact that it accounts for a significantly greater percentage of world military expenditure than the Warsaw Pact countries.

To understand the level of frustration existing in Belgium, the rising expectations and aspirations engendered by the détente period have to be considered. The collapse of détente and the reemergence of hostile East-West relations have created a more favorable environment for the arguments of those dissatisfied with current policies. The nonratification of SALT II and the unsuccessful MBFR negotiations fostered frustration and increased distrust of the superpowers, especially of the United States. The peace movements continually question the goodwill of the negotiators. For instance, they assert that the alleged American preparedness to negotiate with the Soviets was merely a political facade designed to legitimize the stationing of cruise and Pershing II missiles. The same negative attitude exists with respect to the MBFR negotiations. The peace movement insists that Belgium should play a more "constructive role" in the effort to break the present stalement.

The widespread attitude of distrust is further enhanced by a growing feeling of political inefficacy and public powerlessness. These feelings have contributed to the pervading fear that military research and development is outrunning political control. Consequently, the opposition and the peace movements are pushing for nuclear and conventional military balances at a much lower level. And their sentiments are finding favorable responses.

The entire political spectrum supports more active and productive East-West arms-control efforts. The parties differ, however, on their prospective methods for achieving this goal. The Volksunie, the Walloon Regionalists, and the Flemish Communist Party all defend the idea of a nuclear-free zone in Europe. Both Christian Democratic parties, as well as both Liberal parties, advocate negotiations that would lead to a lower armament level, but at the same time they emphasize that this must be done from a position of parity. The French-Speaking Front and the French Socialist Party endorse a European disarmament conference in order to make the Helsinki agreements more meaningful. The Flemish Socialist Party calls for an immediate freeze on the nuclear arsenal, the withdrawal of all nuclear weapons from the nonnuclear European countries, the creation of a European nuclear-free zone, and negotiation of the lowest possible conventional balance. Similar proposals have been drafted and promoted by groups in the peace movement. Thus, there is a strong political consensus over the ends, if not the means. Obviating the need for increased defense expenditure while gaining control of the East-West arms race are shared goals.

A fourth general orientation will be to *prevent a further deterioration of Atlantic solidarity.* The present erosion of trans-Atlantic solidarity is caused by several factors. First, there are conflicts over such problems as burden-sharing, protectionist pressures, and high interest rates. Equally important are the many misunderstandings caused by different concerns and analyses and the American tendency to focus on European minority views of anti-Atlanticism. Despite these eroding pressures, there has always existed a substantial consensus within the government and Parliament concerning NATO membership. Each new government emphasizes its loyalty to the Alliance. As the fifth Martens Government expressed the matter, "Our defense policy is, within the general context of our national foreign policy, only thinkable within the framework of the collective security alliance. . . . In order to achieve more security, the government will base her policy on . . . loyalty to the NATO defense alliance."[93]

This continuous commitment will serve as a stabilizing factor in the face of those who might be tempted to push Belgian policy in a direction of reducing contributions to the Alliance. Although questions are frequently posed and criticisms raised with respect to concrete logistical problems, the basis of the Belgian role in NATO strategy and the acceptance of NATO doctrine have never been seriously questioned. Even Louis Tobback, known for his criticism of Belgian defense policy, has referred to himself as a "cool NATO lover" and "an American ally."[94]

The attitudes of most political parties concur with pro-NATO sentiment in Parliament. Even the Communist Party (KPB) platform does not demand that Belgium should unilaterally withdraw from NATO. The environmentalist group ECOLO is the only party with representatives in Parliament that included a motion in its platform for Belgium's withdrawal from the military structure of NATO. Even this party, however, desires that Belgium should remain a member of the Atlantic Alliance.[95] There are some small extreme leftist parties such as RAL (Revolutionary League of Workers) and the PvdA (Labor Party) that do demand a withdrawal from NATO. A slightly different attitude can be found in the platform of the FDF (French-Speaking Front). This Brussels-centered party demands that Belgium conduct a policy that would make Europe an autonomous entity with respect to defense organization and weapons production.[96]

The positive attitude of the government continues to find widespread support among the public. The majority of Belgians are still convinced that NATO represents the best framework for the country's defense.[97] Belgians, however, register a less favorable attitude toward NATO, 48 percent, when compared to the Germans, 75 percent; the Dutch, 73 percent; the Danish, 59 percent; and the English, 57 percent.[98] Moreover, the evolution of attitudes over time has a negative trend: From 1976 to 1980 positive appreciation of NATO dropped and the negative evaluation increased.[99] This sentiment contrasts sharply with the attitude of Belgian soldiers, who generally have no doubt whatsoever about the vital importance of NATO for Belgian security.[100]

Finally, the peace movement, with its strong pleas for the dissolution of both power blocs, NATO and the Warsaw Pact, must be considered. Despite their demands, it is remarkable that these peace organizations have chosen not to question the Belgian membership in NATO until the moment when both blocs can be dissolved. For example, Pax Christi pleads for the eventual establishment of a collective Pan-European security system that would make NATO and the Warsaw Pact superfluous. Moreover, it requests government support for the development of an alternative defense model in which nonmilitary forms of defense have a major role. Nowhere does it mention a unilateral withdrawal of Belgium from NATO.[101] Other peace organizations, such as the Flemish Action Committee Against Nuclear Weapons (VAKA) and the National Committee for Peace and Development (CNAPD), also urge a simultaneous dissolution of the military blocs.[102] A few radical movements, such as Onkruit, advocate an unconditional and immediate withdrawal from NATO, but their influence is insignificant. Until now, peace organizations have been very critical of NATO strategy. Consequently, they would like to see the government actively oppose NATO policy within the structure of the Alliance.[103] But despite all their efforts, these groups do not seem to have influenced overwhelmingly the attitude of most Belgians.

The fifth basic orientation of Belgian policy in the coming period will be an emphasis on *a more multidimensional approach to security.* In the eyes of many Belgians, the United States has made a great mistake by reducing its analysis of many conflicts to the East-West struggle, and by further aggravating the situation by a singular focus on the military dimension of the conflict at the expense of the other aspects. The significance the United States attaches to the military dimension is understood by those who fear the growing Soviet military potential. But at a time when little difference of opinion exists between the majority of European countries and the United States on the need to maintain a global and regional balance with the Soviet Union, Europeans think that the United States does not place sufficient import on the socioeconomic realities and on the endemic factors of instability in the world.[104] Belgians are very aware of the interdependence of securities—global-regional-national, military-economic-political, internal and external. But they believe strongly that defense expenditure needs to be fitted into an economic policy that gives priority to maintaining a healthy economy and a reasonable level of social welfare. This philosophy has not changed since the end of World War II, and it is not likely to in the next decade.

The final basic orientation will be the desire for *greater Europeanization of Europe's defense*. This conception involves much more than merely finding more efficient means to produce needed weapons systems. The recent pleas for European defense integration can be seen as a response to the growing demands of both the United States and the European Allies for more equitable burden sharing. Many Belgian opinion leaders believe a more integrated European defense would make burden sharing considerably more equal.

In order to understand the burden-sharing issue as seen from the Belgian perspective, it is necessary to distinguish between three kinds of burden sharing—material, risk, and conceptual—and to appreciate their interdependence. All too frequently the issue is simply portrayed as the need for Europe to pay more for its defense. Admittedly, there has been a great deal of tension within NATO surrounding different appreciations of material burden sharing. But perceptions of the current situation are not all similar.

Several years ago, Belgium agreed in conjunction with other NATO members to increase its defense budget by 3 percent annually. It quickly became evident that this commitment could not be fulfilled. Consequently, the Belgian Minister of Defense stressed that the 3-percent goal could only be realized on a long-term average. The government acknowledged the fact that it was not currently meeting the target, but it claimed that in the future it would change that situation. In addition, it stressed that in the previous years defense expenditures had surpassed the annual 3-percent target.

This situation has been frequently criticized by the United States and by NATO. Some time ago, General Bernard Rogers suggested that Belgium make cuts in the social sector so that the defense expenditure could be increased or at least be kept at the present level.[105] The Flemish Socialist Party replied that it was strange that the United States should suggest the need for a 3-percent increase, exactly after an eight-year period in which there had been a real increase in the Belgian defense budget and a real decrease in the U.S. defense budget. The difference between the yearly net change in spending of both countries in this period averaged approximately 7 percent.[106] Another reply to the American criticism was the fact that the 3-percent agreement included a clause referring to the economic conditions that would influence the efforts to achieve the prescribed goal. For Belgium, the domestic financial situation prohibited a 3-percent increase. According to the government, this position would be reevaluated when economic conditions permitted.[107]

It should also be noted that the material burden-sharing gap has significantly decreased since the end of the 1960s. Whereas Europe's 1969 contribution to NATO accounted for only 23 percent of the total budget, by 1979 it equaled more than 40 percent.[108] U.S. Secretary of Defense Caspar Weinberger partially recognized this fact when he stated, "The U.S. had made a major effort in recent years to urge its allies to assume a greater share of the common defense burden. . . . Those efforts have all achieved a measure of success, but more has to be done."[109]

With regard to risk burden sharing, most Belgians accept the need for equality among the Allies. There are, however, differing perceptions of the current balance. Whereas Americans claim, for instance, that INF modernization represents a good step in the direction of redistributing risks, some Belgians argue the converse. They contend that Europe presently bears the greatest dangers, and that after the INF modernization the situation will look even more asymmetric. For many Belgians the modernization process has reinforced the notion that Europe is increasing its role in the Western nuclear deterrent without receiving a commensurate increase in its control. The European fear centers around the concern that during a conflict the United States would try to limit a possible war to the European theater through the use of conventional weapons or the INF weapons and thereby avoid a strategic nuclear exchange.[110]

Finally, perhaps the key dimension of the burden-sharing problem is that caused by the discrepancy between the European material and conceptual contributions. The planning input of Europe in the Alliance has significantly lagged behind its increased military contributions. Since World War II, nearly all important concepts and theories with respect to security and defense have been developed by the United States. This situation is perhaps even more true for Belgium than the other European Allies, notwithstanding some praiseworthy Belgian initiatives.[111] A greater European contribution to the "architecture" of the security and defense policy of NATO represents a precondition for greater effectiveness and solidarity within the Alliance.

These considerations have stimulated renewed and growing interest, at the governmental and nongovernmental level, in the development of an integrated European security policy. While reducing defense costs through weapons standardization, a more integrated European approach to defense would also allow a more faithful articulation of European interests. Such a development would increase the identification of the population with the security of Europe and thereby, it is felt, strengthen its commitment to defense.[112] During the last few years, there has been a widespread proliferation of statements, lectures, articles, colloquia, reports, and books about the need to develop an integrated Euro-defense system.[113] In Belgium, at least, the purpose of more European integration is clearly not to become a third superpower, but rather to strengthen NATO and to bolster popular support for Alliance policies.

A leading exponent of European integration has been Foreign Minister Leo Tindemans. On many occasions he has emphasized that "within" the Atlantic Alliance the European pillar needed to be strengthened, and he has urged that a forum for political contacts between the European Community and the United States, with respect to security matters, be created. He considers the construction of a Western European political and defense organization necessary not only to reinforce security but also to restore European self-confidence.[114]

All the political parties who approve of the NATO framework for Belgian defense also support the idea of a European pillar. Their general line of thinking is that NATO must be the framework for the Belgian defense, but that Europe should be able to take its own stands rather than permit itself to be overwhelmed by the United States. A few political parties go further and argue for European independence with respect to defense. The FDF, for example, included in its 1981 election platform endorsement of an autonomous European defense.[115] The proponents of a fully independent Europe, however, are a small minority.

The European-dimension concept is also present in the minds of the general public. The degree of support, however, is difficult to assess. One indicator could be the opinion poll cited earlier in which 18 percent of the Belgians interviewed consider a European defense organization under European command within NATO as the best defense structure for Belgium.[116] Only the existing NATO arrangement scored higher (25 percent) as the best solution for defense. The pattern seems relatively constant, since a 1980 poll revealed similar results;[117] 23 percent of the Belgian population considered a European entity within the Alliance as the best defense structure, while "NATO as the best defense structure" scored 28 percent. The independent-Europe option was supported by 16 percent of the Belgians overall: 10 percent in Flanders, 23 percent in Wallonia, and 22 percent in Brussels. As the figures indicate, regional differences significantly influenced peoples' choice.

The majority of the public (61 percent), however, seems to be well aware that the military power of Europe alone would not be sufficient to counterbalance successfully the Soviet Union. Younger respondents (18–20) were the most optimistic, with 50 percent believing Europe strong enough to defend itself.[118] Of all the political groups, the Socialist parties' constituencies were the most evenly divided on this issue. In the Walloon part of the country, the Socialist voters (PS) believed the least in Europe's weakness (54 percent). The same is true in Flanders for those respondents who identified themselves as Socialist (SP, 49 percent). The Christian Democrats and the Liberals (CVP, PSC, PVV, and PRL) shared skepticism about Europe's ultimate power potential (70 percent).

In military circles one also finds the conviction that a strengthening of the European pillar is a "necessity." Exponents of this line of thought, such as General Pierre Cremer and General Robert Close, are convinced that Europe must strengthen itself within NATO in order to prevent a further widening of the U.S.-Europe gap. Both, however, emphasize that their proposals do not imply the creation of an independent European defense system.[119]

Consequently, Belgium will urge a stronger reconciliation at two levels: at the Atlantic level, and at the level of the ten European Community members. As a part of this revival of the two-pillar idea, there is a growing awareness of the need to assert more strongly the security dimension in European Political Cooperation. There is a clear belief that a greater effort by the European member-states would result in a more symmetrical contribution in the development of security and defense policy and would significantly contribute to a greater effectiveness and solidarity in the Atlantic Community. Convinced that the West would profit from a pluralistic and competitive market of ideas, Belgium will place a high priority on achieving a better equilibrium of conceptual contributions to Allied planning.

Notes

1. *Economisch Zakboekje* (Antwerp: Kluwer, 1983–84).
2. A. Adam, *The internationale veiligheid van staten: Hoe stelt zich het probleem voor België?* Lecture held at a K.I.B.-colloquium, Leuven, March 1980.
3. J. E. Helmreich, *Belgium and Europe: A Study in Small Power Diplomacy* (The Hague: Mouton, 1976), 14.
4. Helmreich, *Belgium and Europe*, 239.
5. F. Daels, "Weerbaarheid," in *Vos Visies*, no. 2 (1983).
6. L. Wils, *Politieke geschiedenis van België* (Leuven: Wouters, 1980), 90.
7. H. Simonet, "La sécurité de la Belgique dans son contexte futur," *Contact*, 56 (December 1980): 4.
8. Helmreich, *Belgium and Europe*, 347.
9. F. Govaerts, "Belgium, Holland and Luxembourg," in *Small Powers in Alignment*, O. De Raeymaeker, ed. (Leuven: University Press, 1974), 295; P. H. Spaak, *Parlementaire Handelingen Kamer* (1944–45), 6 December 1944, 92 (hereafter *Parl. Hand. Kamer*).
10. Paul F. Smets, ed., *La Pensé Europénne et Atlantique de Paul-Henry Spaak (1942–72)* (Brussels: Goemaere, 1980).
11. P. Van Zeeland (Christian Democrat), *Parlementaire Handelingen Senaat* 1948–49, 11 May 1949, 1891 (hereafter *Parl. Hand. Senaat*); J. Rey (Liberal); *Parl. Hand. Kamer*, 1948–49, 3 May 1949, 13; H. Fayat (Socialist), *Parl. Hand. Kamer*, 1948–49, 3 May 1949, 6–8.
12. Simonet, "La sécurité de la Belgique," 11.
13. House of Representatives: 139 in favor, 22 against, 1 abstention. Senate: 127 in favor, 13 against.
14. *Document no. 1.* (Leuven: Center for Strategic Studies, University of Leuven, 1982).
15. S. Vancaeneghem, "Een paraat leger? Jawel om een oorlog te vermijden," interview with F. Swaelen, Minister of Defense, *Spectator*, 23 (6 June 1981): 12.
16. Simonet, "La sécurité de la Belgique," 9–26; see also P. H. Spaak, "Dès le début

de la crise de Suez, j'eus donc deux préoccupations: Être ferme vis à vis de Nasser et tâcher de contribuer à maintenir l'entente parmi les partenaires de l'Alliance Atlantique," in *Combats Inachevés*, vol. 1: *de l'indépendance à l'alliance* (Paris: Fayard, 1969), 229.

17. Spaak, *Combats Inachevés*, vol. 2: *de l'espoir au déception* (Paris: Fayard, 1969), 336.

18. Simonet, "La sécurité de la Belgique," 23.

19. Ibid., 23.

20. J. Gérard-Libois, "Le conduite et la politique extérieure de la Belgique," *Res Publica*, 5 (1973): 947–64; L. de Smedt, "M. Spaak et M. Harmel. Dix années de politique étrangère belge, deux hommes, une même politique," *Res Publica*, 3/4 (1974): 601–16.

21. L. Colot, "La politique belge en matière de détente et de coopération en Europe," *Chronique de Politique Etrangère*, (January 1969): 53–128.

22. *Parl. Hand. Kamer*, 1965–66, 14 June 1966, 13–15.

23. Govaerts, "Belgium, Holland and Luxembourg," 353.

24. *Parl. Hand. Kamer*, 1953–54, 12 November 1953, 9.

25. Spaak, *Combats Inachevés*, vol. 1, 27.

26. *Parl. Hand. Kamer*, 1953–54, 17 November 1953, 11.

27. *Parl. Hand. Senaat*, 1962–1963, 5 February 1953, 445.

28. *Parl. Hand. Senaat*, 1960–1961, 9 May 1961, 42–45.

29. *Parl. Hand. Kamer*, 1956–1957, 9 May 1957, 7–12.

30. *Parl. Hand. Senaat*, 1962–1963, 5 February 1963, 446–451.

31. *Parl. Hand. Kamer*, 1971–1972, 21 June 1972, 1690.

32. Spaak, *Combats Inachevés*, vol. II, 199.

33. *Parl. Hand. Senaat*, 1962–1963, 5 February 1963, 446–451.

34. The following data and information can be found in J. Smits, *Democratie op straat, een analyse van de betogingen in België* (Leuven: Acco, 1984); and "Les Mouvements de la paix en Belgique," *Courrier Hebdomadaire*, 240 (24 April 1964). Among the participants on 10 April 1960 were: Jeune Garde Socialiste, Kommunistische Jeugd, Jong Socialisten, and Jeunesses Syndicales. The only non-Socialist or Communist movements participating were the Liège-section of the "Jeunesse Ouvrière Chrétienne" and a number of radical pacifist groups; on 24 March 1963 there were, in addition to the earlier groupings, also members of the Katholiek Vlaams Hoogstudenten Verbond (Union of Catholic Flemish University Students), the Union of Humanist Youth, the Francophone Student Youth, and some representatives of Protestant and Jewish organizations. The official slogans were:
• Against atomic weapons and equipment in Belgium and for the Belgian army
• For an immediate stop to all atomic tests
• Against nuclear proliferation
• For destruction of all nuclear weapons
• For general mutual and controlled disarmament
In March 1964 a greater number of Catholic youth organizations participated. There were also a great number of marchers from Holland and Germany, and they were joined by some parliamentarians. In addition to the Communists, there were Socialists (Rolin, Glinne, Hurez, Bracops, and Cudell) and Catholics (Van Cauwelaert, de la Vallée Poussin, and Debecquoy). The slogans were similar to those of 1963, but additional demands were:
• A reduction and reconversion of military expenditures to the social and cultural sector, and aid to developing countries
• A nonaggression pact between NATO and the Warsaw Pact Nations

35. Govaerts, "Belgium, Holland and Luxembourg," 328.

36. Ibid., 330–31.

37. Ibid., 331.

38. In Belgium a distinction is made between defense expenditures and military expenditures. Military expenditures are composed of money allocated to the Ministry of Defense by Parliament and are part of defense expenditures. Defense expenditures are defined for NATO purposes as expenditures made by the government specifically to meet the needs of the armed forces. Under the NATO definition, expenditures for

any given period should represent payments made during that period, even though for national purposes some of these payments may be charged against the budget for a preceding period. Only actual payments are counted. Indirect costs, such as loss of revenue due to tax exemptions on government transactions, do not constitute payments. Nondefense budget items that may be included under the NATO definition are security forces (so far as they are trained in military tactics, equipped with military equipment, and under military authority in wartime), government contributions to military retirement funds, and nonreimbursable military assistance. Items not included in the NATO definition include war damage, veterans' payments and benefits, civil defense, and stockpiling of industrial raw materials. In Table 1.4 military expenditures are used.

39. *Parl. Hand. Senaat,* 1965–66, 1 June 1966, 1056–57.

40. Govaerts, "Belgium, Holland and Luxembourg," 368.

41. *Parl. Hand. Kamer,* 1965–66, 14 June 1966, 13–15; and *Parl. Hand. Senaart,* 1965–66, 14 June 1966, 1236–39.

42. Govaerts, "Belgium, Holland and Luxembourg," 369.

43. Ibid., The "Parti Wallon" had two seats in the Parliament and the "Front Démocratique des Francophones Bruxellois" had three seats.

44. Ibid., 370.

45. M. Vincineau, "Le Parlement belge devant la crise de l'Alliance Atlantique," *Chronique de politique étrangère,* (January 1968): 84–164. The results of the voting were:

House		Senate	
Yes: all Christian Democrats present	74	Yes: Christian Democrats	64
all Liberals present	42	Liberals	31
two Socialists	2	Socialists	1
	118		96
No: the majority of the Socialists	51	No: Socialists	23
the Communists	5	Volksunie	5
Front des Francophones	2	Communists	4
Parti Wallon	2	Front des Francophones	1
l'Union de la Gauche Socialiste	1		33
	61		
Abstained: Volksunie	11	Abstained: Socialists	21
Socialists	5	Christian Democrats	1
	16		22

46. Govaerts, "Belgium, Holland and Luxembourg," 372.

47. Ibid., 372–73.

48. Press service of the Ministry of Foreign Affairs, Speech of Minister P. Harmel on the occasion of the Senate discussion about the budget of the Ministry of Foreign Affairs, Brussels, 16 March 1971, 18–19.

49. *Parl. Hand. Senaat,* 1966–67, 17 January 1967, 416.

50. Govaerts, "Belgium, Holland and Luxembourg," 362–63.

51. The study group of ten was headed by the Belgian Willot. The report was approved by the General Assembly on 12 December 1980.

52. P. Lévy, "L'opinion publique belge, la défense et son adéquation à la menace," in *Acta Colloquia* 1980 (Brussels: Royal Higher Institute for Defense (K.H.I.D.), Defensie Studiecentrum, 1981), 40–41 (hereafter Opinion poll Lévy).

53. "Hoe staat Europa tegenover de U.S.?" *De Standaard,* 8 March 1982, 7–8.

54. "Panorama's grote raketten-enquête," *Panorama,* 20 September 1983, 31.

55. Capt. Delwiche, *La défense nationale et l'opinion publique en Belgique* (Thesis, Krijgsschool, Brussels, 1960), 4. The questions were: Is it preferable to keep an

independent army, or would it be better to integrate? Does Belgium by its adherence to European or international military organizations augment its chances to prevent war on its territory or not?

56. International Research Associates (INRA), *L'implication de l'OTAN et du SHAPE en Belgique. Rapports des résultats d'une enquête concernant les attitudes du publique belge à l'égard de l'implantation de l'OTAN et du SHAPE en Belgique,* Brussels, 19 May 1967, quoted in Govaerts, "Belgium, Holland and Luxembourg," 381.

57. Opinion poll Lévy, 13.

58. A. Van Staden, "The Antinuclear Movement in the Netherlands and Belgium: Impact, Causes and the Future," in *Pacifisme et dissuasion,* ed. P. Lellouche (Paris: IFRI, 1983), 21.

59. Opinion poll "De Belgen vertrouwen voor hun veiligheid op de V.S.," in *De Standaard,* 8 March 1982 (hereafter Opinion poll *De Standaard*). The question was: If Belgian security would be threatened by a Soviet invasion, how much confidence would you have in the United States to do the necessary to defend Belgium, even if this might imply the risk of a direct attack against the United States?"

Answer:

	Men	Women	15–24	25–34	35–54	55 and over
Very much	14.6	9.0	11.6	11.9	11.0	11.9
Some	36.6	30.8	35.4	32.3	32.6	34.1
A little	21.8	23.1	19.0	26.1	25.5	18.9
None at all	8.9	10.8	13.2	10.6	9.0	8.3
N.a./n.o.	18.1	26.4	20.6	19.0	21.9	26.8

	Left	Neutral	Right	Flanders	Brussels	Wallonia	Total
Very much	14.2	11.1	11.6	8.7	7.5	17.2	11.6
Some	31.1	29.8	43.8	32.7	39.6	33.0	33.5
A little	26.2	22.4	24.4	23.5	24.5	20.4	22.5
None at all	16.0	11.1	3.5	8.3	7.5	13.1	9.9
N.a./n.o.	12.4	25.6	16.7	26.9	20.8	16.3	22.5

60. M. Howard, "Reassurance and Deterrence: Western Defense in the 1980s," *Foreign Affairs,* 61, no. 2 (Winter 1982/83): 302–24.

61. Van Staden, *The Antinuclear Movement,* 16.

62. "Verklarung algemene vergadering I.P.B. in verband met de diskussie rond de nieuwe kernwapens (17/10/81)," *Koerier,* 25, no. 1(February 1982): 13–14.

63. B. Adam, "Désarmement et développement," *La Cité,* 6 (April 1982).

64. *De Morgen,* 15 September 1982.

65. M. Deweerdt, "Het Belgisch politiek gebeuren in 1981," in *Res Publica, Politiek jaarboek 1981* (Brussels: Politologisch Institut, 1981), 242.

66. Louis Tobback, "De P.S. begaeft? Uit aan politike prostitutie," in *De Morgen,* 6 September 1984.

67. Charles Osgood, *An Alternative to War on Surrender,* (Chicago: University of Illinois Press, 1962).

68. See L. Reychler, *Vrede, moraal en wetenschap,* AIB Papers 2 (Leuven: University of Leuven, 1983).

69. P. Vandermeulen, "Interview met Ministger van Landsverdediging F. Vreven," *Forum,* 1 (1982): 4—6.

70. Opinion poll Lévy.

71. Ibid.

72. Ibid. 27—30.

73. Opinion poll "Les Belges veulent une meilleure armée," *L'Evénement,* 25 (July 1980): 5—11.

74. Opinion poll "Les jeunes et les problèmes de paix de la défense," *Le Soir*- RTBF (July 1980) published in Groupe de Recherche et d'Information sur la Paix (GRIP), *Dossier Notes et Documents,* no. 32 (30 January 1981).

75. J. Luyten, "België ligt niet wakker van de nieuwe raketten," *De Volkskrant* (16 November 1979).

76. The government then, the first Martens Coalition, was made up of the CVP, PSC, SP, PS, and FDF. H. Simonet (SP) was Minister of Foreign Affairs and J. Desmarets (PSC) Minister of Defense. The main opposition came from PVV, PRL, VU, RW, and KPB.

77. B. Adam, A. de Meulenaere, and A. Zaks, *Le dossier des Euromissiles* (Brussels: GRIP, 1981), 32 (hereafter Zaks, *Le dossier des Euromissiles*).

78. Those members were W. Demeester and T. Declerq (CVP), J. Van Elewijck (SP), and P. Van Grembergen and E. Van Steenkiste (VU).

79. The interpellators were H. De Croo (PVV), L. Tobback (SP), L. Van Geyt (KPB), M. Banneux (FDF), A. Van der Biest (SP), R. Peeters (CVP), P. Van Grembergen (VU), and W. Demeester (CVP).

80. Zaks, *Le dossier des Euromissiles*, 43.

81. *La Dernière Heure*, 10 July 1980.

82. *Le Peuple*, 12 July 1980.

83. "Raketten: Dreiging devaluatie. België onder Duitse druk," *De Morgen*, 11 December 1979, 1.

84. R. Germonprez, "De vredesbeweging een eendagsvlieg? (2)" *De Morgen*, 3 December 1981.

85. *La Lanterne*, 10 October 1981, 5.

86. M. Deweerdt, "Het Belgisch politiek," 242.

87. Opinion poll "Les missiles américains en Belgique: pour ou contre?" *L'Evénement*, 35 (18—24 October 1980).

88. Opinion poll "Les missiles U.S. en Belgique: le nom gagné du terrain," *L'Evénement*, 78 (1 October 1981): 12—13. The question was: "Taking into account the installation of Soviet missiles in Europe, do you think that one should accept the installation of American missiles in Belgium?" Other questions produce different answers. In an opinion poll published in *De Standaard* of 27 October 1981, the reference to the Soviet missiles was eliminated; consequently, a higher number of respondents (66 percent) claimed to be opposed to the installation of nuclear weapons. In an opinion poll published in *l'Evénement*, no. 87 (3 December 1981), this number increased to 89 percent.

89. Opinion poll *De Standaard*.

90. *Pourquoi Pas*, 19 October 1983.

91. *Panorama*, 20 September 1983.

92. Opinion poll *De Standaard*.

93. *Parl. Hand. Kamer*, 1981—82, 18 December 1981, 86.

94. *Parl. Hand. Kamer*, 1980—81, 9 June 1981, 2233.

95. V. Zaks, "La défense dans les programmes électoraux des partis politiques," *Dossier Notes et Documents*, 47 (30 November 1981): 16.

96. F.D.F., *Bruxellois, maître chez toi*, Election program, 1981, 90.

97. Opinion poll *De Standaard;* Opinion poll Lévy, 40.

98. Ibid.

99. Opinion poll Lévy, 41.

100. P. Manigart, "Les relations militaro-civiles en Belgique," *Recherches Sociologiques*, 15, no. 3 (1981): 214-15.

101. Pax Christi Flandre, "1999: Vijftig jaar NAVO," *Kommentaar*, vol. 3, no. 3 (April 1979).

102. E. Van de Begin, *De vredesbeweging in Vlaanderen* (Antwerp: Omega, 1983).

103. K. Van Leuven, "Van Veiligheid en Vrede," *Kultuurleven*, 7 (1982).

104. L. Tindemans, "De defensie van Europa of de Europese defensie," in *Acta Colloquia*, 1982, K.H.I.D., Defensie Studiecentrum, 423-33.

105. General B. W. Rogers, "Increasing Threats to NATO's Security Call for Sustained Response," *NATO Review* (June 1981): 1—6.

106. *Parl. Hand. Kamer*, 1980—81, 9 June 1981, 2232.

107. P. Vandermeulen, "Interview met minister van Landsverdediging F. Vreven," *Forum*, 1 (1982): 4—6.

108. K. Kaiser et al., *La sécurité de l'OTAN: bilan et orientation* (Paris: IFRI, 1981).

109. U.S. Congress, C. Weinberger, Secretary of Defense, *Report on Allied Commitment to Defense Spending*, March 1981, 3.

110. J. Yochelson, "Nouvelles réalités politiques de l'OTAN et politique Américaine," *Politique Etrangère*, 3 (1979): 445—60.

111. L. Reychler, "Wat in Veiligheid?," *Veiligheid en Stratégie*, vol. 1, no. 1 (December 1981): 62.

112. L. Tindemans, "De defensie van Europa of de Europese defensie," *Acta Colloquia*, 1982, K.H.I.D., Defensie Studiecentrum, 423—33.

113. L. Reychler, in cooperation with M. Riga and J. Van Peteghem, "De organisatie van het Europeesveiligheids-en defensieonderzoek," *Acta Colloquia*, 1981, K.H.I.D., Defensie Studiecentrum, 213—28.

114. L. Tindemans, *Het Europens Defensiebeleid*, speech delivered at the opening of the academic year 1981—82 of the Royal Higher Institute for Defense (K.H.I.D.), 25 September 1981. See also the speeches delivered by L. Tindemans at the European Parliament in Strasburg on 21 January 1982 and at the Western European Assembly in Paris on 14 June 1982. See also F. de Moor, "Leo Tindemans: het gevecht met de faiten," *Knack*, 30 June 1982.

115. F.D.F. *Bruxellois, maître chez toi*, Election program, 1981, 90.

116. Opinion poll *De Standaard*.

117. Opinion poll Lévy, 40.

118. Opinion poll "Face à l'impérialisme Soviétique, les Belges souhaitent un renforcement de la puissance militaire Européenne dans le cadre de l'OTAN," in *La Dernière Heure*, 5 May 1981.

119. H. De Meulenaere, and B. van Autryve, "De onbegrepen Close: militair moet Europa niet zelfstandig zijn," interview with General Close, *Forum*, 5 (1980): 12—14.

2

Denmark's Quest for Security: Constraints and Opportunities Within the Alliance

MARTIN O. HEISLER

Introduction

Denmark is a small country in a moderately exposed geostrategic position. Its military capabilities have been substantially short of self-sufficiency for the defense of its territory and maritime domain for more than a century. Its small population and other structural limitations have

*A nonnational could hardly achieve a cogent, nuanced grasp of a subject as intricate and fraught with the risk of misinterpretation as the holistic overview of a country's security policy without the help of indigenous specialists and the opportunity for field research. The former was provided by the generous suggestions (invariably constructive), critical comments, and general assistance of many—most particularly Ib Faurby, Nikolaj Petersen, and Erling Bjøl. While they saved me from several factual errors and gave much good advice, I did not always avail myself of their wisdom and experience. Thus, they should not be blamed either for the errors that remain or for the analyses and policy perspectives in this chapter. I also benefited greatly from discussions with Niels Amstrup, Jørgen Grønnegård Christensen, Niels Jørgen Haagerup, and Ole P. Kristensen. The latter was made possible by a Fulbright Professorship at the Institute of Political Science at Aarhus University (1978–79) and by a regular faculty appointment there from January 1981 through August 1982, and by several subsequent, briefer stays in Denmark. Financial support from the Danish-American Fulbright Commission, the Danish Institute for International Relations, the Danish Social Science Research Council, and the General Research Board of the University of Maryland is gratefully acknowledged. Special thanks are due to Gregory Flynn of the Atlantic Institute for International Affairs for editorial assistance and for both gentle and occasionally necessarily less-subtle encouragement in working the manuscript through several drafts.

precluded any significant increase in its military effort. These factors, combined with Denmark's experience in World War II—it was quickly defeated and occupied by Germany, notwithstanding its neutral status—and the threats to its security perceived to emanate from the Soviet Union in the war's aftermath, militated in favor of alliance as a means to enhanced security.

Denmark entered NATO in 1949 as a charter member after efforts to create a Scandinavian alliance failed. The latter would have been more congenial for many reasons, not least because it would have avoided entanglement in large-power and bloc politics and because it would have permitted the pursuit of more clear-cut policies of nonprovocation or "confidence building" as a means of lessening the threats to be confronted. The decision to join NATO was clearly made *faute de mieux*.

The country was integrated into the NATO structures and performed its Alliance tasks earnestly. As the end of the initial twenty-year term of the Alliance treaty approached, and following a careful and thorough consideration of its future in NATO, a nondecision of sorts was reached. Denmark chose not to exercise the treaty's provision for opting out—but again the choice was made, to some extent, for want of an acceptable alternative master security policy. (Some would say that the issue was buried in a study commission until it became moot.)

Since the late 1960s, foreign and defense policy areas have become increasingly politicized, beginning at the time when the discussions surrounding continued membership in NATO were taking place. This trend has contributed to the erosion of the relatively quiescent position of Denmark in the Alliance in the earlier period, when defense and Alliance policies were largely elite business. Thus, divergence (in public opinion far more than in government thinking) from the policies and actions of the United States has become more noticeable, first in Southeast Asia and more recently in Central America, and with regard to the imbalance, perceived by many in Denmark, in the way that NATO's December 1979 double-track decision has unfolded. For some segments of the political society, cohabitation in an alliance with the United States is sometimes an issue in itself. The democratization of foreign and defense policy has also brought these areas into an already highly democratic general political process, contributing to the increased tendency to weigh defense expenditures against pressing social-policy needs and high rates of taxation. And the historical position, among a segment of the policy-relevant or elite community, that a Danish defense effort is futile has gained a measurable public base.

There remains substantial support for a defense effort and for membership in NATO at both the mass and elite levels. The country's military forces are thoroughly integrated into the Alliance structure. Defense planning is premised on NATO support and reinforcement. Yet, the tension between the European desire to maintain and expand détente and the United States' modulation of this policy track probably affects Denmark more than most other members. This is so not only because the predominant social and political values expressed in the democratic political process tend toward détente but also because throughout the modern history of Danish security policy there has been a steady and growing tendency in that direction.

The current manifestations of increased elite and mass opposition to NATO's Intermediate-Range Nuclear Force (INF) modernization policy, and to the tone set by the Americans in East-West relations more generally, thus should not be viewed as novel or unexpected. The disparate minorities who are disposed against entangling, institutionalized arrangements in foreign affairs can be mobilized (if not thoroughly aggregated into a single bloc or stance) by effective leadership. This was vividly demonstrated in the referendum on membership in the European Communities in 1972, when anti-EC votes nearly prevailed, and in the first direct elections to the European Parliament in June 1979, when the single largest block of votes was cast for a slate opposed to EC membership.

Since its shift from government to opposition in September 1982, the Social Democratic Party—the country's largest—has moved toward such a role. Some may attribute the rhetoric and parliamentary votes of those who, until a short time ago, underwrote such crucial NATO policies as the double-track decision of December 1979 when they were in office to cynical maneuvers designed to facilitate a return to power. But a basic question remains: Why would a major, well-established party assume a controversial position on a critical issue, thereby reaping much criticism, unless its leaders perceived actual or readily mobilizable public support of substantial proportions?

In attempting to match the level and form of the defense effort that is consonant with national tradition, resources, and political support on the one hand, and with externally influenced roles and commitments on the other, Denmark is subject to tensions not unlike several other members of the Alliance. The question becomes whether Denmark will be able to chart a course in security policy that is in greater harmony with domestic possibilities and limitations while at the same time meeting the country's defense needs and Alliance roles.

These are the salient concerns addressed in this chapter. In the next section two key elements of Denmark's security situation will be examined: the changes in the international environment and the historical experiences that were instrumental in shaping defense posture—at least until recently. In subsequent sections the positions and roles of the country in the Alliance will be described and analyzed; the influences currently bearing on the repoliticization of Danish defense policy will be examined; and, finally, the outlook for Danish security positions will be considered briefly.

There can be little doubt that Denmark is going to find it increasingly difficult to identify escape routes, however limited, out of the seemingly inexorably tightening spiral of scarce resources, problematic governance, and an international environment that frequently appears intractable, if not hostile. But alternatives consistent with Danish values and resources, advocated by a growing number of highly respected analysts and political and military leaders in the Alliance, can be envisioned. It remains to be seen whether the political will to move toward them can be mustered.

The Bases of Change and Continuity in Danish Security Policy

A country's experiences in international conflict tend to structure its approach to security. While such structures need not be—and generally tend not to be—determining, in the Danish case they have had significant long-term effects. The cumulative impact of the country's experiences since 1864 is clearly discernible in its current defense posture and is likely to be noticeable at least in the near future. This touches the substance as well as the tone of defense policy in Denmark; and, curious as it may seem to some, it often fuels simultaneously "prodefense" and "antidefense" sentiments and quiescence on defense-related issues. Most important for this chapter is the fact that most Danish attitudes toward the country's associations with NATO—past, current, and foreseeable future—are intricately linked to the country's defense-related experiences in the last 120 years.

The Evanescence of Security

In 1864 Denmark was quickly and badly defeated by Prussia and Austria in the Schleswig-Holstein War, which was a step in the process of German unification. Until then, the country was *relatively* removed from the European international system. It had no substantially more powerful neighbor. The country was able to provide for its security with a manageable commitment of resources for land forces and with a navy that was large for the size of its population because of its extensive merchant fleet and overseas territorial interests.

The Schleswig-Holstein War was a milestone in the evolution of Danish security. It made clear that Denmark could not assure its own comprehensive defense unilaterally against the most likely sources of threat—in particular, its much more powerful neighbor immediately to the south. The war was traumatic, not only because the peace settlement at its conclusion stripped Denmark of about one-third of its territory and population in the south of the Jutland,[1] but also because it demonstrated dramatically the inadequacy of its national military means for self-defense. Following the war, defense forces were reconstructed to serve as a qualified deterrent. That is, the country sought a military capability that, while insufficient to withstand a determined assault by a substantially larger power, would suffice to raise the cost for a potential aggressor above the threshold of easy or worthwhile gain. (This approach to security is somewhat like that taken by Switzerland for some time, and it is not dissimilar from Swedish armed neutrality in modern times.)[2]

Denmark succeeded in preserving its security in World War I through a combination of neutrality, some accommodation of German interest (by mining the Baltic Straits in 1914, thereby contributing to a sectoral defense for Germany), and limited deterrence. Denmark was not deemed an essential military target by the belligerents in any case.[3] World War I would be the last major conflict or threatening situation in Europe in which remoteness, the limited deterrent the country was able to muster, and a formal nonprovocative stance sufficed to provide security.

The creation of the League of Nations in the aftermath of World War I played a part in Danish thinking about security and defense effort. Some major parties hoped the league would enhance security. These, particularly the Social Democrats, were inclined to favor arms limitations and the use of resources, thus freed, for social programs. By contrast, the Conservative and Liberal parties, traditional supporters of stronger defense policies, stressed the league covenant's point regarding members' obligations to provide for their own defense as a justification for higher military expenditures.

These positions reflected a political division among the major parties that can be traced from the 19th century to the present.[4] In the last century, the Conservative *(Højre)* and, to a lesser degree, Liberal *(Venstre)* parties were supporters of significant military expenditures.[5] Also, at that time a proportionately larger officer corps (to which some historians have referred as an "officer class") and a supportive ethos in the upper classes provided political support for such efforts. On the other side, the Social Democrats, once they entered the political arena, questioned such use of resources on two distinct but mutually reinforcing grounds: They shared international working-class aspirations for cross-national solidarity and a concomitant hope that wars among states could be made obsolete, and, as noted, they preferred using resources for social needs. Since their emergence as a separate political party in 1905, the Radical Liberals *(Radikale Venstre*—hereafter, Radicals) could also be counted on to oppose a strong Danish defense profile, having split off from the Liberal Party in large part because of disagreement with the latter on the priorities attached to military expenditures.

Notwithstanding the deterioration of its security position as a result of political changes in Europe and technical developments in offensive warfare, Denmark, like many other states, did not strive to raise its defensive capabilities in the years preceding World War II. Arguably, it could not afford to do so from the standpoint of economic wherewithal, and significant political division on the issue also made any action by the governments of the day in favor of massive armament unlikely. The Social Democrats' opposition to using scarce resources for defense instead of social programs was sufficiently strong to forestall a major military buildup. The Danish political response to the economic crisis of the 1930s was thus a general reduction in government budgets and a disproportionately greater decline in military spending. The country's military capabilities declined substantially.[6]

The German invasion on 9 April 1940 was thus to proceed at negligible cost to the aggressor. Neither Denmark's weakened defense forces nor its neutral status deterred the attack, which was, of course, but a small part of a vast strategic expansion from the German perspective. Overcoming Danish resistance and the political costs of ignoring Danish neutrality proved to be insignificant impediments, given Germany's goals and political resoluteness.

Independent defense and neutrality had failed; and in the post–World War II period Denmark has never again considered going it alone. The era of collective security, or failing that, collective defense, had begun. Denmark entered into it because there was no realistic alternative to alliance for providing security for its population and territory. However, the threads from which the fabric of Danish security policy had been woven for at least 85 years before the advent of NATO can be traced to the present: a national military establishment, supported by majority opinion (varying in magnitude over time); aloofness from most great power confrontations and a persistent quest for détente (positions that may be seen as modern surrogates for a neutrality that could not be pursued formally and explicitly after entry into NATO); and a recurring preference for nonprovocative or confidence-building policies in general. Although less visible and regular in alliance than in earlier periods, the presence of these elements suggests continuity that, although muted by the myriad changes in settings, institutions, forms, and issues, seems persistent.[7]

While Denmark's entry into NATO in a formal sense marked a break with the tradition of nonalignment, both the circumstances of the choice of the NATO framework and the country's behavior as a member of the Alliance reinforce the notion of continuity in general security disposition. This is perhaps most evident in the development of Denmark's accession to NATO.

Entering the Alliance

Having found its modest independent military capability and its neutrality insufficient for its security needs, and with its prewar military structure largely dismantled by the German occupation administration, Denmark emerged from World War II essentially without defense forces and without a security policy. Although the League of Nations had not proved effective as an international mechanism for the enhancement of small states' security, the leaders of most Danish parties looked once more to such a collective security regime—this time to the United Nations, which appeared to have "more teeth" than had its predecessor. This stance was less the product of naïveté than of a combination of general, widely shared values favoring broadly organized international approaches to security. There was a paucity of military and economic means for mounting a go-it-alone defense, of course, and the determination to avoid association with any power bloc was strong in the major parties. The Liberal Prime Minister, Knud Kristensen, voiced such a determination, as did his Social Democratic successor, Hans Hedtoft, in the months following his entry into office in late 1947.

The shift from the universal level was made reluctantly. It can be attributed to the simultaneous realization that the United Nations was not likely to become an effective agency of collective security and that Soviet moves to consolidate recent military gains in Eastern and Central Europe might lead to a significant and threatening alteration in the European system.

The threat perceived to emanate from the Soviet Union was both generalized and specific to the Nordic region. The coup in Prague in February 1948 showed a heavy-handedness that concretized a threat that, until then, some Western European governments could treat in a temporizing manner. In the same month, a letter from Stalin to the President of Finland proposing a defense agreement between that country and the Soviet Union brought the Russian threat directly into the Nordic milieu, for given the war between Finland and Russia a few years earlier and the inequality of the two countries in terms of size and strength, the proposal could be reasonably seen as intimidation.

The threat posed by the Soviet Union in the late 1940s could not be ignored in Denmark. In the south, its border with Germany on Jutland was exposed to a potential land attack from across the relatively narrow barrier of the western zones of occupation. The Soviet position was acquiring substantial depth, since the territories occupied in the war were consolidated politically and militarily. The Danish islands and waterways were vulnerable from the sea and air; and considering the fluctuating, but never negligible, importance of the Danish straits to the postwar Soviet navy for passage to the North Sea and the Atlantic, they were increasingly perceived as potential targets. While Denmark, unlike Norway and Finland, was not in direct land contact with the Soviet Union, it was moderately exposed. Russian withdrawal from the Danish island of Bornholm in 1946 (occupied toward the end of the war against Germany) buttressed Danish confidence for a short time, but the events of 1948 and the general atmosphere of the nascent Cold War reinforced the perceptions of exposure and threat.

Adequate independent defense could not be mustered; global security through the United Nations had become unrealistic; and recent experience with neutrality led to its rejection, at least by the Liberals, Conservatives, and Social Democrats. (The Radicals continued to favor it.) Alliance was the only remaining alternative.

By the spring of 1948 the Danish Government had begun to contemplate some form of collective security arrangement. The Social Democrats had come to accept the need for a modest national military effort—which, in any case, was all that the country's means permitted in the late 1940s. The Conservatives favored a greater effort, which might have entailed considerable public financial sacrifices. The Liberal position fell between those of the two other parties. All three, however, could agree on the need to increase the efficacy of national forces through alliance, preferably outside the framework of the emerging Western and Soviet blocs.

Beyond doubt, the Social Democratic Government's favored approach to collective defense was through a Scandinavian Defense Union (SDU) that was not associated with major powers. As Nikolaj Petersen has written:

> The major objective of the Danish Government was to find a solution which kept the Scandinavian countries together, either independent of or in association with the Western Powers; only when in February 1949 it became crystal clear that Norway and Sweden would not be able to agree on the character of an SDU, did the Danish Government turn toward its reserve option, membership in the Atlantic Pact.[8]

The disagreement alluded to revolved around a strong Norwegian preference for an SDU aligned with the West and an equally staunch Swedish position against any extra-Scandinavian connection. While Denmark's first preference paralleled that of Sweden, it was less adamant on the question of either guarantees from Western powers or formal association between the SDU and the West.[9]

The country's experiences in World War II had a marked influence on these preferences—particularly for the ruling Social Democratic Party. Danish Social Democrats had developed close and positive ties with Sweden during the war. Relations with Norway were interrupted by the war, but that country's response to the German invasion in April 1940 was to have significant influence on Denmark in the period following the war. Norway met the attack with considerable military resistance and fought valiantly for some time, while Denmark capitulated after a few brief skirmishes. Moreover, the former's population showed remarkable resilience under a harsh occupation, and its government-in-exile was associated with the Allied campaign. These contrasting images help to account for the high esteem in which Norway was held in the postwar period by the general public and by policy makers in Denmark. In short, Norway became a "country of reference" for Denmark,[10] which perhaps partially explains its recurring tendency to follow Norway's lead in security-related matters.

The above considerations disclose the most important determinants of Denmark's entry into NATO and for its Alliance posture thereafter. For Denmark, the choice of NATO was made because none of the preferred alternatives was available. *It was not a consensus for or an active seeking of alliance with the major Western powers that led to Danish accession as much as a general recognition of the necessity of alliance and the failure to work out a Scandinavian alternative not tied to the West—all in the presence of threats perceived to be real and significant.* The tendency, especially in the years following World War II, to take the cue from Norwegian foreign and security policy, coupled with *the absence of concerted opposition of great political weight* to entry into a Western Alliance, help to explain the outcome.[11]

It is worth mentioning, in passing, that the principal American interest in Danish membership in the Alliance focused on Denmark's Arctic possession, Greenland. During World War II American bases were established there on the basis of a bilateral agreement (subsequently renewed). There was less concern with Denmark itself, in part because it was perceived as sufficiently exposed to Soviet forces to be difficult to defend.[12]

The Danish profile in NATO is more likely to be understood if one bears in mind the country's positions, preferences, and self-perception at the time the Alliance was formed. The recurring assumption of a "special position" with regard to the stationing of NATO troops, the positioning of weapons, the roles contemplated for nuclear weapons in the various strategic frameworks and defense scenarios that have followed one another in NATO during the past thirty years, and steady—indeed, one might say, structured—pressure in the direction of arms limitations, détente, and, in general, nonprovocative or confidence-building stances are all related to the same values that had made a Scandinavian alliance not formally integrated with the Western block attractive to Denmark at the outset. These tendencies also provide some important clues to understanding levels of defense funding, both in terms of Danish budgets and NATO targets. The manner in which the impacts of the Danish experience through World War II and the decision to seek security through alliance in the late 1940s have influenced the country's approaches to defense in the Alliance will emerge more specifically in the remaining sections of this chapter.

Charting a Danish Path in the Alliance: Structuring a Limited Partnership

Over the past few years, Denmark has become the focus—indeed, for some, the symbol—of "under-performance" of Alliance responsibilities along several lines. Specific criticisms of Danish policy have been based on the perception that it is "free-riding"—shirking its responsibilities—in terms of its budgetary effort for defense, as well as providing less than optimal political support for Alliance policies. The pejorative term "Denmarkization" has come to symbolize a greater or lesser tendency in this direction in the Alliance-related behavior and policies of some states, Denmark most of all.[13]

The criticism of Denmark is the result of a combination of traits in Danish behavior and rhetoric with regard to security policy in general and, more specifically, that directed toward American goals for NATO members. Most of these traits are exhibited by other members as well, but they may appear especially pronounced and frequent by the Danes. In the Danish case they are also probably less alloyed with confidence-building behavior vis-à-vis the Alliance. Notable among such characteristics are steadfastness in the pursuit of détente and the related emphasis on policies of nonprovocation. These can be traced to the first years of

NATO—the height of the Cold War—as indicated by the discussion below of policies toward the stationing of foreign troops, establishment of foreign bases, and the siting of nuclear weapons. Such dispositions tend to ebb and flow for some member-states, but they have been rather consistent in the Danish case. Another such trait is the persistence of a minority sentiment toward neutrality or a nonaligned, "low profile" defense posture.

The central task in this section will thus be to look back and to consider what Denmark did in the Alliance during its first twenty years and why it did it, in order to understand better the elements of continuity and change in recent Danish policy. In addition to the normal overview provided by time-series data in the quantifiable dimensions of policy such as defense expenditures, manpower, and public opinion, one can get an insight into the basic Danish orientation from examining responses to specific items that have arisen on the NATO agenda. Three sets of events in NATO's first twenty years, taken together, depict the patterns of Danish participation in the Alliance: (1) the rearmament of Germany, its accession to NATO, and the resulting reorganization of the areal command structure into COMBALTAP; (2) the barring of the stationing of foreign troops, of the establishment of foreign bases, and, subsequently, of nuclear weapons on Danish territory in peacetime; and (3) the consideration of continued membership in the Alliance as the end of its initial twenty-year term neared.

The first two sets of events arose initially in the 1950s, but they have had salient import for Danish security policy and the country's positions and roles in the Alliance to the present—and their ramifications are likely to continue to be significant in the coming years. The third marked the beginning of a broader participation in, and a noticeable politicization of decision making with regard to security policy; and thus it either began or reinforced some of the important patterns of the domestic politics of defense discernible today. Each of the three also demonstrates the continuity of values and styles in defense policy that the country carried with it into the Alliance—that have come to characterize the Danish style—and that are likely to influence policies in the 1980s.

From German Accession to the Unified BALTAP

When, on 30 August 1954, the French National Assembly rejected the draft treaty of the European Defense Community, it did more than negate the French initiative of 1950 (the Pléven Plan) for providing an internationally integrated framework for German rearmament. It also dismantled the defense plans of five other European countries, frustrated the United States, and—in the only slightly overdramatized words of one analyst—it "plunged the West into one of the sharpest of the series of crises which have punctuated its efforts to organize for unity."[14] At that time a vital hostility toward and trepidation of Germany—especially the specter of a rearmed Germany—still prevailed in Europe. But the rearmament of Germany was deemed essential by Western (primarily, but far from exclusively, American) strategic planners; and, with the failure of EDC, NATO became the setting of choice.

Misgivings about German rearmament were at least as great in Denmark as elsewhere in Europe, and the consequences of the Federal Republic's entry into the Alliance were even more direct and far-reaching. Danish reactions to German accession to NATO were not particularly favorable for several years after the event, and this in spite of a substantial enhancement of Danish security. Instead of merely a tepid U.S. interest in guaranteeing the country's integrity—as distinguished from greater interest in Greenland—Denmark now had Germany's acute concern with the same. As Erling Bjøl, writing in 1968, observed:

> Whereas in 1949 the Americans seemed somewhat reluctant to commit themselves to the protection of Denmark, since in their view the Baltic could be sealed off from southern Norway, and Denmark was, moreover, geographically so exposed that it would be hard to defend, the Germans have indicated a clear interest in assuring that Danish territory should remain under Western control.[15]

Resistance to association with the Federal Republic in NATO was manifested nonetheless on several levels. First, popular sentiments based on wartime memories were awakened, leading to a series of demonstrations and disputes of substantial proportions. In the vanguard of that reaction were members of the resistance during the German occupation and some high-ranking military officers and the Home Guard (militia). Second, the Radicals and at least some members of the parliamentary delegation of the Justice Party (*Retsforbundet*) opposed German membership in NATO, and they tried to force the government's hand by calling for a referendum on the issue. (The Communist Party, which held 8 of the 179 seats in the *Folketing* at that time, was also opposed). Third, concern was expressed in some quarters that, since the German central front was the most likely site of conflict, Denmark, less than 100 miles from the East-West German line, would be in greater jeopardy of involvement in war if Germany were admitted.[16] Foreign Minister H. C. Hansen argued effectively, however, that it was not a question of whether Germany would rearm but, rather, in what context. Moreover, since a German military contribution was far more important for the Alliance than Denmark's position, the latter might be adversely affected.[17]

The Federal Republic's entry into NATO raised, *per force*, questions regarding its adaptation to the existing command structure, in which Schleswig-Holstein was included in the Northern Region, together with Denmark and Norway, while the rest of the Federal Republic was in the Central Region. The basic German preference was for shifting both Schleswig-Holstein and Denmark from the Northern Region to the Central (that is, German); but this was totally unacceptable to Denmark because of the strong political sentiments regarding military cooperation and coordination with Germany. For logistic as well as command-linkage purposes, especially in northern Germany and Jutland, however, the integration of German and Danish forces was considered essential by Bonn—and that judgment was shared by the office of SACEUR.

These differences were resolved by compromise in 1961. A new subcommand, BALTAP (BALTic APproaches), was created under the Northern Region. The commander of the unified BALTAP structure— COMBALTAP—was to be a Dane, with a German officer as deputy commander. This arrangement, which brought German Schleswig-Holstein, Hamburg, and Denmark under a subcommand based in Karup (Denmark), was acceptable to the Danes, since it involved a multilateral command structure (staff officers from other NATO members were to be included in BALTAP) rather than a bilateral German-Danish one. The main parliamentary opposition, coming from the Radicals, was muted, since they were by then in the governing coalition, and in effect they would have had to give up that role in order to persist in their opposition to the unified command compromise.[18]

COMBALTAP is the framework not only for Denmark's integration into the NATO military structure but, in a fundamental sense, for the organization of Danish defense in general. This is due in large part to Denmark's interesting solution to a difficult problem in coordinating national and NATO commands. Under normal circumstances every country would prefer to retain national control of its military units, but in case of need for swift Alliance action, NATO prefers to have those forces under joint command. The current Danish approach to dealing with this built-in tension is to designate the head of COMBALTAP also overall Chief of Operative Defense Forces. Thus, in case of crisis or war, he would have overall command of Danish forces, until these are assigned to NATO, at which time he would command as COMBALTAP. Under COMBALTAP are arrayed the regional commands for Denmark and Schleswig-Holstein, as well as the naval and tactical air commands. The COMBALTAP thus wears a national as well as a NATO hat.

This critical organization resulted from (1) an event outside Danish control (German rearmament and NATO membership), and (2) a compromise constructed to cope with historically based political reactions. While BALTAP appears to be an appropriate and effective security structure from the standpoints of organization and strategic planning, its inception was not essentially shaped by Danish military desiderata, except indirectly: It was a requisite for the country's continued membership in NATO.

Finally, the events leading up to and following directly from the creation of BALTAP adumbrated a change in the political processes involved in making Danish defense policy. Public mobilization on the issue of German entry into NATO and the Danish-German command structure had come to be a factor, although not the most decisive one. By the late 1960s it was to become a very significant element in what had previously been an essentially elite process. It was, however, only the beginning of the transition to the period in which public opinion plays an important part. Even at that time, Danish politicians did not make it clear, in the course of public discussions, that a concomitant of German entry into NATO—particularly in a unified command with Denmark—was likely to lead to the prepositioning of German materiel on Danish soil. The withholding of this information seems to have been deliberate. The emerging, more open process met the ebbing elite process in defense policy making.

Limiting the Partnership: Debarring Foreign Troops and Nuclear Weapons from Danish Territory in Peacetime

It has often been observed that Denmark's—and, in a similar degree, Norway's—motives for joining NATO "were predominantly military in nature. . . . What they were seeking was primarily a credible military guarantee that Soviet aggressions would be met with adequate Western power. . . . Expectations of military assistance [played] an important role in the decisions of the two governments."[19] Yet, Norway and Denmark pursued confidence-building policies vis-à-vis the Soviet Union from the outset, thereby working on the two sides of the security equation—increasing military capability through alliance while simultaneously seeking to decrease the threat confronted.

Norway, faced with diplomatic pressure from the Soviet Union in early 1949, formally assured the Soviets that no foreign troops or bases would be allowed "on her territory, 'as long as Norway is not attacked or exposed to threats of attack.' "[20] Denmark pursued a similar policy from the beginning, although it made no formal commitments of the sort provided by Norway.[21] In 1957 limitations were placed on the stationing of nuclear weapons.

This policy was influenced by domestic political considerations in both countries, as well as by the pursuit of a "Nordic Balance," whereby "Soviet restraint toward Finland was balanced by Norwegian and Danish restraint within the Atlantic Alliance, Sweden being a neutral balancing state which could tip toward the West in case of unacceptable Soviet pressure on Finland."[22] The relative influence of domestic and international factors on these decisions may be interesting to contemplate,[23] but no definitive answer is likely to be available. In any case, it is far less pertinent to the concerns at hand than any ramifications and implications of the policy over time. Three of these are very important, both in terms of the insights they provide into Danish positions in the early years of the Alliance and for their continuing influence on present (and probably future) security issues.

First, by pursuing confidence-building policies virtually simultaneously with the major step of alignment, Denmark continued its pre–World War II pattern of working both sides of the security equation. At the same time, it established within the NATO setting what seems to be at once the essence of Danish security policy—and, in a related sense, foreign policy—and the major source of recurring friction between

Denmark's Alliance posture and its conception of fundamental national interest: the pursuit of military protection through NATO and of maximum attainable détente.[24]

This stance is in itself a focus of American criticism, but it also underlies a variety of forms of "underperformance" in the Alliance—except perhaps for the budgetary. As long as the international situation does not change either toward a greatly heightened threat to the country or in the opposite direction, the tension between the two elements of Danish security policy and the concomitant friction with the Alliance are likely to remain. At the same time, as long as the tension remains, the fear of the gradual "Finlandization" of Denmark is not well founded.

Second, both Denmark and Norway succeeded in institutionalizing limitations or constraints on their Alliance roles with regard to nuclear weapons at an early point in NATO's life. Their unilateral stance, taken in 1957, was not challenged initially by the Alliance, and the longevity of the policy is in itself a source of legitimacy for it. Domestic opinion in Denmark, which may have had a bearing on the initial decision, has been conditioned in terms of the nonnuclear policy to such a degree that it is unlikely that either the public or elites could be moved to alter it, except perhaps in the case of a massive and acute military threat. Such a threat, however, could not be effectively addressed—because of insufficient time—through the installation of nuclear weapons on Danish territory, and in any case they would be of little or no incremental military advantage under such circumstances.

Third, and finally, the debarring of foreign troops and bases has implications for one of the fundamental components of Danish defense policy: rapid reinforcement in case of a security emergency. This subject will be treated below in greater detail. At this juncture, it is sufficient to note the obvious: The existence of Allied bases and foreign troops would probably simplify greatly and expedite the reception of reinforcements. The prepositioning of materiel and the logistic preparations for troops might be facilitated appreciably by members of their own armed forces already in place. Recent joint exercises, however, seem to indicate that no insuperable problems exist with the present arrangements.[25]

The Continuation of NATO Membership: The Nondecision of 1969

Denmark was one of the few members of the Alliance in which the provision of the North Atlantic Treaty permitting a member to opt out (with one year's notice) at the end of twenty years led to serious discussions and studies of that option and alternatives to NATO. As Nikolaj Petersen has pointed out, "while there was never any real probability that Denmark would choose to leave NATO . . . in 1969, the '1969 problem' was widely discussed within the press among the political parties."[26] The "1969 problem" generated voluminous literature in Denmark, but it would be of little value to review it here.[27] A small number of points deriving from it should be noted, however.

First, the occurrence of extensive discussions of Denmark's Alliance relationship was important in itself. What had been, twenty years earlier, an issue area that engaged some politicians and the professional military (and small numbers of specialists in the press and intellectual circles) became, in the late 1960s, a public agenda item. Several diverse factors accounted for this development. In politics, two Socialist splinter parties had emerged, each essentially neutralist and opposed to NATO membership; the Radicals, while no longer programmatically opposed to alliance and to the military dimension of security, were steadfastly skeptical of "automatic renewal" of Danish membership. Having more than doubled their seats in the *Folketing* in the elections held in early 1968, they had entered into coalition with the two traditionally staunch supporters of NATO, the Conservatives and the Liberals. Now they called for a critical examination of Denmark's options. That process was widely reported in the press, stimulating much discussion.

Second, the war in Southeast Asia had contributed substantially to the mobilization and politicization of public opinion with regard to international relations. This development made contact with the coming-of-age of what Ronald Inglehart has called the "post-materialist generation": young people who had grown up without firsthand memories of war or depression and who, therefore, began to turn their attention to value-related and public questions rather than to physical security and material needs.[28]

Third, a significant external development influenced the direction of these discussions: the issuing of the Harmel report in December 1967. Denmark was one of the smaller members of the Alliance that influenced the content of the Harmel Committee's deliberations.[29] The report endorsed a two-track course for the Alliance: military security and détente. This, of course, paralleled Denmark's preferences since the advent of the Alliance and even earlier, and it helped to defuse a large enough segment of the skeptical side to make continued membership likely.[30]

Fourth, and finally, several official and private study groups were assigned the task of assessing Denmark's security situation in anticipation of the 1969 "renewal date." The most prestigious among these concluded in general that, as in 1949, there was no adequate alternative to NATO. These study commissions were at their tasks for several months—and in the case of the most important, years—thereby also contributing to the muting of the issues.

The Radicals had helped to bring about these discussions, but even if the party had been so inclined, it probably could not have forced the issue, since to have done so would have jeopardized its place in the governing coalition. The decision (in reality, a nondecision) to continue in NATO was consistent with Danish public opinion (see Table 2.2). Thus, for both security and political reasons, it was a reinforcing decision.

But the episode is important because it did mark the beginning of greater openness in the formation of foreign and security policy. These issue areas ceased to be the exclusive domain of those for whom they were formal or professional responsibilities. In the markedly egalitarian and democratic ethos that had prevailed in Denmark for several decades, the manifestations first clearly discernible in the course of the discussions revolving around the "1969 problem" took firm root quickly.

The Not-Quite-Free Rider: Denmark's Defense Effort

The difficulties of measuring and comparing countries' military capabilities are well known. But inasmuch as these difficulties are not readily overcome, and because the terms of Alliance discussion and debate revolve around the issues of national defense efforts and burden-sharing—making these money and manpower indicators symbolically significant—one is reduced to using these measures of the unmeasurable.[31] A look at spending and manpower patterns for this earlier period of the Alliance reveals that the Danish "contribution" to the Allied effort was consistent and unambiguous, if limited.

The Danish defense budget represents a bargained, multi-year agreement among the major parties, and the working out of the budget agreement is generally a difficult and prolonged process. Since 1960, the indexation of the military budget to the general cost of living—in terms of salaries for military personnel and purchasing value for materiel—has been gradually extended, and it was fully achieved by 1973. (Given that there is also a "technological inflation" rate of from 3 to 5 percent per year on the average, however, such general indexing leaves a shortfall in funds for procurement in most years.)[32]

There are many ways in which defense-expenditure data can be displayed, each with its shortcomings. In Table 2.1, Danish defense expenditures for the period 1960–80 are in several forms. The first column shows military expenditures in current knoner, while the second represents them in per capita terms for the population as a whole. The values are calculated on the basis of an index, to control for inflation (with 1970 as the base year). Values above and below 100 indicate greater or lesser spending per capita on an arithmetic scale. The third column, also an indexed per capita ratio, represents defense expenditures in relation to the number of military personnel in that year. The fourth column is the percent of the Gross National Product devoted to defense.

It is evident from the second column of this table that Danish military expenditures have increased over the twenty-one-year period from 1960 through 1980 (by 67 percent) in real terms. While in eight of those years there were decreases in this index, the trend has been one of steady increases. (If current kroner are considered, there has been an absolute increase in every year, as the first column shows.)[33] The rates of increase have been quite similar for each of the two decades: approximately two-and-a-half percent per year.

The fourth column shows military expenditures as a percentage of Gross National Product—the most common indicator used in cross-national and diachronic comparisons. Here, too, the regularity of the Danish defense effort is striking: Over the twenty-one years the range has

Table 2.1   **Military Expenditures: Per Capita, Per Capita Armed Service Personnel, and as a Percentage of GNP**

Year	Military expenditures (mill. DKR)	ME/Capita	ME/Capita armed services	ME as percentage of GNP	ME as percentage of government budget
1960	1066	77.1	72.3	2.4	17.0
1961	1210	78.4	75.5	2.5	15.5
1962	1538	95.6	85.7	2.8	16.8
1963	1638	93.9	81.5	2.8	16.2
1964	1838	97.1	79.6	2.7	16.4
1965	1946	101.9	86.1	2.6	14.8
1966	2035	100.1	86.4	2.5	13.1
1967	2387	99.1	91.1	2.6	11.4
1968	2438	104.9	101.5	2.8	9.8
1969	2565	102.6	99.8	2.6	9.3
1970	2881	100.0	100.0	2.5	8.6
1971	3191	108.5	120.2	2.3	8.3
1972	3306	107.4	111.7	2.3	7.6
1973	3563	101.5	115.9	2.0	7.3
1974	4493	110.3	135.7	2.2	7.4
1975	5097	120.1	159.0	2.2	7.0
1976	5732	117.5	155.7	2.2	7.2
1977	6508	118.0	156.7	2.4	7.4
1978	5397[a]	120.0	163.2	2.4	7.0
1979	7635	120.3	160.1	2.0	6.9
1980	8794	128.9	170.8	2.4	7.1

[a]Fiscal year 1978 covered only nine months (April-December 1978).
Note: The 2nd and 3rd columns of data are indexed in constant prices with base year 1970-100.
Source: International Institute for Strategic Studies, *The Military Balance,* 1960-61 through 1982-83, and Danmarks Statistik, *Statistisk tiörs oversigt,* 1978 and 1982. These tables were calculated from data from the above sources with the assistance of Ib Faurby and Franke Snyder.

been between 2 percent and 2.8 percent, with a mean of 2.45 percent for the period. One does note a difference between the decade of the 1960s and that of the 1970s, but the overall consistency is more striking. The final column indicates that military expenditures have remained strikingly constant as a proportion of steadily and sharply rising general government expenditures since the early 1970s.

The average annual expenditure of 2.6 percent of GNP for defense during the earlier years of Denmark's membership in NATO represented an earnest effort for three reasons. First, Alliance strategy became progressively more dependent on (American) nuclear deterrence. This made a more substantial budgetary effort appear superfluous to some and made it politically difficult to negotiate across parties, some of which were either lukewarm to more than token defense expenditures in the first place or, as in the case of the largest party, the Social Democrats, inclined to stress social policy effort. Second, the widely observed and theoretically accepted tendency of smaller members of alliances to provide less than their proportional shares of the costs of collective defense may in fact have operated in the Danish case in this period, particularly in light of the growing reliance on nuclear deterrence in an era widely believed to be one of American strategic nuclear superiority.

If these two factors militated against a higher level of defense spending, a third provided impetus for maintaining the mean 2.6 percent of GNP expenditure and for such more subtle but nonetheless significant increments as those entailed by indexation for inflation. This factor was the combination of the tradition of support from the Conservative and Liberal Parties for the military and the progressive socialization of the military cadres in terms of Alliance norms. As the general officers and even field-grade officers came to have more and more routine and institutionalized contact with their American and other Allied counterparts, their notions of what constituted an adequate level of military preparedness tended to be revised upward. In addition, their experiences served as stimuli for prodefense politicians.

Manpower levels actually rose in the first half of the 1960s—with a peak strength of 52,000 (for all services combined) being reached in 1964. The army in that year had an active force level of 34,000 men, three-quarters being conscripts; the navy was staffed by 8,000 (one-half being conscripts); and the air force's strength was at 10,000 (35 percent conscripts). For all three services the length of service was between fourteen and sixteen months for the lowest grade and eighteen to twenty-four months for noncommissioned officers. At that time the navy consisted of eighteen frigates and escort ships, three submarines, eight mine-layers and twelve mine-sweepers, and a number of patrol boats and landing craft. The air force had eight fighter-interceptor squadron and support units, as well as ground-to-air missiles for air defense.

As will be seen later, force levels and major weapons systems have declined greatly since the mid-1960s, along with the tours of duty served by enlisted personnel and conscripts. While the relative share of the nation's wealth devoted to defense was remaining quite stable, the military capability purchased with these resources began to decline drastically. However, these were events that came later and interacted with a more broadly changing context for Danish policy making. The effort of the earlier period is clearly characterized by constancy, even if the seeds of things to come were already being sown.

Popular Attitudes Toward NATO and Defense

The positions of parliamentary elites with regard to the Alliance in particular and defense policy in general have already been described. In the earlier years of Danish alliance, general public opinion did not play an appreciable direct role in security-policy formulation. It is interesting nevertheless to glance briefly at the data.

The representation of the evolution of Danish opinion on such straightforward questions as "Are you for or against Danish participation in NATO?" since the birth of the Alliance, requires considerable care. There is substantial short-term fluctuation in responses to surveys; and neither theoretical nor situational explanations are adequate. However, while such fluctuations militate against a simple tabular presentation of survey results since 1949, it is possible to characterize such data in summary terms.

As can be seen from Table 2.2, a substantial plurality supported Danish membership in the Alliance during its first decade, but approximately one-quarter of respondents were opposed to it and a somewhat larger proportion answered "don't know." In the second decade—from 1959 to the late 1960s—the proportion of those opposed dropped substantially, *but the gains accrued to the "don't know" category, rather than to those favorably disposed.* Since then, there has been a moderate increase in the proportion of responses indicating support for membership, as well as opposition to it.

Inasmuch as security policy in Denmark was largely the domain of a fairly small political and sectoral elite until a few years ago, the relevance of the data from the earlier period is most important not for its relative weight at the time, but as a base of comparison with later periods, when

Table 2.2   Levels of Support for Danish Membership in NATO

Year	For %	Against %	Don't Know %
1949	47	26	27
1954[a] (April)	39	25	36
1954 (August)	47	24	29
1959	42	15	43
1964	49	13	38
1969	45	13	42
1970	52	15	33
1972	45	18	37
1973	49	25	26
1974	52	19	29
1975	51	22	28
1976	49	17	34
1977	52	26	22
1978	57	21	22
1979	55	19	26
1981	59	18	23
1982 (December)	58	21	21

[a]Such fluctuations in surveys taken a few months apart were not unusual.

Sources: Gallup Institute. Reproduced in *Dansk Udenrigspolitisk Årbog,* 1979, 1981, 1982.

public opinion began increasingly to influence elite positions. For the first twenty years of the Alliance, the balance in favor of membership neither impeded elite-formulated policy nor moved it in specific directions. As will be shown, this did change in the decade that followed, with the public becoming a more discrete brake, stimulus, or, in a limited degree, perhaps even the shaping instrument.

The First Twenty Years: Well-Defined Alignment

The three sets of events reviewed here, combined with the assessment of Denmark's quantifiable contribution to Alliance defense, provide a basis for understanding the Danish profile in NATO during its first twenty years. The summary profile that emerges is one of a country that, while becoming integrated into the structures and processes of NATO, retained the orientation with which it entered the Alliance and, to a considerable extent, managed to institutionalize it. In the main, that orientation consisted of maintaining a limited but well-defined national military capability, augmented through alliance, while pursuing a long-term policy of nonprovocation or confidence building. The former goal was achieved not only through protection under the American nuclear umbrella in the collective security arrangement that NATO represents but also through the integration of local defense capabilities with the Federal Republic in the BALTAP framework. The latter could at least be pursued, although, perhaps because of its nature, not attained. The emergence of détente as an Alliance posture during the last phase of the period in question and its acceptance through the Harmel Report represented a movement by NATO in a direction that Denmark had begun to follow before 1949. By assuming special positions on some Alliance issues—in particular, concerning the stationing of foreign troops and the acceptance of foreign installations and of nuclear weapons on its territory—the country did less than many other members; but the limitations it placed on its collective defense roles were shared by one or more members in each case.

This profile reflected a careful equilibrium of political preferences and the weight of historic experience and material constraints. The factors that produced this equilibrium all constitute constraints or parameters not only for Danish security policy and Alliance behavior in the past, but for the future as well.

The decade of the 1970s witnessed a tightening of these constraints, but it was marked by continuity with, at least as much as change from, the period following World War II. The major factors conditioning this process of tightening were, from the external environment, large-power and general Alliance policies and general economic conditions, and, from within, the continued and perhaps exacerbated limits of weak coalition governments and the increasing influence of antinuclear (energy as well as weapons) and peace movements on left-wing parties and the Social Democrats. The level of defense effort—in terms of expenditures, weapons systems, and manpower—and the basis for security-policy orientations in public opinion link the external and internal domains. The ways in which this transpired are the subjects of the next section.

Converging Constraints on a Macilent Defense

It is a major theme of this chapter that the factors of continuity are at least as important as the changes in Danish society in explaining Danish security-policy choices. One does not find in the late 1960s and early 1970s, for instance, the same breakdown in the domestic consensus underpinning Danish defense policy as that described in the chapter on the Netherlands. It is certain that the decision-making process did become more "open" than in earlier periods, when such matters were largely decided by a small group of political elites, but it should be clear from the discussion above that the nature of "consensus" was very special during the first two decades of alignment. It rested on a multiparty bargain that adequately regulated political differences among the major

Table 2.3 Composition of Danish Opinion on NATO Membership, 1981

	For %	Against %	Don't Know %
Total	59	18	23
Supporters of parties to the right of Social Democrats	77	12	11
Social Democrats	55	17	28
Supporters of parties to the left of Social Democrats	25	71	4
Men	72	16	12
Women	47	21	32
Age Group			
15-24	47	22	31
25-39	60	21	19
40-59	66	14	20
60 and older	61	16	23
Education Level[a]			
I	59	16	25
II	66	15	19
III	52	34	14

[a]Level I = folkschools (9 or 10 years of education); II = middle school education; III = gymnasium or above.

Source: Dansk Udenrigspolitisk Årbog, 1981, 378.

actors. This embodied a certain number of special Danish positions on a number of Alliance issues and a general orientation that placed as much emphasis on a historically founded preference for confidence-building efforts with the potential adversary as on maintaining national defenses. Increased openness did not challenge this "consensus," and, at least at the outset, it may have reinforced its character.

What happened during the 1970s, however, was that the specific political bargain that had functioned effectively for over two decades became more and more difficult to maintain. By the early 1980s it had become virtually untenable, and with the departure of the Social Democratic party from government into opposition in 1982, the repoliticizing of defense policy in Denmark had entered a new, more virulent phase. This section explores in turn those factors in Danish society and those changes in the external environment that interacted to create the context in which this important shift occurred.

The Conditioning Context

Two basic points about Danish society and its political system need to be understood in order to appreciate the ways in which new external challenges came to have the impact they did on political choice in Denmark. Neither is unique to Denmark, but each is more accentuated there than in other countries of the Alliance.

THE ADVENT OF POSTMATERIALISM: THE PSYCHOLOGY OF SECURITY. Perhaps the least quantifiable and hence most speculative element that seems to have been operative during the 1970s is the rise of the so-called postmaterialist orientation in Western populations.[34] This stems, according to Ronald Inglehart, from the combined conditions of physical security from war and freedom from deprivation.

Denmark has constructed a comprehensive welfare state that makes it virtually impossible for Danes of today to experience the economic insecurity of the generation that lived through the Great Depression. Although high unemployment and generally weak economic conditions have prevailed in the country for nearly a decade, with declines in real take-home income having occurred in several years, the welfare state has served as an effective cushion for virtually all. In this regard, Denmark surpasses nearly all its partners.

At the same time, physical security has been complete and sustained for the majority of Danes living today. This is undoubtedly attributable in large part to the success of the Atlantic Alliance as a deterrent. This success, however, commonly breeds disregard for its own sources and requisites. The aftermath of World War II and the advent of the Cold War did not enter the consciousness of most Danes directly; they had either not yet been born or they were too young to have a personal recollection of the climate in which the country entered NATO.

Under these conditions, publics (and often members of decision-making elites, particularly parliamentarians) find it increasingly difficult to see direct connections between security based on a nuclear deterrent, especially someone else's deterrent, and the resources expended on a small state's conventional military apparatus.[35] Moreover, with the passage of several decades of peace, possibly but certainly not demonstrably owed to that deterrent, military force—one's own and that in the arsenals of the members of one's own alliance—becomes an abhorred, threatening element of *in*security.

A postmaterialist orientation tends to emphasize confidence-building paths to security more than military preparedness. It shows a marked concern with development assistance to the Third World,[36] impatience not only with American foreign policy—formerly in Vietnam, currently in Central America—but also with regard to American competitive armament policies and nuclear weapons in particular, and similar values. These underlie much of the tension between Denmark and the United States, as well as the recent and emergent politics of Danish security policy.

None of this is peculiar to Denmark, of course. Political and financial support for defense has declined among specific segments of the populace and elites not only in the smaller NATO states but also in the United States. The roots of the change are the same: judgments about the utility of force in the thermonuclear era. Yet, in Denmark, such tendencies have become particularly pronounced during the last twelve to fifteen years.

This seems to be particularly true for the younger cohort, at least among the politically most active. Younger people are less sanguine about a path toward security through NATO than are members of older generations. In surveys of the participants of the Danish parties' congresses, conducted in 1978–79, two scholars found very marked divergence by age, for the Social Democrats in particular, in responses to questions regarding "continued membership in NATO being the best guarantee of Danish security" and "affinity for the U.S."[37] Those who had been adults during World War II placed considerable reliance on NATO membership as an assurance of Danish security, while younger delegates did not. It would also appear from the survey that the "postmaterialist" generation of Social Democrat activists feels less affinity toward the United States than do its elders.

There is no direct evidence to indicate that a desire to "cater to the youth" of the party or of the country was at the roots of the decision by the Social Democrat Party's leadership to reverse the positions it had held while constituting the government, but given the strong antinuclear energy movement of the mid- and late 1970s, largely populated by markedly "postmaterialistic" young people, and the substantial overlap between the movement's membership and more recently coalesced antinuclear weapons groups, guarded inferences seem warranted. Further, the attraction by the Left Socialists—in particular, of younger, more radical Social Democrats—may also have served to motivate the party leadership to reinforce its boundaries.

PROBLEMS OF GOVERNANCE. One need not develop at length the general theories about the problems of governability in modern democratic societies,[38] but some specific dimensions of this problem particular to Denmark must be grasped if the nature of the constraints that operate on the formulation of Danish defense policy are to be understood.

As was noted, coalition government has been the rule in Denmark in this century. Coalitions have tended to be plagued either by immobilism—an inability to rise above rather low common denominators among the parties comprising them—or fragility. Internally, more stable coalitions or single-party governments have not, of late, disposed of parliamentary majorities. Thus, they govern by sufferance or because no alternative to them can succeed.

The structural sources of this problem can be found in the party system and electoral behavior. Since the "fragmenting election" of December 1973, the *Folketing* has generally had to accommodate ten parties. None approaches a majority. The Social Democrats, long the largest, customarily constitute 30 to 40 percent of the membership. The five or six other "large" parties—the Conservatives, Liberals, Progress Party, and, more recently, the Socialist Peoples Party and the Center Democrats—tend to hover slightly above or below 10 percent. Voters' loyalties are not as firm as in some other European states, but they are sufficient to make it unlikely that shifts in party strengths will be of such magnitude in the near future that these patterns will be broken.

Neither left-of-center nor the more conservative governments are able to satisfy more than a minority of the fragmented electorate across a sufficiently wide range of salient issues—for example, the pressures for the growth of public expenditures, unemployment, and Alliance policies—if they act decisively. When the numbers of those thus alienated are added to those already disposed to oppose them, the arithmetic against effective governance is overwhelming. During the past ten to fifteen years the problem has been exacerbated by seemingly increasingly firm demarcation lines between left and right, both on domestic—essentially in the past decade, public sector and macroeconomic policies—and foreign- and defense-policy issues.[39]

Thus, the parties to the left of the Social Democrats—the Socialist People's Party and the Left Socialists—have pushed increasingly hard for higher expenditures for social programs, not simply at the expense of the defense effort, which, in any case, they oppose, but also of general economic viability. Although the left wing of the Social Democrats might have been amenable to maintaining the growth of social expenditures if the requisite resources could have been taken from the defense sector, it could not carry the party as a whole, because such a course would have required increasing the domestic and foreign debts, which already were exceedingly high. Faced with politically potent organized interests in favor of sustained domestic expenditures—including clients of the welfare state and its "providers," those employed in the very extensive public sector[40]—and with the inexorable consequences of Denmark's position in a world economy in recession, the party's position as a minority government was not tenable by mid-1982.

It was in this circumstance that the four-party right-of-center "bourgeois" coalition replaced the Social Democrats as a minority government. The new government's constituents were more inclined than those of its predecessor to support attempts to hold down the growth of the public sector. While the parliamentary opposition might criticize the scaling down of the growth of government expenditures and the cutting in real terms of some programs, within six to nine months after taking office the coalition's efforts began to bear fruit. In January 1984 they were "rewarded" for their attempts to deal with the "chronic economic crisis" and returned to power with a 2 percent increase in their still tenuous, minority parliamentary base.

The "bourgeois" coalition, however, is tolerated rather than enthusiastically supported by the electorate. They do tend to alienate those in the electorate who did not vote for them, with their relatively—that is, in the Danish context—hard line on Alliance policies and defense-expenditure proposals.[41] But the alternative—a government left-of-center composed of or based on the Social Democrats—is seen as less able to deal with the cardinal issue of the "economic crisis," since it is less likely to curb public expenditures. Thus, the Social Democrats remain vulnerable, even if they align themselves more closely with voters' sentiments regarding Alliance policies in general and nuclear weapons and defense expenditures in particular.

The Changing External Environment

The particular political bargain that amounted to a form of "consensus" during more than two decades of Danish alignment was struck under a set of permissive conditions. They were permissive in the sense that they allowed a political bargain to pass as if there were a real consensus. There was certainly both public support and substantial elite agreement on Danish membership in NATO—that the country's defense should first and foremost be based on the Alliance—but at no time could a "consensus" be said to have been present on the substance of such membership.

Among the four most important parties in modern Danish politics— the Conservatives, Liberals, Social Democrats, and Radicals—the Radicals have been reluctant supporters of membership and not-infrequent opponents of its consequences. They and the Social Democrats have generally tended to put domestic priorities ahead of Alliance requirements. In recent times, the Socialist People's Party and the Left Socialists, as well as the very small Communist Party, have been generally vocal critics of the Alliance and occasional challengers of membership. Yet the combination of traditional support for a military effort (from the Conservative and Liberal parties) and the absence of realistic alternatives (in the eyes of the Social Democrats, eventually the Radicals, and substantial pluralities of the body politic) seemed to add up to something like consensus. The environment remained conducive, not forcing any of the parties to make trade-offs incompatible with the central bargain.

The semblance of consensus began to erode in the late 1960s, with the advent of the "1969 problem," and during the 1970s, with two major changes on an international level bringing to a head the contradictions inherent in the situation. The first was the end of sustained economic growth in the Western world and with it the advent of difficult choices about how to spend limited resources. The second was the changing balance of forces between East and West and the decision by Allied leaders to modernize NATO's nuclear arsenal as well as to seek negotiated limitations on these systems.

THE ECONOMY AND THE DEFENSE EFFORT. The generalized economic downturn that has prevailed with scant relief for approximately ten years has been a critical factor affecting both the politics and the economics of the Danish defense effort. Again, the Danes are not unique in this regard, but some of the consequences for Denmark have been sharper than for many other countries in the Alliance.

National economies as "open" to the international economy as that of Denmark have particular difficulties in managing public resources. An economy as dependent as Denmark's on exports of finished industrial goods and agricultural products and on oil imports is difficult to manage from within. Moreover, in the Danish case, high proportions of national income are cycled through government for mandated social expenditures, thereby limiting economic flexibility and policy control even further. The interactive consequences of these circumstances amount to a vicious circle: slowed economic activity leads to high levels of unemployment (Denmark's is among the highest in the OECD), and that, in turn, burdens public resources even more.[42]

Second, another effect of declining exports and sharply increased import costs (particularly, but not exclusively for fuels) is the need to borrow heavily, especially abroad. This has produced ever-increasing debt-servicing costs and a chronic capital shortage over the past decade, and particularly in the last several years, given the high interest rates prevailing in world money markets. (By 1983, the country's net foreign debt stood at about one-third of its GDP.)

The fiscal crisis of the Danish state became one of the most acute within the industrial world during the past decade. The resources available for defense thus came under increasing pressure, and this at a time when the same factors were also augmenting the cost of performing even the same military tasks. Not only did the budget for procurement of military equipment have to absorb inflation and currency devaluations, but the cost of training, particularly in the air force and navy, has skyrocketed over the past decade as a result of a nearly 450 percent increase in fuel costs and also because modernized systems have generally been more fuel-intensive. This is discussed in greater detail later.

The political side of these phenomena has tightened the constraints on defense even further. The attempts of succeeding governments to control doméstic expenditures through cutting the rate of growth of wages and social policy outlays have generated a zero-sum perception among the numerous active special-interest groups and within the general public. As a consequence, defense spending is seen to come at the expense of social programs. The psychological sense that such a trade-off may exist is quite independent, of course, of whether or not there is an actual "substitution effect" at work. Moreover, by the end of the decade being considered here, the association in both the general public's mind and in that of at least some policy makers that high American interest rates were partially responsible for Denmark's economic malaise (or at least the decreased ability to deal with it) has aggravated reactions to calls for increased defense expenditures and to recurring charges of "free-riding."

It is in this context that the seeming incongruity in public opinion of strong support for a Danish military effort and the simultaneous unwillingness to see an increase in defense expenditures should be viewed (see Table 2.4). There are strong variations in attitudes across political orientations, but some recent data (see Table 2.5) would indicate that none of the major segments of the public supports increased defense expenditures. Moreover, according to other recent data, the majority of Danes do not feel that defense should be exempted from a general attempt to curb public-sector expenditures (see Table 2.6). Favoring the maintenance of a viable defense effort but declining to underwrite its funding is not a peculiarity of the Danish public, and it can be explained in terms of theories of political dynamics and behavior that apply to several other

---

Table 2.4   Public Support for the Danish Defense Effort

| | Aggregate of strongly and moderately positive responses | | | |
	May 1975	Oct 1976	Oct 1978	May 1980
Can Danish defense forces be effective?	23.7	26.2	29.7	34.3
Will the populace support the defense forces?	81.6	83.5	85.0	82.8
Does the Danish defense effort help to assure peace?	53.1	56.9	59.9	63.8
Is a (Danish) defense desirable?	68.8	74.7	77.4	78.3
Should more money be spent on defense?	10.3	14.9	17.5	30.3

Source: The Danish Military-Psychological Institute's surveys, as reported in *Dansk Udenrigspolitisk Årbog,* 1980, 431.

Table 2.5 Composition of Opinion on Defense Expenditures

	Raise Expenditures %	Maintain Present Level %	Lower Expenditures %	Don't Know %
Total[a]	20	41	27	12
Supporters of parties to the right of Social Democrats	33	47	12	8
Supporters of Social Democrats	15	48	28	9
Supporters of parties to the left of Social Democrats	8	17	71	4

[a]Note that the source is different from that cited in Table 2.4.

Source: Gallup Institute survey, originally published in *Berlingske Tidende,* 15 September 1980, reproduced in *Dansk Udenrigspolitisk Årbog,* 1980, 433.

Table 2.6 Should Defense Expenditures Be Exempt from a General Cut in Public Spending?

	Yes %	No %	Don't Know or In Doubt %
Total	36	51	13
Supporters of the Governing Coalition:			
Conservatives	61	26	13
Liberals	67	19	14
Center Democrats	56	30	14
Christian Peoples Party	72	17	11
Supporters of:			
Social Democrats (Opposition)	14	73	13
Radicals	11	74	15
Socialist People's Party	10	82	8

Note: The question asked a representative sample of 1,228 persons on 6 December 1982: "Should the existing defense agreement (among the parties and embodied in law) be maintained unchanged even if there are reductions in public expenditures in general or should defense appropriations also be decreased?" (author's translation). A "Yes" indicates the maintenance of the expenditures agreed to in the current defense accord; a "No" signifies that if public spending is cut defense should not be exempted from such cuts.

Source: Observa Institute Survey, originally published in *Jyllands-Posten,* 16 December 1982, reproduced in *Dansk Udenrigspolitisk Årbog,* 1982, 424.

policy areas as well.[43] Nevertheless, as general economic conditions have deteriorated, there can be no doubt that the pressure on defense spending has increased.

The task of Danish governments in meeting defense obligations has thus been made more difficult by both the actual and the perceptual conditions to which the transnational economic downturn contributes. On the one hand, it reinforces the historically anchored disposition to pursue security through confidence building rather than increased armament. On the other hand, the convergence of three factors—(1) prolonged, adverse transnational economic conditions; (2) a thoroughly institutionalized, effective welfare state in a political framework that is sensitive to the Babel of electoral and organized interest voices from below; and (3) the extremely steep rise in the money costs of maintaining an up-to-date, balanced military capability—precludes a more substantial budgetary effort and forces an extremely difficult set of trade-offs on any government if it wants just to maintain existing defense efforts. This being said, it is nevertheless important to keep these difficulties of managing the Danish defense effort in perspective. With the caveats regarding cross-national comparison of defense expenditures and the meaning of quantified money and manpower data, it remains possible to assess the Danish defense effort in relation to the efforts expended by some other members of the Alliance. In doing so, one sees that difficult or not, political choice did not unilaterally sacrifice the defense effort on the altar of domestic political exigency.

The charge of "Denmarkization" has been leveled in the last few years, with particular focus on Denmark's perceived tendency to lag behind in budgetary efforts for defense. Yet, a straightforward comparison of the evolution of defense expenditures since 1969 in Denmark and six other NATO countries does not provide clear evidence for the charge. In Table 2.7 the changes in per capita military expenditures are presented for an eleven-year period, 1970 to 1980—the period during which the "Danish lag" supposedly developed. Three of the six states, most notably the United States and Canada, spent less per capita at the end of the period than at its outset, while three others spent more. But only one among the latter—Belgium—increased its per capita defense expenditures more than Denmark. Clearly, a more discriminating analysis is required. Four specific factors need to be considered if recent Danish efforts in defense are to be better understood.

First, even hard-pressed minority governments managed to maintain the level of defense expenditures under economically and politically extremely difficult circumstances. Beginning in the mid-1970s, the Danish economy faltered, but in terms of both indicators noted in the preceding paragraph, the share of defense expenditures was maintained, *in the face of actually declining personal and national incomes and steep increases in legally mandated domestic expenditures.* The latter were driven by incremental and, to a substantial degree, demographically determined costs attached to social security, health care, and similar programs and, begin-

Table 2.7   Net Changes in Military Expenditures and Armed Forces, 1970–1980: Selected NATO Members

Country	Change in Per Capita Military Expenditure, 1970–1980 %	Change in the Size of Military Forces, 1970–1980 %
Belgium	+53.9	+ 0.9
Canada	− 9.8	−12.1
DENMARK	+28.9	−16.7
Netherlands	+ 5.0	− 4.5
Norway	+10.6	+ 5.4
United Kingdom	− 1.4	−14.6
United States	−22.0	−24.6
TOTAL NATO[a]	+ 3.8[b]	−12.7

[a]Aggregate data for all NATO members except Iceland.
[b]Aggregate NATO data for this indicator cover only the period 1973–1980.

Source: Calculated from NATO Information Service, *The North Atlantic Treaty Organization, Facts and Figures,* 10th ed. (Brussels, 1981), 321–22. (Expenditure data in constant units.)

ning in 1975, extremely high unemployment rates. (Unemployment averaged 3.6 percent for the fifteen years between 1960 and 1974 and jumped to 11 percent beginning in 1975.)[44] The political structure militates strongly in favor of continued incremental increases in domestic spending, and the internal constituencies for defense expenditures are much less substantial. Therefore, the fact that the level of the budgetary effort for defense has been sustained under these conditions may be taken as a sign of substantial governmental or elite commitment to it.

Second, as noted earlier, the combination of unfavorable macroeconomic conditions and continuing growth in domestic public programs has generated a high foreign debt and accompanying debt-servicing costs for the country. What is important here is that the increases in the public sector's domestic and foreign debt-servicing costs have been so high in the past decade that they absorbed a greater share of the Danish GNP than the 1.4 percent share lost by defense in that period.[45]

Third, the structure of Danish defense expenditures is such that a substantially higher proportion of it is spent abroad than is the case for most other members of the Alliance. This is because Denmark produces virtually no armaments and fuel for its armed forces. In economically good times, this loss of jobs and money for the national economy can be— and was—offset by the country's high productivity and exports. Since the general economic downturn in the mid-1970s, however, this characteristic pattern in Danish defense expenditures has meant that the *burden on the economy*—as distinguished from the governmental budget—has been growing substantially more rapidly than either the GNP or the defense burden gauged by budget figures, particularly because of the increased foreign debt and debt-servicing costs. Thus, *the cost of defense to the Danish economy has grown substantially over the past decade and is considerably greater than the magnitude of the defense budget would indicate.*

Fourth and finally, the magnitude of *security-related economic effort*—as distinguished from government expenditures for military forces—can be and arguably (given the conceptions of security and responsible international roles prevalent among large segments of Danish society and decision makers) ought to be thought of as encompassing several categories of spending not included in the defense budget. Some of the elements of a more broadly conceived financial effort are the massive Danish subsidies to the populations of Greenland and the Faroe Islands, both of strategic significance to NATO; the costs of international peacekeeping forces such as in Zaïre, Gaza, and Cyprus in the past, and a high probability of such contributions in the future; and foreign economic assistance to underdeveloped countries at levels (as percentages of GNP) measurably higher than most other countries.

If some or all of these categories of expenditure are taken into account, Denmark's financial contribution to security is much more substantial than would appear initially. Greenland obtained home rule in 1979, and while it entered the European Community with Denmark, its populace remained opposed to membership. It is not self-sufficient economically and has recently voted to sever its ties to the Community. Danish subsidies to Greenland amount to more than 20 percent of the current level of the Danish defense budget and may now increase.[46] While Denmark disposes of 1.2 percent of the aggregate GNP for all of NATO and expends only 0.7 percent of aggregate NATO defense costs in budgetary terms, it contributes 1.1 percent of the total spent by NATO countries for international peacekeeping and more than 2.5 percent for foreign economic aid.[47] Leaving aside for now the question of whether international peacekeeping and foreign economic assistance are appropriately considered a part of the security effort in terms of expenditures, the argument that the massive subsidies to Greenland ought to be so treated seems strong in the context of NATO. It will be recalled from the discussion above that it was Greenland's strategic value that generated most of the American interest in having Denmark in the Alliance at the outset; and Greenland's continuing—probably increasing—importance as the site of strategic early warning and communications installations remains high not only for the collective defense of the Alliance but for American continental security as well.

Regardless of whether the financial effort for defense is actually greater than Denmark is given credit for, it is evident that this level of expenditure has yielded smaller military forces and fewer copies of major weapons with the passage of time. With both manpower and materiel costs increasing substantially in the past two decades—a trend likely to continue or to become even more accentuated in the future—the Danish response has been to reduce manpower *and* the numbers of major weapons while striving to maintain an arsenal that is, in its major components, as close to state-of-the-art as possible. This trend is demonstrated in part by the figures in column 3 in Table 2.1 above and in Tables 2.8 and 2.9. The number of active-duty military personnel has declined sharply, and the ratio of defense spending (which has remained essentially constant after adjustment for inflation) to those forces has increased correspondingly. In short, despite substantial increases in personnel

Table 2.8   Military Manpower, 1960–1982

Year	Active Duty	(Number of whom are conscripts)[a]	Reserves	Home Guard	Armed Forces per 1,000 pop[b]
1960	44,000				9.6
1961	43,000				9.4
1962	46,500			55,000	10.0
1963	49,000	(36,750)		56,000	10.0
1964	52,000	(33,000)		56,000	10.0
1965	51,000	(32,250)		55,000	10.0
1966	50,000			58,600	10.0
1967	45,500			69,000	9.4
1968	45,500			69,000	9.4
1969	45,500			69,000	9.3
1970	44,500			69,500	9.0
1971	40,500		43,000	64,000	8.1
1972	43,400		79,500	55,100	8.7
1973	39,800		91,000	67,300	7.9
1974	37,100		80,500	65,800	7.4
1975	34,400		74,000	68,100	6.8
1976	34,500[c]				6.8
1977	34,700	(12,270)	82,000	70,800	6.8
1978	34,000	(12,270)	82,500	72,900	6.6
1979	34,650	(10,500)	82,500	71,760	6.7
1980	35,050	(11,800)	81,500	72,960	6.4
1981	32,600	(11,000)	81,500	73,300	6.4
1982	31,200	(9,500)	79,300	74,100	6.1

[a]Length of service for conscripts: 1960–1964   16 months
                                       1964–1965   14–16 months
                                       1966–1969   12–14 months
                                       1970–1973   12 months
                                       1974–1982   9 months

[b]Active duty calculated from the same sources as Table 2.1.
[c]Estimate.

Source Same as Table 2.1

Table 2.9 Military Manpower: Distribution by Service

Year	Army	Reserve	Home Guard	Navy	Reserve	Home Guard	Air Force	Reserve	Home Guard
1960	29000			7500			7500		
1961	29000			7000			7000		
1962	32000			7000			7500		
1963	33600		56000	7000			8400		
1964	34000		56000	8000			10000		10500
1965	33000		55000	8000		3500	10000		10500
1966	30000		55000	7200		3600	12600		10500
1967	28000		55000	7200		3500	10300		10500
1968	28000		55000	7200		3500	10300		11000
1969	28000		54000	7000		4000	10500		11000
1970	27000		54000	7000		4000	10500		8000
1971	24000	40000	52000	6500	3000	4000	10000		11500
1972	27000	65000	51000	6600	3000	4100	9800		11500
1973	24000	80000	51000	6300	4000	4300	9500	7000	11500
1974	21500	69500	50000	6000	4000	4300	9600	7000	11500
1975	21500	69500	52000	5800	4500	4600	7100	8000	11500
1976									
1977	21800	69500	54400	5800	4500	4800	7100	8000	12000
1978	21000	69500	56100	6100	4500	4800	6900	8000	12000
1979	21400	74500	56600	6100	4500	4860	7150	8500	10300
1980	21000	74500	56200	6200	4500	4860	7850	7500	11900
1981	19300	70000	56500	5700	4000	4900	7600	7500	11900
1982	18000	65000	57300	5800	4200	4900	7400	10000	11900

Source: International Institute for Strategic Studies, *The Military Balance,* 1960–61 through 1982–83.

costs, such as salaries and fringe benefits, the Danish military has become progressively more equipment-intensive; but because equipment has become more costly, this shift has been accompanied by a reduction in the quantity of such equipment.

By 1982 the total number of personnel had been reduced to 31,200 (including 670 women, who are excluded from battlefield units), 30 percent being conscripts. (The tour of duty for conscripts was cut to nine months in 1973.) Of the total, the army's share had fallen to 18,000; the navy's strength to 5,800; and that of the air force had been reduced to 7,400. The equipment disposed of by each of the services had been substantially modernized but also cut in numbers.

The army is presently comprised of five mechanized infantry brigades and three regimental combat teams and disposes of 256 tanks (120 being Leopard 1s). It is supported by an "Augmentation Force" reserve of 6,000, subject to immediate recall, a "Field Army Reserve" of 43,000, and a regional defense force of 16,000, as well as an Army Home Guard of 57,300. The air force has 112 combat aircraft, approximately half of which are F-16s; and while the numbers of combat aircraft are still dropping, the upgrading of the equipment continues apace. By the end of 1984 there were 92 combat aircraft, 80 of modern design (mostly F-16s). The navy's present complement has declined to five submarines, five frigates and corvettes, a number of patrol craft, seven mine-layers and six mine-sweepers, as well as minor support craft. The navy also continues to lose units as the costs of replacements continue to rise.[48]

The progressive shrinkage of active-duty manpower and equipment has, of course, been a response to the massive increases in the costs of both of these components of military preparedness. In late 1981 and early 1982, during discussion of the three-year defense budget, the direction and the serious implications of this trend were occasionally acknowledged with dark humor in the defense-policy community, with the argument that at the rate it was going it would not be long before the Danish defense effort would consist of one soldier, serving in the army on Mondays and Thursdays, in the navy on Tuesdays and Fridays, and in the air force on Wednesdays and Saturdays—and, while he might have his own Danish rifle, he would have to rent a ship and an airplane for use in his navy and air force roles.

The budgetary, manpower, and materiel-related constraints on Denmark's defense effort are serious, but the most significant ramifications may not be the slow growth of defense expenditures, with manpower and equipment declining in numbers. For Denmark's defense posture is not premised on independent viability in terms of security; and its contributions to NATO's overall military capability, under any realistic circumstance, would be so slight, given the inherent limitations of size and national resources, that marginal increases in terms of money and/or manpower border on the negligible. The country's defense is based on collective security through NATO in general and on a holding action in particular, until Allied reinforcements can join combat.[49]

Viewed in this light—that is, assuming the continuation of reliance on collective defense through the Alliance—three less-evident elements are crucial. First, the symbolic and political significance of the country's visible defense effort (especially in budgetary and manpower terms) reverberate in relationships within the Alliance and, as the issue of "Denmarkization" indicates, especially with the United States. Second, military forces other than standing, active-duty units become important both qualitatively and quantitatively. Third, the complex of questions related to Denmark's readiness to receive reinforcements in appropriate numbers, in good time, and with particular equipment, weapons, and configurations must be dealt with.

The first has already been treated in part. With regard to military manpower, it is noteworthy that while active-duty force levels have declined steadily and substantially during the past twenty years, the number of trained and equipped personnel—reserves and Home Guard, in addition to standing forces—has actually increased. The growth has come in both the reserve and Home Guard categories, as the figures in Tables 2.8 and 2.9 show. It thus may be feasible for Denmark to marshal sufficient military manpower to meet the strategic requirements of a holding action (until reinforcements are in place) and to satisfy such other desiderata as the maintenance of a substantial citizen role in national defense. The country's readiness to receive appropriately equipped allied reinforcements is more problematic, however, especially given the restrictions on nuclear weapons in peacetime, which may affect prepositioning. Since these issues bear on current and prospective strategic considerations, their treatment is more appropriate in the final section of this chapter.

Tying together the strands of the argument made earlier, one arrives at the following: Economic stringency for Denmark has been painful. It clearly has not been alone in this regard. All of the countries studied in this volume have gone through extremely difficult periods beginning in the mid-1970s. The effects on the Danish defense effort have nonetheless been real. The direct effects on the budget, however, have been perhaps the least important. Uncontrolled inflation in the defense sector is primarily responsible for the same money buying less defense; economic conditions and readily understood political constraints have simply prevented the government from doing much about it.

It is the indirect effects that have been most damaging. In the minds of many people, there clearly has been the reinforcement of the image that defense is being purchased at the expense of social security. The fact that defense spending has been maintained during a period of cutbacks in other areas has increased pressure, above all within the Social Democratic Party, whose preferences for domestic programs and for confidence-building became difficult to reconcile with positions it felt compelled to take on defense. But the pressure has been more general than that of guns versus welfare and, the difficulties of bringing the state budget under control had a great deal to do with the departure of the Social

Democrats from power in September 1982 and the profile they adopted thereafter.

INF AND DENMARK. This is not an appropriate place to review the evolution of the strategic basis of the Atlantic Alliance since its formation to the present. Changes in it, occasioned by technological developments—for example, the advent of Intercontinental Ballistic Missiles (ICBMs)— American commitments to and recurring direction of attention toward interests outside the region, changing economic balances, and political mood have been extraordinarily well documented and analyzed, and there is wide agreement, if not consensus, on the import of such changes for NATO and for its European members. The "doctrine of 'flexible response,'" the "fear of 'decoupling,'" and the shifting regional balance of nuclear power (leading to the "double-track" INF policy) have not only altered and complicated the initial positions of the United States and European members but, arguably, progressively weakened the belief that an attack on the latter would be prevented through deterrence. They have also increased the perception that NATO-Europe would be *defended* instead—that is, that it might become the battleground.

No appropriate time-series data exist on the evolution of Danish perceptions of the capability of the United States to extend an effective umbrella for NATO-Europe or on the perceived willingness to use its strategic deterrent for that purpose; but the conjecture that perceptions of both capability and credibility have declined in recent years seems warranted. The failure of the United States to achieve its goals in Southeast Asia and to protect its proclaimed interests effectively elsewhere have doubtless contributed to such impressions, as has the shift in the balance of theater forces that gave rise to the Long-Term Development Program (LTDP) and to the double-track INF decision within the Alliance.

These objective and perceptual aspects of the current strategic situation apply generally to NATO-Europe, but they have particular ramifications for Denmark for several reasons. Salient among these are the nuclear issues as these have reentered the agenda, through the double-track INF decision in particular, and the difficulties of managing détente, which is linked in the perceptions of many with INF and arms reductions—the "other track". These issues stress the policy-making capabilities of the regime—not just those of the government of the day, but those of any likely alternatives to it in the foreseeable future.

Notwithstanding the long-established policy to refuse nuclear weapons on Danish territory and the fact that the 1979 NATO decision to deploy 572 Pershing II and cruise missiles with nuclear warheads did not envision such installations in Denmark, INF became a burning issue in the country. At the heart of the debate have been the broader questions of the role of nuclear weapons in NATO's strategy and the possibility of a nuclear-free zone in the Nordic Region, rather than nuclear weapons in Denmark itself.[50]

In the fall of 1979 a split developed in the governing (but minority)

Social Democratic Party regarding INF-related discussions in NATO. The left wing of the party pressed the government to propose, at the December 1979 ministerial meeting from which the double-track decision emerged, a six-month delay in the decision, while the possibility of arms-control discussions was pursued with the Soviet Union.[51] Since then, pressures from its own left wing, from the Socialist People's Party and the Left Socialists, as well as from peace groups outside the *Folketing,* continued until it was forced out of office (essentially on domestic, economic policy issues) in September 1982.

The difficulties the Social Democrats had in controlling this pressure became evident at the party's annual meeting in 1981. Delegates to the congress passed a resolution "to work toward keeping nuclear weapons off Danish soil," pointedly omitting the words "in peacetime," contrary to the leadership's wishes and notwithstanding the fact that a peacetime ban on such weapons had been established twenty-four years earlier.[52] The 1981 party congress vote can be seen as an indication that many in the party were moving toward a more radical antinuclear-weapons position than that of the party's leaders, who were also the Government. This position was buttressed by the prevailing public sentiment on the issue of nuclear weapons in general and INF in particular. In a survey conducted in December 1979, a substantial plurality (48 percent) agreed with the statement that, with the deployment of the SS-20, the Soviet Union had assumed a position of superiority vis-à-vis NATO in intermediate-range nuclear weapons in the European theater, versus 18 percent dissenting and 34 percent indicating that they "did not know". Yet, a plurality believed that it would be wrong for NATO to modernize and augment *its* intermediate-range missiles (43 percent versus 31 percent, with 26 percent responding "don't know"). Among those who said they had followed discussions of the issue, the distribution of opinion was 37 percent in favor of a NATO response, with 47 percent believing it would be inappropriate or undesirable. A large majority opposed changing Denmark's policy of precluding the stationing of nuclear weapons on Danish soil if, in the light of the perceived Soviet superiority in intermediate-range nuclear weapons, NATO should make such a proposal.[53]

By December 1982 survey results showed that a bare majority (51 percent) favored adhering to the 1979 NATO agreement; 29 percent wanted to abrogate it, while 20 percent were in doubt or did not know.[54] But, significantly, opinion on the issue was sharply divided by party. Not only among the supporters of the traditionally antimilitary parties (the Radicals, Socialist People's, and Left Socialists), but among the historically pro-NATO and moderately prodefense Social Democrats, strong majorities favored breaking the agreement. (Among the respondents who identified themselves with the Social Democrats, 44 percent opted for breaking the accord of December 1979 on the double-track decision, while only 27 percent wanted to adhere to it.) Among the Radicals, voters' opinion was more nearly divided, with 37 percent favoring breaking the agreement and 35 percent wishing to maintain it.

The "second track" in NATO's 1979 INF decision is clearly the chosen path for a majority of Danes. Elites and public alike would doubtless prefer the removal of all theater nuclear weapons from Europe—most especially intermediate-range missiles—by both the Warsaw. Pact and NATO.[55] While it appears to have no chance of acceptance as government policy, the venerable "Nordic nuclear-free zone" proposal revived by Norway in 1980—it was originated many years ago by Finnish President Urho Kekkonen[56]—entered the Danish security-policy agenda in the following year. The Social Democratic Government rejected it as essentially "uninteresting," since it would unilaterally give up an option that, even though it is not exercised in the region, might be useful in theaterwide arms reduction bargaining, and also as incompatible with fundamental NATO strategy and, thus, Danish membership in the Alliance. Nonetheless, the proposal became, in 1981, one of the rallying points of the emerging peace movement in Denmark.[57]

Three factors thus point to a portentous resurfacing of the deeply rooted tension-reducing component of security policy in the late 1980s: the call by the party's activists for a general, rather than specifically, peacetime ban on nuclear weapons on Danish territory; the embrace by the young and relatively small but serious peace movement of the Nordic nuclear-free zone proposal; and the disinclination of the public to support INF modernization by NATO even in the face of a perceived Soviet superiority in such weapons. They form the specific combination of pressures that were brought to bear on the Social Democratic Party by the fall of 1982, when it moved into opposition.

A New Political Polarization?

Within a short time after going into opposition in September 1982, the Social Democratic Party began to shift its position on defense-spending commitments and on several key aspects of the INF issue, signaling an end to the multiparty bargain that had been operative since the 1950s.

The issue of defense expenditures is significant as much for what it symbolizes as for the substance. Approximately a year and a half before entering into government, the new coalition had proposed increasing force levels to the higher targets set for 1983 and for a three-year period—in the context of the defense agreement then being negotiated among the parties—annual increases of 2.2 percent in expenditures.[58] The Social Democratic Government, largely through the efforts of Prime Minister Anker Jørgensen, pared down the increase to a total of 2 percent stretched over the three-year accord. In late 1982, in the context of a general effort to curb the growth of public spending, the Social Democrats proposed to cut the defense budget as well as domestic spending. While the constituents of the governing coalition favor exempting defense from general public-sector savings, larger majorities among the voters of the other parties believe that if government expenditures are to be cut, those for defense should be included (see Table 2.6). The Social Democrats were able to force a compromise with the conservative parties on a cut for 1983–84 slightly more than half of the original proposal.[59]

On the nuclear issue, the Social Democrats first decided in December 1982 to block the appropriation of funds for INF infrastructure costs— funds they had agreed to provide while in government—with the prospect of the actual deployment of the INF weapons and with the lack of progress along the arms-limitation track of the 1979 decision. Then, using their parliamentary strength, they pushed the minority-governing coalition toward a position in the NATO ministerial setting to delay the beginning of deployment until some agreement could be reached between the Soviet Union and the United States in the Geneva INF talks. This shift by the party, mirrored in the opinions held by its constituents and buttressed by even stronger views from the left, augurs ill for the capacity of the major parties to pursue a consistent course in the Alliance. (In the spring of 1984 similar political pressure, coupled with increased public opinion against INF deployment, led the Danish Government to renege on the balance of the country's share of intrastructure payments.)

Neither generational changes in dispositions toward NATO or the United States, or security policy in general, nor any of the other factors operating on current Danish policy will suffice to explain the shift by the Social Democrats since the summer of 1982—or, for that matter, the current substance and form of the country's security policy. However, taken together, the elements considered in this section and the preceding one point to a set of constraints on most of the larger parties' leaders *and on any likely future coalition*. A large minority—essentially the supporters of the four parties in the coalition that came to power in September 1982 and, to a lesser extent, of the now troubled and declining Progress Party—supports a strong pro-NATO stance, and it supports sustained or increased defense expenditures as well. A numerically roughly comparable minority is strongly opposed to NATO's nuclear weapons-based defense posture in general and the deployment of Pershing II and cruise missiles in particular, and it is unfavorable to what it considers financial sacrifices for military purposes. A large segment of the same minority is, for that matter, not particularly happy with Denmark's membership in the Alliance.

Until recently, the Social Democrats and Radicals made the pivotal difference for managing these divergent perspectives. Now, in different ways and probably for somewhat different reasons, they have moved from lukewarm support for Denmark's Alliance roles toward challenging the means that had for several decades been used to fulfill those roles.

The country's long-lived economic malaise has contributed directly and indirectly to these recent developments. First, the Social Democratic minority government could not continue in power as long as it could not effectively mute the pressures of labor and other organized interests toward continued growth of public expenditures. (It is not at all certain, of course, that the party would have adhered fully to the NATO agreements it had entered into had it stayed in power.) Second, the pressures on both public and household budgets emanating from poor economic conjuncture worked toward perceptions of defense expenditures as being too costly—if the choices were between the real growth or even the maintenance of such spending, on the one hand, and the continued use of resources for social programs on the other. The massive foreign debt and concomitant debt-servicing costs played a considerable part in reaching this crossroads. To support NATO policies that were distasteful or frightening to many and simultaneously to incur major financial burdens strained both the dispositions of substantial segments of the public and also the political resources of parties when faced with selling such a Hobson's choice from the position of a governing minority or a minority coalition.

The reasons for the Social Democratic switch should be sought less in a "collapse of consensus" on security policy among the major parties than in increasing problems of governance, especially under severe economic constraints in a democratic welfare state such as Denmark. As Ole P. Kristensen's insightful analyses have clearly shown, it is likely that even when agreement can be reached on the proposition that public expenditures in general need to be curbed in the common interest, it is difficult, if not impossible, to get the publics organized around particular interests to absorb their shares of those cuts.[60]

As long as public sector growth was not effectively curbed, it was likely that growth in defense expenditures would be seen to be at the expense of more readily divisible, tangible programs and benefits only by those— the Radicals, the Socialist People's Party, the Left Socialists, and some on the left of the Social Democrats—who were not favorably disposed toward such expenditures in the first place. Once cuts in the growth of domestic programs—and absolute cuts in some of them—loomed as real possibilities, the majorities opposed to increased defense spending made their political weight felt. A minority government is in a singularly weak position to resist such a public mood in a democracy.

At the same time, it is clear that a new coalition is vulnerable politically on security-policy issues and that the Social Democrats, once they entered into opposition, sought to exploit the problems in governance faced by their successors. The *volteface* of the party on defense expenditures, INF deployment, and relations with NATO in general is most likely to be understood if it is viewed as part of the tactical maneuvering to construct a political base from which to return to government, with still little or no more than 30 percent of the votes and of the seats in the *Folketing*.

From the historical discussion above, it will be recalled that the party has been principally concerned with domestic issues: it joined the Conservatives and Liberals in supporting the national defense effort later and less wholeheartedly, and, especially when in opposition in recent times, it softened that support when such a posture seemed politic.[61] Splits inside the party on security policy in general and the INF decision and defense expenditures in particular were evident in recent annual meetings. The push from the two Socialist parties to the Social Democrat's left and an articulate, if small, segment of the party itself probably accounted for this. However, between September 1982, when it went into opposition, and late May 1983, the internal divisions were erased: The entire parliamentary party (with the exception of one back-bencher, who abstained) voted in the *Folketing* to instruct the government to strive to change three specific policy positions underwritten by the party between 1979 and the summer of 1982, when it constituted the government.[62]

The parliamentary vote called for a freeze of the Alliance's intermediate-range missiles at currently deployed levels while negotiations between the United States and the Soviet Union continued in Geneva; and it advocated the removal of all time limits for such negotiations. This position, in sum, amounted to the proposition that unless negotiations on intermediate-range missiles in Europe succeed in eliminating them, no new NATO weapons of that type should be deployed.

Second, the party's parliamentary initiative accepted the Soviet negotiating demand that French and British missiles presently in place be counted as part of NATO's INF strength—a position directly in conflict with both long-standing Alliance policy and the American bargaining posture. Third, it argued for lumping together the on-going INF and START (that is, strategic) arms-limitation talks in Geneva.

As with the December 1982 vote to withhold further appropriations for INF infrastructure costs—and so too with the May 1983 vote—Conservative Prime Minister Paul Schlüter chose not to treat the challenge to the government's position as a vote of no-confidence; but in the end this was largely irrelevant. What counted was that the ability of the minority government to implement steps involving Denmark's Alliance responsibilities was thrown into question, since a blocking majority sits in opposition.

The retention of the conservative coalition in the elections of January 1984 may have enhanced Denmark's governability in the short run, particularly in that the government's much-needed policy of curbing public expenditures can thus be continued. However, there is scant reason to believe that the election weakened the Social Democrat-led Opposition's potential for blocking or, as the events of 1982–83 showed, occasionally dictating defense-related policies. It may be argued, in fact, that the government has the best of both worlds: It is absolved (in the eyes of the electorate, but also perhaps of the Alliance) from responsibility with regard to defense policy as long as the Opposition can exert telling influence in that domain, and it can reap benefits from its economic policy. However, this changes little with regard to the realities of the situation.

Yet one should avoid the temptation to accept at face value the "simple" explanation of the Social Democrats' drastic and rather comprehensive reversals. The thoughts and actions of the party's leadership may well have been guided by the desire to return to power with the support—active or tacit and emanating from mixed motives—of those who oppose INF deployment, sustained or increased defense spending, earnest burden-sharing in the Alliance, or American foreign policy. But by itself such an explanation is dangerous for what it ignores. First, the Social Democrats' current stance is at least as consistent with long-term Danish dispositions toward security as their earlier position was. Second, there is a substantial manifest opinion base with which the recent positions are consistent, and perhaps additional latent opinion that may be mobilized by the recent departures. Third, in any event, short of strong and sustained economic growth, Denmark is not likely in the forseeable future to be able to satisfy its NATO-targeted goals in a way consistent with the general strategic path set by both Danish governments and the Alliance.

The discussion above of the evolution of Danish security policy prior to World War II, and with regard to NATO, demonstrates both the deep roots of the confidence-building side of the country's concerns and the reluctance of substantial segments of the polity to become enmeshed in East-West confrontations and in the politics of the nuclear-arms race. For at least one substantial portion of the body politic—in a society histori-cally divided by party and opinion on important defense and foreign policy related issues—this dimension of long-term tendencies has not been eclipsed by participation in NATO. And, far from being eroded over time, it is possibly stronger at present than at any other time in the period since World War II.

The question of Denmark's future in NATO is a real one again—for the first time in at least fifteen years, and possibly since 1949. The internal divisions brought to the surface by the Social Democrats' change of position since mid-1982 are not likely to be quickly or easily bridged. It is doubtful that, even if it wanted to, the party's leadership could carry off yet another about-face in the near future. Not only would such a reversal devastate the party's already severely damaged credibility for "serious-ness" and reliability, but it would also, in all likelihood, drive away large numbers of supporters among its younger constituents and from its left wing.

The foregoing discussion contains little or no reason for optimism regarding a return to the *relatively* more harmonious relations between the mainstream NATO positions on the one hand, and Denmark's on the other, as one might think of the period up to the late 1970s. The politicization of security and foreign-policy issues in general and nuclear weapons in particular, the lack of stable governments with the ability to make commitments within the framework of the Alliance and good expectations of being able to live up to them, the substantial recent shift in the positions taken by the leaders of the Social Democratic Party and their impressive ability to array the parliamentary party behind them do not augur well for the future. Even if some or most of these factors that have affected the formulation of security policy recently could be neutral-ized, there remains the massive set of economic problems faced by Denmark.

Thus, neither politically nor economically is the country going to be able to do *more* by way of meeting its NATO responsibilities as these have been traditionally conceived. There may, however, be possibilities for doing things *differently*, while enhancing both national and collective security. It is with a view toward such alternatives—alternatives that may be more realizable than changes in approach to more traditional items on the agenda—that prospects for some major issues for the 1980s are considered in the final section.

W(h)ither Denmark in NATO?

To reiterate the point of departure, Denmark entered NATO *faute de mieux* in 1949. Alliance was preferred as a means of enhancing the clearly insufficient national capabilities to provide security only because there were no attainable alternatives. It is reasonable to assume that it will remain the preferred collective security arena for Denmark through the 1980s—but still *faute de mieux*.

The thoroughly integrated national defense establishment, through BALTAP, provides a predictable, stable relationship, both from NATO's perspective and from that of Denmark. However, large segments of both the populace and political elites would like to be dissociated from some aspects of Alliance policy. Neither at the time the Alliance came into being nor for any sustained period since has Denmark as a society been fully comfortable in NATO. (A sharp distinction needs to be made, of course, between the society in general and governments-of-the-day and the "defense establishment" in the country.) Policies of confidence building and a general disposition toward détente have a venerable basis on the country's history.

That disposition has been stimulated many times in the past thirty-five years by strong divergence between the values that underlie it, and American actions and NATO policies that appear to many Danes to be contrary to it. This has been the case with the war in Southeast Asia, American policy in Central America, the erosion of détente between the United States and the Soviet Union, and, more recently, the divisive issue of INF deployment. The point is that the results should not be read as cause of a breakdown in consensus on NATO-based security policy inside the country, or of a new dissensus between Denmark and others in the Alliance. Rather, such phenomena stimulate and bring to the surface long-standing underlying differences within Denmark and within NATO.

These differences, essentially "present at the creation," have also been considerably accentuated by both the continued evolution of Danish society and the specific divergences on policies and actions of the sort just noted. They strongly affect the country's positions on such issues as arms control, détente, "burden sharing" within the Alliance, and, in general, the quality of relationships within the NATO framework. Denmark's position in NATO is thus likely to continue to be ambivalent for some time. The consistent support for membership in the Alliance *per se*, which remains in the abstract, will be in recurring conflict with opposition to specific responsibilities evoked by particular policies.

In sum, the country's political economy, its problems of governance, its intrinsically limited resources, and its security-related political culture all point to a continuation or accentuation of the tendencies and problems that have already marked its membership in NATO, particularly in the last ten to fifteen years. All foreseeable Danish governments will be strained to accommodate demands from the Alliance and reluctance from within. They are likely to continue to defer or avoid security-related decisions that exacerbate such strains. They are likely also to strive to assuage public concern by trying to find the confidence-building angles in security issues and simultaneously to pay Denmark's dues in the Alliance to the maximum extent that is politically feasible.

Precisely how this will all translate into actual policy cannot, of course, be predicted with assurance. The critical factor will involve the extent to which what one might call a "minimalist" position gains a more substantial foothold in Danish political life. For the moment, such a position is not being articulated in a comprehensive or programmatic manner by any organized group in Denmark—not in the way, for instance, that similar ideas are being put forward by the Norwegian Johan Galtung.[63] However, the positions adopted by the Left Socialist Party and many in the Socialist People's Party[64] clearly move in this direction as do those of peace movement organizations such as "Nej til Atomvåben." More important, those of a seemingly increasing number of Social Democratic parliamentarians, first on the left wing of the party and now closer to the center, seem to be moving in the same direction.

It is not possible to measure the numerical strength or political position of a "minimalist" policy alternative in Denmark at present. To the extent that such views are held by members of the public and of parliamentary and other policy elites, they are clearly piecemeal and internally inconsistent. Only the Socialist Peoples Party and the small Left Socialists are clearly opposed to NATO membership; and while they have been joined by the Radicals and important and growing elements of the Social Democrats in opposing NATO's INF modernization, there is clearly no majority in Denmark for jeopardizing, much less withdrawing from, membership in the Alliance.[65] But the dramatic *volte face* of the Social Democrats since they entered into opposition in September 1982 is what makes prediction so difficult. Without such support that the largest, pivotal party had been provided for defense efforts throughout most of the period of NATO membership, the levels of economic and political effort that will prove feasible may indeed be lower. Moreover, if the party opts to make the defense effort—or the opportunity costs associated with it in terms of social policy needs—a major feature of its opposition strategy, the realities of Danish politics would make it exceedingly difficult to prevent a further slide toward "minimalism."

The Social Democrats have been reinforced in their departures by the transnational social democratic forum "Scandilux," a consultative forum in which the parties from the Low Countries, the Federal Republic, Great Britain, Norway, and Denmark meet periodically. While the influence of the views from this quarter, particularly from the Norwegian Labor Party and the Federal Republic's SPD, on the Danish Social Democrats is not quantifiable, it is clearly present. Some of the substantive points in the latter's positions on the payment of INF infrastructure costs, the revival of the Nordic nuclear-free zone idea, the extension of the INF limitation talks in Geneva before the deployment of NATO's new missiles, and others articulated in Denmark in early February 1983 are echoes of points advanced by Egon Bahr of the German SPD and other participants at a Scandilux meeting a few weeks earlier.[66] Yet, if the Danish party's recent turnaround on security-policy issues in general and NATO policies in particular is based mainly on (i) domestic political maneuvering on the part of the leadership, with a view to returning to government; (ii) a *realpolitik*-based nod in the direction of the party's left wing and the two smaller leftist-socialist parties; and (iii) an attempt to capitalize on antinuclear weapons and antidefense expenditure sentiments in the party's electoral constituency, then the reinforcement of such positions by other countries' social democratic parties is less instrumental than it is merely convenient.

Assuming that this is the case, as was argued earlier, then what can one say about the actual substance of Denmark's contribution during the coming period to fulfill the basic requirements of Danish and Alliance strategy? Denmark's defense strategy, should NATO's deterrent fail and defense become necessary, has been to conduct a holding action until Allied reinforcements arrive. Such a strategy hinges on three basic conditions. First, national forces must be able to conduct effective defensive war long enough to make it possible for reinforcements to reach the country. Second, allies must have the political will and the military means to deploy such reinforcements in a timely manner and with adequate strength and appropriate form. This is in part contingent on the third condition: The country to be supported must facilitate the arrival, emplacement, and effective operation of reinforcements. The second requirement is essentially outside the control of a small country planning for such contingency. The two key issues that remain from the Danish perspective, then, are the preparation to receive reinforcement and the adequacy of the national defensive capability to maximize their effectiveness.

Preparing to Receive Reinforcements

Perhaps more progress has been made, during the early 1980s, in the political and technical preparations for receiving Allied reinforcements than in any other aspect of Danish defense. The long-standing Danish policy regarding the stationing of foreign troops or the establishment of foreign bases made such preparations a complicated issue for some time. Unlike Norway, which faced this issue earlier, Denmark was reluctant to confront it.[67] While an agreement on establishing "Colocated Operating Bases" (COBs) for receiving five American air squadrons and providing full repair and maintenance facilities for them at four Danish installations in Jutland was concluded without much public discussion in 1976, the matter of establishing stockpiles of ammunition, fuel, spare parts, and in general preparing the ground for receiving substantial numbers of British and American land forces in case of a security emergency became politicized in the late 1970s and early 1980s.[68] The argument, emanating mainly from the Socialist Peoples Party and the Left Socialists, was essentially that extensive prepositioning amounted to the establishment of foreign bases. The left wing of the Social Democrats joined in opposition in September 1981 at the party's annual congress.[69] This reluctance to facilitate the implementation of NATO's "Rapid Reinforcement Plan"—again, the basis for Danish military security—was manifested in the Social Democratic government's unwillingness to press the issue until the spring of 1982. At that time, a substantial majority in the *Folketing* approved a prepositioning plan, and the four-party coalition that entered into government later that year has proceeded with its implementation.

At present, strategic planning and Danish preparations envision receiving rapid reinforcement by a British light brigade (approximately 13,000 men), the American fighter squadrons noted above, two British squadrons, and, under certain circumstances, a portion of an American marine amphibious force.[70] For several reasons, perhaps most notable among them the image in Denmark of American marines as a bit too "rough and ready" for operations in that country, reliance on a larger proportion of British reinforcements has been politically more attractive.[71] Be that as it may, this crucial dimension of Danish security policy has been managed adequately, after several years of practiced avoidance of the issue, and nothing on the horizon indicates that this will come unraveled politically.

Maintaining Defense Adequacy

There can hardly be a precise calculus for determining beforehand what force levels and weapons would be required for fighting an effective holding action, given Denmark's position. Under these circumstances, however, the same amount of money has been buying less defense in Denmark over the past decade, and it is reasonable to assume that defense capacity is lower than officials would prefer. What are the chances, therefore, of at least maintaining, if not increasing, the current level of effort?

PAYING THE BILLS FOR DEFENSE. When the problems of governance that accompany a highly fragmented party system in the context of a thorough-going democracy confront the differing perspectives on security that exist within the Danish political system, it is readily apparent that no Danish government likely to be in office in the foreseeable future will be able (even if it were so inclined, as the "bourgeois" minority coalition is) to increase the budgetary effort for defense, except in conjunction with greatly increased, sustained economic growth. That, alas, is not on the horizon. The current level of effort may nevertheless be both economically and politically maintainable, as long as the buying power of Danish defense-Krone is not further eroded by higher costs for imported weapons and fuel. This problem clearly is not unique to Denmark—in fact, it is common to all countries studied in this book—but it will be a critical factor in determining whether, during the coming period, Denmark finds the will to afford a defense effort comparable to that of today, let alone that of yesterday.

At the same time, one must continue to bear in mind that, while the Danish defense effort may not be as substantial as the Alliance would like, the overall costs of defense to Denmark's economy are not accurately reflected by the sums contained in the defense chapter of its public budget. The net costs of defense for the Danish economy are substantially higher than budgetary expenditures might indicate. This is so because a larger portion of such expenditures is expended outside the economy than for virtually any other member of NATO.

Denmark, because it produces almost no military goods and almost none of its defense-related fuel, must import both of these goods—and it must import them under chronically unfavorable balance-of-payments conditions in the presence of an already high foreign debt (with attendant high debt-servicing costs) without the benefit of substantial "offsets" through military exports. Thus, while some members of the Alliance—most notably the United States and France—realize substantial returns to their economies through military exports and thereby stimulate private sector productivity, Denmark does not. Even such small members of NATO as Belgium (small arms exports) and Norway (fuel production) can offset some of their defense expenditures or contain them in their own economies to a greater extent than can Denmark.

By one set of preliminary estimates, more than 22 percent of Denmark's defense budget is lost to the national economy, while comparable figures for the United States, Norway, and Belgium are 5, 17, and 19 percent, respectively.[72] This suggests not only that the net economic efforts of some of the smaller states in the Alliance are substantially higher than those of some of the larger members but also that the economics and the politics of the defense budgets may be stretched considerably more in a country like Denmark than is generally perceived. While in most countries defense expenditures currently provoke lively debates about alternative uses for resources, the circumstances of Denmark—the need to import very substantial portions of its defense materials, chronic difficulties in terms of growth rates, domestic and foreign public debts, and unemployment—mean that more than marginal increases for security simply fall outside the realm of the politically feasible. From the vantage point of Danish workers and interest organizations in many sectors of the economy, the expenditure of public funds without visible job-creating or economy-stimulating consequences borders on the irresponsible. In the slow-growth, high-unemployment conditions that have prevailed since the mid-1970s, it has been increasingly difficult to sell politically the sending abroad of approximately 0.6 percent of the GNP—the amount accounted for by that share of the country's defense expenditures that are lost to the national economy.

This means that Denmark is condemned to finding ways to get more defense out of each defense-Krone and to maximize the return to its own economy of money spent on defense. In this connection it may be useful to look briefly at the problems Denmark faces in protecting the island of Bornholm and the Baltic approaches. The exposed position of Bornholm makes its effective defense problematic against a concerted attack, considering the island's proximity to East Germany and Poland. Mine defense is, and is likely to continue to be, an important component of the BALTAP (joint Danish-German) effort. Patrolling and reconnaissance operations in the Baltic can be maintained in the near future at present levels (generally deemed adequate) with existing resources. However, the naval and air forces required for such operations are also declining in numbers as a result of the cost squeeze, and operational or combat sufficiency may become questionable by the end of the 1980s.

Part of the problem can be attributed to the economic constraints already discussed, but two additional points need to be made. First, Denmark's formerly substantial ship-building industry has declined somewhat in recent years. Although the three newest corvettes to join the fleet in the late 1970s and early 1980s were built in the country (with much of the design work being done in Britain), and possibilities exist for constructing at least portions of multinationally developed naval vessels there as well, neither the optimal utilization of domestic industrial capabilities nor substantial exploitation of foreign markets has been pursued aggressively. At present, it is not clear whether the next generation of submarines, motor torpedo boats, and mine-layers will be partly or mostly built in Denmark. From the point of view of overall economic position, it will be necessary to consider the industrial policy aspects as well as the costs accruing strictly to the defense budget in order to retain as much of such work as possible for the economy. In brief, what may appear to be more cost-effective when only the defense outlays for ships are calculated may prove more costly to the Danish economy as a whole when lost jobs and industrial decline are also taken into account.

Second, the purchase of approximately eighty F-16 aircraft and the general endeavor to maintain a state-of-the-art air force has led not only to the decline in the total number of front-line combat aircraft but also has exacted an opportunity cost in terms of patrol and reconnaissance planes (of the AWACS and Nimrod type) that may be of greater value in the protection of the Baltic approaches. The balanced and state-of-the-art force-structure policies, so long a determining influence on Danish military thinking, may thus have to be reconsidered in the mid-1980s. For, clearly, the patrolling and defense responsibilities in the Baltic cannot be adequately fulfilled if the cost-induced erosion of appropriate naval and aircraft systems continues beyond the present levels. The choices between buying—and, from the perspective of such larger members of the Alliance as the United States, selling—more copies of sophisticated fighter aircraft, on the one hand, and maintaining appropriate systems of more specialized (if less exciting) patrol craft, on the other, must be confronted from different perspectives than the historic ones in the next round of procurement decisions. The maintenance, let alone the enhancement of Danish defensive capability, may no longer permit adherence to a balanced-force structure.

ALTERNATIVE MEANS TO ENHANCE DEFENSE? A land attack on Denmark could only come over the German-Danish border in Jutland and presumably could only follow from a generalized attack that penetrated Allied defenses on the Central Front in considerable depth. Here a "holding action" would be fought in Germany by that country's forces and by the Allied troops committed to the Central Front. The defense of Danish territory—and the provision of land forces for a forward defense in, for example, Schleswig-Holstein—could be mustered through rapidly mobilizable reserve and Home Guard manpower since presumably the massive concentration of land-defense capabilities on the central German front would provide at least several days for such mobilization. In short, Denmark's defense requirements could be met through reliance on reserve forces, the bulk of which could be mobilized within several days of an attack on the Alliance's forward positions. This aspect of the country's geostrategic position obviates the need for a substantial standing army. Moreover, it may permit taking advantage of that dimension of Danish military capability least eroded by the economic and political factors responsible for the steady decline in manpower and materiel: reserves and the Home Guard.

As can be seen in Table 2.8, reserves and Home Guard force levels have increased more rapidly during the last twenty years than active-duty strength has declined. In general, manpower for reserve and Home Guard service is adequate in numbers and is likely to remain so. While demographic projections point to a steady (though, in comparison with such other states in the Alliance as Germany, not drastic) decline in the 18-to-25-year-old population, such factors as seemingly chronic shortages of entry-level jobs for youth and a shift in recent years toward a greater willingness on the part of young people to serve in some military or paramilitary capacity,[73] suggest that if a reserve and militia-based (Home Guard) manpower-intensive ground-defense option is pursued it would have the necessary human wherewithal.

The reserve and Home Guard components of Danish defense are, then, relatively bright spots in both the country's relevant resources and public support for a national effort.[74] Gradual increases in both the quality and the size of these components would substantially enhance "holding action" capability in the face of land attack on Danish territory, or even (an unlikely but not unimaginable) seaborne invasion, since this would be detectable well before landings could be effected. The recruitment, training, equipping, and keeping current of such forces at levels that would extend the holding-action capabilities necessary in a strategic posture, which hinges on defense through Allied reinforcement, would be appropriate in economic, political, and social terms, as well as from a military standpoint.

Economically, the training and keeping current of reserve forces is far less costly than the maintenance of larger standing units. Further, materiel support can be provided domestically in greater degree than state-of-the-art systems with which active-duty troops are presently equipped, particularly if such forces are equipped (in greater proportion than standing forces are at present) with simpler, more reliable, and easier to operate and maintain antitank, infantry, and antiaircraft weapons most appropriate for their missions.[75]

Political support for an expansion of reserve and Home Guard capability is likely to be substantial in Denmark, because such an effort is clearly defensive and nonprovocative. Symbolically, an enhanced conventional land-force alternative focused on expanded reserves represents a national effort for territorial defense, rather than an effort that is perceived as making a minuscule incremental contribution to a broad collective undertaking, controlled by larger powers, the goals and leadership of which often fail to generate substantial support.

A final argument supporting the expansion of reserve and Home Guard forces is essentially social, but it may have potential political payoffs as well. The training of larger numbers of young citizens for military duties and integrating them into reserve units will minimize the prospect—of concern to at least some high-ranking officers in Denmark[76]—of the defense forces "becoming a state within the state." In Denmark, at least as much as in most other European members of NATO, this socializing function of military service is viewed as significant and it is frequently cited as a reason for the continuation of conscription.[77] The reserve and Home Guard traditions are deeply engrained in Danish culture, but the steady decline in the numbers of young adults serving on active duty during the last twenty years has made such service a select rather than a general experience—thereby distinguishing the minority in each cohort that is inducted from most of their peers. Providing substantial training and sustained periods of retraining or field-exercise experience for reserves and Home Guard would reverse this effect and would contribute to the integration of the military into the society.

Innovation or Stalemate?

Neither the movement away from a balanced-force structure nor one toward increased reliance on the reserves and the Home Guard figures highly on the current agenda in Denmark. In fact, two types of opposition may prevent either from ever being seriously considered, or at least they will delay consideration until more damage is done, both in terms of Denmark's declining force posture and its relations with its Allies. First, a concentration on reserves for conventional land defense may not meet prevailing notions of appropriate contributions to the collective efforts of the Alliance. Second, the preferences—and the politics—of the professional military establishment tend to support the continuation of a "balanced" force structure that embodies as much as possible the most up-to-date and technologically most sophisticated weapons available, even if economic constraints necessitate the miniaturization of the Danish military.

Yet, the facts and analyses presented in the preceding sections would indicate that few other alternatives exist for escaping from the vicious spiral into which Danish defense policy has been trapped. While there is public support for a national military effort in Denmark, the general impression that such an effort is not likely to make much difference in time of need is widespread (see Table 2.4). These feelings are reinforced by the historic and current inclinations toward a nonprovocative security posture. If an expansion and upgrading of reserve capabilities, including the Home Guard, can increase holding time against a conventional attack, it will enhance defensive effectiveness in a nationally controlled, nonprovocative manner. Further, given the increasing attention accorded to building up conventional capabilities in the Alliance, such an undertaking could be seen as consistent with NATO goals. Arguably, by concentrating on upgrading conventional reserve forces, Denmark would be taking a modest, first national step toward an evolution of the Alliance currently advocated by some respected strategic thinkers.[78]

Calls from NATO leaders for expanding the Alliance's conventional capabilities are, of course, generally made in terms of the desirability of approaching more closely the force levels disposed of by the Warsaw Pact. However, there are other, less-reactive values to be derived from such an endeavor.[79] It is commonplace to observe that increased conventional capabilities will raise the nuclear threshold in Europe. This argument is apposite for Denmark, notwithstanding the *de facto* denuclearization of the country in peacetime. Allied defense is clearly contingent on the use of nuclear weapons if conventional arms fail to hold off an attacker. An increased Danish capability to resist attack through enhanced reserves would raise the threshold for the use of nuclear means by allies coming to its defense and possibly obviate recourse to these weapons altogether in the country. Thus, a reorientation of Danish defense efforts would not be inconsistent with some significant Alliance goals, and, perhaps more important, it may address the prospective rather than the retrospective needs of European and NATO defense in a manner that is more harmonious with general public values than does the present course.

The second source of opposition—that of the Danish defense establishment to the renunciation of a balanced-force structure—is more understandable if unfortunate. There are several forces supporting the prevailing (and traditionally well-established) defense structure. Interservice politics, underpinned by political support in the *Folketing*, especially from the Conservative and Liberal parties, militates in favor of a "balanced" force structure; and competition for resources among the army, navy, and air force is similar to the patterns found in many other countries. Further, especially in the higher ranks, the professional military exhibits a tendency common to smaller members of the Alliance: the dual aspiration of "keeping current" in terms of state-of-the-art weaponry and conforming as closely as possible to NATO forces' structure and distribution desiderata. The reason for this disposition probably stems from the desire of the higher ranks in the officer corps to be as thoroughly "respectable" as possible; but the desire to obtain and benefit from the most up-to-date technical developments emanating from the major powers in the Alliance is also present and important. Arguably, as long as Denmark is a member of the Alliance, its military establishment ought to strive to be taken seriously by its counterparts in other member states, but if the balanced, up-to-date force structure of the country is being reduced in quantity because of high inflation rates in weapon and fuel procurement and conscript pay, loss of Allied esteem is likely to occur in any case.

In the absence of a capacity to overcome this type of opposition, neither the political nor the economic means will exist for Denmark to break out of its current impasse. Even if the opposition is overcome, the outlook is only for marginal improvements in a far less than optimal situation during the rest of this decade. Denmark's security problems and its relationships in NATO are of the sort to which it is necessary to become inured, rather than the kind that have "solutions." The country has, as the experience of the last thirty-five years indicates, become inured. The important question is whether the Alliance—and the United States in particular—is prepared and willing to also become inured to the Danish way of alignment.

Notes

1. Approximately 200,000 of the 800,000 people who thus fell under German jurisdiction were Danish-speaking; the rest were German-speaking.

2. Although their *problématiques* are different from Denmark's, the patterns of defensive security policy followed by Switzerland and Sweden are worth comparing with both the historical and current postures assumed by Denmark. See especially Dietrich Fischer, "Invulnerability Without Threat: The Swiss Concept of General Defense," *Journal of Peace Research,* 19, no. 3 (1982): 205–25.

3. This is not to say that Denmark's location removed it from the military calculations of larger European states. In fact, great power-jockeying for advantage in the balance of power extended to such concerns as the utility of the Baltic Sea. Thus, for example, in the years immediately preceding and following the turn of the century, Germany sought to avoid Russian and British ascendancy in the Baltic, since that would have put it in jeopardy of a two-front war. Other instances in the latter part of the 19th century and in the years preceding World War I abound. However, these were generally not major concerns for the larger states, and, in any case, they neither threatened Danish security nor drew Denmark into significant power politics. Remoteness is clearly relative.

4. Of course, when attempting such an exercise, one must compensate not only for the proliferation of parties and shifts in their relative strengths, as well as Denmark's very different position in a changed world, but also for the transformation of Danish society and political system. These issue areas were, until the late 1960s, in the elite domain. The greater openness of foreign and defense policy making has induced important changes.

5. The Liberals disagreed with the Conservatives both with regard to how to defend the country and on the level of military expenditures.

6. For a brief summary, in English, of the policies and events prior to the war, as well as an account of the electoral and coalition politics that led to the replacement of the Liberal Government (in 1929) by a Social Democrat–Radical Liberal coalition that was to last until April 1940, see Eric. S. Einhorn, *National Security and Domestic Politics in Post-War Denmark* (Odense: Odense University Press, 1975), 10–12. The great irony of this event and of the consequent effects on Denmark's military posture was, as Einhorn points out, that it was pressure from the Conservatives on the Liberal Government for higher defense expenditures that brought about its downfall and opened the door to the left-of-center coalition that was far less favorably disposed to spend on defense.

7. Cf. Nikolaj Petersen, "The Alliance Policies of the Smaller NATO Countries," in *NATO After Thirty Years*, ed. Lawrence S. Kaplan and Robert W. Clawson (Wilmington, Del.: Scholarly Resources, 1981), 83–106. The accounts of events and their analyses presented here and in Petersen's chapter are similar, yet his conclusion with regard to the meaning of Danish entry into NATO in terms of continuity and change is the opposite of mine (ibid., p. 94). The reason for this divergence seems to be that Petersen considers *formal* Alliance membership and roles more important that I do. It *is* an important discontinuity, in the sense that it represents a clear break with Denmark's history of nonalignment and brief experiment with neutrality. However, the continuities discernible in Danish behavior in the Alliance with the past patterns discussed above are also important. The position taken in this chapter and developed further below is that continuity in spirit and outcome is more important than form.

8. Nikolaj Petersen, "Danish and Norwegian Alliance Policies 1948–49: A Comparative Analysis," *Cooperation and Conflict*, 14, no. 4 (1979): 196. See also N. Petersen, "Britain, Scandinavia, and the North Atlantic Treaty 1948–49," *Review of International Studies*, no. 8 (1982): 251–68.

9. The Danish position indicated here reflected the preference of the Social Democratic Government. The Liberal and Conservative parties preferred the Norwegian approach, but they were prepared to accept the Swedish.

10. I am grateful to Professor Erling Bjøl for pointing out the importance of this relationship.

11. Cf. Petersen, "The Alliance Policies of the Smaller NATO Countries" and "Danish and Norwegian Alliance Policies 1948–49."

12. See Erling Bjøl, "Nordic Security," *Adelphi Papers*, no. 181 (London: International Institute for Strategic Studies, 1983), 2–4.

13. Ibid., 33ff., and on p. 36 a quote from a letter by then U.S. Secretary of Defense Harold Brown to the Danish Minister of Defense. See also Nikolaj Petersen, *Dansk Sikkerhedspolitik i 1980erne: Tendernser og Problemer* (Oslo: Den Norske Atlanterhavskomité, 1982), 11.

14. Ben T. Moore, *NATO and the Future of Europe* (New York: Harper and Brothers, for the Council on Foreign Relations, 1958), 53.

15. Erling Bjøl, "NATO and Denmark," *Cooperation and Conflict*, no. 2 (1968): 101.

16. Ibid.

17. Harald Westergård Andersen, *Dansk politik i går og i dag*, 3rd ed. (Copenhagen: Fremad, 1982), 180.

18. Ibid., 180–82; and Bjøl, "NATO and Denmark," 101.

19. Petersen, "The Alliance Policies of the Smaller NATO Countries," 98.

20. Bjøl, "Nordic Security," 6. See also Anders C. Sjaastad, "Geopolitical Realities and Alliance Military Contingencies: The Northern Flank," in *NATO: The Next Thirty Years*, ed. Kenneth A. Myers (Boulder, Colo.: Westview Press, 1980), 166.

21. Bjøl, "Nordic Security," 6.

22. Ibid.

23. See, for instance, Einhorn, *National Security and Domestic Politics*, 30–34.

24. See, for instance, Petersen, "The Alliance Policies," 102.

25. Interview with General O. K. Lind, COMBALTAP, Karup, Denmark, August 1982.

26. Petersen, "The Alliance Policies," 98.

27. An overview and a summary of the most influential, official "Expert Subcommittee of the Government Committee on Security Policy" report (generally referred to as the "Seidenfaden Committee Report") is given in Bjøl, "NATO and Denmark." (Erling Bjøl was one of the members of the Seidenfaden Committee).

28. Ronald Inglehart, *The Silent Revolution: Changing Values and Political Styles Among Western Publics* (Princeton: Princeton University Press, 1977).

29. Petersen, "The Alliance Policies," 98.

30. Ibid., 98–99.

31. On the shortcomings of "measuring the measurable" and the increasing tendency toward it in economics, see Robert L. Heilbroner, "On the Limited Relevance of Economics," *The Public Interest,* 21 (Fall 1970): 80–93. For a parallel argument related to the pitfalls of such measurement in policy studies, see two related works by B. Guy Peters and Martin O. Heisler, *Government: What Is Growing and How Do We Know?* Studies in Public Policy, no. 89 (Glasgow: University of Strathclyde Centre for the Study of Public Policy, 1981) and "Thinking About Public Sector Growth: Conceptual, Operational, Theoretical and Policy Perspectives," in *Why Governments Grow: Measuring Public Sector Size,* ed. Charles L. Taylor (Beverly Hills and London: Sage Publications, 1983), chap. 10.

32. See V. Güntelberg and O. H. Eggers, *Våbenteknologi, Økonomi og beskæftigelse* (Copenhagen: Danish Defense Ministry, 1980), 23–24.

33. See Nikolaj Petersen, *Forsvaret i den politiske beslutningsproces* (Copenhagen: Danish Defense Ministry, 1979), 7, for the period 1960–77, and International Institute for Strategic Studies, *The Military Balance, 1982–83* (London: IISS, 1982) for later years.

34. Inglehart, *The Silent Revolution.*

35. See Gregory Flynn et al., *The Internal Fabric of Western Security* (Totowa, N.J.: Allanheld, Osmun, 1981), 43–46.

36. Cf. Hans-Henrik Holm, *Hvad Danmark gør . . .* (What Denmark does . . .) (Aarhus: Forlaget Politica, 1982), chap. 6.

37. Studies conducted by Ib Faurby and Ole P. Kristensen, Aarhus University. I am grateful to them for sharing some of their findings with me.

38. See, for instance, Michel J. Crozier et al., *The Crisis of Democracy* (New York: New York University Press, 1975).

39. Cf. Ib Faurby, "Party System and Foreign Policy in Denmark," *Cooperation and Conflict,* 14 (1979): 163ff.

40. Depending on the mode of calculation, between 40 and 50 percent of all adults in Denmark receive their primary income from government, through employment or transfer payments. See Don S. Schwerin and Martin O. Heisler, *Government as Paymaster: Public Employment and Dependence on Transfer Payments for Primary Income in the Nordic Countries* (Aarhus: Institute of Political Science, 1982), 27–28, 42.

41. See Table 2.6 and cf. Ole P. Kristensen, "Voter Attitudes and Public Spending: Is There a Relationship?" *European Journal of Political Research,* 10 (1982): 35–52.

42. See, for instance, OECD Economic Surveys 1981–82, *Denmark* (Paris: OECD, 1982).

43. See Kristensen, "Voter Attitudes and Public Spending."

44. H. Haue, J. Olsen, and J. Aarup-Kristensen, *Det ny Danmark, 1890–1980,* 2nd ed. (Copenhagen: Munksgaard, 1981), 311–13, provides the longest internally consistent time-series on Danish unemployment figures. For more recent figures, see Danmarks Statistik, *Statistisk tiårsoversigt, 1982* (Copenhagen: Danmarks Statistik, 1982), 40.

45. Ibid., 104ff.

46. Bjøl, "Nordic Security," 33. While the Danish Government's position is that it will not make up for lost subsidies, political pressure (particularly from the parties of the Left) may reverse that stance.

47. Calculated from Ruth Leger Sivard, *World Military and Social Expenditures, 1982* (Leesburg, Va.: World Priorities, 1982), 27, representing 1979 data.

48. These data are from the International Institute for Strategic Studies, *The Military*

Balance, 1982–83 (London: IISS, 1982), and Danish Ministry of Defense, *Styrke-strukturoversigter for Hæren, Søværnet, Flyvevåbnet* (Copenhagen: Forsvarsminsterens skrivelse, 10 February 1982).

49. See, for instance, Bjarne F. Lindhardt, *Allierede forstærkninger til Danmark* Dansk Udenrigspolitisk Institut Forskningsrapport, no. 5 (Copenhagen: Samfundsvidenska-beligt Forlag, 1981), and *Forsvarslove 1982* (Copenhagen: Schults-Forlag, 1982).

50. Petersen, "Dansk sikkerhedspolitik i 1980erne," 15.

51. Ibid., 16.

52. Ibid., 15.

53. Gallup Institute survey, December 1979, reproduced in *Dansk Udenrigspolitisk Årbog,* 1979, 372–73.

54. *Dansk Udenrigspolitisk Årbog, 1982* (Copenhagen: Dansk Udenrigspolitisk Insti-tute og Jurist-og Økonomforbundets Forlag, 1983), 423.

55. See, for instance, Petersen, "Dansk sikkerhedspolitik i 1980erne," 17.

56. Cf. Bjøl, "Nordic Security."

57. Petersen, "Dansk sikkerhedspolitik i 1980erne," 17–18.

58. Nikolaj Petersen, "Konsensus eller Konflikt? Dansk sikkerhedspolitik 1979–83," *Dansk Udenrigspolitisk Årbog* (1983): 44–45.

59. Ibid., 45.

60. Ole P. Kristensen, "The Logic of Political-Bureaucratic Decision-Making as a Cause of Governmental Growth: Or Why Expansion of Public Programs is a Private Good and Their Restriction Is a Public Good", *European Journal of Political Research,* 8 (1980): 249–64, and "Voter Attitudes and Public Spending."

61. See, for example, several of the essays in *Forsvaret til debat* ed. Kjeld Olesen (Copenhagen: Fremads Fokusbøger, 1970). Olesen was Foreign Minister in the Social Democratic Government that held office until September 1982. The book was pub-lished while a multiyear defense agreement was being negotiated and discussed.

62. *Berlingske Tidende,* 27 May 1983.

63. See especially his "NATO and the States of Western Europe: The search for an alternative strategy," in *Debate on Disarmament,* ed. Michael Clarke and Marjorie Mowlam (London: Routledge & Kegan Paul, 1982), 45–61. See also Dietrich Fischer, *Preventing War in the Nuclear Age* (Totowa, N.J.: Rowman & Allanheld, 1984).

64. See, for instance, Gert Petersen, *Om nødvendigheden af dansk fredspolitik* (On the necessity of Danish Peace Policy) (Copenhagen: Vindrose, 1982). Petersen is a member of the *Folketing* and long-time leader of the Socialist People's Party. He is generally acknowledged, even by his political opponents, to be a well-informed and thoughtful, if highly partisan, voice on security policy.

65. A survey taken in December 1982 showed 58 percent in favor of Danish membership in the Alliance, with the balance of the sample evenly divided between opponents and those who did not know or had no opinion. Survey findings reproduced in *Dansk Udenrigspolitisk Årbog, 1982,* (Copenhagen: Dansk Udenrigspolitisk Institute, 1983), 422. Only the Socialist People's Party and the Left Socialists' supporters show majorities in opposition to membership in NATO.

66. On these most recent events in the Scandilux setting as they relate to the Social Democrats' positions, see Petersen, "Konsensus eller Konflikt," 56ff.

67. See Bjøl, "Nordic Security," 36.

68. Petersen, "Konsensus eller Konflikt?"

69. Ibid.

70. Ibid.

71. Bjøl, "Nordic Security," and interview with General Lind.

72. For detailed argumentation and analysis, see M. O. Heisler, "Domesticating Defense Expenditures: Theoretical Considerations in Comparative Perspective," Insti-tute of Political Science, Aarhus University (1982), presented at the 1982 Annual Meeting of the International Studies Association (Cincinnati, March 1982). A more comprehensive statement of this broader view of conceptualizing and operationalizing economic defense effort is contained in Heisler, "Thinking About the Costs of Defense: Economic vs. Budgetary Perspectives," forthcoming.

73. "Tusindvis af unge vælger forsvaret" (Thousands of Young Choose Defense) *Weekendavisen* (14–20 May 1982): 1, 11.

74. Consider in this regard the assessment of a member of a NATO committee that explored the situation in the field relatively recently:

> It's fascinating the attitude that certain countries and people have to the need for defense. I was very struck when I was in Denmark by this very simple fact. They have a Home Guard, and 60,000 men in that Home Guard keep their weapons and ammunition in their own homes. That's a fantastic symbol, I think, of the attitude they have to defense and also of the stability of their society. Now, it wouldn't be feasible in some countries. (U.S. Congress, House Subcommittee on Military Personnel and Compensation of the Committee on Armed Services, *Defense Manpower Policies and Problems Among Member Countries of NATO*, 97th Cong., 1st sess., 1981, 26.)

75. Cf. Frank Barnaby and Egbert Boeker, *Defense Without Offense: Nonnuclear Defense for Europe*, Peace Studies Papers, no. 8, School of Peace Studies, University of Bradford (London: Housmans, 1982), esp. chap. 4.

76. As indicated by COMBALTAP, General O. K. Lind, in an interview with the author, August 1982.

77. See, for instance, the source cited in note 73 above.

78. See, for instance, General Bernard W. Rogers, "The Atlantic Alliance: Prescriptions for a Difficult Decade," *Foreign Affairs*, 60, no. 4 (Spring 1982).

79. See Hedley Bull, "European Self-Reliance and the Reform of NATO," *Foreign Affairs*, 61, no. 4 (Spring 1983): esp. 881ff.

3

The Netherlands Depillarized: Security Policy in a New Domestic Context

JAN G. SICCAMA

Introduction

In 1981 Walter Laqueur coined the term "Hollanditis" to indicate the direction in which the security debate in the Netherlands was moving at that time.[1] He was referring to a certain kind of public-policy illness that had the potential to spread throughout the world like an epidemic. However, Lacqueur left the precise nature of the disease unclear.

Did he believe that the renewal of the ban-the-bomb movement in the Netherlands had already infected government policy, and if such were the case, what would be the content of that policy? Would it be purely *neutralist*? If so, then one must remember that neutralist policies do not coincide *per se* with antidefense or antimilitaristic attitudes in general, as the examples of Sweden, Switzerland, and Yugoslavia show. Or did Laqueur indeed want to suggest that *pacifism* in the classical sense of the word—that is, policies directed against *any* kind of military preparation—would spread over Europe? If not, did "Hollanditis" then refer only to *antinuclear* feelings and responsibilities?

In this respect, Laqueur's term was as ambiguous as the peace movement itself, which has, until now, refused to declare whether it is anti-American, antidefense, antiarms race, antinuclear, or simply antiwar. Perhaps Lacqueur intended "Hollanditis" to refer to a *nationalistic* movement rising out of security issues. If so, it is surprising that he singled out the Netherlands at the very time that the German peace movement had in some respects already outstripped its Dutch predecessor. It was clear that the German peace movement had nationalistic overtones, as exemplified by the proposals by its leading group, *Aktion Sühnezeichen Friedensdienste,* for a nuclear-free Germany. Or, if Lacqueur meant "Hollanditis" to refer to the recent increase in the antinuclear (but not necessarily anti-NATO) organizations, then why did he choose to ignore the United States, with groups such as Ground Zero and the Freeze Movement, which are certainly not inspired by their Dutch counterpart. Why not, then, "Germanitis" or "Americanitis?"

All of these questions do indeed point back to one central issue: Why did Lacqueur choose Holland as a focal point of the changing attitudes toward security and defense? What is the Netherlands' security stance, and does it deserve to be deemed special? This chapter is devoted to analyzing the security profile of the Netherlands and the factors that are most likely to influence that profile in the coming period. A large part of this analysis will be confined to factors that are specific to the Netherlands. However, as the above questions illustrate, the Dutch security outlook cannot be understood without reference to alterations in the international system and specifically within the Atlantic Alliance.

This chapter will first discuss how the security calculus of the Netherlands has developed over time, which reference points in history have been crucial, and how the country views its present international position. Second, the elements of consensus for the period during which the Netherlands was perceived as a "staunch ally" will be described.[2] Usually the period in which Dutch security policies were almost completely in accordance with American and West German foreign policies is dated from the establishment of NATO in 1949 to the growing criticism on the American intervention in the Vietnam War in 1968.

In the subsequent section, the nature of and the reasons for the crumbling of the consensus will be discussed. Was the period from 1949 to 1969 really an exception, and is the Netherlands, perhaps along with other nations, simply returning to "normalcy?" Or is the picture more complicated, in that a complete return to a neutralist and pacifist policy is precluded by new circumstances—for example, the change in the configuration of military power that took place after World War II—or by internal factors? Finally, the future of Dutch security policies and its possible consequences for the Atlantic Alliance will be dealt with. Will the Netherlands stay in NATO, and what will be its future contribution to NATO's programs?

Cross Pressures from History

Following the conclusion of the Eighty Years' War with Spain by the Peace of Munster, the Republic of the Seven Provinces emerged, although only for a short period of time, as one of the major powers in international politics. During the course of the 17th century, there were three Anglo-Dutch military confrontations over trade, prompted by the desire for commercial freedom and, in particular, the right of neutral trade (a

Dutch policy goal ever since). After 1658 the Republic also sought to counter the threatening growth of Sweden and, until the end of the Spanish Succession War (1713), remained involved in European power politics in order to balance French expansionism.

Throughout the 18th century the position of the country declined in terms of economic and military power. Three years after the conclusion of the Treaty of Utrecht in 1713, the Republic had to enter into a renewed alliance with Great Britain, mainly because the latter wanted to prevent Dutch neutral trade with its enemies. With the outbreak of the Seven Years' War in 1756, a period of Dutch abstentionism began, with Dutch neutrality being politically pro-French and anti-British. The fourth Anglo-Dutch war (1780–84) precipitated the further decline of the Netherlands in the international hierarchy, which led eventually to annexation in 1810 by the French under Napoleon.

After the liberation from the French in 1813 and the decisions of the Congress of Vienna, the three Low Countries (the Netherlands, Belgium, and Luxembourg) together played the role of a buffer state at the northern border of France. This period, however, was short-lived, ending with the Belgian rebellion against Dutch domination in 1830. Following the secessions of Belgium, the Netherlands dropped to an even lower status among the nation states, with its chief interests being the exploitation of the Dutch Indies and the establishment of domestic tranquillity. It is this long period of neutralist abstentionism (1839–1940) to which people refer when they use phrases such as "a return to normalcy" to describe an alternative foreign policy for the Netherlands today.

The term "neutral" is slightly misleading when referring to Dutch policy during this period. From 1839 to 1866 Dutch neutrality was anti-French, from 1866 to 1901 it was anti-Prussian, and from 1870 on it was anti-German. Policies from 1901 to 1905 can be characterized as nonaligned but pro-German, which can be attributed partly to Calvinist sympathies for the Boers in their struggle against the British. After 1906 a turn to more passive neutrality could be observed.

World War I marked the beginning of the fourth subphase of this long neutralist-abstentionist period. Neutrality withstood the test of war. While the Great War swept over almost all other European nations, the leaders of the Social Democratic parties of Norway, Sweden, Denmark, and the Netherlands endeavored to bring peace by supporting common neutral initiatives.[3] Undoubtedly, this positive learning experience determined the continuation of neutrality during the interbellum period (although it might also be responsible for the failure to avoid war in 1940).

After the conclusion of the Treaty of Versailles, neutrality became part of the Dutch ideology. The Netherlands was reluctant to join the League of Nations, since league members might have to apply sanctions against aggressor states. The term "zelfstandigheidspolitiek" (policy of autonomy) was used to differentiate the policies in the 1920s and 1930s from absolute neutrality. As one of the so-called Oslo states, the Netherlands in

1936 rejected the binding force of Articles 10 and 16 of the Covenant of the league by joining in the Copenhagen Declaration.

Even after France and Great Britain had declared war with Nazi Germany, an important foreign-policy spokesman in Parliament, Mr. Serrarens, observed: "We who, as neutrals, are not being carried away by the passions of war, have the duty in these days to guard the higher ethical values for mankind and in particular for Europe."[4] His colleague, Mr. Rutgers van Rozenburg, depicted the Netherlands as an island of sanity amidst "the folly of the peoples."[5] Prime Minister Dirk Jan de Geer maintained that his country was "a lighthouse" in this dark world.[6]

Those statements, exemplifying the claim to the moral superiority of self-reliance that is so typical of the present policies of a neutral country like Finland, were accompanied by a last-minute attempt to strengthen the defensive capabilities of the country. Even the Social Democrats, who had gradually given up their absolute antidefense viewpoint ("broken rifle"), contributed to this military buildup when they entered government for the first time in 1939. Nevertheless, on 10 May 1940 the German army launched its long-awaited attack, forcing the country to capitulate after five days. Similarly, the Dutch Indies, which had shared the neutrality of the homeland, fell to the Japanese on 8 March 1942.

As could be expected, the negative learning experience of 1940 contributed to the abandonment of neutrality after the war. In 1943 Eelco N. van Kleffens, the Foreign Minister of the exiled Dutch Government in London, already sketched the outlines of an Atlantic alliance by expressing the hope that the United States would join in the containment of Germany after the war:

> If, in fact, developments were to proceed in this direction, there would emerge in the West a strong formation in which America with Canada and the other British dominions would function as an arsenal, Great Britain as a base (particularly for the air force) and the Western parts of the European continent—I refer to Holland, Belgium and France—as bridgehead. In this manner we would be dependent, it is true, on the Western powers; but these powers would, conversely, have a need of us. It is difficult to think of a stronger position for our country. This formidable bloc in the West would find its balance in Russia, which will be covered, after Japan's defeat, by natural boundaries in the North, East and South: [Russia] must and will continue—as we must and will—to pay full attention to the security of its open frontier vis-à-vis Germany.[7]

Six years later, the basic idea of Dutch participation in a large Western bloc came true, although it was not Germany but the Soviet Union that would become the main object of containment. First, however, the Netherlands went through an intermediate phase, beginning in 1945, in which they looked toward collective security through the United Nations. The postwar government, very much engaged in rebuilding the country and reinstalling control over the Dutch Indies, adopted a wait-and-see policy, hoping that an agreement between the four occupying powers would keep Germany unarmed. In this phase the government rejected the idea of military alignment in a Western European defense bloc outside the United Nations, since bloc formation might provoke hostile reactions from the Soviet Union. In particular, the inclusion of Germany in such a bloc was initially regarded as impossible and undesirable.[8]

Only after the failure of the four-power conference in London in November/December 1947 and the Gottwald coup of 25 February 1948 in Prague did the long tradition of Dutch neutrality come to and end with the signing of the Brussels Pact by France, Britain, and the Benelux countries.[9] Although the treaty still mentioned Germany as a possible aggressor, it was clear that this regional defense pact was designed against the Soviet Union.

On 6 July 1948 negotiations started in Washington between the five parties to the Brussels Treaty and representatives of Canada and the United States for a possible association of the latter two with the original five. As a result, on 4 April 1949, the North Atlantic Treaty was signed. With the exception of the Communists, the entire Dutch Parliament approved the pact.

As one foreign observer of Dutch foreign policy recently noted, Dutch security since that time has not been defined independently but "is seen only in terms of Europe and NATO."[10] This represents the foundation of consensus upon which security policy has been constructed and maintained. In the formulation of policy, international organizations, international negotiations, and international initiatives dominate, and few references to the Netherlands appear. Consequently, "national 'interest' is not a concept of much relevance to Dutch foreign policy."[11] One analysis of the use of the concept of "national interest" in Dutch foreign policies concluded that such a concept was, except for some cases of economic affairs, utterly nonexistent: "[There are no] political criteria selected from a specific Dutch angle."[12]

To what extent has history shaped the present security policies of the country? First, it is clear that the failure of neutrality in 1940 enhanced the tendency toward alignment after World War II in the same way as the success of neutrality in 1914 had fostered the continuation of that policy during the interbellum period. Second, a tangible remnant of the country's history as a major and colonial power is illustrated by the relatively large size of the navy in comparison with other Western European countries, as well as in comparison to the other branches of the armed forces. Perhaps because it once occupied a more prominent position in the international hierarchy, there is a continuing concern with the question of whether the Netherlands should be categorized like all other small states. The self-image of the Netherlands is one of being small "yet rather influential, perhaps not in international confrontation, but certainly in international cooperation."[13] Consequently, the issue of how international influence can be maximized, either by "setting a good example" for the rest of the world or by participating actively in NATO, remains an important one in the Dutch security debate.

Third, and very relevant to the political heritage of the Netherlands, is the constant debate over the "continuity or discontinuity in the international orientation of the country."[14] For example, in the most elaborate survey of postwar Dutch foreign policy, J. J. C. Voorhoeve considers the policies during the postwar period as deriving from three diplomatic traditions dating from before World War II: (1) maritime commercialism, (2) neutralist abstentionism, and (3) internationalist idealism. Voorhoeve's approach assumes an overwhelming *continuity* in the foreign policy of the Netherlands. In his view the maritime commercial interests frequently prompted an aloofness from power politics, which in its turn fostered the emphasis on idealistic values—pacifism, legalism, and moralism—instead of realism. Postwar security policies have, according to Voorhoeve, simply pushed the tradition of neutralist abstentionism to the background. But "it is still alive, however weak, and supports the idealistic elements of Dutch policy in the regional and 'mondial' policy spheres."[15]

Actually, Voorhoeve maintains that the *Pax Americana* has only replaced the *Pax Brittanica* covering the neutralist stand between 1839 and 1940. In that period:

> Holland had no other task in the European power system than the maintenance of its own integrity. Even that responsibility was light, because Great Britain would throw in its weight against any preponderant continental Power threatening Dutch independence. Not the virtuousness of the Dutch, but the balance of power enabled Holland to abstain from power politics.[16]

Voorhoeve even compares the present position of Western Europe with the position of the Low Countries in the multipolar European system before World War II:

> Western Europe, since 1945 no longer the center of world politics, remains a crucial area. The United States fends off the potential power of the USSR over Western Europe much as Britain once kept France, and later Prussia, out of the Rhine delta. Western Europe of today resembles, in a way, the Northern and Southern Netherlands of yesterday. Well to do and free, the culturally and commercially active grouping lies prostrate militarily and has abandoned an independent world role (with the exception of France).[17]

Unfortunately, it is doubtful whether the existence of certain "constants" in Dutch foreign policy really sheds much light on questions of continuity or discontinuity. To start with the obvious, there have been considerable periods in the 17th, 18th, and 20th centuries during which active participation in power politics prevailed over neutralist-abstentionist tendencies. It also remains unclear how rather dramatic changes in actual policies, which obviously have taken place, can ever be explained by diplomatic traditions assumed to be present all the time.

Second, the explanation of foreign policy through "constants" assumes that Dutch behavior is not susceptible to changes in the international environment. This is clearly contradicted by the facts. In the 17th century, Holland as a major power more or less shaped its own international environment: After the Congress of Vienna, however, Dutch policies conformed primarily to British interests in order to prevent one of the other powers from establishing hegemony over the European continent. Finally, there are contradictions between the constant "traditions" themselves.[18] As one skeptic remark in this respect: "When it is not the merchant [that can explain Dutch foreign policy behavior], it is the clergyman."[19]

Third, using the "traditions" depicted by Voorhoeve to explain Dutch policy in terms of "constant factors" does not yield falsifiable statements, since no policies are excluded as contradictory to the theory. For all these reasons it is unlikely that the debate on constant or changing factors in Dutch foreign policy will yield any clues about the direction in which the nation is heading. It is rather the preoccupation with this debate within circles of foreign-policy analysts that is an important fact in itself. Under present conditions, it seems to reveal the fear that the Netherlands will shift from "realist" (pro-NATO) to "idealist" policies. By emphasizing continuity, it is possible to presuppose that at least some control will be retained, and that the shifts that do occur will not be as dramatic as they might look. In addition, since continuity in policies is considered "better" than discontinuity, the argument also serves to discredit opponents.

The contents of these pro-NATO policies in the Netherlands are analyzed below. The question of whether "idealism" really has taken over in Dutch security policy will then be addressed.

The Nature of Consensus, 1949–68

In 1945, 50 percent of those polled in the Netherlands expected a new world war within their lifetime (32 percent even within ten years). This percentage rose to 71 percent in 1948 (52 percent in ten years), but it decreased to 31 percent in 1953 (11 percent in ten years).[20] This fear of war was clearly a fear of the Soviet Union. A public-opinion poll in 1948 showed that 75 percent of the respondents thought that "certain countries" wanted to dominate the world. Three in four holding that opinion pointed to the Soviet Union; one in four pointed to the United States.[21] The publics' perception of a communist threat was also shared by the political parties (except the Communists) and the postwar governments. Once collective security arrangements in the framework of the U.N. had proved to be impossible, Dutch security policies were framed in defense pacts with other nations.

Basically, the Dutch security consensus from 1949 to 1968 was centered around four primary assumptions: (1) NATO interests should prevail over other policy goals; (2) U.S. leadership should be accepted and supported; (3) West Germany should be tied to NATO; and (4) within NATO, strategic deterrence should be emphasized.[22] In order to define better the basis of the consensus, each of these four priorities shall be examined individually.

The Basis of the Consensus

PRIORITY FOR NATO. The priority assigned to NATO confirms the old rule that security interests must prevail over other objectives. Two examples of policy objectives that might have been or were in conflict with the Atlantic Alliance include the retainment of Dutch colonies and the efforts toward European integration. To a lesser extent, mondialist policies such as fostering human rights and promoting the development of an international legal order also fall into this category. (The Dutch refusal to protest the Salazar regime in Portugal is an example of the latter.)

The priority assigned to Atlantic security was not an immediate factor in Dutch policy making after World War II. At that time the Netherlands was much more concerned with reestablishing control over the Dutch Indies than it was with the Cold War. Many people rallied around the slogan "Indonesia lost, catastrophe born," and even the Labor Party supported military intervention. However, in March 1949 Averell Harriman, the U.S. Assistant Under-Secretary of State, made clear to Dutch Foreign Minister Dirk Stikker that the United States was willing to supply its future allies with arms, but not until the allies had solved their colonial problems. Stikker was convinced that the Netherlands would not join NATO if he revealed Harriman's message to the Dutch Parliament at that time.[23] His colleagues in government were not as sympathetic as he toward Indonesian nationalism and American security interests.[24] However, Indonesian independence was inevitable in the end, and thus the Netherlands' entry into NATO was facilitated without the issue having to be confronted directly. Eventually, the signing of the North Atlantic Treaty was made possible by a promise from the American Secretary of State, Dean Acheson, that the Netherlands would not be excluded from military assistance.

Similar American pressures, in which Atlantic security interests prevailed, were exerted during the New Guinea crisis at the beginning of the 1960s. Dutch Foreign Minister Joseph Luns was working intensely for a gradual process of decolonization that would result in an independent West New Guinea. But when Indonesia attacked New Guinea, the Netherlands was not able to defend it without the assistance of their major ally, the United States. American unwillingness to provide this assistance forced Luns to accept a rapid Dutch withdrawal, although he was able to save face by negotiating the provision that Indonesia could get control over the western part of the island only after a period of interim rule and a plebiscite within the framework of the United Nations.[25] Although Luns was bitter about the lack of American support in this situation,[26] he continued his strong support for the United States. Narrower interests were sacrificed in favor of collective European security through NATO.

The Dutch attitude toward European integration evolved in much the same way. There is little doubt that a politically and militarily united Western Europe would change Atlantic security relationships dramatically. Thus, the successive Dutch governments (and the political parties in Parliament) have always strongly opposed the establishment of an independent European nuclear force as a substitute for American nuclear protection. Officially, however, Dutch governments have denied that there is even a latent conflict between Atlantic and European cooperation. In 1963 Foreign Minister Luns stated in Parliament that:

> In the vision of the Netherlands, those two aspects are not contradictory. Quite the opposite, they are complementary insofar as we have always believed that the Atlantic Alliance can be strengthened in an essential way by a new cooperation between the European countries and that the EEC itself will be implemented fully only if it encompasses a wider circle of countries and keeps its windows open to the other parts of the world.[27]

Implicitly, Luns was referring to the Dutch wish for the British entrance into the EEC, which at the time was blocked by France. It was precisely the anti-Gaullist European policies of the Netherlands that enabled the Dutch Government to prevent any contradiction of the military security arrangements in NATO. As one analyst has summarized Dutch objectives: "At all costs, the Netherlands wanted during the sixties to prevent France from succeeding to merge the European continental Powers into a newly established Political Union, which would mean the formation of a disruptive block within NATO."[28]

These policies clearly placed priority on NATO. As many observers have noted,[29] European politics were considered a corollary of Atlantic politics and, according to C. L. Patijn, Dutch policies were simply "NATO politics disguised as European federal purism."[30]

SUPPORT FOR U.S. LEADERSHIP. After the decolonization of Indonesia, the Netherlands welcomed the establishment of a *Pax Americana*. Economic reconstruction was greatly enhanced by Marshall aid. Between 1948 and 1952 the country received one billion dollars from the United States, which was considered a crucial contribution to the recovery of the war-stricken economy.[31] Furthermore, U.S. military aid accounted for half of the military equipment that the Dutch acquired during the 1950s.[32]

Thus, the Netherlands was not enthusiastic about the proposed Pleven Plan for a European Defense Community. Whereas Belgium, Luxembourg, Italy, and Germany accepted the French invitation to take part in the negotiations, the Dutch, like Great Britain, Norway, and Denmark, sent only observers. Foreign Minister Stikker feared that the plan would put a heavy financial burden on the country, and he doubted the plausibility of trying to forge six national armies together.[33] But after America had taken its position on the plan and the negotiations seemed to make real progress in October 1951, the Netherlands decided to support fully the EDC, with the hope of furthering European economic integration and facilitating the rearmament of Germany. However, the formation of a Western European military entity was not in itself valued as an aim. The importance of integrating the EDC into NATO was stressed by the Dutch, and direct entry of West Germany to NATO would have been considered an acceptable alternative. This position can be seen as an early indication that the military alliance with the United States prevailed over other forms of political and military cooperation in Europe, especially if the latter ones did not have the consent of the United States.

In the same vein, the Dutch opposed the development of independent British and French nuclear forces. Also, the government did not initially favor the Multilateral Force (MLF) idea, since Defense Minister S. H. Visser did not see how it could help to restrict the number of independent nuclear powers within NATO. The Dutch participated in the MLF discussions only to explore the narrow range of possibilities to which it would agree, and to prevent what it considered to be harmful developments, such as nuclear cooperation between the French and the Germans.

Likewise, the priority of the military alliance with the United States was evident in Dutch European politics. Examples include the Dutch wish to incorporate the United Kingdom (as a pro-Atlantic element) in the Community, the desire to check the big members, and the attempt to keep Europe out of antagonistic power politics. Together, these policies highlight the successful resistance of Minister Luns against a Gaullist Europe.

De Gaulle had rejected military integration in NATO and proposed a nonsupranational form of political cooperation between the EEC members. Luns feared that de Gaulle's political union would serve to orchestrate the member nations as instruments to accompany French diplomacy in the world. Such a union could serve as a bloc inside NATO, which, under French influence, could become increasingly independent of the United States and therefore disrupt Alliance cohesion. At the summit of 17 April 1962, Luns (and Paul-Henri Spaak, who had initially supported the Fouchet proposals) vetoed the French initiative.[34] In Parliament, Luns's resistance against de Gaulle was greatly lauded, although it caused a major crisis in the European Community. Thus, the support of U.S. leadership in the West was an indispensable element of consensus in the Netherlands' security policies during the 1950s and 60s:

> The Netherlands, like the other small European Powers, preferred the gentle hegemony of a remote Atlantic Super Power over what would be a less credible leadership, but a more immediate domination by Britain, Germany, France, or any combination of them in a militarily independent Europe.[35]

TYING WEST GERMANY TO NATO. After the war the Dutch Government had a long list of claims against Germany concerning war damages. Although there were various proposals to claim German territory, the government demanded only small frontier corrections. In January 1947, in a note to the four occupying powers, the Netherlands supported the American proposal to demilitarize Germany, but it rejected—in the hope of restoring Dutch exports—geographical dismemberment. At that time the inclusion of Germany in a Western defense pact was still regarded as impossible and undesirable.

With the Cold War in progress, however, the Netherlands' position shifted to favor the military integration of Western Germany into the Western bloc. By 1950 several speakers in Parliament had already pointed to the need for a German contribution to the defense of the West, and Foreign Minister Stikker agreed with the American proposal to study German rearmament in the North Atlantic Council. In 1951 the government began to see the EDC as a means of facilitating Germany's rearmament, but when the EDC failed in 1954, the agreements of London and Paris were reached, with only the Communists in opposition. As a result, Germany entered into NATO and joined the Brussels Treaty, which was thereby transformed into the Western European Union (WEU). Even the Dutch Social Democrats, who once had a pacifistic tradition, now tried to persuade the German Social Democratic Party (which at that time still followed a policy of neutrality, or at least one against rearmament) of the need of a West German military contribution against the Soviet military threat.

Since the policies of the Federal Republic of Germany remained "low key" and in accordance with American security interests for quite some time, it is difficult to determine whether the Netherlands gave priority to the policy of supporting the American leadership or to a policy that would tie the Netherlands to a German Federal Republic fully integrated in the West. In any case, the far-reaching harmonization between Dutch and German foreign policy remains a remarkable fact. Already by 1960 a treaty was signed in order to normalize relations between the two neighboring countries by providing accommodations on financial problems and border questions. What factors explain this quick shift to support for a full acceptance of Germany?

First, there was the clear perception that a German contribution against the Communist threat was indispensable. Second, there was the opinion that the economic reconstruction of the Netherlands could be accomplished only with a recovery of the German economy. Third, the Dutch public and major political parties were confident that the Federal Republic would develop into a stable democracy. Fourth, and most important, Dutch policies tried to avoid having West Germany opt for any of the four other alternatives, all of which were considered undesirable. They wanted to prevent a separate deal between West Germany and the USSR to attain German reunification; a militarily independent Western Germany (possibly with its own nuclear weapons); a European Community dominated by a directorate (specifically military cooperation between France and Germany); and finally, an Atlantic alliance dominated by a Washington-Bonn axis.

CONCENTRATION ON STRATEGIC DETERRENCE. Although NATO had agreed at its Lisbon meeting of 1952 to build a conventional force of ninety-two divisions, it soon became clear to the Dutch that this goal would not be attained. When, in 1957, the North Atlantic Council decided to introduce nuclear weapons into the armed forces of the Western European nations, the Netherlands was the first ally to accept them. In Parliament only the pacifist Socialist Party and the Communist Party questioned the transfer to the Netherlands of weapon systems capable of delivering nuclear warheads. All the other parties favored the position of the minister of defense, that "the shield should not be broken in a short time. . . . Thus, the shield forces should be equipped with tactical nuclear weapons. They are extremely effective against enemy concentrations of armed forces . . ., supply routes, means, airports and other bases."[36]

There were three main reasons for the Dutch acceptance and even for the welcoming of nuclear weapons in the late 1950s. First, the Dutch saw these American nuclear weapons primarily as an alternative to the creation of fully independent nuclear forces, such as the French *force de frappe*, to which the Dutch were strongly opposed. Also, the Dutch preference for the continuation of the American veto on the use of the nuclear weapons was provided for in the security arrangements. Second, the tactical nuclear forces were regarded as a compensation for conventional weakness vis-à-vis the Warsaw Pact nations. Third, nuclear weapons diminished the necessary increases in defense spending. This was especially favored by the Labor Party, which had, during the formation of the fifth Drees Cabinet, succeeded in establishing its demand that defense outlays would no longer have absolute priority, but that in the future "military demands [would] have to be compared with other government programs."[37]

Following President Johnson's decision to bury silently the Multilateral Force proposal, the United States suggested that the Netherlands become a member of a select committee to study various possibilities for Allied participation in nuclear planning and the use of nuclear weapons. However, the Netherlands opposed the formation of such a select committee, since it went against the principle of equal rights within the Alliance. The Netherlands had always rejected the principle of restricted Alliance meetings such as those between the United States, Britain, and Germany or General de Gaulle's 1958 proposal to form a *triumvirate*. The Dutch preferred the formal equality of all NATO members except the United States (because of its nuclear hegemony), since the creation of a class of middle powers would put the Netherlands in a tertiary position. Furthermore, a representation of only one small power (in this case, the Netherlands) on a committee consisting of the United States, Great Britain, West Germany, and Italy would have ultimately prevented the possibility of enlarging Dutch influence by means of the combined efforts of the small allies.[38] Eventually, in 1966, the Dutch had to accept a compromise whereby the newly created Nuclear Planning Group (NPG) would include three seats, to be alternated every eighteen months between six small Allies.

Like the Dutch reliance on NATO and American leadership in the Alliance, Dutch security policy, until 1977, relied heavily on American strategic nuclear weapons to deter the use of violence by the Warsaw Pact nations against Western Europe, rather than building a capacity to fight an actual war. Any doubts on the credibility of American nuclear protection of Europe were denied, since such speculations were thought only to promote American disengagement, thus functioning as self-fulfilling prophecies.

The unlimited faith in the American strategic arsenal is well illustrated by two limitations in the defense efforts of the Netherlands. First, it deliberately maintained inadequate conventional defense forces. It was only after the building of the Berlin Wall in 1961 that the Netherlands met NATO's request to station permanently a Dutch brigade in northern Germany. A request to deploy a second brigade was not honored (and has not been honored to date). Likewise, civil and national territorial defense, which is considered of great importance to NATO's lines of communication, were kept deliberately weak. In 1977 the Advisory Council on Defense Affairs (ADA) concluded that there was hardly any system for defense of airports, harbors, and supply routes.[39]

The second illustration is provided by the Dutch stance on the role of nuclear weapons. Although tactical nuclear weapons were accepted as a necessary nexus between the conventional and the strategic nuclear levels, the Dutch Government and Parliament opposed predelegation of the authority to use these nuclear weapons to Dutch military commanders. They also opposed a "miniaturization," which would result in nuclear systems (the so-called mininukes) having almost the same status as conventional weapons. As a result, nuclear systems such as the "Davy Crockett," suitable only for use at the micro level of armed conflict, were not introduced in the Dutch army.

The Netherlands' concentration on strategic deterrence rather than on direct defense seemed to have been based on three considerations. First, it was believed that NATO's conventional and tactical nuclear forces alone were inadequate to deter an attack. Therefore, emphasis on deterrence by nuclear punishment was considered a necessary complement to direct defense.

Second, for a vulnerable and densely populated country like the Netherlands, the consequences of large-scale conventional and tactical nuclear hostilities were as unacceptable as those of a general nuclear war. Consequently, the Dutch believed that not too many options below the strategic level should be kept open. The Netherlands therefore felt much more comfortable in the days of American nuclear superiority and the corresponding threat of "massive retaliation" than in the period of "flexible response."[40]

Third, reliance on the American strategic arsenal was not only effective against the Soviet Union, since the costs of using violence were extremely high to the USSR, but was also a low-cost solution to the Dutch. Other military postures would have required considerably higher levels of defense spending (which were considered incompatible with the welfare state) and/or the introduction of a new generation of tactical nuclear weapons better fit for the actual fighting of a war in the so-called European theater. Until 1977 both options were rejected.

This is the complex of themes and priorities that guided Dutch security policies during the period of consensus, but was it translated into policies? It may be instructive to examine the answer to this question by reference to three policy areas: (a) support for policies in NATO; (b) defense efforts; and (c) attitudes toward emerging détente and arms control.

Consequences for Policy

SUPPORT FOR POLICIES IN NATO. During the period immediately following World War II, the government of the Netherlands could count on the solid support of the political parties (except the small Communist Party and some antimilitarist Socialists), as well as the silent support of the public. Public support for alignment in Western defense pacts was strong from the start. In April 1948, just after the Brussels Treaty had been signed, 71 percent of the Dutch surveyed were in favor of the pact. Shortly after the conclusion of the Atlantic Pact, 52 percent of the people polled in the Netherlands were in favor of NATO, while only 9 percent opposed it.[41] By 1967 support for NATO membership had risen to 85 percent, while the number of those opposing it had dropped to only 7 percent.[42]

Possibly, faith in NATO had increased because the Alliance was considered to function effectively. The strong fear of a new major war culminated in 1948, when 52 percent of the population expected that a new European war would break out within ten years, but by 1967 the percentage had dwindled to 10.[43] Quite naturally, these elements reflected a combination of fear of the Soviet Union and support for the United States. In 1948, 75 percent of the respondents thought that "certain countries" wanted to dominate the world. Among them, 75 percent thought that the USSR was striving for this goal. Similarly, in 1968, 79 percent of the Dutch population held the opinion that "certain countries" wanted to dominate the world, with 72 percent of them saying that the Soviet Union strived for world domination.[44]

At the same time, the United States was rated in very favorable terms. In a 1948 poll, 76 percent of the interviewees had a "friendly" attitude toward the United States, and in 1971 this percentage had risen to 83— 17 percent "very friendly" and 66 percent "rather friendly."[45] The Dutch rated the Americans as more progressive and practical than themselves, and the United States was considered, in polls taken in 1965, 1968, and 1969, to be the second-best friend of the Netherlands; Belgium was mentioned first.[46] The relatively strong support for the United States was also apparent in a cross-national poll in 1957. When questioned about a hypothetical war between the United States and the Soviet Union, only 22 percent of the Dutch responded that their country should try to stay out of it, whereas the corresponding percentages elsewhere were 54 percent in Britain, 63 percent in Germany, 66 percent in France, 74 percent in Belgium, and 94 percent in Sweden.[47]

The Dutch policy-making elite could thus rightly claim public support for its stance that NATO—and the military alliance with the United States, encapsulating Germany in the West—was the "cornerstone" of Dutch security policies. Dutch policy makers also believed that the Netherlands could maximize its influence by actively supporting NATO. Specifically, they were convinced that a small power could acquire essential security information in NATO that it might otherwise have missed, and that the Netherlands could effectively help steer the course of the Alliance by participating actively in NATO consultations. These consultations in NATO have in fact been described as the "Dutch method of compensation for being small and lacking any automatic claim to a special relationship with the United States."[48]

All things considered, there are indeed indications that the Dutch contribution to NATO was evaluated positively by the United States.[49] Nevertheless, there is reason for skepticism about the effective influence of the Netherlands, if only because it almost always chose the side of its major allies.

DEFENSE EFFORTS. In 1945 a Dutch army and navy under national command did not exist; only the navy had been able to retain an independent structure during World War II. In 1947 and 1948 numerous, lightly armed forces were established in an attempt to prevent the decolonization of Indonesia. Defense in the European part of the kingdom was kept at a minimum size, since "police" actions in Asia absorbed almost all military manpower during this period.[50] However, in 1950, after Indonesia had become independent, a crash program to build up the armed forces in Europe was initiated. This reflected the sense of urgency felt after the outbreak of the Korean War: Europe had to be able to counter a similar invasion, which was expected within three years.[51] In fact, the program was so ambitious that during the first four-year period it was impossible to spend the money allocated for defense.

During the subsequent four-year planning period, "defense ceilings" were reduced from 1,500 million guilders to 1,350 million guilders per year. Apparently, the sense of urgency of the military threat had waned, so the defense bureaucracy shifted to the maintenance rather than the building of the armed forces. During this period, actual outlays exceeded defense ceilings, since money that had not been spent in the first planning period could be transferred to the second four-year period. As a consequence, real defense outlays increased uninterruptedly between 1950 and 1957. Even so, half of the newly acquired equipment was provided by the United States (and Canada) within the framework of the Mutual Defense Assistance Program (MDAP).

Dutch defense expenditures peaked in 1957, then dropped for two consecutive years. This was partially a consequence of general budget cuts during the second postwar economic recession, although it also reflected the lower priority assigned to defense spending, made possible by the "New Look" strategy—the introduction of nuclear weapons and the contribution of Germany to Western defense.

In 1960 a program for "mechanization and motorization" marked the start of a third postwar upswing in defense expenditures. The Dutch army was transformed from a five-division force that relied heavily on mobilization capacities to a three-division force consisting of two combat-ready divisions and one mobilization-ready division. This process involved a reduction in manpower, especially in the number of conscripts, and the acquisition of new materiel in order to make the army more mobile. From 1964 onward, however, increases in the general defense budget no longer kept pace with increases in the wages and salaries of military personnel and price increases of new equipment.

In general, these defense efforts needed only to be justified to Parliament by a reference to "NATO obligations." Data on public support for the Dutch armed forces in this period, available only for the years 1963 through 1968, seem to reflect the public's general attitude during the entire period of consensus: At least four in five Dutch considered military defense "necessary" or "a necessary evil."[52]

EMERGING DÉTENTE AND ARMS CONTROL. The Dutch role as a staunch NATO ally made the government a follower rather than an initiator in the slow process of relaxing tensions with the East, beginning after the Cuban missile crisis of 1962. According to Foreign Minister Luns, it was not that the true objectives of the Soviet Union had changed, but rather that the Kremlin had been forced to admit that Communist expansionism could not be attained by military means. Nevertheless, political relaxation was, for Dutch governments of the 1960s, compatible only with sustained military efforts.

Furthermore, as a result of their support for U.S. leadership, the Dutch saw détente primarily as a task for the United States, and not the small European states, in dealing with the Soviet Union. Accordingly, Luns visited Moscow only in 1964, and the Netherlands did not join the "Group of Nine" smaller European states—Rumania, Hungary, Bulgaria, Yugoslavia, Finland, Sweden, Austria, Belgium, and Denmark—which was formed in 1965 in order to promote a relaxation of tensions in Europe in an informal way. Although the Foreign Minister had traveled to some Eastern European countries in 1967, he was willing to enter the "Group of Nine" (consequently becoming the "Group of Ten" in November 1967) only after the Second Chamber had pointed out that Belgian ministers Spaak and Harmel were playing an active role in that organization.

The Soviet intervention in Prague confirmed the government's skepticism about the limited chances for détente. As a result, Dutch politicians were rather doubtful about the Russian motives for the Conference on Security and Cooperation in Europe (CSCE). However, the Netherlands supported NATO's proposal of 1968 for negotiations on mutual force reductions, although concrete dealings should, in the Dutch view, be left for bloc-to-bloc negotiations.

Not long afterward, though, it would become obvious that détente and arms control would turn out to be the last tenets of Dutch foreign policy that had the guaranteed support of the main political parties. Both issues would evolve into areas where there were conflicts over nuclear policy and the appropriate level of defense efforts. Eventually, divergence would start to dominate.

Crumbling Consensus

It is of course rather arbitrary to pinpoint 1968 as the year in which a gradual erosion of consensus on Dutch security policies started. Nonetheless, three events indicate the beginning of the crumbling process.

First, the growing American military involvement in Vietnam aroused a wave of criticism in the Netherlands. For the first time, at least in the eyes of large sections of the public, the United States was not behaving as an exemplary superpower, especially since the global struggle between the Free World and totalitarian Communism was not particularly important for the Dutch. Perhaps it was not accidental that this upswing of criticism came at the very time that it became clear that the United States might lose the war, reflecting the ever-increasing limits of a superpower. In politics, success breeds support, while failures diminish it. With the American failure came a corresponding loss of Dutch support, although the government remained reluctant in fulfilling the demand of the Second Chamber to inform Washington of Dutch criticisms. Thus, this can be seen as one of the first moments of dissension between the authorities on the one hand, and public opinion, supported by major components of the party system, on the other.

Second, following the Warsaw Pact intervention in Czechoslovakia, a fierce debate over the level of defense expenditures developed. According to the government, the Soviet intervention in Prague had shown that détente was still uncertain. Thus, it proposed an increase in defense expenditures of Df1.225 million, distributed over the years 1969–71, to improve the armed forces. It was hoped that this move would signal to the East that NATO was willing to resist military threats. But this proposal met with opposition from large parts of the public: According to a poll in 1968, 61 percent of those who had heard about the proposal were against it, while only 35 percent approved of it.[53] Prime Minister Piet de Jong was even forced to take the unusual step of going before the Dutch public in a special television broadcast to advocate the Netherlands' contribution to Western vigilance. Although the government's proposal was eventually adopted in Parliament, a large number of negative votes (including some from the Labor Party) were cast against it.

A third example illustrating changes in the security debate is the success of the New Left within the Labor Party (PvdA). This group, in a list of "ten red points," questioned for the first time the Netherlands' membership in NATO by suggesting that it should be dependent upon the disappearance of dictatorial states (Portugal, Greece) from the Alliance. Furthermore, the New Left wanted to recognize the German Democratic Republic (GDR) as a second German state. However, the government took the position that unconditional recognition should await the normalization of relations between the Federal Republic and the GDR, including an agreement on the access routes to Berlin. It was claimed that unilateral Dutch moves would weaken the bargaining position of West Germany. Nevertheless, the New Left did succeed in changing the position of the Labor Party on this issue, thereby reflecting the growing impact of détente and the emerging dissension between major political parties in the Netherlands.

Although developments were more gradual in nature than would be suggested by pinpointing 1968 as the year of disruption, it is clear that it became increasingly difficult during the 1970s and 1980s to speak of *the* security policies of the Netherlands. It had become necessary to differentiate among several policy fields, as well as among the viewpoints of various governments, various political parties, and various segments of public opinion.

The main reason for the breakdown of the consensus was a social transformation that was taking place in the Netherlands at that time. Increasingly, Dutch security policy found itself working in a new domestic context that no longer allowed differing perspectives among the various political groups to be effectively managed. The difficulties were augmented by a changing international situation that forced the Dutch political system to confront issues that brought these differences to a head. In order to understand changing Dutch attitudes toward the Atlantic Alliance and its policies, it is necessary to examine the shifts that have taken place.

The Changing Context

PUBLIC OPINION. Although it is difficult to argue that public opinion was a major factor directly contributing to the breakdown of the consensus, it nevertheless was an indispensable element in the emergence of differing political views after 1968. Even though there remained a general agreement on overall goals in Dutch security policy, increasing dissension arose over the specific policies that were appropriate to achieve these goals. And the discord found a positive echo in the public at large.

In general, support for the Netherlands' membership in NATO has remained present among the public, the major parties, and the various coalition governments. A chronology of public support for Dutch membership in the Western defense pact is presented in Table 3.1. Despite certain fluctuations, such as a dip at the peak of warfare in Vietnam, a solid majority—two-thirds to four-fifths of the population—still favors Dutch membership in NATO. This finding is reinforced by a majority of

Table 3.1 Support for Netherlands' Membership of NATO

	% positive	% negative
1967	85	7
1969	65	13
1970 (1st poll)	66	14
1970 (2nd poll)	60	18
1971	71	12
1972 (1st poll)	66	16
1972 (2nd poll)	63	21
1974 (1st poll)	71	8
1974 (2nd poll)	76	9
1976	81	4
1977	78	11
1979 (1st poll)	76	12
1979 (2nd poll)	57	3
1980	76	14
1981 (1st poll)	73	17
1981 (2nd poll)	62	21
1981 (3rd poll)	56	18
1981 (4th poll)	72	2
1982	76	13
1983	82	15

Sources: Philip. P. Everts, "Wat denken 'de mensen in het land'?" (What Do 'the People in the Country' Think?), *Acta Politica,* 16, no. 3 (July 1981): 314; Ph. P. Everts, "The Mood of the Country: New Data on Public Opinion in the Netherlands on Nuclear Weapons and Other Problems of Peace and Security," *Acta Politica,* 17, no. 4 (October 1982): 509; NIPO, 1982; Atlantische Commissie, 1983.

similar size (65–70 percent), which agrees that Western Europe needs a military counterweight to the Soviet Union (Table 3.2). Moreoever, support for the Dutch armed forces in 1982 is as strong as it was in the 1960s (Table 3.3).

Seemingly inconsistent with support for NATO (Table 3.1) and the preference for a balance of power (Table 3.2) are the firm majorities against specific NATO weapons' programs. As early as 1975, 60 percent of the respondents in a poll were opposed to nuclear missions of the Dutch armed forces. This percentage decreased to 53 percent in 1979 and rose to 56 percent in 1980.[54] In 1983, 50 percent of the interviewees did not agree with the statement that "the Dutch armed forces should remain equipped with nuclear weapons."[55] In March 1981, 58 percent opposed deployment of the neutron bomb; in October 1981 it was 69 percent.[56] In 1981, 40 percent opposed deployment of cruise missiles in the Netherlands under any conditions. This percentage, over an average of seven polls, was 45 percent in 1982 and 41 percent in 1983.[57] Other

Table 3.2. **"Do you think that Western Europe needs a military counterweight to Russia and the other countries of Eastern Europe or is there no need for such a counterweight?"**

	7/74 %	11/74 %	79 %	80 %	12/80 %	5/81 %	10/81 %	1/82 %
Need	70	66	67	65	68	62	63	67
No need	14	24	21	22	21	29	18	22
Do not know/no answer	16	10	12	13	11	10	19	11

Source: Everts, *Acta Politica,* 3 (1981): 315.

Table 3.3 **"The armed forces are . . ."**

	1963 %	1964 %	1965 %	1966 %	1967 %	1968 %	1974 %	1982 %
Necessary	59	48	46	46	40	47	45	51
A necessary evil	34	35	35	34	40	35	41	29
Hardly necessary	3	5	4	6	7	6	8	8
Superfluous	3	7	8	6	9	6	6	9
Do not know	1	5	7	8	4	6	0	3

Source: Foundation Society and the Armed Forces, *Public Opinion and Armed Forces in the Netherlands* (January 1982).

surveys show that a majority opposed the stationing of cruise missiles in the Netherlands, while the percentage in favor of deployment varies between 26 percent and 44 percent.[58]

At the same time, surveys concerning the publics' expectation of a coming war are inconclusive. Table 3.4 presents data that indicate a secular decrease in the public's fear of war over the period from the late 1940s until the late 1970s. Data collected by Eurobarometer over a number of years, however, would suggest that the fear of war seems recently to be on the rise. In July 1971, 22 percent of the respondents thought that there was a likelihood of 50 percent or higher that a new world war might break out within ten years. In 1977 this percentage was 35 percent, in 1980, 29 percent, and in 1981, 40 percent.[59]

Similarly, concern about the Soviet threat reveals a certain ambiguity. In 1972, 64 percent of those questioned thought that other nations wanted to dominate the world: 48 percent of them pointed to the USSR, 35 percent to the United States, and 29 percent to China.[60] But in October 1981 only 10 percent were "very concerned" that the Soviet Union would attack Western Europe within the next five years, whereas 32 percent

Table 3.4   Expectation That a World War Will Break Out Within the Next Ten Years

1945	32%	1962/1 (October 15)	10%
1948	52%	1962/2 (October 20)	19%
1950	41%	1962/3 (November 15)	19%
1953	11%	1967	10%
1957	18%	1971	10%
1960	10%	1977	7%

Source: Netherlands Institute for Questions of Peace and Security, *Oorlogsverwachting en Overlevingskans* (Expectation that a war will break out and the likelihood to survive) (The Hague: Netherlands Institute for Questions of Peace and Security, 1978), 3ff.

were "fairly concerned," 25 percent were "not very concerned," 17 percent were "not at all concerned" and 7 percent did not know or gave no answer.[61]

These response patterns are not unique to the Netherlands, and they illustrate the particular difficulty one has in measuring accurately public attitudes. One of the problems is that the phrasing of the question may influence the answers. For instance, in a 1981 poll 54 percent of the respondents agreed with the Interchurch Peace Council (Interkerkelijk Vredesberaad-IKV) slogan "free the world of nuclear weapons and start with the Netherlands."[62] Similarly, in 1981, 56 percent agreed with the proposal that "the Netherlands should, irrespective of what other countries in Western Europe do, set a good example and not allow nuclear weapons on its territory, regardless of whether or not a guarantee existed that Eastern Europe would follow"[63] However, in another poll only 29 percent wished "to remove all nuclear weapons from the Netherlands," while 64 percent thought that this was "not yet possible" or opposed such a removal.[64] These and other contradictory results may have been caused by the assumption implicit in the IKV slogan that nuclear disarmament in the Netherlands will indeed result in global nuclear disarmament (first question), and by the phrase "to give the good example" (second question). The public in general desires mutal (nuclear) disarmament or would be willing to set a "good example."

A second problem in public-opinion data is that, from a theoretical viewpoint, it is impossible to confront people with the correct trade-offs. People tend to choose for the immediate "good" without considering the ramifications. Finally, respondents may not have spent much time thinking about a subject before being asked a question about it. While a majority of the Dutch population seemed to be in favor of removal of nuclear weapons from the country, 74 percent disagreed with the statement that such a move will decrease the chances of nuclear war.[65] Although opposition was strong against nuclear weapons' programs, in

1981 only 13 percent were in favor of a reinforcement of conventional defenses.[66] In 1983, 33 percent of the respondents agreed that diminishing nuclear armaments should be accompanied by strengthening conventional defense.[67] Another interesting finding was that only 18 percent of the respondents thought that the Second Chamber would reject deployment of cruise missiles in the Netherlands, while in the same poll 58 percent of the respondents opposed deployment.[68] In spite of the negative attitude toward cruise missiles, the percentage of interviewees expecting a positive decision concerning deployment increased from 46 percent in 1981 to 60 percent in 1982 (an average of three questionnaires), and up to 76 percent in 1983 (an average of seven polls.)[69] It remains an open question as to whether these findings reflect a supreme insight into the realities of politics or simply a low intensity of preferences, even with respect to the nuclear issue.

Comparisons of public-opinion data over time thus do not allow one to draw definite conclusions on shifts in public attitudes. At present, there seems to be as large a majority supporting pro-NATO/promilitary balance policies as a majority opposing specific weapons programs. What this provided, however, was a fertile environment for the rise of significant new interest groups in Dutch society. These groups soon began to play an important role in the making of security policy, mostly through their effect on the political process. Once consensus had begun to fray, actors in the Dutch political process found new ways to exploit these ambiguities and the developing *depillarization* of Dutch society.

DEPILLARIZATION AND THE POLITICAL PROCESS. The changes that have taken place in the political process can be understood only within the framework of the *depillarization* of Dutch society in general. Until the mid-1960s, the Netherlands was characterized by religious and ideological subsocieties: Protestant, Roman Catholic, Socialist, Liberal, and so on. These subsocieties, called "zuilen" (pillars), comprised not only the political parties and the churches but also the schools, trade unions, broadcasting associations, newspapers, hospitals, and voluntary associations; for example, sports, choirs, and so on. Citizens channeled their demands and support through their respective "pillars" and through their political parties. Surprisingly enough, this fragmented political process resulted in stable governments, since the leaders of the pillars compromised between conflicting demands from their clients. This has been characterized by some as the politics of accommodation in a "consocietional democracy."[70] Until the mid-1960s, this political system worked smoothly, since there was considerable consensus among the political elites on the desirability of the welfare state, and since security was defined as "security through NATO."

However, in the late 1960s, the "pillars" of Dutch society gradually crumbled. Church membership and attendance declined. Dutch Catholics, who had been among the most faithful to Rome, started to criticize almost every view expressed by the pope. This deconfessionalization subsequently led to critical losses for the religious center parties. As indicated in Appendix 1, the parties of the Catholic (KVP), Calvinist (ARP), and Reform (CHU) churches have, since 1972, held less than a third of the seats of the Second Chamber, whereas until 1967 they occupied a total of more than half. To halt further decline, they merged to become the Christian Democratic Appeal (CDA), and in 1977 they entered Parliament as one faction.

Another change has been that political demands and support have increasingly been channeled through pressure or action groups that focus on single issues. The Catholic and Socialist trade unions, for instance, decided to join hands, addressing their demands directly to the government, sometimes bypassing the political leaders of their pillar. Consequently, the settling of conflicts has become much more difficult for the political elites, who have to rely on neocorporatist compromises between the government and specific pressure groups.[71]

With a certain amount of instigation coming from within the Dutch educational institutions—in contrast to other countries, the student revolution has remained successful in the Netherlands—a "progressive" political culture has come to prevail. Because of the lack of conservative tradition in Dutch politics, politicians seldom identify themselves with the conservative label. Once the welfare state had been firmly established, foreign policy became a field in which politicians could give themselves a "progressive" profile—for example, by opposing American military interventions or condemning nuclear weapons on moral grounds. These tendencies to "progressiveness" in the political culture are partially identified with the youth, since until recently, youth had a tendency toward more or less "leftish" political viewpoints and party preferences. However, it has not been demonstrated that members of the new generation, who lack the direct experience of World War II, do not change their views as they grow older. Recently, the relatively conservative Liberal Party (VVD) has been the most popular party at the high-school level, and observers were shocked to find out that 10 percent of Dutch youth had "ultraright" views with respect to foreign laborers in the country.

In the specific area of security policy, analysts point to societal changes as the impetus behind the *democratization* of policy making and the advancement of *populist* elements in social values. Foreign policy had previously remained one of the last bastions in which the formal elite—government, parliamentarians of the major parties, officials in the bureaucracies—shared the same priorities and formulated policies without direct intervention by other actors. Gradually, informal elites have penetrated the decision-making process. The most important among them are the churches, various single-issue groups, and the political parties.

The churches have been particularly important in emphasizing the moral aspects and questions of foreign policy. Originally, development aid and human rights were among their main concerns. However, during the 1970s the churches (and their umbrella organization, the IKV) shifted their focus in order to criticize nuclear policies both with respect to specific programs and on normal grounds.[72] Some analysts maintain that the churches, finding their places of worship emptying, are looking for a new role and a fresh reason to exist, which they seek in political involvement—for example, the ban-the-bomb movement. However, even though there is a definite parallel between the drop in church attendance and the increase in political involvement of the clergy, a causal chain between deconfessionalization and increasing societal involvement of the churches has thus far not been demonstrated. (The extent of deconfessionalisation in the Netherlands since 1966 is represented in Table 3.5 below.) On the other hand, there can be no doubt that Dutch enthusiasm for NATO has declined because of its long association with Dr. Luns, who is considered by progressive Dutch circles to be ultraconservative, especially in view of his past indulgence toward authoritarian regimes, and because he is traditionally Catholic, pro-American, and proarmaments.

Single-issue group include "country groups" (in most cases opposed to right-wing regimes, such as in Chile and South Africa) and organizations concerned with specific policy areas (such as development aid and "peace"). Organizations such as "Stop the Neutron Bomb," and the IKV in particular, have been very effective in influencing actual security policies during the last few years.

This influence can, however, be explained only by examining the changes that have taken place within the political parties. In the period of consensus, political leaders and parliamentarians of the major parties agreed on the fundamental premises of security policy. Now, because of the depillarization of society, the party elite's traditional priorities have to compete for legitimacy with the public mood or with the mood of the party rank and file. Populism has thus become an alternative means of enhancing the career prospects of politicians.[73]

In the Labor Party, for example, the sharing of the peace movement's nuclear concern serves as a more potent method of legitimizing political authority than unconditional support for NATO and the United States. Potential candidates for parliament, for instance, may increase their

Table 3.5   Religion Adhered to by Respondents (in percentages)

	1947	1960	1971	1981
No religion	17.1	18.3	23.6	27.0
Roman Catholic	38.5	40.4	40.4	37.8
Dutch Reformed	31.1	28.3	23.5	22.0
Calvinist	9.7	9.3	9.4	8.9
Other	3.7	3.6	3.1	5.1

Source: Central Bureau of Statistics, *Statistisch Zahboeh* (Statistical Compendium) (1983): 75.

chances of being nominated over the established parliamentarians by being more critical toward nuclear weapons. This reflects a general rule that PvdA voters are more "conservative" than PvdA members; that PvdA delegates at congresses, who decide the rank order of candidates for the Second Chamber, want to express the more leftish views of the party's members; that PvdA council members are usually further to the right than the Party Congress; that elected PvdA parliamentarians are more to the right than PvdA council members; and that PvdA ministers are further to the right than PvdA parliamentarians. Nevertheless, there may have been changes in the recent past. In 1980 there were twice as many PvdA voters adhering consistently to nuclear pacifism than to pro-NATO views.[74]

The Christian Democratic Appeal, with its nuclear dissidents, also draws 20 percent of its vote from nuclear pacifists, but 41 percent are fully supportive of NATO policies.[75] Because of the party's fragile character as a result of its recent merger, opponents of nuclear programs have been influential, since the leaders of the party have wanted to avoid a split at all costs. Particularly for the Calvinists, formerly belonging to the AR party, nuclear scruples have become a symbol of identification, indicating, in addition, their preference for a coalition with the Social Democrats. Coalition governments with small majorities in Parliament—two seats for the CDA-VVD administration during the period 1977–81, six seats for the administration of the same colors governing since 1982—were of course vulnerable to pressure from these nuclear objectors and, through them, to pressure from the churches and the Interchurch Peace Council (IKV). This most probably remains true: Two opponents of the cruise missiles have left CDA, forming a new fraction in Parliament and consequently reducing the majority in the governing coalition to four seats.

The new leader of VVD in Parliament, Mr. Ed Nijpels, has indicated that his party—which is rapidly approaching the size of CDA and PvdA—should be regarded as more "leftish" than the Christian Democrats, and that their attitude toward nuclear weapons would be an important factor in making this clear to the public.[76] This could signify a move to enlarge further support for the VVD, which has developed from a small one-pillar party with twenty-two seats in 1972 to a truly popular party with thirty-six seats in 1982.

However, the transformation from consensus among all the major actors on security policies to agreement at a general level, although with much more divergence on specifics, cannot be attributed only to changes in Dutch society. For a substantial part the political system of the Netherlands has been influenced by shifts in the international environment. As usual, it is necessary to consider external factors that have contributed to the breakdown of consensus.

EXTERNAL FACTORS. Among the many changes in the external context of Dutch security policy, four have been of particular importance within the framework of this analysis. First has been the relative decline in the global position of the United States; second, the success, although only partial, of European integration; third, the relative decline of Dutch influence in Western Europe; and fourth, the increasing importance of other issues in comparison with military security.

There can be no doubt that the decline in the relative position of the Western superpower has produced a decline in support for the United States. Daily life shows that Japan and the EEC are now able to compete vigorously with North America, and that the yen, the deutsch mark, or the Dutch florin have sometimes been harder currencies than the U.S. dollar. At the same time, events in Southeast Asia, Teheran, and Afghanistan have illustrated that the leader of NATO is not always capable of policing the world effectively. Moreover, when it comes to military struggles between liberation movements and autocratic regimes supported by the United States—for example, in Central and South America—the sympathies of the active political community are no longer with their major ally.

In addition, the rise in Europe's relative power position within the Alliance has produced a willingness to challenge U.S. assessments of Western interests. In the 1950s and 1960s, one of the chief reasons for the partial success of the federation of Western Europe had been that the United States dominated Western European politics.[77] The United States did not tolerate violent struggles between traditional archrivals like France and Germany. Deterrence of the Soviet Union implied that European members of the Alliance submitted to American management of relationships with the East. This resulted, for example, in the renunciation by the Federal Republic of the use of force in its pursuit of German reunification. But with the relative decline in American economic and military power and the relaxation of tensions with the East, the Western European nations no longer accept American desires as dictates. A pacified and partially united Western Europe has acted in a less, and not—as the American federators of Europe had expected—in a more friendly manner toward the United States.

Numerous examples illustrate this paradoxical result. With respect to specific international crises—Iran, Afghanistan, the Middle East, Poland, the Soviet gas pipeline—European policies have tended to be coordinated more in the framework of European Political Cooperation than in NATO. Most frequently, this has resulted in European attitudes that are somewhat different from those of the United States. For certain European nations—for example, West Germany with its *Ostpolitik*—détente has been so fruitful that they have been less willing to return to a policy of confrontation with the Soviet Union than has the Western superpower with its global responsibilities. One of the most revealing episodes was the statement by Helmut Schmidt and Valéry Giscard d'Estaing that they could, with respect to Poland, not accept a second Afghanistan. This implied that for the moment they were willing to accept the Russian occupation of Afghanistan, despite heavy criticism by the United States and Great Britain. Although official statements maintain that détente is indivisible, many Europeans seem to be willing to persist in good relations with the USSR in Europe, even if the Soviets are violating global détente in, for instance, Asia. For the moment, it may be that Western Europe can show its new political identity only by distinguishing its policies from those of the United States, but the magnitude of differing assessments has grown, and there is a direct effect on the degree of willingness to place priority on strengthening American leadership.

The perception of diminished Dutch influence in NATO is a phenomenon particularly important to understand the Dutch. This change may stem from the reversal of very particular conditions that gave rise to an overestimation of the position of the Netherlands in the 1960s. At that time West Germany still kept a low profile in "high politics," France had withdrawn from the military organization of NATO, and the United Kingdom was not yet a member of the EEC. These factors together created an artifically elevated role for the Netherlands. However, when all those major powers shifted their power position during the 1970s, the Dutch fell back to a more "normal" position, which is somewhat lower than that to which they had become accustomed when Dr. Luns was the Minister of Foreign Affairs. The importance of the psychological effect of this on the Dutch approach to the Alliance should not be understimated.

Finally, during the period of détente, international issues other than military security in NATO have come to the forefront. For example, the Dutch consider human-rights policies as perhaps even more important than the Carter Administration did. By channeling 1.5 percent of its GNP into the developing countries, the Netherlands ranks as the top donor (as a percentage of GNP) of development aid. Even in this period of economic recession, all the main political parties give absolute priority to attaining this target: They argue that this aid is necessary not only from a viewpoint of international justice but also that development cooperation is a necessary component of security policies concerning North-South relations.

This priority in fact reflects the Netherlands' general tendency to incorporate its economic concerns into its security policies, chiefly as a result of the 1973–74 Arab oil embargo (because of its supposedly pro-Israeli policy during the fourth Arab–Israeli War). As a highly industrialized country depending heavily on trade, the Netherlands is vulnerable not only to modern conventional and (limited) tactical warfare but also to cutoffs of its energy supply. In October 1981 only 10 percent of the respondents said they were "very concerned" about a Soviet military attack on Western Europe; 32 percent were "fairly concerned," while 18 percent answered that a cutoff of oil from the Middle East by the Soviet Union is "a great danger" and 35 percent that "it is not a very great danger."[78] Economic threats seem particularly to concern the Netherlands, probably because they cannot be managed in the traditional NATO framework of European security.

These changes in the international environment have interacted directly with the internal changes in Dutch society to transform the context in which Dutch security policy must be formulated and consensus managed. To see how these changes have affected actual policies, it will be best to examine the evolution of attitudes in the same three policy areas that were discussed previously: (1) support for NATO policies; (2) defense efforts; and (3) détente.

Consequences for Policy

SUPPORT FOR NATO POLICIES. Tension has emerged in Dutch society between support for NATO membership *in general*—a majority of roughly two-thirds of those surveyed—and a tendency toward discussion once it becomes a matter of *specific* policies. With the "depillarization" of Dutch society, this tension has been played out both in the formal political process and in many other levels of everyday life.

Among political groupings, only the small Pacifist Socialist Party (PSP) unconditionally rejects NATO membership, while the other small parties of the left (the Communist CPN and the Radical parties PPR and EVP) are content with being extremely critical in their attitude toward NATO. However, NATO membership had become an important issue within the Labor Party by the beginning of the 1970s. In 1975 the Party Congress adopted a resolution to the effect that the Netherlands should leave NATO if the Alliance had not made "an essential contribution to détente within three years." They also proposed that the decision to stay in NATO should be debated regularly, and that membership should be discontinued immediately if French tactical nuclear weapons were given a role in Central Europe, or if a European nuclear force were developed in any other way. The position of the delegates at the Congress was, however, not shared by all the Labor parliamentarians and by even fewer Labor politicians holding offices. Since then, the issue of NATO membership as such has disappeared from the political agenda, perhaps because even the emerging antinuclear movement advocated continued membership in the Alliance.

The problem of divergent approaches to specific policies, however, has only become greater, especially with regard to the nuclear issue. In April 1970 Defense Minister Willem den Toom (VVD) was questioned extensively by Parliament on NATO's general nuclear strategy, interpellation Imkamp. The first real confrontation focused on the replacement of "Honest John" missiles by "Lance" missiles. The Labor Party Minister of Defense, Henk Vredeling, and his State Secretary for Equipment, Bram Stemerdink, advocated a reshuffling of military assignments within the Alliance, whereby the responsibility for the nuclear mission of the Honest John/Lance missiles would be shifted to the Federal Republic of Germany. Such a shift would have satisfied the rank and file of their party who were opposed to the nuclear capacity of the Lance missiles, but because West Germany was unwilling to support the Dutch army corps in the northern part of their country with Lance, it was finally decided to deploy a nuclear-capable Lance in the Dutch armed forces, despite the fact that the Labor Party Cabinet risked a severe confrontation with its party in taking this step.

A second confrontation was set off in 1977 by President Carter's announcement of plans to deploy Enhanced Radiation-Reduced Blast (ERW) weapons in Europe. Until that time, the Dutch representatives to NATO had fully supported NATO's Long-Term Defense Program, including both the proposal for strengthening conventional means and the damage-limiting programs for Theater Nuclear Forces. However, this time Dutch defense analysts concluded that the ERW weapon might run counter to the idea of strategic deterrence, which was a traditional element of Dutch security policy; their arguments were not decisive for the outcome of the debate on the "neutron bomb" (as the weapon is commonly called), but they may well have tipped the scales. While the government retained a noncommittal attitude in the early phase, a newly formed action group, "Stop de Neutronenbom" ("Stop the Neutron Bomb"), mobilized public opinion and collected 1,200,000 signatures against the bomb's deployment and production. They argued that the N-bomb was *more,* rather than less, destructive than the A-bomb and the H-bomb, even though it would "respect buildings but kill people." Despite the fact that "Stop de Neutronenbom" was inspired by the Dutch Communist Party, members of the Labor Party and the Christian Democrats participated in its activities as well. It was not long before the only party still advocating deployment of the ERW weapon was the liberal-conservative People's Party for Freedom and Democracy (VVD).

The condemnation of the neutron bomb on moral grounds by the Christian Democrat Minister of Defense, Roelof Kruisinga, who resigned because of his nuclear stance, drew the attention of Christian Democrats in other countries, as well as diverse political groups at home. One important result was that a majority in Parliament, consisting of the Labor Party (PvdA), the left-of-center party Democraten 1966 (Democrats '66), and the Christian Democrats (CDA) began to raise serious objections to short-range nuclear systems in general. Consequently, in 1979 the Second Chamber adopted a resolution not to make the 155 mm Howitzer dual-capable, although NATO had demanded the expansion of nuclear-capable artillery forces for quite some time. This Dutch opposition to the neutron bomb, as well as Egon Bahr's verdict "Perversion des Denkens," was very influential on other allies.

Since 1979, nuclear opposition has concentrated on the issue of the deployment of cruise missiles in the Netherlands. It is no secret that key members of the CDA-VVD Government personally supported NATO's double-track decision of 12 December 1979. However, resistance to the decision, and specifically to the stationing of forty-eight Ground Launched Cruise Missiles (GLCMs) in the Netherlands, was considered to be so widespread and intense that Foreign Minister Cris van der Klaauw added a footnote to the NATO communiqué, thereby deferring the deployment decision of the Netherlands until December 1981 and making such a decision conditional on the arms-control negotiations between the United States and the USSR.

At grass-roots level, nuclear opposition has been led by the Interchurch Peace Council (IKV), which has become much more effective in galvanizing public opinion than "Stop the Neutron Bomb." Until 1977 this organization limited itself to trying to educate people on peace questions during the annual "Peace Week." However, in 1977 they adopted the slogan "Free the world of nuclear weapons and start with the Netherlands" and succeeded in forming some 400 groups at the local level, encompassing some 20,000 active citizens.

The churches participating in the IKV approved of its activities without taking responsibility for its views. Thus, the members of these various churches served as the first group targeted to support the condemnation of nuclear deterrence by the IKV. The relationship between religion and support for IKV activities is depicted in Table 3.6.

The Dutch Reformed church, which had in 1962 already adopted a resolution condemning the *use* of nuclear weapons—but still accepting their possessions pending general and complete disarmament, *Gnadenfrist*—organized a new debate at parochial level. In 1981 this debate resulted in a resolution that included the rejection of the possession of nuclear weapons also. However, because of internal differences of opinion, the Dutch Episcopate produced a pastoral letter so vague that proponents of unilateral as well as multilateral disarmament were satisfied by it. The Catholic church has debated the issue at the local level, mostly because of a *Pax Christi* publication in support of IKV.

In the main Calvinist church, views have split between moderate support for IKV and a countermovement (Interkerkelijk Comité voor Tweezijdige Ontwapening-ICTO) favoring only mutual disarmament between East and West. In 1984 the synod of the Calvinist church followed the Reformed Synod in condemning the deployment of cruise missiles in the Netherlands.

Discussions in the churches have also spilled over to the political parties. A crucial target of IKV actions was the newly formed Christian

---

Table 3.6 Religion Adhered to and Support for IKV (in percentages)

	Roman Catholic	Dutch Reformed	Calvinist	No religion
Agree	31	29	20	38
Neither agree nor disagree	39	42	27	39
Disagree	30	29	53	24

Source: Netherlands Institute of International Relations "Clingendael"/NIPO, (September 1983).

Democrat Party (CDA) (which was the result of a merger between the Catholic People's Party (which had been participating in all postwar governments), the Protestant Christian Historical Union, and the Calvinist Anti-Revolutionary Party. With a majority of only two seats in Parliament, the center-right Van Agt Government was extremely vulnerable in 1979, since a group of ten so-called dissidents (all but one descending from the Calvinist branch) had rejected all responsibility for deployment of the 572 missiles in a previous vote. Their pivotal position explains why IKV pressures were so successful and how the first Van Agt Government almost fell in December 1979 because of the INF issue.

While the CDA remained divided over the issues, the peace movement was extremely successful in propagating its view within the Labor Party. By 1975 the Congress of the Labor Party had already decided that NATO should adopt a no-first-use policy, that there should be nuclear-free zones in Europe, and that the Dutch military forces should not perform any nuclear tasks in NATO. In 1979, while they were in the opposition, they rejected deployment of Long-Range Theater Nuclear Forces (LRTNF) *at the present time.* However, the Labor Party objections to the double-track decision gradually hardened, and by 1981 deployment of Intermediate-Range Nuclear Forces (INF, as it was then called) was unconditionally rejected. Nonetheless, their party leader, Joop Den Uyl, made his leadership in the election of that year conditional on his demand that the Netherlands should retain at least one or two nuclear missions. Apparently, the 1975 desire to remove all nuclear weapons from the Netherlands had been placed on the back burner in order not to preclude the incorporation of the Labor Party in any future coalitions. After the long process of cabinet formation, which has become ritual in the Netherlands, a coalition government of CDA, PvdA, and D'66 succeeded only because of an "agreement to disagree" on the cruise-missile issue. It was decided that the government would accept the double-track decision as a fact, but the PvdA ministers would be obliged to leave the cabinet as soon as factual preparations for deployment in the Netherlands began. The D'66 party was and still is, "under the present circumstances," unwilling to accept "Tomahawks" on Dutch soil.

Both the PvdA and D'66 left the government after the September 1982 elections, so the agreement was never officially put to the test. But the INF issue illustrates how changes in the political system of the Netherlands have made it almost impossible to comprise on nuclear matters. Although NATO in general is still supported, decisions on specific weapon programs are fully supported only by the relatively conservative People's Party for Freedom and Democracy (VVD).

DEFENSE EFFORTS. Even for a country as abundant in statistical sources as the Netherlands, it is very difficult to collect reliable data on defense efforts. First, depending upon the function for which the data will be used—for example, political authority to spend, cross-national comparison of burden sharing, or the effects of defense spending on the national economy—different organization, such as the Ministry of Defense, NATO, and the Central Bureau of Statistics in the Netherlands, use different definitions. Second, actual outlays may differ substantially from budget figures. For these reasons defense ceilings and budget figures from the 1950s and later in the 1970s are not reliable indicators for defense spending. Military-force goals framed only in financial terms—for example, NATO's recommendation to increase real defense expenditures by 3 percent—should thus be regarded cautiously.

Despite these caveats, it can be shown that the pattern of total defense efforts since 1968 does not differ substantially from previous developments. Between 1900 and 1965, 80 percent of the variation in Dutch defense expenditures can be explained by increases in national per capita income and population growth.[79] External crises—for example, mobilization during World War I and in 1939—caused upward shocks, and in accordance with the so-called ratchet effect, military spending dropped after periods of external violence, although not to the level that would be consistent with the long-term trend in national income.

As Table 3.7 shows, real defense expenditures by the Netherlands continued to grow almost uninterruptedly during the 1960s and the 1970s.

Table 3.7   Total Defense Expenditures of the Netherlands (in millions of guilders) Deflated by the Index for Consumer Prices (1975 = 100)

1950	2,694	1965	5,418
1951	3,008	1966	5,241
1952	3,861	1967	5,902
1953	3,793	1968	5,833
1954	4,285	1969	5,923
1955	4,578	1970	6,309
1956	4,684	1971	6,478
1957	4,405	1972	(6,559)
1958	3,879	1973	6,597
1959	3,642	1974	7,219
1960	4,020	1975	7,524
1961	4,580	1976	7,449
1962	5,078	1977	(7,873)
1963	5,298	1978	(8,087)
1964	5,442	1979	(8,510)
		1980	(8,262)
		1981	(8,219)

Sources: Central Bureau of Statistics, *Tachtig Jaar Statistiek in Tijdreeksen 1899–1979* (Eighty Years Statistics in Chronological Order) (The Hague: Staatsuitgeverij, 1979); figures in parentheses published by the Ministry of Finance, "Ten Years Review" in *Miljoenennota 1984.*

This growth in real defense expenditures does not, however, signify that there are no great problems in financing the military apparatus. First, although the military has certainly succeeded in obtaining a part of the increases in national income and tax revenues, its part has become proportionately smaller in relation to spending for private purposes and most other government outlays. This is represented in Tables 3.8 and 3.9.

Second, the main problems of financial management concern not only the total *level* of defense expenditures but also the *composition* of the budget. If one splits defense outlays into personnel costs (deflated by the indicator for wages and salaries) and equipment costs (deflated by an indicator for investments), real defense outlays dropped from Dfl. 4,199 million in 1956 to Dfl. 4,071 million in 1977.[80] This result does not

---

Table 3.8   Defense Expenditures (DE) as a Percentage of Federal Spending and Gross Domestic Product

Year	DE as % of Spending by the federal government	DE as % of GDP
1962	19.0	4.7
1963	18.7	4.5
1964	18.4	4.4
1965	16.1	4.0
1966	14.9	3.8
1967	15.5	4.0
1968	13.6	3.7
1969	13.6	3.6
1970	13.4	3.5
1971	12.7	3.4
1972	13.1	3.4
1973	12.0	3.2
1974	12.0	3.3
1975	11.3	3.5
1976	10.3	3.3
1977	11.0	3.3
1978	10.1	3.3
1979	10.4	3.4
1980	9.9	3.3
1981	9.9	3.4
1982	9.5	3.4
1983	9.5	3.5
1984	9.0	3.4

Note: Figures in the third column are similar to those used by NATO.

Source: Ministry of Defense, *Financiële kerngegevens* (Main Financial Figures on Defense), 1983, 27.

Table 3.9   Breakdown of Government Expenditures: Comparison Between 1974 and 1984 (millions of guilders)

	1974	1984	Index 1984. 1974 = 100
Social security	9.059	32.627	360
National debt	3.304	23.563	713
Development assistance	1.125	3.834	341
Housing	4.487	14.243	317
General government	2.221	4.744	214
Culture and recreation	1.140	2.941	258
Judicature and police	2.479	5.310	214
Health and environment	475	1.315	277
Education and universities	14.158	26.402	186
Defense	6.275	13.020	207
Public works	4.206	10.890	259
Agriculture and fisheries	1.409	2.060	146
Other	1.843	4.618	251
	52.181	145.567	279

Source: Ministry of Finance, *Miljoenennota's 1983 and 1984.*

contradict the findings in Table 3.7, since price increases for new armaments exceeded increases in consumer prices but were lower than increases in wages and salaries.

In an attempt to limit the defense burden, the number of personnel engaged in defense has been reduced by 20 percent since 1962, as shown in Table 3.10. As a percentage of the total labor supply, the armed forces have dropped from 3.11 percent in 1961 to 2.23 percent in 1980; as a percentage of the population, the total has dropped from 1.41 percent to 0.93 percent over the same period. The most important contribution to these percentage decreases in military personnel can be found in the number of conscripts. Until 1968 there was a shortage in the supply of conscript-aged youth. Since then, there has been a substantial decrease in the number of available positions per eligible conscript, reflecting both a desire to cut back on personnel costs and an increase in the supply of conscript-aged youth caused by the postwar "birth peak." Consequently, the number of eligible conscripts actually drafted decreased dramatically, from 69.9 percent in 1954 to 32 percent in 1976.[81]

The transition of the Dutch army from "armed men" to "manned arms" can only partially explain these changes, since in 1978 the number of conscripts actually doing service started to rise again. Perhaps another factor is the strength of trade unionism in the army. Peaks in the percentage of eligible conscripts declared unfit for actual service or exempted from the draft clearly coincided with a high degree of unioni-

Table 3.10   Military Personnel

Year	Volunteers	Conscripts	Administrative	Total	
1947	n.a.	n.a.	n.a.	(182,000)	
1948	n.a.	n.a.	n.a.	(180,000)	
1949	n.a.	n.a.	n.a.	(182,000)	
1950	n.a.	n.a.	n.a.	(126,000)	
1951	n.a.	n.a.	n.a.	(110,000)	
1952	n.a.	n.a.	n.a.	(127,000)	
1953	n.a.	n.a.	n.a.	(150,000)	
1954	n.a.	n.a.	29,634	(167,000)	
1955	50,434	76,175	30,634	157,243	(167,000)
1956	49,535	77,264	32,713	159,512	(167,000)
1957	48,522	77,267	33,103	158,892	(166,000)
1958	48,624	79,140	32,695	160,459	(163,000)
1959	48,825	80,380	32,156	161,361	(161,000)
1960	48,735	82,044	31,467	162,246	(163,000)
1961	49,531	82,470	31,214	163,215	(165,000)
1962	50,770	84,860	30,773	166,403	(169,000)
1963	51,902	79,160	30,988	162,050	(165,000)
1964	53,332	72,490	30,820	156,642	(158,000)
1965	53,302	66,356	30,955	150,613	(153,000)
1966	54,528	67,948	31,670	154,146	(157,000)
1967	57,030	67,472	31,419	155,921	(159,000)
1968	59,608	58,008	31,591	149,207	(152,000)
1969	60,602	54,413	30,949	145,965	(148,000)
1970	59,871	49,151	30,138	139,520	(142,000)
1971	60,311	51,299	29,978	142,241	(143,000)
1972	60,150	54,134	30,515	145,298	(145,000)
1973	58,883	49,139	29,797	138,269	(139,000)
1974	57,220	50,610	28,949	137,279	(138,000)
1975	56,189	48,398	28,506	133,593	(135,000)
1976	56,375	45,200	28,248	130,323	(130,000)
1977	56,011	46,159	28,215	130,895	
1978	55,874	49,137	28,032	133,563	
1979	55,799	49,749	26,410	132,558	
1980	56,974	49,310	26,440	133,983	
1981	57,058	49,324	26,932	134,448	
1982	56,975	48,757	27,117	133,191	
1983	56,664	47,500	27,050	131,214	
1984	56,899	46,368	27,242	130,509	
1988	56,958	45,756	27,392	130,106	
1993	57,708	46,296	27,662	131,666	

n.a. = figure not available.

Sources: Figures have been made available by the Ministry of Defense. Data on total manpower (in parentheses) are estimates of the Central Planning Bureau.

zation in the Association for Conscripted Military (VVDM). In 1978, when almost all VVDM demands—requests to be treated as civilians as much as possible, including financial benefits similar to the minimum wage paid in business—had been honored, the size of the armed forces stabilized at some 105,000 persons, including approximately 49,000 conscripts. Since then, VVDM membership has dropped from a peak of 30,000 to the present level of 8,000, and a new, more moderate union, also representing some 8,000 members, has shown up as a competitor.

Have decreases in manpower indeed resulted in a substantially increased capacity to buy new armaments? This has been one issue on which the defense debate has focused. In 1970 a leading Dutch historian on World War II, Lou de Jong, drew a parallel between the 1930s and the 1960s, charging that the Dutch army was too ill-equipped to perform its missions in NATO. A year later, the government appointed a commission to look into defense policy. The majority advocated returning the level of defense spending to 4.25 percent of the GNP by 1975, although the minority felt that stabilization at 3.945 percent was adequate.[82] They also suggested that operating costs be reduced by 10 percent in order to increase "investments." The need for this recommendation can be deduced from Table 3.11.

As a result, Labor Party Minister of Defense Vredeling subsequently drafted a defense white paper outlining physical and financial military planning for 1974–83.[83] Ready troop strength would be reduced by 20 percent in the expectation that the Mutual and Balanced Force Reduction (MBFR) talks would soon lead to an agreement. However, his plans were criticized by the United States, West Germany, and the NATO Secretariat (headed by former Minister Luns), with the result that the government partially revised its policy, although it maintained that NATO was paying attention only to Dutch quantitative reductions and not to qualitative improvements.

Indeed, a significant modernization has been implemented in recent years. The navy has acquired several new ships (for example, a series of S-frigates), although the total number of vessels has diminished. Similarly, Vredeling defied opposition within his own party—"Political congresses don't buy aircraft"—by replacing F-104 Starfighters and Northrop F-5s with F-16 combat aircraft. Likewise, demands by the 1975 Labor Party Congress to cut unilaterally the army's combat-ready troop strength and to reduce defense spending to 3 percent of the GNP before 1978 were not implemented in government policies either.

One problem has been that those allies who have been asked to take over military tasks within NATO have tended to see such requests as attempts to diminish the Dutch defense burden unilaterally. On balance, one can conclude that the armed forces have been trimmed to a smaller scale, but not as substantially as the Labor Party would have wished. Furthermore, the economy drive was not just the work of a Labor-led coalition instigating the boom in "investments" during the 1970s, but it also stemmed from reductions that started as far back as the beginning of the 1960s. The drive has been necessitated by three structural factors.

Table 3.11 Breakdown of the Defense Budget by Percentages

Year	Personnel costs	Other operating costs	Total operating costs	"Investment" costs
1952	34.4	32.9	67.3	32.7
1953	35.2	36.9	72.1	27.9
1954	37.6	33.3	70.9	29.1
1955	39.8	31.9	71.7	28.3
1956	39.6	28.6	68.2	31.8
1957	43.7	29.8	73.5	26.5
1958	49.5	30.0	79.5	20.5
1959	54.0	32.4	86.4	13.6
1960	51.4	30.2	81.6	18.4
1961	50.9	24.4	75.3	24.7
1962	52.6	24.2	76.8	23.2
1963	52.0	23.4	75.4	24.6
1964	53.2	20.2	73.4	26.6
1965	58.1	21.0	79.1	20.9
1966	62.3	22.9	85.2	14.8
1967	61.8	20.8	82.6	17.4
1968	64.1	20.2	84.3	15.7
1969	63.1	19.9	83.0	17.0
1970	63.6	18.4	82.0	18.0
1971	64.2	20.7	84.9	15.1
1972	66.0	20.8	86.8	13.2
1973	66.8	18.6	85.4	14.6
1974	66.4	17.3	83.7	16.3
1975	64.6	16.7	81.3	18.7
1976	64.4	17.1	81.5	18.5
1977	57.8	18.2	76.0	24.0
1978	61.2	17.7	78.9	21.1
1979	59.3	18.3	77.6	22.4
1980	59.0	20.4	79.4	20.6
1981	56.2	20.8	77.0	23.0
1982	55.0	20.8	75.8	24.2
1983	54.2	20.8	74.3	25.7
1984	53.0	21.0	74.0	26.0

Source: Ministry of Defense, *Financiële Kerngegevens Defensie* (Main Financial Figures) (1983), 29.

First, because of Dutch tradition, the navy remained an inordinately important part of the armed forces.[84] This becomes especially clear if one compares the size of the Dutch fleet with its Belgian counterpart and considers the fact that the quality of the navy is highly regarded. Second, the military requirements for fighting in Indonesia, as well as American military aid between 1950 and 1961, had pushed Dutch defense to a level that the country could not, or at least was not willing to, sustain on its own, especially in a time of decreased international tension. Finally, economic growth and increases in general government spending tended to hide the dwindling position of defense for a long time. Increases in wages and rank inflation were partly countered by reductions in manpower. Similarly, increases in the prices of new weapons' systems were partly compensated for by delaying their acquisition or by buying smaller numbers. But because economic growth has almost stopped, financial difficulties can no longer be so easily obscured. Drastic reductions in scale or even the elimination of complete tasks have almost become inevitable for the future.[85]

Eventually, these fiscal constraints may bring defense efforts back to the front page, from where they have been chased away by the nuclear issue. During the 1982 defense budget debate, PvdA spokesman Klaas De Vries, came out in favor of a nuclear-free Western Europe, adding that, if necessary, his party was willing to pay the price for this goal in the form of higher expenditures for conventional defenses. However, since the welfare state is at stake in the present economic crisis, old spending patterns will have to be scrutinized before parliamentarians will be willing to increase the defense burden. For example, the 1:2:1 rule of division of the budget between the navy, the army, and the air force, respectively, which was already rejected in the 1974 white paper but has remained in practice ever since, can hardly be maintained any longer. Moreover, defense planning, which is at present still largely left to the individual services, will have to become more centralized.

Internationally, criticisms on the process of "societalization" of the armed forces (the image of long-haired Dutch soldiers) have been rejected by many military experts from other countries, who point out that in international maneuvers the Dutch have operated effectively in spite of relaxed discipline. Furthermore, the Dutch share in NATO's defense expenditures, excluding U.S. spending, has increased from 4.6 percent in 1971–75 to 4.7 percent in 1976–77 and to 4.8 percent in 1981.[86] From the viewpoint of financial *burden sharing,* the Netherlands has thus remained a loyal ally, and as yet defense spending has not provoked the same dissension as nuclear questions.

DÉTENTE AND ARMS CONTROL. The Dutch consensus in favor of détente and arms control, nascent at the end of the 1960s, became full-blown in the 1970s. However, for most Dutch politicians, détente was defined as the elimination of the causes of East-West tension by exchanges at the societal level, rather than by accommodations accepting the status quo in Europe at the diplomatic level. Thus, in the Final Act of the Helsinki Accords and at the followup conferences in Belgrade and Madrid, the Netherlands particularly emphasized human rights and the free flow of persons, ideas, and information across national borders. When the Soviet Union was not forthcoming in the fields of human rights and fundamental liberties, many Dutch were disappointed by the results of détente. Nevertheless, an almost uniform support for friendly contacts with the East has persisted.

This degree of ambiguity can be found in the church peace movement as well. At first, the IKV had advised Lech Walesa, the Polish Solidarity Trade Union leader, to operate cautiously, since a Soviet intervention in Poland might result in the deployment of LRTNF in Western Europe. But after the military coup in Poland, the IKV came out as one of the strongest supporters of Solidarity, arguing that only a "crumbling of the blocs" could bring an end to the nuclear stalemate in Europe. This view called attention to the question of whether the IKV advocated a reunification of Germany, which would be a likely result of a disintegration of the military alliances. At first, the IKV supported *Aktion Sühnezeichen Friedensdienste* (its equivalent in the Federal Republic), which called for Reunification, but at the meeting of the Second Special U.N. Session on Disarmament, the chairman and secretary of the IKV switched their position to oppose German reunification and succeeded in deleting this demand from a collective petition that was being issued by the peace movements on that occasion.[87]

Contrary to the wide range of opinions in many other areas, adherence to arms control can count on almost unanimous verbal support in the Netherlands. For conservative parties and groups, it is a diplomatic move to gain public support for retaining an East-West military balance, while for progressives, it is the first step to disarmament. For example, the Dutch Foreign and Defense ministers proposed to NATO in December 1974 that the reduction of tactical nuclear weapons should also be discussed in MBFR talks. In December 1975, at the Vienna MBFR talks, the West presented the so-called third option indicating an American willingness to reduce the number of Pershing 1A missiles and nuclear-capable F-5 aircraft, including 1,000 warheads, in exchange for a Soviet withdrawal of one tank army from the GDR. Although Foreign Minister Max Van der Stoel claimed that this proposal was an example of Dutch influence in NATO, one should not overlook the fact that similar ideas had been previously discussed in the United States. Furthermore, Dutch doubts about the deterrent value of short-range Theater Nuclear Forces (TNF) were not reflected in NATO's proposal, which, on the contrary, as observed by Labor Party member Pieter Dankert[88], offered the withdrawal of delivery systems capable of hitting Warsaw Pact territory.

In their 1975 white paper on "Disarmament and Security," Foreign Minister Van der Stoel and his State Secretary, Peter Kooijmans, favored "deemphasizing the role of nuclear weapons,"[89] They stated that a "reduction of the role of nuclear weapons" should be accomplished through establishing an equilibrium of conventional military forces in Europe. When the MBFR talks did not prove to be overwhelmingly successful by the end of the 1970s, and since the politicians wanted to show the public that they took arms control seriously, the center-right government supported the demand that deployment of INF should be accompanied by an offer to negotiate with the USSR. They also required that the decision on the deployment of GLCMs in the Netherlands be made conditional upon the state of affairs of the negotiations after two years, and upon the elimination of some nuclear missions of the Dutch armed forces within the framework of NATO's so-called Shift Study (later called "Comprehensive Study"). Furthermore, the Netherlands "assumed" that SALT II would be ratified by the United States Congress.

Excessive optimism over bilateral arms control by the major political parties was at that time severly criticised by the antinuclear movement. The IKV considered the existing mutual arms-control limitations as stimulating rather than dampening the arms race, since technological innovations remained unrestricted and the ceilings did not necessitate large reductions in numbers. Instead, they called for unilateral steps, including the removal of nuclear weapons from Dutch territory, which was presented as an application of Osgood's GRIT theory[90], since it was supposed to trigger a process of mutual steps.

Calls for nationalistic unilateralism in the Dutch peace movement have become so strong that President Reagan's 1981 proposal for a "zero option" was rejected as sheer propaganda. Although the American negotiating position in Geneva fully accommodated the main demands of the 400,000 demonstrators who marched through the streets of Amsterdam on 21 November 1981, it was clear that the ban-the-bomb movement would oppose the deployment of cruise missiles in the Netherlands even if the Soviets refused to reduce their SS-20 arsenal. As soon as it comes to specifics, it seems that consensus on détente and arms control turns out to be as fragile as the apparent harmony in the other policy areas.

The above presents the changes that have taken place in the conduct of Dutch security policy over the past decade or so. Despite these changes, there remains a general foreign-policy consensus—although not the same consensus of earlier years—and this disappears only when one gets down to the level of specific policy proposals, in particular those concerning new nuclear programs. This phenomenon is to be explained by a combination of well-known international developments—dwindling power of the United States, the eroding strategic "guarantee" for Western Europe, and so on—and, above all, on important changes within Dutch society. Undoubtedly, the "depillarization" of society is in some respects peculiar to the Netherlands' political system, but its consequences—democratization of foreign policy making, domestication, lack of latitude in decision making—are also known in other Western industrialized countries. To conclude, the implications of these processes for the profile of the Netherlands as a member of the Atlantic Alliance will be addressed.

The Emerging Dutch Profile in the Alliance

In March 1981 Karl Kaiser, in an interview with a Dutch newspaper, wondered what had happened to the usual Dutch loyalty to Allied policies. Ironically, not long afterward (by the time the term "Hollanditis" had been coined), a huge rally of West German Protestants voiced exactly the same concerns as those of the confessional peace movement in the Netherlands. Soon one SPD district after another began renouncing the NATO decision on INF in much the same manner as their counterparts in the Netherlands' Labor Party had done a year before. In fact, in the early months of 1979 politicians in Bonn, such as Herbert Wehner, were even quicker and more bitter in their opposition to new medium-range armament programs than most socialist and centrist parliamentarians in The Hague. As far as criticism of the U.S. Government is concerned, the Dutch Government lagged far behind Chancellor Schmidt when he intimated that Carter's leadership was irresponsible and could have brought about an unstable world situation, similar to that of 1914.

Thus, the Netherlands is not—nor is the European continent, when one considers the Labour Party in Britain—an isolated case. European waves of antinuclear feelings occurred both in the late 1950s, starting in Britain, and again in the late 1970s and early 1980s, originating from, among other sources, the German *Ostpolitik* and the Dutch weariness with mere lip service to arms control. Moreover, all references to pacifism based on moralist and neutralist traditions have only limited relevance. The Netherlands, as opposed to some other European countries, remains willing in the case of high alert to provide ten brigades for the Central European sector, and in peacetime it is prepared for six nuclear missions, four of which have first-line weapons systems deployed in the framework of a forward defense. (For a review of current defense efforts of the Netherlands, see Appendix 2.) Furthermore, the Dutch people are second to none of their allies in raising their voice in protest against the military crackdown in Poland and the treatment of dissidents in Eastern-bloc countries.

However, government measures in the Netherlands can be implemented only if a supporting consensus exists within Dutch societal organizations, although the Netherlands is not a special case in this regard either. Implementation of government macroeconomic policy, for instance, is possible only with the support of trade unions and the employers' associations. Governments' decision-making latitude in foreign policy is similarly constrained. In the nuclear area, above all, it is no longer possible to speak of a security policy, since political authorities are paralyzed by the existence of two veto groups. On the one side, the traditional elite still functions as a pro-NATO lobby. Members of this elite, which is strong in departmental bureaucracies and in political parties like VVD and CDA, tend to accept more readily Allied or American decisions as corresponding to Dutch security interests. On the other side, an antinuclear lobby—consisting of the peace movement and represented heavily in the PvdA, and, in view of the small margins coalitions tend to have, sufficiently in the CDA—wants to prevent the Netherlands from assuming any new nuclear responsibilities. This deadlock between the two veto groups is accompanied by a rather diffuse but deep-rooted antinuclear feeling among the Dutch population that competes with traditional desires to remain a faithful NATO ally and to be sufficiently armed against the USSR.

The situation is made worse by the fact that politicians do not excel in confronting their party members and voters with clear policy choices and trade-offs. Instead, most have chosen escape routes from the nuclear dilemmas. These paths include the unconditional propagation of dé-tente, or the throwing around of slogans without a clear meaning—for example, "deemphasising the role of nuclear weapons." Others call for bilateral arms control; rejected by the antinuclear movement as an instrument only fueling the arms race, this policy is embraced with extreme optimism by the strong supporters of NATO. Other escape routes are attempted in policy areas in which a fundamental consensus still prevails, such as development aid or in moral indignation, such as protests against apartheid in South Africa and military régimes in Latin America. With respect to some issues, EPC viewpoints have functioned as an escape route, providing the possibility of delaying national decisions by first settling differences of opinion with the European partners. Similarly, initiatives by the Labor parties in Scandilux can be seen as attempts to gain support against policies of the United States and Western European middle powers, but they have until now resulted only in the postponement of decisions and of the selection of criteria for later decisions. But the fact is that these are only escape routes. The conduct of Dutch security policy has reached an intractable stalemate at its core, and this is the first of three key factors that will affect its formulation in the coming period.

This nuclear stalemate is accompanied by a second factor: the fragile nature of governing coalitions more generally, another major effect of "depillarization." Given the breakdown of consensus, this has produced ever-shifting political positions and even more frequent changes of government. By 1982 the Labor Party again had strengthened its nuclear opposition and entered the election campaign as a party unconditionally opposed to the deployment of cruise missiles. It claimed that a compromise with the Christian Democrats, as had happened in 1981, was no longer possible, since the CDA refused to say " 'no' in all circumstances" to the new European missiles. Since the PvdA regained its position as the largest political party, its antinuclear label was obviously not a hindrance in attracting voters. But, at the same time, the definitive Labor Party stance on the cruise-missile issue paved the way for a CDA-VVD coalition. Naturally, no settlement was possible between the "unconditional no" of PvdA and the "possible yes" of CDA, as was so between the "possible no" of CDA and the "yes" of VVD.

Nevertheless, even this center-right coalition refused to take a clear position on the new European missiles. By making deployment conditional upon INF negotiations in Geneva, as was wished primarily by the Christian Democrats, they created opportunities for further delays in decision making. Moreover, either of the two parties—the Christian Democrats, faced with rather chronic losses of seats in Parliament, or the Liberals, in search of new coalition opportunities to undermine the monopolistic position of CDA—could decide to change partners and form a coalition with the PvdA. For the Netherlands this would certainly mean that the INF would suffer the same fate as the MLF did in the mid-1960s.

A final factor that will determine future choices is whether the ban-the-bomb movement loses momentum. Although the November 1981 demonstration in Amsterdam indicated massive antinuclear feelings, a poll among the 400,000 demonstrators showed that, at most, 4 percent of them belonged to the CDA or the VVD, the parties with a majority in the Second Chamber; 45 percent of the demonstrators were voters from small left-wing parties, who have obviously already succeeded in convincing the Labor Party to reject the cruise missiles.[91] The demonstration on 29 October 1983 in The Hague, which attracted 550,000 people, showed a similar partisan bias in the composition of its participants.[92] Moreover, the demonstrations may have represented a peak in the antinuclear movement, and it might be extremely difficult to show such massive support once more. For the present, discussions in the PvdA and the IKV have focused on the acceptability and the effectiveness of civil disobedience to halt cruise-missile deployment. But attitudes diverge substantially in regard to the use of these methods, thus putting the functioning of representative democracy, through majority decisions, to the test. The committee "Kruisraketten nee" ("No to Cruise Missiles") designated May 1984 as "action month," while a national campaign to collect signatures is under construction.

One palpable result has been that both the peace movements and the Dutch people have had to address the nuclear issue in the wider context of the real world situation. For example, the IKV has widened its interests to look at questions other than the morality of nuclear weapons. The leaders of the IKV decided that they were not willing to support the blockade of American conventional munition transports through the Netherlands. This made clear that the IKV should, for the moment, be considered an antinuclear movement, and not—like the organizers of the blockades—a pacifistic movement in the classical sense of the word. (This also illustrates that "Hollanditis" lacks a clear definition.)

Also, attempts "to crumble the blocs" in Europe following the Polish military coup were much more controversial than the frightening campaigns portraying the disastrous effects of nuclear war. It seems that reliance on strategic deterrence is much more comforting than the idea of nuclear war is discomforting. According to the results of a 1977 questionnaire, two-thirds of the Dutch population were already convinced that they would not survive a nuclear conflict in Europe, although, in the same poll (in accordance with the assumptions of deterrence doctrine), only a small minority considered such a conflict likely within the next ten years.[93] In the same vein, in the 1982 "Peace Journal," published annually during the Peace Week, the IKV agreed that it was important to address structural problems such as unemployment, since they were preoccupying public opinion. Finally, reactions were not favorable, particularly among church members, to the IKV advice of

1982 to vote only for political parties that unconditionally opposed the deployment of cruise missiles. The Dutch people have begun to realize that the issues are very complicated and offer no black-and-white choices.

Notwithstanding these uncertainties of party and coalition politics and the growing or declining influence of peace movements, it is almost certain that the nuclear issue will remain at the top of the Dutch political agenda during the next few years. One reason is that the NATO decision of 1979 not only planned deployment for the Netherlands in 1986, but it made it inevitable that opposition would remain mobilized for the same period of seven years. The Labor Party has become deeply committed to the antinuclear calls from the Dutch public. Unlike in the interbellum period, however, they now are the strongest single party in Parliament. Moreover, the party's contribution to the reconstruction of the country after World War II has gained it the respect of the public. For these reasons it will be very difficult—and it may not even be very beneficial— for the Christian Democrats and the Liberals to keep the PvdA out of coalition bargaining for a long time. Yet, as soon as the Labor Party does not get its way on the cruise missile issue, any settlement with the coalition partners is likely to be out of the question. The chairman of the Labor Party, Max van den Berg, and the parliamentary leader, Den Uyl, have already announced that their party will fight any positive deployment decision in any future coalition in which their party is asked to participate. Since nuclear questions are thus considered to be so overwhelmingly important in the Netherlands, they will to a large extent determine Dutch contributions to future NATO programs. Of course, this will also be determined by the fact that some Allies, in particular the United States, regard willingness to deploy GLCMs as a test case for Alliance solidarity. Dutch politicians feel they have to sail between the Scylla of being rejected as an unfaithful ally in NATO and the Charybdis of neglecting popular antinuclear feelings.

Obviously, the Labor Party will lean more heavily toward the ban-the-bomb movement, and the Liberals (VVD) will, in the immediate future, give priority to solidarity with the North Atlantic Allies. The crucial factor might be that the Christian Democrats will no longer be able to compromise, on the one hand, because they are divided on nuclear matters themselves and, on the other, because the polarization between the major parties has gone too far. This will almost certainly result in a party attitude that shows support for very general policies but withdraws support for specific policies that require a positive contribution or stand. If this dilemma is applied to various policy areas, it is likely that Dutch security policies in the 1980s will be guided by five main themes, each of which is explored below.

Stay in NATO but Avoid Commitments to New Nuclear Responsibilities

In view of present nuclear discontent, it is perhaps surprising that NATO membership is not today a political issue, as it was a decade ago in the

Labor Party. American proposals to deploy ERW bombs in Central Europe, the size of the proposed INF deployment (indicating that a Eurostrategic balance separated from the strategic arsenals of the super-powers may develop), accusations that the European Allies do not share their part of the conventional defense burden, and plans of the Reagan Administration to deploy a defense system against ballistic missiles in space are all in contradiction with the traditional Dutch emphasis on strategic deterrence. Indeed, they all seem to weaken deterrence. It is increasingly difficult for the Dutch Government to convince progressive and centrist party intellectuals that NATO, in its approach to armaments and arms control, is seeking stability and trying to put an end to the technological arms race.

Nevertheless, the question of NATO membership is an issue only for the small parties of the left. There are three basic reasons why the three large political parties will probably continue generally to support Dutch membership in NATO. First, since Dutch security has been defined since World War II as "NATO's security" by most party members and voters, the discontinuation of participation in the Western defense pact would be regarded as too great a rupture with the past. By lending general support to NATO, a feeling of continuous military protection is kept alive.

Second, there is a lack of acceptable alternatives to NATO. In 1981 only 17 percent of those polled chose alternative security options: 11 percent wanted to establish an independent Western European defense force not allied to the United States, and 6 percent chose to rely on a greater accommodation of the interests of the Soviet Union. Even though 27 percent of those polled "did not know" or did not answer the question, 57 percent favored a continuation of NATO membership: 31 percent preferred NATO as it operates now; 15 percent preferred a changed NATO, in which Western Europe has more say in return for paying more of the costs; and 11 percent wanted to withdraw Dutch military forces from NATO but remain in the Alliance for such things as policy consultations.[94]

Third, opposition to nuclear weapons tends to have—at least in its consequences—nationalistic overtones. For example, the IKV's immediate target is to prevent deployment of cruise missiles *in the Netherlands*, and subsequently remove nuclear weapons from *Dutch* territory. Likewise, opposition to President Reagan's 1981 decision to produce the neutron weapon was much smaller than in 1977, when his predecessor, Jimmy Carter, proposed to incorporate ERW bombs in the armed forces of the European Allies (including the Netherlands). The first Van Agt Government partially followed this nationalistic line by making deployment of cruise missiles in the Netherlands conditional on the elimination of nuclear missions presently performed by the *Dutch* armed forces, and not on changes in NATO's military posture as a whole.

However, priority for NATO is no longer unconditional: Popular resistance to nuclear weapons may result in objections to new nuclear responsibilities or to the retention of traditional nuclear roles. It has already been argued that the present center-right government could not take a positive deployment decision, even on the order of sixteen or thirty-two missiles, because of divergences within the CDA. However, the VVD has been blocking a clear "no" response to the cruise missiles. Since its formation, for the first one and a half years, the government could hope to escape a deployment decision following a successful conclusion of the INF negotiations. The designation of the Woensdrecht airbase as the eventual missile site in the Netherlands, in June 1983, was recommended in order to stimulate Russian concessions in Geneva. During the Woensdrecht debate, Minister of Defense Job de Ruiter (CDA) promised that infrastructural preparations, which had to start in the summer of 1984, would be preceded by a deployment decision. Further delays, the favorite alternative of the divided coalition, therefore seemed precluded. Another alternative, joint deployment with Belgium, undoubtedly proved to be unacceptable to the southern neighbors of the Netherlands.

Two other factors that could have eased the painful deliberations in 1984 in fact worsened the situation. First, the Russian walkout in Geneva, after deployment in the FRG had been approved by the *Bundestag*, has made the Dutch fight for arms control an uphill struggle. Second, by accepting, for the most part, NATO's Montebello decision to withdraw an additional 1,400 warheads from Western Europe, the Dutch Government has made a trade-off between cruise missiles and nuclear artillery almost impossible. For a long time, Prime Minister Ruud Lubbers (CDA) had hoped to find a compromise to such a trade-off, which would have accommodated objections by CDA defense specialists in Parliament against battlefield nuclear systems. The government decided to replace the dual-capable, but obsolete, "Nike-Hercules" antiaircraft missiles with the conventional Patriot system. In addition, Atomic Demolition Mines (ADM's) probably will be removed, while the dual-capable "Lance" will be continued, if only because PvdA authorities share responsibility for the introduction of these systems in the armed forces. Preparations to give F-16 combat aircraft and Orion-LRPM a nuclear capability continue, although the final decision has yet to be made.

In June 1984 Prime Minister Lubbers, who previously had threatened that his Cabinet would not be able to reach a decision[95], showed that he was a master in finding compromises by winning parliamentary approval for a policy: (a) promising that the Netherlands will deploy a "proportionate share" of the 572 NATO systems if an arms-control agreement has been concluded between the United States and USSR in November 1985; (b) rewarding the Russians unilaterally if they freeze the number of SS-20s at 378 (in which case the Netherlands will not deploy GLCMs), while threatening them at the same time by saying that Holland would deploy its full number of 48 cruise missiles if the USSR added to the 378 SS-20 missiles supposedly present in June 1984. While satisfying nuclear protests in the immediate future—the building of shelters at Woensdrecht has been delayed by one and a half years—this decision made deployment far more probable than it had been since 1979.

Although nuclear upheaval in The Hague should not be exaggerated (no Cabinet has yet been forced to resign over a nuclear issue), it is clear that any Dutch Government will think twice before accepting new nuclear responsibilities, and this will perhaps be even more true after cruise missiles have been accepted on Dutch soil.

Accept American Leadership but Try to Preserve Détente and Arms Control

From being an extremely staunch and faithful supporter since the decolonization of the Far East, the Netherlands has turned into a rather critical ally of the United States. Dutch criticisms of the United States tend to be concentrated on the American intervention in the Third World and the lack of American concern over human-rights violations. Likewise, confrontation policies toward the Soviet Union can expect to draw criticism from the Netherlands. This can be explained in part by geographical position: Western European countries, situated in the direct vicinity of Soviet occupation troops, tend to react differently than an "island" with global responsibilities, like the United States.

One can expect that this situation will continue in the near future. Interviews published in 1978 showed that formal elites supported U.S. leadership in the Alliance more strongly than members of the informal (and in part, counter) elites. However, once the question was raised over what should happen if the American nuclear guarantee of Western Europe was no longer considered credible, opinions were widely divergent: 22 percent expected a fragmentation of Europe; 20 percent anticipated a greater influence by, or rapprochement with, the Soviet Union; 33 percent expected increases in conventional and nuclear armaments; 3 percent proposed a political unification of Europe; and 8 percent gave still other answers (13 percent do not know or did not answer).[96]

One factor that helps to explain the almost absolute priority for détente in the Netherlands is that arms control is considered an indispensable instrument to solve the nuclear dilemmas of the politicians. Bilateral arms control, after all, can allow one to delay or avoid difficult nuclear decisions; thus, all major political parties will tend to pay lip service to negotiations. Even though American strategic superiority has disappeared and the credibility of the nuclear guarantee of Western Europe has diminished, any formula for parity in SALT or a treaty prohibiting ballistic-missile defenses in outer space is warmly supported by the Netherlands. The MBFR talks are still seen as a way to establish an equilibrium in conventional forces in Europe and of enabling reductions in the numbers of nuclear warheads. Similarly, the American "zero solution" in INF negotiations was considered unrealistic but still welcomed, since it would eliminate intermediate-range nuclear weapons completely. However, "linkage politics"—that is, making progress in arms-control negotiations dependent upon cooperative Soviet behavior in other policy areas—is criticized by the Netherlands, since it does not give absolute priority to arms control. As long as the United States continues to promote such policies, as President Carter did in his refusal to submit the SALT II treaty for ratification, and as the Reagan Administration has done this far, an uneasy relationship between the United States and the Netherlands will probably continue to exist.

Concentrate on the Conservation of a Minimal Degree of Cohesion Within Western Europe

The days of clear priorities in the Netherlands' European policy seem to have passed. Dutch adherence to the idea of a federal Europe has been frustrated, not only by various kinds of summitry between the major powers of the Western world and Franco-German cooperation on decision making within the EEC, but also by the antifederalist attitude of the United Kingdom, the country so much welcomed as a European partner by the Netherlands. Because of this stagnation in European integration efforts, priority will be given to retaining, in day-to-day conflict management, what has been accomplished in the past.

This may give rise to a fundamental reevaluation of the position of West Germany. Following a period of intense concentration on what would be Germany's position after World War II, the German problem has ceased to be a major concern, since the Federal Republic was thought to have found a new identity in the West. However, several developments in the 1970s may indicate that German-Dutch relations are still uneasy below the surface. Willy Brandt's *Ostpolitik* was, in fact, supported by the Netherlands. But in the early 1970s, the Dutch Labor Party began to criticize harshly the German practice of denying official positions to people of the far left *(Berufsverbot)*. This severely strained relationships with the West German SPD. Later, in a television interview, Helmut Kohl was confronted with a candid and critical Dutch public, an event that further troubled bilateral relationships. Ironically, Helmut Schmidt, who first had the image in the Netherlands of being the "iron chancellor," was regarded much more positively as soon as the New Right in America showed its strength, while Helmut Kohl appeared to be too colorless a figure to attract much opposition.

It is not clear which direction future German-Dutch relations will take. The natural tensions between a major power and a small power may be diminished by cultural bonds, such as the increasing Dutch attachment to German television networks. As for military security affairs, the Van Agt Government already missed an opportunity for the improvement of German-Dutch relations in the spring of 1979, when an agreement could have been reached with Chancellor Schmidt on deployment of a substantially smaller number than the planned 572 missiles. Since that time, the Schmidt and Kohl governments have voiced their criticisms of the Dutch reluctance to deploy cruise missiles, even though the German "nonsingularity principle" required the cooperation of only one other continental NATO power (Italy). Prime Minister Ruud Lubbers, of the present CDA-

VVD Government, stated several times that the German decision on the missiles would be a very important guideline for the Dutch decision, but it still remains to be seen how he will act.

A recent study by the Scientific Council for Government Policy has indicated that an accommodation between Dutch and West German security interests might be found in "a Western European position more independent of the United States."[97] But it has not been made clear what the contents of these Western European policies should be. For example, an independent West German nuclear retaliatory force, although it would be a radical substitute for American nuclear protection, might destabilize relationships with the USSR. Similarly, a separate accommodation between the USSR and Germany, and possibly the Benelux countries, offers the prospect of "Finlandization" and possibly German reunification, with the latter of course being desired only by the Germans. Franco-German nuclear cooperation is not only an unlikely alternative but also a prospect that the Netherlands has always opposed. The Dutch conclusion therefore will be that "grand designs" for independent European policies are not plausible as long as viable alternatives for security arrangements are lacking.

Emphasize Conventional Defense Within NATO's Strategy of "Flexibility in Response" but Give Priority to the Welfare State

Recently, two Dutch security analysts argued that conventional warfare in the Netherlands could produce the same number of casualties as limited nuclear warfare. The bombing of continental ports and the setting loose of poisonous clouds from surrounding chemical industries would be devastating. Massive conventional warfare in cities like Hamburg and Frankfurt would also cost millions of lives. For these reasons, they proposed that it would be in the interest of highly centralized and industrialized societies like the Federal Republic and the Benelux countries to shift from NATO's current reliance on the uncertainty of nuclear escalation against Russian territory to a policy that makes clear to the Soviet Union that the costs of a European war would be equally high for them as those incurred in Western Europe.[98] Such a strategy would require only limited numbers of INF ("some dozens instead of hundreds"), while nuclear battlefield systems could be drastically reduced. In sum, their findings reinforced the Dutch predisposition toward strategic deterrence.

Although this proposed change in NATO's strategy is in accordance with the traditional Dutch emphasis on strategic deterrence, it is unlikely that it will be supported sufficiently in the Dutch political system. First, traditional elites are fearful that discussions about changing NATO strategy might bring an end to the Alliance. They feel that deemphasis of the role of nuclear weapons should be attained by strengthening conventional defenses, even if this shift may contradict an "equal sharing of risks," a concept to which the Americans claim to adhere. Second, the peace movements, in their struggle against all nuclear weaponry, have deliberately kept the public uninformed of what conventional warfare in Western Europe might be like. Although the antinuclear movement might in the future turn into an antidefense movement, politicians are likely to try to outflank recent nuclear protests by unilaterally increasing the conventional capabilities of NATO. Third, the military, which has always regarded nuclear warfare as unmanageable and uncontrollable, tends to be in favor of reducing the role of nuclear weapons, especially because of all their political liability. Finally, the idea of strategic deterrence is also losing support in the United States, as shown by the no-first-use proposal of McGeorge Bundy et al.[99] and statements of former American secretaries (Henry Kissinger and Robert McNamara). Many Americans still prefer not to become involved in a nuclear war as a consequence of conventional warfare in Europe.

These four groups potentially form a firm coalition in favor of new strategic concepts such as FOFA, which has recently been put forward by SACEUR. Paradoxically, General Rogers's request for an additional 4-percent spending on conventional defense over the period 1983–87 may gain added support because of the nuclear protestors in the Netherlands. In the last two years, budget cuts for defense have been smaller than those for several other government programs. Moreover, for 1983, even the Dutch Labor Party was willing to spend an additional 1.2 percent on defense in real terms; the CDA-VVD coalition finally agreed to increase real military expenditures by 2 percent. (In 1982 the rise was 1.5 percent.) Looking ahead to the period 1984–93, the Defense Whitebook foresees a growth in real expenditures of 2 percent for the first five years.

These percentages still fall short of the 3-percent increase goals targeted by NATO, although real spending for the period 1989–93 is projected to increase annually by 3 percent. Moreover, in the long run, defense spending will have to be traded off for cuts in social welfare and other expenditures deemed necessary for the maintenance of a welfare state. The choice will have to be determined in the political process. However, this is no longer an easy task, since settlements between the political leaders (who granted priority for defense spending in 1950–57) are no longer possible, and various pressure groups directly demand from "the state" that their interests be protected. In all, the most that can be expected is that the defense budget will be treated equally vis-à-vis the social sector.

For the reasons indicated above, some skepticism is warranted with respect to the possibilities of escaping from nuclear dilemmas by means of arms control, adaptation of NATO's strategy, or the strengthening of conventional defenses. In 1979 the first Van Agt Government attempted to tackle part of the dilemma by seeking to abolish several Dutch nuclear missions through a proposal to shift from short-range to intermediate-range systems. But it has become sufficiently clear that the NATO Allies are not very enthusiastic in supporting such a Dutch initiative as long as it is unlikely that the Netherlands will deploy part of the INF on its own territory.

Accept Military Responsibilities Outside Europe Only in a Mondialist Multilateral Framework

Although the Dutch are interested in maintaining an uninterrupted flow of oil from the Persian Gulf, it is unlikely that they will cooperate militarily in the protection of the Middle East oilfields and shipping lanes. First, the effectiveness of military action in attaining these goals remains questionable. Second, military action south of the Tropic of Cancer has been all but excluded—although this may not be the consequence of the wording of the NATO treaty—from Dutch policy. As Dutch participation in its various programs shows, actions within the framework of the United Nations can count on Dutch support. However, Dutch political support is probably too weak even for the participation of the Dutch navy in protecting the sea lines around the Cape (as has been suggested by the "principal nations" approach), mainly because such actions would take place in a NATO and not in a mondialist framework.

In summary, one can conclude that the fragmentation of consensus has added restrictions to guidelines in all areas of security policy. Whether this will result in a "muddling through" in NATO or in a fragmentation of the Alliance itself is a question beyond the scope of this chapter. It can be assumed with respect to this issue that American and German attitudes will prevail.

As far as the Netherlands is concerned, it is feared that a negative deployment decision would give the country the role of an outsider in the Alliance (even though it would not come down to the "footnote status" of Denmark and Greece). In its economic policies, the governing coalition has pursued a program of budgetary cuts and savings in social security with a vigor regarded as impossible some years ago. It is unlikely, however, that such a full-scale "turn to the right" will be accomplished in nuclear policies. The reason is that nuclear scruples have become symbolic of progressive views in a "depillarized" society.

Paradoxically, nuclear protests might indeed result in a substantial increase in conventional defense efforts. This is being supported not only by Americans, military men, and sections of the peace movement, but it is also seen as an instrument to show that Holland is still a good ally. Unfortunately, such a large-scale preparation for prolonged conventional war in the vulnerable rear of the combat area of central Europe not only contradicts the traditional Dutch preference for strategic deterrence; it also runs counter to the vital security interests of this nonnuclear ally.

Appendix Table 3.1 A Percentage Breakdown of Seats in the Second Chamber by Political Party 1946–82

	46	48	52	56	59	63	67	71	72	77	81	82	
Small left parties (CPN, PSP, PPR, EVP)	10	8	6	5	3	5	6	7	11	4	6	6	
Labor Party (PvdA)	29	27	30	33	32	29	25	26	29	35	29	31	
DS'70	—	—	—	—	—	—	—	5	4	1	—	—	
right-wing split off PvdA													
D'66	—	—	—	—	—	—	5	7	4	5	11	4	
Christian parties (center)	53	54	51	51	50	51	46	39	32	33	32	30	before 1977 KVP (Catholic), ARP (Calvinist), and CHU (Reformed); since 1977 CDA
VVD	6	8	9	9	13	11	11	11	15	19	17	24	
Small right parties (SGP, GPV, RPF, Farmers Party)	2	3	4	2	2	5	7	5	6	3	4	5	
	100	100	100	100	100	101	100	100	101	100	99	100	

Cabinets:

1945–46	Schermerhorn-Drees (Socialists and KVP)
1946–48	Beel (KVP and PvdA)
1948–51	2nd Drees (KVP, PvdA, CHU, and VVD)
1951–52	3rd Drees (KVP, PvdA, CHU, and VVD)
1952–56	4th Drees (KVP, PvdA, CHU, and ARP)
1956–58	5th Drees (KVP, PvdA, CHU, and ARP)
1958–59	Beel (interim Cabinet) (KVP, ARP, and CHU)
1959–63	De Quay (KVP, VVD, ARP, and CHU)
1963–65	Marijnen (KVP, VVD, ARP, and CHU)
1965–66	Cals (KVP, PvdA, and ARP)
1967–71	De Jong (KVP, ARP, CHU, and VVD)
1971–72	Biesheuvel (KVP, VVD, ARP, CHU, and DS'70)
1972–73	2nd Biesheuvel (KVP, VVD, ARP, and CHU)
1973–77	Den Uyl (PvdA, PPR, D'66, KVP, and ARP)
1977–81	Van Agt (CDA and VVD)
1981–82	2nd Van Agt (CDA, PvdA, and D'66)
1982–82	3rd Van Agt (CDA, D'66)
1982–	Lubbers (CDA, VVD)

Appendix Table 3.2 Current Defense Efforts

Except for the defense of the Netherlands Antilles, current defense is completely assigned to NATO.

Army (67,000—including 43,250 conscripts; 145,000 reserves): 2 armored brigades and 4 mechanized infantry brigades (part of which are on immediate recall) are incorporated in NATO's defense of northern Germany (approximately 30,000); 1 brigade (5,500) is permanently deployed in Germany. During wartime approximately 80,000 forces (10 brigades) should be available. Low priority for territorial defense (except for harbors and transit routes to Germany). Presently, one armed infantry battalion takes part in UNIFIL (Lebanon). Armaments include 343 Centurion 1, 468 Leopard I and 105 Leopard II tanks (340 Leopard II tanks are on order), and YP 765 and AMX armed personnel cars.

Navy (17,350—including 1,250 conscripts; 2,800 marines; and 1,700 naval air arm): takes part in SACLANT's efforts to secure transatlantic ship routes and to defend the North Sea (main task: antisubmarine warfare). The fleet has been modernized almost completely and consists of 2 guided missile-destroyers, 6 submarines, 12 frigates, and several mine-sweepers and other vessels.

Air Force (17,500—including 3,900 conscripts); assigned to 2 ATAF and consists of 182 combat aircrafts (F-104G and NF-5, being replaced by F-16s), 3 SAM squadrons with "Nike-Hercules," and 11 SAM-squadrons with improved "HAWK."

Defense expenditure 1983: Hfl. 12,646 bn ($4.556 bn)

Total armed forces: approximately 103,000 (including 49,000 conscripts)

Total civilian personnel: approximately 27,000

Nuclear missions: 1. "Lance" (army)
　　　　　　　　　2. 8-inch Howitzer (army)
　　　　　　　　　3. ADM's (army)
　　　　　　　　　4. F-104 Starfighter F-16 (air force)
　　　　　　　　　5. "Nike-Hercules" (air force)
　　　　　　　　　6. Nuclear depth charge (navy)

Appendix Table 3.3.   Defense Goals and Subgoals

1.   To provide a (military) contribution for the peace and security of the Kingdom of the Netherlands and its allies.

1.1   To maintain and adapt the national contribution to NATO to the quantitative and qualitative demands formulated by the Alliance.

1.1.1   To contribute to maritime security of the Atlantic Ocean, the Channel, and the North Sea (including contribution to the Standing Naval Forces and participation in the Maritime Contingency Force).

1.1.2   To provide a contribution by the army to the defense of central Europe.

1.1.3   To integrate a contribution by the air force with the Second Allied Tactical Air Force; if necessary, to provide a contribution by the air force to ACE Mobile Force (North).

1.2   To maintain peace and security for the kingdom.

1.2.1   To provide security for the Netherlands' territory in Europe.

1.2.2   To provide security for the Netherlands Antilles.

1.2.3   To protect Dutch interests at sea.

2.   To provide within the framework of international cooperation a contribution (military or otherwise) to peace and security.

2.1   To contribute to peace operations of the U.N.

2.2   To contribute aid in cases of natural disasters (for example, Disasterbrigade).

2.3   To execute other tasks that are, by treaty obligations, assigned to the armed forces (for example, Detection and Rescue Agency, Inspection of Fishing).

3.   To execute tasks that are, from a point of view of efficiency, or as a consequence of special tasks, assigned to the armed forces (for example, Hydrography, Removal of Explosives Service, Regulation of Air Traffic).

4.   To provide conditions that make efficient execution of the aforementioned subgoals possible (for example, training and logistical support).

Notes

1. Walter Laqueur, "Hollanditis: A New Stage in European Neutralism," *Commentary* (August 1981): 19–26.
2. A. van Staden, *Een Trouwe Bondgenoot: Nederland en het Atlantische Bondgenootschap 1960–1971 (A Faithful Ally: the Netherlands and the Atlantic Alliance 1960–1971)* (Baarn: Anthos, 1974).
3. *De Prins*, 2 June 1917, 261.
4. H. Daalder, "Nederland en de Wereld, 1940–1945" ("The Netherlands and the World: 1940–1945"), *Tijdschrift voor Geschiedenis*, 66 (1953): 171–72, reprinted in *The Foreign Policy of the Netherlands*, ed. *J. H. Leurdijk* (Alphen van den Ryn: Sijthoff & Noordhoff, 1978), 51.
5. *Ibid.*, 172 (in Leurdijk, 51).
6. Quoted in J. J. C. Voorhoeve, *Peace, Profits and Principles: A Study of Dutch Foreign Policy* (The Hague: Nyhoff, 1979), 52.
7. Radio broadcast to occupied Holland, 28 December 1943, quoted in Voorhoeve, *Peace, Profits and Principles*, 102.
8. S. I. P. van Campen, *The Quest for Security: Some Aspects of Netherlands Foreign Policy, 1945–1950* (The Hague: Nijhoff, 1958), 30–32.
9. For an analysis of government documents signifying this policy change, see H. A. Schaper, *The Security Policy of the Netherlands 1945–1948*, reprinted in *The Foreign Policy*, ed. Leurdijk, 89–116. According to a Dutch memorandum for the Benelux Conference, 29–31 January 1948, the Dutch Government at that time did not view the proposed Western European cooperation as an end in itself, but as a means to achieve three of the principal objectives of its foreign policy: participation in the international consultations concerning Germany; support for its policy in Indonesia; and a security guarantee from the United States.
10. William K. Domke, "Compromise, Consensus and Populism in Dutch Defense," *Transaktie*, 12, no. 2 (1983): 159–72.
11. *Ibid.*, 8.
12. S. Rozemond, "Buitenlandse politiek en Nederlands belang" (Foreign Policy and Dutch interest), *Acta Politica*, 18, no. 1 (January 1983): 125.
13. Voorhoeve, *Peace, Profits and Principles*, 12.
14. On this debate, see, for example, Voorhoeve, *Peace, Profits and Principles;* J. L. Heldring, "De Invloed van de Openbare Mening op het Buitenlands Beleid" (The Influence of Public Opinion on Foreign Policy), in *Nederlandse Buitenlandse Politiek*, ed. L. G. M. Jacquet (The Hague: Nederlands Genootschap voor Internationale Zaken, 1970); J. L. Heldring, "Preoccupatie met het Beginsel" (Preoccupation with Principles), in *Gelijk Hebben en Krijgen*, ed. A. L. Constandse, J. L. Heldring, and P. van 't Veer (Amsterdam: De Bezige Bij, 1962); J. L. Heldring, "Between Dreams and Reality," in *The Foreign Policy*, ed. Leurdijk, 307–22; C. B. Wels, *Aloofness & Neutrality: Studies on Dutch Foreign Relations and Policy-Making Institutions,* (Utrecht: Hes, 1982); and B. R. Bot et al., *Lijn in de Buiterlandse Politiek von Nederland* (The Hague: Staatsuitgeverij, 1984).
15. Voorhoeve, *Peace, Profits and Principles*, 300.
16. Ibid., 48.
17. Ibid., 288.
18. On pp. 296–300 of his book *Peace, Profits and Principles*, Voorhoeve mentions seven of these "inconsistencies."
19. A van Staden, "Review of Peace, Profits and Principles," *Internationale Spectator*, 33, no. 12 (December 1979): 785.
20. Nederlands Instituut voor de Publieke Opinie (NIPO) Poll no. 915.
21. NIPO Poll no. 213.
22. Cf. Voorhoeve, *Peace, Profits and Principles*, chap. 5 and 6.
23. Van Staden, *Een Trouwe Bondgennot*, 34.
24. L. G. M. Jaquet, *Minister Stikker en de souvereiniteitsoverdracht aan Indonesië* (Minister Stikker and the Transfer of Sovereignty to Indonesia) (The Hague: Martinus Nijhof, 1982).

25. A. Lijphart, *The Trauma of Decolonization: The Dutch and West New Guinea* (New Haven and London: Yale University Press, 1966), 63–64.

26. *Luns, ik herinner mij* . . . ((Luns, I remember . . .) (Leiden: Sijthoff, 1971), 79–80, 89, and 109.

27. Proceedings of the Dutch First Chamber, 24 April 1963, 345.

28. Van Staden, *Een Trouwe Bondgenoot*, 26.

29. R. W. Russell, "The Atlantic Alliance in Dutch Foreign Policy," *Internationale Spectator*, 23, no. 13 (July 1969): 1203; L. G. M. Jaquet, "The Role of a Small State within Alliance Systems," in *Small States in International Relations*, ed. A. Schou and O. A. Brundtland (Stockholm: Almquist and Wicksell, 1971), 65; Van Staden, *Een Trouwe Bondgenoot*, 26; and Voorhoeve, *Peace, Profits and Principles*, 146.

30. C. L. Patijn, "Het Nederlandse Buitenlandse Beleid" (The Foreign Policy of the Netherlands), *Internationale Spectator*, 24, no. 1 (January 1970): 23.

31. J. Tinbergen, "The Significance of the Marshall Plan for the Netherlands Economy," in *Road to Recovery: The Marshall Plan: Its Importance for the Netherlands and European Cooperation*, (The Hague: Ministry of Foreign Affairs, 1954), 22–27.

32. Explanatory Statement to the 1958 Budget of the Department of War, 1957, 3.

33. Voorhoeve, *Peace, Profits and Principles*, 110.

34. Recently, a German defense expert has attributed the failure of the Adenauer-De Gaulle initiative to American diplomacy. See U. Nerlich, "Change in Europe: A Secular Trend?" *Daedalus*, 110–11 (Winter 1981): 101.

35. Voorhoeve, *Peace, Profits and Principles*, 115.

36. Letter concerning the defense efforts in the years 1961 through 1963. Proceedings, Second Chamber of Parliament 1959–1960. From 1956 onward, successive ministers of Defense pleaded openly for the introduction of new nuclear weapons. For this reason, the suggestion that Parliament has never taken a serious decision about their deployment is not correct.

37. Explanatory statement to the 1957 Budget of the Ministry of War, 1956, 3. Cf. also for a view in retrospect, H. Hansen, *De zes atoomtaken van Nederland* (The Six Nuclear Missions of the Netherlands) (Amsterdam: Van Gennep, 1982).

38. Voorhoeve, *Peace, Profits and Principles*, 114–15.

39. *Teritoriale Verdediging* (Territorial Defense), Rapport van de Adviesraad Defensie Aangelegenheden (The Hague: Advisory Committee for Defense, 1977).

40. Voorhoeve, *Peace, Profits and Principles*, 150.

41. NIPO Polls nos. 252 and 299.

42. See Table 3.1.

43. See Table 3.4.

44. NIPO Polls nos. 231 and 1230.

45. NIPO Polls nos. 181 and 1407.

46. NIPO Polls nos. 1068, 1223 and 1302.

47. International Research Associates 1957.

48. Russell, "The Atlantic Alliance," 1198.

49. Voorhoeve, *Peace, Profits and Principles*, 122 (fn. 4).

50. See Table 3.10.

51. J. H. Lubbers, *Van Overloop naar Overheveling: Mogelijkheden tot vergroting van de Doelmatigheid in het Nederlandse Financiële Defensiebeleid* (From the Impossibility to Plan Financially in Time to Transfers: Opportunities to Increase the Efficiency of Financial Planning in Dutch Defense Policies) (Leiden; Stenfert Kroese, 1962), chap. 2; *Defensienota 1954* (Defense Memorandum 1954) (The Hague: Ministry of Defense, 1954), 89.

52. See Table 3.3.

53. NIPO Poll, no. 1244.

54. Reported in Philip P. Everts, "Wat vinden 'de mensen in het land'? Openbare mening en kernwapens," *Acta Politica*, 3 (1981): 327.

55. Instituut voor Sociaal-wetenschappelijk en Economisch Onderzoek (ISEO).

56. Reported in Philip P. Everts, *Acta Politica*, 4 (1982): 531.

57. Ibid., 528; see also *Elseviers Magazine,* 22 October 1983.
58. Reported in Everts, *Acta Politica,* 4 (1982): 528.
59. Ibid., 498.
60. NIPO Poll no. 1508.
61. USICA data reported in Everts, *Acta Politica,* 4 (1982): 499.
62. Reported in Everts, *Acta Politica,* 4 (1982): 516.
63. Ibid., 517.
64. Ibid., 519.
65. KRO Broadcasting company, 1981.
66. AVRO Broadcasting company, 1981.
67. J. G. Siccama, ed. *Wapens in de Peiling: Opinie Onderzoek over Internationale Veilijheid* (The Hague: Staatsuitgeverij, 1984).
68. KRO Broadcasting company, 1981.
69. NIPO. Cf. *Elseviers Magazine,* 4 December 1982 and 22 October 1983.
70. A. Lijphart, *The Politics of Accommodation: Pluralism and Democracy in the Netherlands* (Berkeley: University of California, 1975).
71. For an analysis, see J. Th. J. van den Berg and H. A. A. Molleman, *Crisis in de Nederlandse Politiek* (Crisis in Dutch Politics) (Alphen aan den Rijn: Samson, 1974).
72. Incidentally, it should be noted that the church leaders responsible for these viewpoints are much more "progressive" than average church members, and that their viewpoints regarding peace movements are supported more widely by nonreligious people than by people belonging to a church. For a discussion of this phenomenon, see Ph. P. Everts, "Kerken, kerkelijkheid en buitenlandse politiek" (Churches, Religiousness and Foreign Policy), in P. R. Baehr et al., *Elite & buitenlandse politiek in Nederland* (Elite and Foreign Policy in the Netherlands) (The Hague: Staatsuitgeverij, 1978), 197–226. See also Table 3.6.
73. Domke, *Compromise, Consensus and Populism.*
74. J. G. Siccama and O. Schmidt, *Hoe dachten de Nederlanders werkelijk over de kernwapens?* (How Did the Dutch Really Feel about Nuclear Weapons?) (The Hague: Netherlands Institute for Questions on Peace and Security, 1981).
75. Ibid.
76. Interview in *NRC-Handelsblad* 6 November 1982.
77. E. Weede, *Weltpolitik und Kriegsursachen in 20. Jahrhundert: Eine quantitativ-empirische Studie* (München: Oldenbourg Verlag, 1975).
78. Reported in Everts, *Acta Politica,* 4 (1982): 499–500.
79. H. W. Houweling and J. G. Siccama, "Vijfenzestig jaar defensieuitgaven in Nederland" (Sixty-Five Years of Defense Expenditures in the Netherlands), *Vredesopbouw,* 13, no. 5/6 (May/June 1976): 23–25.
80. Computation based on figures provided by the Central Planning Bureau. For the whole time-series since 1949, see J . G. Siccama, "De defensiebegroting tussen 1945 en nu" (The Defense Budget Between 1945 and Now), in *De Prijs van Defensie* (The Hague: Foundation Society and the Armed Forces, 1983).
81. Figures provided to the author by the Ministry of Defense. See also Siccama, "De defensiebegroting tussen 1945 en nu."
82. Commission of Civil and Military Experts, *De Toekomst van de Nederlandse Defensie* (The Hague: Staatsuitgeverij, 1972). For a summary in English, see H. J. Neuman, "The Future of Dutch Defense," *Survival,* 14, no. 6 (November/December 1972): 293–300.
83. The title of the text published in English is *Our Very Existence at Stake* (The Hague: Ministery of Defense, 1974).
84. N. Choucri, "In Search of Peace Systems: Scandinavia and the Netherlands 1870–1970," in *Peace, War and Numbers,* ed. B. M. Russett (Beverly Hills and London: Sage, 1972), 239–74.
85. On 3 June 1983 Jan van Houwelingen, State Secretary of Defense for Material, announced that "the armed forces cannot be maintained in their present quantity." See *De Prijs van Defensie,* 6.
86. Based on data in successive SIPRI Yearbooks.

87. *International Herald Tribune,* 7 June 1982.

88. Proceedings, Second Chamber, 26 August 1976.

89. Ministry of Foreign Affairs, *Ontwapening en Veiligheid* (Disarmament and Security) (The Hague: 1975).

90. Charles Osgood, *An Alternative to War or Surrender* (Urbana: University of Illinois Press, 1962).

91. In addition, 6 percent of the demonstrators had voted D'66 in May 1981 and 20 percent had voted Labor Party; 22 percent had no party preference. See *De 21 november demonstranten* (The Demonstrators of November 21) (Nijmegen: Center for Peace Studies, 1983), 45.

92. Preliminary reports on a followup questionnaire among the 29 October (1982) demonstrators by the University of Nijmegen.

93. *Oorlogsverwachting en Overlevingskans* (Expectation That a War Will Break Out and the Likelihood to Survive) (The Hague: Netherlands Institute for Questions of Peace and Security, 1978).

94. USICA data reported in Everts, *Acta Politica,* 4 (1982): 511.

95. Interview in *NRC Handelsblad,* 14 April 1984.

96. J. H. Leurdijk, "De buitenlands-politieke elite en het veiligheidsbeleid van Nederland" (The Foreign Policy Elite and Dutch Security Policy), in Baehr et al., *Elite & buitenlandse politiek in Nederland,* 37.

97. Scientific Council for Government Policy, *Onder invloed van Duitsland* (The German Factor) (The Hague: Staatsuitgeverij, 1982), 143.

98. J. G. Siccama and S. Rozemond, *Evenwicht van de kwetsbaarheid* (Equilibrium in Vulnerability) (The Hague: Netherlands Institute for Questions on Peace and Security, 1982).

99. McGeorge Bundy, George F. Kennan, Robert S. McNamara, and Gerard Smith, "Nuclear Weapons and the Atlantic Alliance," in *Foreign Affairs,* 60, no. 4 (Spring 1982): 753-68.

4

Norwegian Security Policy: Defense and Nonprovocation in a Changing Context

ARNE OLAV BRUNDTLAND

Lessons of Neutrality

The history of independent Norwegian foreign and security policy is not very long. National responsibility for foreign policy came only when the union with Sweden ended in 1905. During the first years of independence there was a strong preference to keep the lowest possible foreign policy profile in order to avoid international entanglements. This was summed up in the famous slogan of the first Foreign Minister, Jørgen Lovland, when he said, "The best foreign policy is to have none."[1] The first attempt to achieve this desired profile was an examination of the conditions necessary for guarantees of Norwegian integrity by the great powers. This effort resulted in the Act of Integrity of 1907, in which Britain, France, Germany, and Russia promised to respect and uphold Norway's territorial integrity, while Norway pledged not to relinquish any part of its territory to any foreign powers. This policy, however, was soon to change.

Norway's break with Sweden in 1905 was made largely because of the conflict over the organization of the consular service. This was a critical foreign-policy matter for Norway because key national economic interests were at stake. Norway had become a nation whose well-being was greatly determined by its international shipping and, to a lesser extent, by its trade. Consequently, the Norwegian economy had developed in a distinctly different direction from the Swedish economy, which was much more protectionist.

Norwegian commercial interests could be satisfied only within an international system of free trade. Such a system could be upheld only by the great powers, of which the most important from the Norwegian perspective was Great Britain. Yet at the same time, Norway's dedication to neutrality was so strong that the importance of the British link could not be stated in public without provoking serious political criticism.[2]

Norway's union with Sweden dissolved without war. Bilateral arms-control agreements proved to be an integral part of the dissolution. These agreements helped reduce the level of bitterness that might have resulted from the separation, and they eased the way for Norway, Sweden, and Denmark to adopt common policies of neutrality during World War I. Foreign policy during the war nevertheless had to consider the expectations and demands of the warfaring parties. Two factors—the gradual German demise and the Norwegian dependence on a British-dominated sea—led Norway to adopt a more pro-British attitude. Norway became what historian Olav Riste has termed "the neutral ally."[3] The war never expanded to threaten Norwegian territorial integrity, and the British sealing off of the German Hochseeflotte guaranteed Norwegian independence. In its wake, Norway was to ignore the risk that hostility among great powers could ever affect its independence.

During the interwar period Norway believed that it had no enemies, for the country was not involved with any power in a political conflict that could be solved by military means.[4] Its geographical remoteness from Europe was taken as a guarantee for peace. Thus, in political circles it was widely believed that military means as an instrument of Norwegian national security policy were unnecessary. In 1933, the year that Hitler seized power in Germany, Norway even adopted a new defense plan that further reduced its armed forces. Only immediately before the German attack on Norway on 9 April 1940 did the Norwegian Parliament finally approve substantial sums for defense.

Norway was a member of the League of Nations. When tensions rose in the 1930s, however, the government sought release from the obligations under Article 16 of the League's Convenant. During this period the alternative of a Scandinavian defense arrangement was considered: Finland feared the Soviet Union; Denmark feared Germany; Sweden could not make up its mind which of the two it feared most; but Norway feared none and was not willing to consider any such arrangement. Attempts to create Nordic defense arrangements never managed to enlist Norwegian support simply because of Norway's unique geographical position.

Nevertheless, when tensions continued to increase, Foreign Minister Halvdan Koht stated publicly that Norway, while adhering to its policy of neutrality, was determined not to end up on the wrong side if hostilities did break out. Geographically isolated, Norway gambled on British interest in preventing Germany from acquiring bases in Norway, while assuming that Britain would never need to use Norwegian territory. The Royal Navy was thought to rule the North and Norwegian seas and thus would not require bases on Norwegian territory. But policy makers failed to appreciate sufficiently the development of military technology and new modes of warfare. Above all, they neglected the increasing importance of territory near the sea for basing airpower for naval protection.

Since its independence in 1905, the single most important foreign-policy event for Norway was the German military attack on 9 April 1940. It shattered the Norwegian belief in pursuing national security based on strict neutrality and left a lasting imprint on her security policy. The legacy of 9 April contains three elements. First, Norwegian territory proved too important to major European powers for them to refrain from attempting to occupy it. Second, Norwegian forces proved insufficient to deter or repel such an attempt. Finally, those states naturally allied to Norway acted too late to deter the attack, had insufficient strength to repel it, and withdrew too early to prevent occupation. This legacy influenced the Norwegian postwar-security outlook, both before entry into the Atlantic Pact and in the final decision to become a member of the Alliance.

In the immediate postwar period, national reconstruction became the Norwegian political aim. This was directed, first and foremost, toward civilian redevelopment, but gradually reconstruction of national defense was also undertaken. Norwegian security policy makers understood that their territory could be of interest to belligerents in a new war in Europe. Although the likelihood of such a war was minimal, Norway's geographical position could serve as an invitation for early involvement if an outbreak of hostilities did occur. Norwegian postwar-security thinking also assumed that military assistance would be received from nonattacking great powers whose strategic interests would be jeopardized by aggression against Norway.[5] Time provided the key factor in the attempt to maintain Norwegian neutrality. As long as the risk of attack seemed distant, it did not matter that Norway's own national defense could only be rebuilt slowly. Time would also allow Norway the opportunity to consider more formal alliance arrangements for the future.

The foreign policy of the immediate postwar years was directed toward avoiding anything that would undermine this strategy. The success of the United Nations formed the basic international precondition for Norwegian neutrality. It was reasoned that as long as the great powers could cooperate in the Security Council, Norwegian security would be assured. Norway could concentrate primarily on national economic reconstruction while gradually rebuilding its armed forces, and foreign-policy activities could focus on mediation and bridge building between East and West. It soon became apparent, however, that the hoped-for cooperation among the great powers would not be forthcoming. Consequently, Norway had to reexamine the assumptions underlying its security policy. Mounting East-West tension in 1947–48 graphically demonstrated Norway's geostrategic exposure.

At the beginning of the Cold War in Europe, Norway had three security options: First, it could continue its neutrality while strengthening national defense; second, it could turn to an international-security arrangement on a regional basis in Scandinavia; or third, it could join the countries that were in the process of forming the Western alliance.

Two particular events in 1948 influenced Norwegian thinking: the Communist coup in Czechoslovakia and the Soviet offer to Finland of a friendship treaty.[6] Czechoslovakia was in a sense regarded as the bridge between East and West, since it combined a Western-model multiparty political system with a foreign policy that adapted to Soviet security needs. As long as the Soviet Union was satisfied with this arrangement, tension in Europe was low enough to make bridge building possible. The coup showed that the foundation of bridge building was crumbling.

The Soviet offer to Finland of a friendship treaty demonstrated that the Soviet Union was also dissatisfied with its bilateral relations with Finland and possibly with other Nordic states as well. Helsinki was among the few capitals of warfaring nations that had never been occupied by any foreign power. Finland received its peace treaty in 1947 and the Soviet-dominated allied control commission left Helsinki in the same year. In the postwar years the Finnish Government pursued the "Paasikivi line," a policy of national independence based on avoiding any conflict with Soviet security interests. As a sign of concern for Soviet security needs, President Juho Paasikivi publicly declared that Finland would not allow any state hostile to the Soviet Union to use Finnish territory; attempts to do so would be countered by Finnish armed forces. Without stressing the concept of neutrality, Finland in effect strived to follow such a policy.[7]

The invitation for a friendship treaty on the model of the friendship treaties that the Soviet Union had concluded with several Eastern European states challenged Finnish independence. The offer to Finland was thus interpreted as an attempt to change the international status of Finland. It was also seen as a forerunner to subsequent Soviet offers to Norway.

The events of February 1948 provoked a series of Norwegian responses: First, the Storting voted a dramatic 50-percent increase in the defense budget without regular committee discussion; second, the Cabinet decided to reject categorically any Soviet offers to Norway; third, the government increased military preparedness, including the transfer of naval units to the extreme north; and finally, the Norwegian Government informed its Western friends about the policy and appealed for support.

The international prerequisite for Norwegian neutrality—low-level East-West tension—had disappeared. Norwegian efforts for a more substantial defense posture were undertaken as far as was politically possible under the circumstances of national postwar reconstruction, but the government soon realized that defense-budget increases would endanger reconstruction without providing adequate national protection. The geographical exposure because of the proximity of the Soviet Union led the government to calculate that a new world war could possibly start on Norwegian territory. The task thus became to find a satisfactory international arrangement that would enhance Norwegian security above what could be achieved by strictly national efforts. Membership in the emerging Western alliance was to be the ultimate choice, but not before a Scandinavian defense arrangement had been examined in great detail.

The Scandinavian initiative was Swedish. Sweden had observed the Western orientation of Norway's crisis management following the Soviet offer of a friendship treaty with Finland. As a result, it asked Norway and Denmark for formal consultations in order to prevent Norway from moving into the emerging Western security arrangements. A prime motive in Swedish thinking was to avoid provoking the Soviet Union into further involvement in Finnish politics. To make the Scandinavian option attractive to Norway, Sweden offered defense cooperation, but it did not promise direct protection of its Scandinavian neighbors.

The Soviet-Finnish Treaty of Friendship, Cooperation, and Mutual Assistance had been concluded in Moscow on 6 April 1948 with recognition of the Finnish wish to stay outside any great power controversy, thus defining Finnish neutrality. The terms of the treaty would be applied in the case of aggression against Finland or on the Soviet Union through Finland by Germany or any state allied with Germany. The friendship treaty was a potential military alliance, but it allowed Finland in peacetime to continue to be a sovereign state pursuing independent policies.

Basic Soviet security considerations were satisfied by the friendship treaty. Sweden's problem was to avoid arrangements in the north of Europe that might prompt the Soviets to reassess their security interests in that area. For the Swedes, well-armed neutrality had the perceived virtue of nonprovocation, which contributed to the success of the Paasikivi policy on Finnish-Soviet relations. The Swedish offer for a Scandinavian defense pact was seen as a further consideration to these nonprovocative policies: an attempt to enhance Finnish neutrality and thereby Swedish security by preventing Norway and Denmark from joining the Atlantic Pact.

Swedish thinking reflects Sweden's geopolitical position. Swedish territory was less exposed than Norwegian territory to an early attack from any of the great powers, and Swedish national defense was substantial. The Swedish air force, for instance, was bigger at that time than the French air force. Lacking geographical exposure and having a strong national defense, the Swedish Government decided not to enter into any international agreement that would foreclose the possibility of staying outside a future war in Europe. The Swedish offer for a Scandinavian defense arrangement would compromise the principle of neutrality only with regard to the Nordic area. The Swedish Government was precise about the nature of the arrangement: It should be both formally and practically based on neutrality.

Norwegian thinking differed. Cooperation with larger Swedish forces would have provided a stronger military base for the defense of Norway. But the different geostrategic situation and the relative weakness of Norway's armed forces made Norway seek a stronger basis for national security than that offered by Sweden. Thus, while the Norwegian Government contemplated a Scandinavian arrangement, it wanted to make certain that the arrangement would not only earn Western support but would also be perceived in the West as part of Western security interests. A formalized recognition of this fact would have been incompatible with the Swedish desire for neutrality, but the Norwegian Government wanted the Western powers to give at least strong de facto recognition through arms deliveries.[8]

Norwegian efforts to persuade the British and American governments to support a neutral Scandinavian pact, prior to its establishment, failed. The Americans in particular had placed top priority on the formation of a collective, regional security arrangement that would be supported by an American guarantee and supplied with American weapons and materiel. Little room existed for neutralism and subregionalism in this overall concept.

It is possible that a Scandinavian pact would have been supported in the West if the Swedish Government had adopted the Norwegian approach. But this was out of the question from the Swedish point of view; it would have been tantamount to bringing all of Scandinavia into the Atlantic Alliance. It seemed to the Swedes that this would bring the Soviet Union further into Finland and thus offset the security gain of a Western arrangement. They assumed that the Soviet Union, after having secured the Soviet-Finnish friendship treaty, would oppose any changes in the security policies of the Scandinavian countries.

The breakdown of Scandinavian negotiations came as a result of the disagreement on the nature and political basis of the defense arrangement. In the end, the national-security needs of Sweden and Norway simply were not similar enough to warrant a pact. There were differences in geographical exposure, in historical experience, and in national defense efforts. Sweden was better shielded from early entanglement, was better armed, and consequently was in a better position to wait before asking for foreign help in the case of aggression. The success of Swedish neutrality during World War II made it impossible to consider any arrangement that was not based on the continuation of neutrality.

The breakdown of the Scandinavian defense negotiations in late January 1949 cleared the path for Norway to join the Atlantic Alliance. By going through the Scandinavian deliberations, Norway had demonstrated that there was not a real Scandinavian alternative, thereby preventing subsequent accusations that this possibility had not been examined. In general, it always remains imperative for a Norwegian Government to explore the Scandinavian or Nordic option in order to avoid criticism of policy.[9] Some commentators later maintained that the round of Scandinavian explorations was a routine the Norwegian Government and Labor Party leadership went through in order to pave the way for NATO membership. But the Scandinavian deliberations were, in fact, more important than a tactical maneuver: By having demonstrated that there was no lost opportunity, the government broadened support for Norwegian NATO membership.

Entering into a military alliance with great-power participation in peacetime was a new experience for Norway and a definite break with its historical tradition. During the anti-Hitler coalition from 1940 to 1945, however, there were already some who desired this arrangement.[10] Although the war years initially saw Norway in alliance with Britain, representatives for the Norwegian government-in-exile in London spoke of the prospects for a more enduring Atlantic Alliance with a perspective beyond the war effort. The war experience also left its imprint on Norway's future relationship with the Soviet Union.[11] The image of victorious Soviet armies projecting Russian power westward was not lost on Norwegian Government circles. The Soviet help in liberating northern Norway in 1944–45 demonstrated to Norwegian policy makers the permanence of great-power proximity. Fear of the Soviet Union increased as the ideological and geographical divide between East and West hardened. The introduction of Cold War polemics, especially hostile Soviet propaganda that claimed that Norway was part of a Western plan for an "Arctic strategy" attack on the Soviet Union, widely illustrated that an isolated Norway could not withstand a Soviet threat. These considerations undoubtedly affected Norwegian judgment at the time of alignment.

Just at the moment the Scandinavian negotiations collapsed, the Soviet Union intervened, asking Norway in a diplomatic note for information about the rumored future Norwegian membership in the Atlantic Alliance. The Soviets characterized the Alliance as an aggressive pact directed against the Soviet Union and the socialist states of Eastern Europe. They asked in particular for information regarding the possible establishment of bases for foreign naval and air forces on Norwegian territory. In addition, they proposed a Soviet-Norwegian nonaggression treaty in a bid to help prevent Norwegian membership in the Alliance.[12]

The Norwegian reply was prompt, indicating that it had been thought out well in advance. In its note of February 1949, the Norwegian Government outlined its position on nonbasing, which henceforth became a centerpiece of Norwegian security policy. The government assured the Soviet Union that Norway had only peaceful intentions and that Norwegian territory never would be placed at the service of any hostile policies. It "promised" that no foreign bases would be established in Norway unless Norway was exposed to a military attack or to the threat of such an attack. The Norwegian pledge was thus conditional, making the continued absence of foreign bases on Norwegian territory dependent on Soviet good behavior.

Initially, Norway did not envisage the Atlantic Alliance as a well-developed international organization with an international secretariat, a number of regional military commands, joint strategies, and regular common maneuvers and exercises. The primary purposes of Norwegian membership were to gain protection under a security system based upon deterrence provided by the Western superpower with a monopoly of nuclear weapons, and to obtain deliveries of arms and military equipment under conditions that would not jeopardize civilian reconstruction.

Norwegian national means of defense were insufficient for the period of high international tensions in the late 1940s. At the same time, Norway tried to lessen existing tension by distinct measures of reassurance, such as the restrictions embodied in the nonbasing policy. Political leaders, like Defense Minister Jens Christian Hauge, asserted that the clarity of purpose with which Norway had joined the Alliance actually helped ease international tension. Thus, the two pursuits were not incompatible under prevailing circumstances.

Norway entered the Atlantic Alliance under very particular circumstances. On the one hand, it enjoyed the protection of the American nuclear monopoly and a vast supremacy in naval forces. On the other, by avoiding foreign basing, it lowered tension and enhanced stability in Northern Europe. The nonbasing policy was critical in avoiding domestic strain that Atlantic Alliance membership would otherwise have created. This balance has been a permanent feature of Norwegian Alliance policy ever since.

The Soviet Union also emerged from this period in a favorable position: A friendship treaty was established with Finland; Sweden continued her traditional neutrality on a renewed isolationist basis; and although Norway and Denmark were in NATO, they had distinctly defensive profiles. At the same time, NATO received a clear commitment from Norway and Denmark; a low-tension security guarantee was provided without other members having to be present militarily in that region of the Alliance. The Nordic states had met their security needs without bringing the military power of the West too close to the Soviet Union in the north of Europe.

Moreover, all concerned, in particular the Nordic countries, had learned from the experience of a combined search for security. As Norwegian Prime Minister Einar Gerhardsen stated in Parliament after the breakdown of the Scandinavian negotiations, the Scandinavian countries had nevertheless been brought closer together and had gained new insight into the security problems of each. This understanding has been important in determining security policy in all of the Nordic countries since then. Nordic states have tried to avoid complicating the security position of one another. The stability created has been termed the Nordic Balance. The different possibilities of change checked by a wish for stability is often termed the dynamic Nordic Balance.[13] It is upheld by the determination not to change national-security policies unless strongly provoked and the recognition that security changes made by one Nordic country may prompt corresponding changes by other Nordic states.

Although breaking sharply with past peacetime preferences, Alliance membership received broad domestic political support. The Labor Party national convention voted for Alliance membership with a substantial majority, subsequently leading to near-unanimous support from the Labor Party parliamentary group. The non-Socialists also voted almost unanimously for membership. The small parliamentary opposition came from pacifists and lingering neutralists. Predictably, the Communist Party parliamentary group voted against the bloc.

The public discussion in 1948–49 pitted the Communists against the combined forces of the Labor and the four non-Socialist parties. The public political fighting that occurred was the Labor Government's battle against the influence of the Norwegian Communist party, whose representatives numbered 11 out of a total of 150 members of Parliament. Until this time the Communists were regular members of the Foreign Relations Committee in the Storting. But the Communists' defense of the coup in Czechoslovakia was interpreted as support for a Soviet takeover of neighboring states and a direct danger for Norway. The Storting thus established a special committee for security affairs that excluded the Communists from participation. The sharp confrontation between the Communist Party, which supported Soviet policy lines, and the Labor Party and non-Socialists, who rejected them, was disastrous for the Communist Party in the 1949 Storting elections. The Communist Party was never again represented in the Storting by more than one member. The entering into the Alliance thus caused the eradication of the far left from the Norwegian political spectrum.

Popular support for entry into the Alliance was, overall, as broad as the elite support. Nevertheless, Labor Party leaders had to work hard to persuade some rank and file of the necessity of a Western alliance and Norwegian membership, and opposition to NATO continued, particularly in the trade unions, where the fight between Labor and Communists lasted for some years. The party leadership's view prevailed, however, The government enjoyed a majority and could also count on support from the non-Socialist opposition. If needed, the intraparty opposition could be presented with *faits accomplis*.

Norwegian entrance into the Atlantic Alliance came about very much as a consequence of elites appraising the risks of the international situation and leading the country into this new security arrangement. But comprehension of the way in which this occurred is critical to understanding Norwegian policy within the Alliance. Norwegian sensitivity to the Nordic aspects of Norway's security could not be ignored. Deterrence through NATO membership was from the outset counterbalanced by reassurance of peaceful intentions through the no-foreign-basing policy. The compromise was clear: Defense concerns were met by NATO membership, and the Norwegian neutralist tradition was embodied in the nonbasing policy. The nonbasing option was, moreover, particularly important for the acceptance of NATO membership by the Labor Party because it helped to give the security profile a distinctly defensive image. This was the precondition for the broad consensus with which Norway entered the Alliance, and it has remained a major influence on the maintenance of that consensus over the years.

The Practice of Alignment

Membership in the Alliance formed the central platform for postwar Norwegian participation in international politics. Membership also created a new basis for Norwegian relations with the Soviet Union. Seen as a guarantee against possible aggression, it instilled self-confidence in Norway. The Soviets, however, argued that the Alliance served the purpose of planning war against the socialist states. At times, this propaganda presented an unpleasant burden for Norwegians. Although no prominent policy maker would acknowledge it, Norwegian security had been achieved at the price of a higher level of international tension. The challenge of continuously, and perhaps indefinitely, having to pursue security politics in such a hostile environment was not easily accepted. Yet it was clear that security could no longer be obtained by aloofness and dissociation.

During the first three decades of NATO membership, Norway had to adjust to a multitude of changing circumstances, but the basic orientations that came with the choice of NATO membership—a substantial national defense effort and a continuous struggle to find moderate, broadly supported policies—continued to be central to Norwegian policy. Political consensus supporting this two-pronged approach to security remained as broad as when the basic orientation was established in the late 1940s.

Naturally, changes in the international scene were felt in the country, but both nationally and internationally Norway stood for moderation. It had no international demands and experienced no problems that could not be solved by mediation. It was largely a status-quo country. Rising international tensions provided stronger support for the Alliance and national-defense spending, while any international relaxation of tensions was of course welcomed. Norwegian policy makers, however, never saw NATO and Norwegian membership as an end in itself. It was a means to an end, that end being security. A long-term objective was to help create international conditions that would obviate the need for military alliances. Hopes of relaxation of international tensions have always been nurtured by many, with the desire for an eventual relaxation also in the defense effort. But in trying to help bring such conditions about, Norway never took initiatives at the expense of NATO solidarity. Norway has always stressed the need to pursue efforts through NATO, and not outside it.

The Politics of Defense

Compared to the three other countries under study in this book, Norway is the odd man out because of its direct proximity to the Soviet Union. The perception of threats that derive from this position, combined with the degree of "independence" within NATO because of the nonbasing policy, has helped give Norwegian defense and security policy a raison d'être that has been widely understood and accepted. A free ride on Allied policy is no option for a country thus located geographically.

Neither the entry into NATO, nor the adaptation to NATO policies, have been free of problems. However, the framework of debate and disagreement during the first thirty years of alignment was well-defined and carefully circumscribed. Differences of opinion over the balance between defense and nonprovocation, while real, were seldom a matter of major political import. It is instructive nevertheless to look briefly at how the political system dealt with major defense issues during the period up to the late 1970s, if only to provide a point of comparison with what transpired thereafter.

Norwegian political parties have tried to maintain the broadest possible national consensus in security affairs. By and large they have succeeded. This success does not mean, however, that there has been no discussion or that consensus has always come easily. Opposition has been marked both by the left wing of the Labor Party and, since 1960, by the Left Socialists, who are, in principle, against NATO membership. Yet it is only recently that signs have emerged of a breakdown in the broad national consensus. This collapse, however, is primarily related to nuclear strategy and arms-control approaches, which will be discussed later.

Security policy decisions were almost exclusively a problem for the Labor Party during the period in which it enjoyed an absolute majority in Norwegian national politics. Although the party managed to conceal disagreement from the public, the internal struggle was considerable.[14] The most visible sign of discontent and opposition within the Labor Party parliamentary group was the 1958 "Easter Revolt," when more than half of the group signed a petition to protest any Norwegian support of a possible introduction of nuclear weapons to the armed forces of the Federal Republic of Germany. The debate over security issues influenced, perhaps decisively, such events as the stepping down of Prime Minister Einar Gerhardsen in 1953 and his return to power in 1955 after a short period, during which his successor, Oscar Torp, had given a higher profile to military issues. In retrospect, it is evident that Mr. Gerhardsen was the only Labor Party leader during the postwar period who managed to keep the party reasonably united behind the new security approach. But even he suffered opposition from the left, which ultimately led to the exclusion of the "Orientering" group. As a consequence, Labor lost its majority in the election of 1961, never to be reestablished.

The splinter group had organized itself as the Socialist Peoples Party in 1960. Two principles guided the new party: opposition to NATO membership and a request for "more socialism." Both in its original form in the 1960s as well as its reorganized form, the Sosialistisk Venstreparti (Socialistic Left Party), it did its utmost to influence the left wing of the Labor Party.

The minority Labor government of the parliamentary period following the 1961 elections could still rely on solid support for its NATO approach because of the four non-Socialist opposition parties: Hoyre (Conservative), Kristelig Folkeparti (Christian Peoples Party), Bondepartiet/Senterpartiet (Farmers' Party, since 1959 the Center Party), and Venstre (Liberals). In security affairs, the fault line divided the Storting into two unequal parts: the two members of the Socialist Peoples Party on one side and the combined 148 representatives of the five other parties on the other. As long as the Labor Party leadership could maintain party discipline, there were no parliamentary conflicts.

The nuances of Norwegian security policy under the Labor government were determined without any serious consultation with the non-Socialist opposition. Prominent political figures among the four opposition parties did criticize Labor's softness on particular security matters, but their parties never chose to challenge the government's policies. The Conservative Party, which portrayed itself as the most ardent supporter of NATO membership and solid defense spending, left security policy to the Labor Party leadership in order to help avoid provocation of and protest by left-wing opposition.[15] Both Conservative skepticism that the nonbasing policy lacked military logic and their greater willingness to accept nuclear weapons on Norwegian territory were thus kept in check by the desire not to disrupt the broad consensus.

Between 1965 and 1971, the period of non-Socialist coalition majority rule, the government also experienced internal opposition to its security policy. Officials within the Liberal Party voiced concern about certain consequences of NATO membership, and the leaders of the coalition, particularly Conservative Foreign Minister John Lyng, decided not to challenge the Liberals unduly. Under the coalition Norway delayed, for instance, before joining the Nuclear Planning Group in order to convince critics that joining this group would not constitute a violation of the nonstorage policy or alter its low nuclear profile.[16] The non-Socialists were not without their own problems when it came to constituting broad-based support for NATO policies.

The two competing groups in Norwegian politics have thus had similar problems. When in power, they have shown a preference for achieving the broadest possible consensus. The strategy of both was to avoid unnecessary confrontations between the government and party dissidents. They also avoided attempts at linking the "right wings" of the party with that of the alternative.

For most of the 1970s, Norway was ruled by a minority Labor government. Except for the 1971–72 debate on EEC membership, foreign policy and security issues seldom represented a major focus of concern. The only other significant point of political contention came with the split over the "gray zone" agreement with the Soviet Union in 1977–78. Essentially, broad consensus continued until the INF question.

Thus, three decades of Norwegian NATO membership witnessed broad political support both for membership and for national defense. Part of the basis for this broad support was the policy of moderation practiced by consecutive governments. The absence of major political conflict also produced public support for defense and the Alliance. Public-opinion polls taken over the years demonstrate the existence of this broad consensus.

Several polls reveal that there did exist strong public support for the development of Norwegian defense forces in the immediate postwar period.[17] In 1946, 69 percent of those questioned responded favorably to "a strong defense." Support among followers of the non-Socialist parties was higher than among Labor Party supporters, while even the Communists gave relatively strong backing to the idea; 90 percent of Conservative supporters answered in the affirmative, while those of the Center and Liberal parties followed with 78 percent and 74 percent, respectively. The Christians registered 67 percent, while 60 percent of Labor supported a "strong" defense; 44 percent of the Communists were in favor while 52 percent opposed.

In 1948 Norwegians were asked if the country should join a great power bloc; 61 percent answered yes, and 69 percent answered that Norway would likely have to join a great power bloc. Conservatives had the highest numbers willing to join, registering 82 percent, followed by the Center (77 percent), Liberals (72 percent), and Christians (68 percent). A majority of Labor sympathizers (51 percent) indicated willingness to join, while 47 percent objected. This poll was taken before the Scandinavian deliberations started (6 percent answered that Norway should join a Scandinavian bloc).

In July 1949, after having joined the Atlantic Alliance, a majority (56 percent) felt that the risk of a major war had decreased and (54 percent) that Norway's security had increased. Predictably, the non-Socialist sympathizers showed a higher score than Labor sympathizers, but there was also a majority among the latter group.

Systematic opinion polls were not taken until the end of the 1960s, but a series administered by the organization Folk og Forsvar (People and Defense) demonstrates a broad consistency in popular attitudes toward defense and the Alliance since then. The results of these studies are presented in Tables 4.1 and 4.2.

In Table 4.1, one is struck by the high and growing belief in the

Table 4.1   The Need for Military Defense

Total Percent	1969	1971	1973	1974	1975	1976	1977	1978	1979	1980	1981	1982
Yes	75	77	75	79	75	79	79	79	84	86	80	86
No	10	9	10	7	6	5	7	6	6	4	6	6
Undecided	8	8	8	9	11	9	8	10	7	5	6	3
No opinion	7	6	7	5	8	8	7	5	4	6	8	5
Total	100	100	100	100	100	100	100	100	100	100	100	100
Persons asked	1633	1638	1635	1593	1659	1599	1675	1657	1709	1437	1376	1404

Question: Do you think that Norway should have a military defense in the present situation?

Source: Kontakt Bulletin Folk og Forsvar, no. 5 (May/June 1982).

Table 4.2 Support for NATO Membership

	1965	1966	1967	Sept.[a] 1968	1969	1970	1971	1972	1973	1974	1975	1976	1977	1978	1979	Jan.[a] 1980	1980	1981	1982
Contributes to security	55	53	49	65	61	62	56	58	64	61	62	65	62	64	62	66	60	64	65
Increases danger	11	11	12	7	10	9	8	7	6	5	7	6	6	8	10	7	14	10	10
No role	22	23	24	11	11	12	16	17	17	17	14	11	12	10	10	11	10	10	12
Don't know	12	13	15	17	18	17	19	13	18	17	19	18	19	20	18	16	15	17	13
Total	100	100	100	100	100	100	100	100	100	100	100	100	100	100	100	100	100	100	100
Persons asked	2150	1628	1624	1618	1628	1630	1627	1632	2101	1574	1649	1515	1607	1614	1520	1519	1499	1348	1367

Question: Do you think that Norwegian membership in the Western Defense alliance NATO contributes to the security of the country against attack by a foreign power, or do you think that our membership in NATO increases the danger of attack, or do you think that our NATO membership plays no role in these matters?

[a]The polls are taken in the month of November each year. Extra polls were taken in September 1968 following the invasion of Czechoslovakia and in January 1980 following the invasion of Afghanistan.

Source: Folk og Forsvar
Kontakt Bulletin, no. 1 (January 1983) and no. 1 (January 1975) and Holst II, 246–47.

necessity of defense. The high level of affirmative responses remains relatively consistent throughout the Norwegian political spectrum. Conservative and Center Party followers supported defense most strongly— 97 percent in 1982. Labor and the Christian Peoples Party followers reflected more moderate opinion (86 and 87 percent, respectively, in 1982). The Left Socialists evinced wider variations in opinion, but support for Norway's defense in recent years has been as high as 72 percent (1980), 64 percent (1981), and 63 percent (1982).

As seen in Table 4.2, public support for Norwegian NATO membership is smaller than support for general defense. Nevertheless, the table indicates solid support for NATO. Since the late 1960s, the backing has exceeded 50 percent. Once again, Conservative followers represent the strongest advocates of the Alliance. The Christians and the Center followers need to be grouped on a slightly lower level, while Labor followers, although the majority believed that NATO contributed to security, demonstrated less enthusiasm. Not surprisingly, the Left Socialists showed little support for NATO.

Thus, public opinion concerning NATO and Norwegian defense corresponds to the political elite attitudes. But while general approval remains high, there are times when considerable apprehension exists. Norwegian sensitivity to international politics can be detected in the number of applications made for nonmilitary service as an alternative to regular military service. In 1950, 2.1 percent applied for nonmilitary service. Just one year later, the figure increased sharply to 6 percent. Conscripts cited conscientious objection to military service because Norway's most important ally was engaged in the Korean War. The following years witnessed a gradual decline, and by 1964 only 1.1 percent asked to be exempted. However, a new height was reached in the early 1970s. In 1970 the yearly figure was 3.9 percent, but by 1974 the figure had escalated to 8.2 percent. Hereafter, the figures slowly decreased, reaching 5.9 percent in 1978. The impact of the Vietnam War dictated these trends. But it should also be added that resisters of military service have been much better organized since the end of the 1960s. This fact might explain why, after the turmoil of the 1970s subsided, the number of applications for nonmilitary service remained higher compared to the post-Korean period. In 1979 the figures again rose above 7 percent. By 1982 the figure reached 7.9 percent. The impact of sharpened international tension and the awareness of dilemmas over nuclear weapons undoubtedly influenced these figures. In the future, acceptance as a conscientious objector may be easier to obtain, since both the Christian Peoples and Labor parties are considering the notion that serious political motivation is sufficient justification for alternative service.

Defense and Deterrence

An important argument supporting Norwegian membership in the Atlantic Alliance revolved around economics. Norway did not have the means to create a national defense sufficient to deter or to thwart a great-power attack. The 1948 policy to increase the defense budget as a response to increased security threats could not be continued without jeopardizing the vitally important policy of national reconstruction. There was also the problem of foreign currency and the Western policy of giving priority to military hardware deliveries to countries willing to join the collective security scheme of the North Atlantic pact. Norwegian authorities opted for a policy of reconstruction and further development of defense on terms that could be achieved within the limits of the Norwegian economy.

Entry into NATO was partly justified by the argument that by benefiting from pooled NATO resources, Norway would be able to make do with a smaller defense budget. Norway would become a net importer of assistance to equip its armed forces, both with regard to military materiel and to various installations under the NATO infrastructure program. If Norway had chosen neutrality, both would have had to have been provided on a national basis. It was argued that if Norway remained neutral, like Sweden, it would have to spend as much as Sweden on defense. While Norway spent about 3 percent of its GNP on defense in the 1950s and 1960s, Sweden spend 4.5–5 percent. It must be admitted, however, that this argument was weakened when in the 1970s Sweden gradually lowered its spending toward the 3-percent mark.

Norwegian supporters of NATO argued that membership made Norwegian defense policy realistic. For Norwegian politicians, so long as Norway was spending as much as was economically possible, Alliance membership was not seen as an economic bargain, but rather as a political arrangement that provided security and infused a sense of realism into national spending.

During the first half of the 1950s the Norwegian defense budget continued to grow, as it did in most NATO countries. Opponents argued that the economic benefits of Alliance membership had been exaggerated. The standard argument against this complaint was that increased defense spending resulted not from Alliance membership, but rather as a consequence of the international climate and the increased risk of war. Nonetheless, Norwegian defense policy, which absorbed increasingly larger amounts of the national budget and which continually demanded justification, strained both political consensus and economic resources. The political strain, particularly acute within the Labor Party, helped provoke the change of prime minister in 1953. Nevertheless, high defense spending continued and may have contributed to the further change of prime minister in 1955. Public perceptions of overspending and waste in the armed forces heavily influenced the political debate. It appeared that Norway would have to accept a relative decline in defense expenditure during the second half of the 1950s.

The reversal of the defense-spending trends in the mid-1950s was only temporary. In the latter part of the 1950s defense spending again increased. In real terms the Norwegian defense budget absorbed 3.4

percent of the GNP almost every year from 1957 to 1972, as illustrated in Table 4.3. From 1972 to the present, allocation has oscillated between 2.9 and 3.2 percent. In real terms the budget has more than doubled from 1956 to 1983. The system of rolling defense five-year plans introduced in the 1960s has helped stabilize annual defense budgets.

Demands to increase defense spending beyond government proposals were rebuffed with arguments that because of NATO membership excessive spending was unnecessary. The logic was that Norwegian defense should be seen as part of a larger alliance framework. For example, the government countered opposition claims in the first half of the 1950s for a more substantial investment in the royal navy with repeated references to the new situation created by Norwegian NATO membership. In the first half of the 1960s the Labor government attempted to fix Norwegian defense outlays to a particular percentage of the state budget. This policy, however, was not accepted by the Storting because Labor desired to be free to enlarge public-sector spending without a concurrent increase in defense spending.

Defense allocation, which for many years represented the biggest share of the state budget, gradually gave way to other policy areas—social security, communications, and education. The share of the state budget for the ministries responsible for these three fields of policy were all less in 1965 than the defense budget, but they were higher in 1983. In 1965 defense absorbed 1.9 billion, while health took 1.2, education 1.3, and communications 1.8. The corresponding figures in 1983 were 12 billion on defense, 17.8 on health, 13 on education, and 14.2 on communications. While the defense allocation represented 16.4 percent of the state budget in 1965, it had shrunk to 8.2 percent in 1983.[18]

These trends reveal the economic and social preferences of Norway. Because of its particular geographic position, Norway demands considerable financial capital to operate. The government has steadily enlarged the public sector. Roughly 50 percent of the GNP is now channeled through public budgets. Population patterns of the country also make it imperative to maintain high public spending in order to give incentives to maintain population in the more distant parts of the country. If, for example, the county of Finnmark was seriously depopulated, it would create a major defense problem, since mobilization would become considerably more complicated. Thus, money channeled to Finnmark in the civilian sectors might "buy" a better security policy because the advantages to be gained from helping to keep people from moving would be greater than the corresponding sums spent for defense in the area.

As far as manpower is concerned, Norway has remained faithful to the principle of general conscription that was embodied in the 1814 constitution. The length of service has varied between twelve and eighteen months, despite the NATO recommendation for twenty-four months' service. Conscription represents one area where the Labor Party leadership adopted a more moderate line than it did on defense spending. Approximately 69 percent of those called up fulfill their duty.

Table 4.3 Defense Spending in Norway (in millions of Kroner)

Year	Current defense spending	Defense spending as % of GNP
1945	215	
1946	406	
1947	296	
1948	252	
1949	220	
1950	259	1.7
1951	292	1.6
1952	424	2.0
1953	581	2.8
1954	649	2.8
1955	702	2.9
1956	771	2.8
1957	826	2.8
1958	938	3.2
1959	1,119	3.6
1960	1,189	3.6
1961	1,220	3.4
1962	1,448	3.7
1963	1,522	3.7
1964	1,719	3.8
1965	1,912	3.8
1966	2,010	3.7
1967	2,256	3.8
1968	2,420	3.8
1969	2,551	3.7
1970	2,750	3.4
1971	2,994	3.4
1972	3,203	3.3
1973	3,503	3.1
1974	3,960	3.1
1975	4,762	3.2
1976	5,304	3.1
1977	5,948	3.1
1978	6,830	3.2
1979	7,628	3.2
1980	8,383	2.9
1981	9,634	2.9
1982	11,037	3.0
1983	12,450	3.1
1984	12,673	2.9
1985	14,327	3.0

Source: Royal Norwegian Ministry of Defense (on request, 1985).

Nonprovocation: A Key Policy Ingredient

The indispensable counterpart of maintaining a strong defense, indeed the prerequisite for maintaining support for that effort, has been the careful practice of nonprovocation as the twin pillar of Norwegian security policy. The nonbasing declaration was the first step in this practice, but in fact it had been an integral part of Norwegian policy throughout the postwar period. Its importance and the forms it has taken can be illustrated by examining four specific policy areas: the implementation of the nonbasing decision; the decision to rearm and integrate Germany into NATO; the conduct of Norway's "Northern policy"; and the nuclear controversy of the late 1950 and early 1960s.

NONBASING POLICY IN PRACTICE. For many, the nonbasing policy represented first and foremost a concession to public opinion in order to facilitate Norway's entry into NATO. But political leaders never lost sight of the fact that nonbasing appeared to mute Soviet reactions to Norwegian membership and served to relax tensions in the whole of Northern Europe. Whatever the reasons for its origins, nonbasing has evolved into an important instrument of foreign and security policy in Norway.

When Norway joined NATO in 1949, the Alliance was a general security guarantee. At that point a development of military integration was not foreseen. Yet within little more than a year perceptions changed dramatically. If the coup in Czechoslovakia provoked the Atlantic pact, one could say that the Communist attack on South Korea in June 1950 provoked the "O" of NATO; namely, the establishment of its international organization and joint headquarters. These developments provided the first need to clarify the nonbasing policy.

In 1951 the Norwegian Defense Minister made an important speech on national security in the Storting. In this statement he declared that the Norwegian nonbasing policy represented no obstacle to: (1) preparation for reception of Allied forces in times of need; (2) entering into agreements to provide for such an emergency; (3) joint exercises and thereby short-time stopovers of Allied forces on Norwegian territory for training purposes; and (4) the establishment of Allied military headquarters on Norwegian soil.[19] Later, it was similarly made clear that the nonbasing policy was no obstacle to the establishment of depots for Allied forces on Norwegian territory in peacetime. These depots could belong to other NATO members, but they would in peacetime always remain under Norwegian maintenance and protection. The government made it clear that a depot was distinctly different from a base.

This example illustrates the effective approach used by the Norwegian Government with regard to the nonbasing policy. The government has never stated explicitly the positive and exclusive content of the policy apart from using the original phrases. Rather, it has stated at appropriate times what would not be hindered under the nonbasing policy. It has always been stressed that the nonbasing policy was a Norwegian policy, defined and exercised by the Norwegian Government, and not something under the control of foreign powers. At no point was the government willing to allow the nonbasing policy to hinder adequate defense preparation.

The nonbasing pledge to the Soviet Union in 1949 was made conditional by the clause: "unless Norway is attacked or under the threat of attack." Attack is easy to interpret as compared with "threat of attack." The Soviets have tried to interpret the Norwegian nonbasing policy as strictly as possible in order to constrain Norwegian freedom of action.[20] The Soviets also have tried to make the Norwegian nonbasing policy a matter of bilateral negotiations, based on the fact that it originally was proclaimed in a diplomatic note to the Soviet Union. Repeated Soviet attempts to negotiate with the Norwegian Government about a further definition of the nonbasing policy have always been rejected. Norway has been willing to explain to the Soviets the significance of the policy, but it has never been willing to give them any negotiating position with respect to it.

A prolonged series of Soviet criticisms of Norwegian security policies during the aftermath of the U-2 incident in May 1960 provoked more explicit use of the nonbasing policy as an instrument of influence. The Foreign Minister, in October 1960, told the Storting that such attacks from the Soviet Union would make it much more difficult for the Norwegian Government, vis-à-vis its own population, to pursue consistently its nonbasing policy. Such a policy, the Minister stated, had been determined with due regard to the security interests of Norway's neighbors.[21] The Soviet Union ceased its charges and relations returned to normal.

Nonbasing has also been used most effectively by the Norwegians as a tool for helping to maintain a Nordic Balance since the signing of the Finnish-Soviet friendship treaty. The concept is one by which the Nordic countries seek to maintain their security on the basis of the status quo. On the one hand, Finland has based its security policy on the principle of neutrality while being a partner in the Soviet-Finnish friendship treaty. Norway and Denmark, on the other hand, have based their security on NATO membership while refusing Allied reinforcements unless attacked or under the threat of attack, to use the Norwegian phrasing. Finnish neutrality is one of the preconditions for Norwegian and Danish nonbasing. Changes in either the nonbasing policy or Finnish neutrality are thus mutually held in check in order to preserve the balance of the status quo.

The "note crisis" of 1961 highlighted the Nordic Balance concept and the role of the nonbasing policy as an instrument of Norwegian policy. The Soviet Union sent a diplomatic note to Finland requesting consultations under Article II of their Treaty of Friendship, Cooperation, and Mutual Assistance. Norway responded by indicating possible revision of the nonbasing policy. Soviet-Finnish consultations never occurred. Finnish President Kekkonen persuaded Nikita Khrushchev that commencement of consultations could stimulate "war psychosis in Norway and Denmark which are members of NATO," while postponement "would be instrumental to calm public opinion in Scandinavia and would lead to a reduction in the need for military preparation not only in Finland and Sweden, but also in Norway and Denmark which are members of NATO."[22] This was a successful policy move because it helped to maintain the status quo in the Nordic region.[23] The outcome of the 1961 note crisis reflected the impact of a warning about a possible change in the Norwegian—and presumably Danish—policy. This crisis represents a classic example of how the Nordic Balance functions.

However, such pressure can work in more than one direction. Changes in Norwegian and Danish policies, which were motivated by perceived challenges unconnected with Finland, could bring forth additional Soviet pressure on Helsinki. As will be seen in the next section, the lifting of restrictions on German participation in maneuvers on Norwegian territory could be used by the Soviet Union as an excuse to pressure Finnish neutrality. Thus, the Nordic Balance functions as a two-edged sword. The fact that the Soviets cited increased German military influence in Norway and Denmark, and the preparations for a joint German-Danish military command within NATO's northern headquarters, in the note of 1961 further illustrates this point.

Nonetheless, the conditions of the nonbasing policy have made it an important instrument for influencing international behavior. It has been criticized for being a policy of weakness, representing a military risk. While this opinion is understandable from a military point of view, insofar as the policy represents an obstacle to peacetime military deployment in remote areas that are difficult to defend, the benefits that have accrued from threatening to change the policy, especially in the U-2 and Finnish note crises, have been considerable. Also, in order to reduce the strategic vulnerability inherent in the nonbasing policy, the Norwegian Government put new emphasis, in the late 1970s, on the policy of prepositioning of heavy equipment for Allied forces on Norwegian territory in peacetime. Prepositioning lessened dependence on shipping lines vulnerable in war and represents a precondition for establishing an effective fighting force by means of swift air transport of personnel. Thus, it remains likely that nonbasing will continue to play a distinct role in the Norwegian practice of security by nonprovocation.

GERMAN REARMAMENT. Among the more difficult challenges to Norway's Alliance profile was the question of West German "rearmament" and integration into NATO. Although it probably aroused stronger opposition on the Continent than in Northern Europe, Norwegian acceptance of the new German role did not come easily. In the end, however, Norway saw it as a necessary evil.

The question of German participation in NATO was viewed from two different perspectives. The first stemmed from the memories of World War II and the German occupation of Norway. The possible security gained by German participation in the Alliance had to be measured against the possible erosion of the broader political support for Norwegian security policies. Here, as in other cases, political leaders placed substantial stress on maintaining the broadest possible public support for national security policy. The idea that German rearmament should coincide with integration into NATO and that the Federal Republic would participate in the European Economic Community made acceptance easier to justify. The fact that no independent German general staff was to be created became a standard argument in favor of the new German role. Although the consequence of this policy—namely, that some high command posts were allocated to German officers—was more difficult to accept. Germany, of course, had no senior officers without some wartime experience.

The second perspective on German entry into NATO was linked to possible Soviet reactions. If a stronger military position for the Federal Republic should provoke strong Soviet reaction, security would be undermined rather than fortified. From the outset Norway wanted security to be pursued at the lowest level of international tension. Care was always taken to underline the defensive posture of Norwegian NATO policies. Norway, allied to the strongest military power, consistently pursued a policy of moderation to reduce the possible provocative effects of this policy. In particular, during periods of tension between the Soviet Union and the Federal Republic of Germany, Norwegian policy makers did not want to stir Soviet reactions by demonstrating a high profile of cooperation with West Germany.

The special relevance of this concern for Norwegian policy is best understood in its relation to the Soviet-Finnish friendship treaty. The treaty is based on a military scenario in which Germany and its allies play a pivotal role. Thus, while military cooperation with the Federal Republic could provide a substantial security asset, especially for the defense of southern Norway, it also could risk Soviet moves toward Finland. A stronger Soviet role in Finnish security would represent a potential danger to Norway's national security. The additional security gained by cooperation with the Federal Republic could be lost through the undermining of Finnish neutrality.

Thus, it is not surprising that the idea of rearming Germany never aroused particular enthusiasm in Norway. Together with Denmark, it experienced a particularly uneasy period during German integration into the Alliance because both belonged to Allied Forces Northern Europe. This station assumed responsibility for the defense of the two northernmost German states, Schleswig and Holstein. The problem of finding the proper defense structure once Germany entered NATO continued for several years in Danish and Norwegian politics and was not resolved in principle until 1961, after four years of controversies, including SACEUR threats to pull Germany's northernmost states out of AFNORTH. Danish hesitation in the fall of 1961 to accept the creation of Allied Command Baltic Approaches (COMBALTAP) even helped provoke the Soviet note to Finland in late October 1961. This note, in turn, accelerated Danish acceptance of COMBALTAP. Yet if the Danes initially felt the problem more strongly than the Norwegians, even in Norway there was reluctance to accept German officers filling their quotas at AFNORTH headquarters near Oslo. This was a recurrent point of domestic controversy in Norwegian politics until the late 1960s.

The German role in the defense of the Baltic Straits was always regarded as very important for the defense of southern Norway. In order to provide the German defense effort with some depth, supply depots for the German navy were established on Norwegian soil. This policy of "prepositioning" was for many years attacked by domestic opponents (within the Labor and Liberal parties) and by the Soviet Union as a move away from the nonbasing policy. But the government persistently defended both its right to define what was compatible with the nonbasing policy and what was necessary for the defense of the country. It resolved that the nonbasing policy was no obstacle to the establishment of such supply dumps, which in peacetime would be under Norwegian control.

Nevertheless, relations with Germany were not completely normalized. Among the residual restrictions was the practice of not allowing German participation in Allied military maneuvers on Norwegian territory. This had the dual function of not provoking domestic or Soviet opposition. During the 1970s, however, the Norwegian Government felt that this restriction should be gradually lifted. In particular, since regular Allied military maneuvers on Norwegian soil became a standard and important feature in demonstrating that the Alliance could work during a crisis, restrictions on German participation were believed to be outdated. Yet the normalizing of relations with Germany, which occurred during the 1970s, stopped short of German infantry units actually participating in maneuvers.

The main reason this military limitation still exists is the continuing fear of Soviet reaction toward Finland. Finnish President Kekkonen indicated the possibility when he stated in public in 1977 that, for Finland, it was important with whom Norway cooperated militarily. He warned that political reactions might develop that neither Finland nor Norway would find in its interest. Essentially Kekkonen was asking for a policy that would avoid any new Soviet demands for consultations. Norway complied by announcing that the policy of normalization had been completed. The Norwegian security interest in the continuation of Finnish neutrality was explained by the Norwegian Foreign Minister, Mr. Knut Frydenlund, on a visit to the Federal Republic.[24]

Aside from this military restriction, however, no further limitations on Norwegian-German cooperation exist. In fact, cooperation between the government of the Federal Republic and both Labor and Conservative governments in Norway has become increasingly smooth and fruitful over the years. Important changes occurred when Willy Brandt became Chancellor in 1969. His promotion of détente, his particular prestige, derived from his anti-Hitler efforts and the fact that he was well known in Norway, where he had spent many of his war years in exile as a political activist, his marriage to a Norwegian, and his practice of cultivating regular contacts with the Norwegian political milieu helped open up a new era in relations. The increased role and political prestige of the Federal Republic has resulted in more political and societal attention being directed toward Germany, whose pivotal role in NATO has been increasingly recognized. German attitudes in security affairs have thus become more important to Norwegian positions, irrespective of the governments' party political composition.

NORWAY'S NORTHERN POLICY. Since the Federal Republic entered NATO and gradually assumed security tasks in the southern part of the Allied northern region, Norwegian defense efforts have been directed more toward northern Norway. It is in this area that Norway finds itself most exposed to the superpower confrontation, principally a naval confrontation. The main reason is the presence in the Kola Peninsula of the most important of the four Soviet strategic naval installations. The transformation of the Soviet navy from a coastal and auxiliary instrument of the army into a blue-water navy with a possible reach to all corners of the world has had a particular impact in the north. Nearly two-thirds of the Soviets' nuclear submarines are deployed in this northern area. In order to enter the North Atlantic, the Soviet navy must pass through a channel of water that lies between the Norwegian coast and islands of the Svalbard archipelago. This route to the high seas is wider than any of the other three outlets (Baltic, Black Sea, and Sea of Okotsk), and consequently the northern fleet has received a particularly important role in Soviet grand strategy.

This combination of circumstances has presented a challenge to Norwegian security policy makers as they attempt to strike a balance between deterrence of war and reassurance of peace. Although the Soviet buildup was considered not to have been motivated by anti-Norwegian designs, the new capabilities nevertheless could be directed against Norwegian interests. In securing against possible Soviet pressure during international crises, Norway must demonstrate that the Soviets have nothing to fear from Norway. Norway, by itself, is unable to provoke the Soviet Union by normal defensive dispositions. But would Norway, as a member of NATO and in particular with forces from other NATO member states, be able to do so?

A low profile guided Norwegian politics in the 1960s, when Allied maneuvers on Norwegian territory acquired increasing importance, as NATO moved from a doctrine of massive retaliation to flexible response.[25] The result has been military limitation, both for Norwegian troops and for Allied forces. For the former, Norway has deployed only a limited number of armed forces to the county of Finnmark, located in the extreme northeast. The bulk of the standing Norwegian forces has been deployed in the county of Troms, which lies west of Finnmark. The distance from Troms to the Soviet border is about 400 kilometers by air and about 900 kilometers by road. Moreover, Norway allows no Allied land maneuvers in Finnmark and never permits Allied airplanes to fly east of 24 degrees, a demarcation that runs through the middle of Finnmark. Allied naval vessels are not allowed to enter Norwegian territorial waters east of the north cape. Allied maneuvers can take place in Troms and in other Norwegian counties, but even here there are special rules and regulations for taking Allied forces into northern Norway, which also includes Nordland county.

It is important to note that while the Soviet Union embarked on an unprecedented naval buildup in the 1970s, it did not follow with a similar development in land and air forces on the Kola Peninsula. There is one Soviet mechanized division in the Murmansk area and one further south in Kondalasksa. A small marine unit is also deployed in the area. With regard to the air force there is a concentration of air-defense planes, but attack bombers have not been regularly deployed in the Murmansk region. Even though there is not a local military balance in the area, the security situation—principally because of Norwegian membership in NATO—is considered reasonably stable.

While Norwegian northern policy has been generally successful, the Soviets have occasionally shown their military muscle. In 1968 they moved a full division to the Norwegian border for some unknown reason. In 1977 they fired missiles into the Barents Sea, an area that both Norway and the Soviet Union claim sovereign rights for economic development. There have also been occasional incidents in the air and at sea, the latter involving both civilian and naval conflicts. Such incidents have been handled bilaterally. Since they have occurred against the background of solid NATO backing of Norwegian security, Norway has had the strength to handle the incidents firmly without raising tensions.

The situation at Svalbard merits some particular observations. According to the Svalbard Treaty of 1920, which came into force in 1925, Norway has full and unlimited sovereignty over the islands. There are some restrictions, however, with regard to economic exploitation, the environment, and defense. Norway cannot discriminate against foreigners with regard to economic activities—mining, hunting, or fishing on land or within the territorial limits of four nautical miles—and has obligations to monitor and maintain the ecological balance. Norway is also prohibited from using the islands for warlike purposes and from creating either a naval base or fortifications. The security of the thus nonmilitarized Svalbard Islands is placed under SACLANT and not CINCNORTH and SACEUR.

The Svalbard situation is complicated by the fact that there are two Soviet mining communities there and only one Norwegian. The Soviet population outnumbers the Norwegian two to one. Norway has been virtually left alone with the Soviet Union at Svalbard because of the lack of interest shown by all the other forty signatories to the treaty. During the 1970s, as people became increasingly concerned with the economic development of the sea and continental shelf, interest in the Svalbard Islands increased. Until this point security policies were the main and almost only basis for a Norwegian-Soviet relationship. The 1970s, however, witnessed interest in the possibility of constructively coexisting with the Soviets at sea and at Svalbard. While a key aspect of security policy has remained the desire to keep the Soviets from doing anything undesirable, the primary focus of economic relations with the Soviets has been to induce them to accept the Norwegian point of view concerning both the situation at Svalbard and in the Barents Sea. The challenge has been to demonstrate the appropriate blend of deterrence and reassurance in order to create a stable situation and thereby prevent security considerations from permeating discussions on matters such as offshore exploration and fishing.

Thus, Norwegian policy makers clearly understand that the Soviet Union considers the northern area vital to its national security. Consequently, Norway is likely to continue the strategy of strength and moderation, especially since this policy of unprovocative security has so far proven successful.[26]

THE NUCLEAR CONTROVERSY 1957–1961. The question of nuclear weapons was introduced into the Norwegian security debate in 1957. The period between 1957 and 1961 was critical to future Norwegian pursuit of deterrence and nonprovocation, and there is also a striking similarity between the problems treated in the first great nuclear debate in Norwegian politics at that time and those which emerged at the end of the 1970s.

The early nuclear debate stemmed from the Soviet triumph with Sputnik and the consideration of what the general Alliance response should be to the perceived increased Soviet nuclear threat. The issue was examined at the NATO summit of prime ministers in 1957.[27] Norway declined participation in possible joint NATO decisions to deploy new Intermediate-Range Ballistic Missiles (IRBMs). In fact, Norwegian Prime Minister Gerhardsen advocated renewed attempts to negotiate with the Soviet Union to avoid deployment of American IRBMs in Europe. Eventually, the deployment in Italy and Turkey took place not on the basis of a unified NATO recommendation, but on the basis of bilateral arrangements.

A second problem created by the IRBM decision concerned eventual direct Norwegian participation in deployment. Interestingly, this problem was approached primarily in terms of its implications for the nonbasing policy. The Prime Minister believed that nonbasing contributed to the low level of international tension in Northern Europe. Thus, the government argued that the same reasoning that had guided the nonbasing policy should also guide the government's IRBM policy. IRBMs could not be deployed on a national basis; therefore, deployment would in effect mean relinquishing the nonbasing policy.

The third aspect of the nuclear question concerned the role of Norwegian forces. In 1957 Norway was offered dual-capable "Honest John" field artillery rockets from the United States. The defense chief argued in favor of their acceptance as a piece of standard modern military equipment. He received the necessary political clearance, although it was widely regarded as a step toward equipping Norwegian forces with tactical nuclear warheads. The official explanation, also used by the Prime Minister in letter exchanges with the Soviet Prime Minister, was that the Honest Johns were modern rockets and standard equipment in most national military establishments. No outside pressure or encouragement should, according to the Prime Minister, lead Norway to forfeit such options. Dual-capable weapons should not be ruled out *en principe* if the weapons were deemed necessary for national defense.

The introduction of Honest Johns nevertheless did have a "dual motivation," at least for some. In the late 1950s the military chiefs asked the government to evaluate the possibility of introducing tactical nuclear weapons, which, among other things, could have been nuclear warheads for the Honest Johns. In 1957 the Labor Party had adopted a program to the effect that nuclear weapons would not be placed on Norwegian territory. This policy had been adopted on the basis of an unannounced motion from the floor during the 1957 party convention. The military chiefs, however, recommended that tactical nuclear weapons be introduced. They presumed that battlefield nuclear weapons could press the opponent to disperse conventional forces in order to avoid being nuclear targets. As long as the presumed opponent, the Soviet Union, had nuclear weapons that would force the Norwegian troops to disperse, the chiefs asked for a similar capability.

The government took its definite stand in late 1960 by refusing to initiate any change in the Norwegian nuclear weapons' policy.[28] The principal argument for not acquiring nuclear weapons was the wish to avoid the tension that presumably would result from their introduction into Norway in peacetime. The wider political considerations of not introducing changes in the stable Nordic situation took precedence over the tactical military arguments. The debate in the Storting in April 1961, which approved the government's program, laid the foundation for a strictly conventional Norwegian defense policy. In order to emphasize that the Norwegian security effort should be completely conventional, the government proposed an extraordinary defense budget increase of one hundred million kroner. The division within the Alliance between conventional Norwegian armed forces and Alliance partners with nuclear weapons had begun.[29] Since U.S. Secretary of Defense McNamara's strategy stressed command and control of nuclear weapons, with no particular wish to deploy them in forward geographical positions, the Norwegian nonstorage policy neither met nor created an obstacle in overall American strategy.

Stressing the conventional role of Norwegian armed forces has been a policy strictly adhered to ever since. Norwegian military personnel has been trained only in defensive measures against the effects of nuclear blasts, and military equipment received from Alliance partners has been stripped of all extra "control and safety equipment" necessary for nuclear

Table 4.4 Norwegian Armed Forces

Year	Army	Navy	Air Force	Total Active	Total Reserves	Total Home Guard	Total
1963	18,000	8,000	10,000	36,000	75,000	100,000	211,000
1964	18,000	8,800	10,000	36,800	75,000	100,000	211,800
1965	16,000	5,400	8,800	32,200	75,000	100,000	207,200
1966	17,000	6,000	9,000	34,000	75,000	70,000	179,000
1967	18,000	8,000	9,000	35,000	75,000	70,000	180,000
1968	19,000	7,000	9,000	35,000	130,000	70,000	235,000
1969	21,000	8,000	9,000	38,000	130,000	70,000	238,000
1970	23,500	8,600	9,000	41,100	130,000	70,000	241,100
1971	18,000	8,500	9,400	35,900	179,600	75,000	290,500
1972	18,000	8,500	9,400	35,900	179,600	75,000	290,500
1973	18,000	8,000	9,400	35,400	157,600	80,000	273,000
1974	17,700	8,300	8,900	34,900	174,500	80,000	289,400
1975	18,000	8,000	9,000	35,000	170,000	80,000	285,000
1976	20,000	9,000	10,000	39,000	170,000	80,000	289,000
1977	20,000	9,000	10,000	39,000	160,000	80,000	279,000
1978	20,000	9,000	10,000	39,000	160,000	85,000	284,000
1979	20,000	9,000	10,000	39,000	160,000	85,000	284,000
1980	18,000	9,000	10,000	37,000	162,000	85,000	284,000
1981	18,000	9,000	10,000	37,000	162,000	85,000	284,000
1982	24,400	9,400	8,300	42,000	158,000	85,000	285,000
1983	24,175	8,850	9,840	43,170	168,000	89,000	299,500

Length of compulsory military service since 1966: army, twelve months; navy and air force, fifteen months

Source: International Institute for Strategic Studies, *The Military Balance* (London: IISS).

tasks. This policy was particularly emphasized when Norway received new dual-capable aircraft. Military maneuvers take place without nuclear scenarios. Even Allied aircraft that are dual-capable never bring nuclear weapons into Norway. Allied naval vessels are assumed not to carry nuclear weapons when on port calls, but there is an American tradition of neither affirming nor denying the existence of nuclear weapons on board U.S. ships. These ships are never physically inspected by Norwegian authorities.

Norway, however, has never explicitly ruled out the possibility that nuclear weapons could be placed on Norwegian soil. At the time the government adopted its nonnuclear position, it emphasized that it would always be the responsibility of the constitutional authorities to take adequate measures for the nation's defense and security. In the view of many, this stipulation means that Norway has reserved a nuclear option for itself. In the early 1960s the Foreign Minister stated that the Norwegian contribution to Nordic stability rested, among other things, on the fact that Norway had never been willing to dismiss the possibility of receiving nuclear weapons.[30] Apart from its other purposes, this statement helped thwart the Finnish proposal for a Nordic nuclear-free zone, first put forward by Finnish President Kekkonen in 1963. This is often termed the Norwegian nuclear option. Although it certainly played a role at a time when NATO had a preponderance over the Warsaw Pact in tactical weapons, the option has not been emphasized in Norwegian politics.

It is difficult to determine what remains of the nuclear option for crisis management. At present, it cannot be ruled out that tactical nuclear weapons could be brought into Norway in time of war.[31] But a warning, such as was given in 1961, that the Norwegian nonstorage policy might be reconsidered if Norway confronted a crisis seems much less likely to happen today. A replay of the Norwegian role in a Soviet-Finnish note crisis is difficult to envisage with regard to the nonstorage policy. The international system has altered drastically in the past twenty years, and although the Soviet Union still desires to keep American forces and weapons as far away as possible, a change in the nonstorage policy would not have the same military impact as before. Moreover, there are still significant ambiguities as to the possibility of Allied forces sent to assist Norway bringing tactical nuclear weapons with them. Another aspect of this is the possible existence of nuclear weapons on board Allied naval vessels or military aircraft outside Norwegian territorial waters and airspace. All these problems and uncertainties with regard to Norway's nuclear option remain unresolved. It is significant to note that since 1961 Norway has not warned of a possible change in the nonstorage or nonbasing policies.

Everything considered, for the past thirty years Norwegian security policy based on membership in NATO has been a considerable success. Essentially, both broad political and public support has been the rule. Sufficient defense spending provided the Norwegian Government with a basis for a distinct national-policy line. The balancing of deterrence with moderation has been steadily and patiently pursued, thus creating a reasonably clear and stable policy. This has contributed to a lessening both in regional and international tension. Norway has thus been in a privileged position.

But security does not differ from other aspects of politics. It is a continuous process that encounters new challenges both from within the political spectrum and from outside. As the end of the 1970s and early 1980s were to show, challenges must be met with perseverence yet patience, with commitment yet caution.

Consensus at Risk

The reintroduction of nuclear-weapon problems into the NATO Alliance in the late 1970s laid the foundation for a new debate about national security in Norway, as it did in many other Alliance member states. The prelude came in 1978 with the neutron bomb episode, but the most important issue was, and remains, the question of long-range theater nuclear weapons' deployment and arms control. These issues were introduced to the public with the NATO double-track decision of December 1979. They provoked a major controversy in Norwegian society and threatened a breakdown in the broad national consensus.

The INF debate was a catalyst for discussion and disagreement regarding a whole range of nuclear issues, for it increased interest among the public and politicians in security affairs. Yet only the INF issue produced sharp political confrontations, with the government surviving by a margin of one vote on several occasions. The debate raised a number of problems concerning how elites exercise leadership and how they respond to the task of integrating reliable policy with domestic demand for democratic participation. Because of public concern over the nuclear issues, the challenge has been strongly felt during the early 1980s and is likely to persist in the future. The question is therefore whether fundamental change has taken place in the way the Norwegian system is able to manage security policy.

Changing Internal Context

The single most controversial foreign-policy issue in the postwar period was not INF, but the question of Norwegian membership in the European Economic Community. Two particular consequences of this debate are important to this study. First, it led to a temporary breakdown in the representative system of government traditional to Norwegian politics. Internal disagreement brought down a non-Socialist majority government in 1971 because the Conservatives favored membership and the Center (Agrarian) Party opposed it. This led to a minority Labor government, which put the issue to the public in a ref .endum in 1972. When the pro-EEC position was defeated, the governnent chose to step down, since it had made the matter a vote of confidence. A coalition of three parties—the Center, the Christians, and the Rump-Liberals—with the support of only 38 members of Parliament out of 150—formed the new government. From 1972 until 1983 Norway was to experience only minority governments. Labor lost the election of 1973 but in the end was given the task of forming a minority government. Its 62 members combined with the 16 Left Socialists to create a Socialists' majority in the Storting, giving them one more than the combined strength of 77 members of the opposition. This "majority of one" was maintained during the elections of 1977, although Labor membership increased to 76, while the Left Socialists, troubled by internal division, were reduced to 2 representatives.

The Storting election of 1981 produced a non-Socialist majority, which laid the foundation for a Conservative minority government. The Conservatives were supported by the Center Party and the Christian Peoples Party, in addition to the Progressive Party of the extreme right. Finally, in the summer of 1983, this government was expanded to a three-party majority government of Conservatives, the Center, and the Christians.

The second consequence of the referendum closely coincides with the first. The popular majority against Norwegian EEC membership is generally considered a success of democracy over foreign policy. It created unrest within parties, which made leadership more difficult, and alerted leaders to popular demands. Foreign Minister Frydenlund summed up the situation by pointing out that foreign policy no longer existed as a province for experts and political elites.[32] Popular arguments and considerations would have to be increasingly taken into account.

This development was reinforced by, perhaps even the consequence of, the educational explosion in Norway that has occurred since the beginning of the 1960s. The number of university students has increased markedly. Societal values toward more freedom for the individual have emerged. Interest in politics has risen, as evidenced by increased public attention to matters such as the nomination process in the political parties. While, in the 1950s, no newspaper regularly covered political-party nominations, the situation now is quite different. Every party strives to broaden political participation in the nomination process. The same can be argued with regard to the development of party platforms. People are constantly invited to contribute views and suggestions. The Conservative government, from the very beginning of its tenure in October 1981, made a pledge to increase openness. A number of questions that previously were never raised in Parliament have subsequently been examined, for instance, in the questions-to-the-minister sessions.

Diverse interest groups have also begun to direct their activities toward the political process. The result is that the state seems to be becoming more and more fragmented. The activities of the state have expanded, with about 50 percent of the GNP now channeled through public budgets. But sector and group involvement have led these participants to think that they "own" part of the budget. At the same time, the state itself has been forthcoming in inviting participation. Since the 1970s, no important piece of legislation has been introduced without a proper "hearing" of the viewpoints of concerned groups and institutions.

This higher degree of *democratization* is also felt in the field of foreign and security policy. Press reporters and television journalists persistently investigate these areas. Thus, the political milieu has changed and the task of leadership has evolved accordingly. Leaders can no longer maintain cohesion by command. Argument and persuasion have become more important for effective political leadership.[33]

The changes in the domestic political environment have been real. The Labor Party that returned to power in 1973 was distinctly more radical than the Labor Party that had governed until 1965. This posture sharpened Conservative opposition, which gained popularity by riding on, and thereby stimulating, what has been termed the "Conservative wave." When domestic politics take precedence in Norwegian postwar policies, there is a sharp confrontation between the two governmental alternatives, the Socialist and non-Socialist. With regard to foreign policy, Labor has proven more vulnerable to public and party dissent. The Conservative Party, on the other hand, experienced less internal debate and gradually became more intolerant of what it perceived to be the soft foreign-policy leadership of Mr. Frydenlund.

Despite these changes, however, there has been clearly no political crisis in the Norwegian system. Even though national-security politics has been brought into the open by the more frequent parliamentary debates on security, the basic bargaining process remains dominated by leaders of the major political parties. A more open security policy has not produced a system in which policy priorities emanate from below. Moreover, while some aspects of security policy have become the source of major political and popular controversy, overall Norwegian policy, both the process and the priorities, is as much characterized by continuity as change.

Continuing Commitment to a Strong Defense

The headlines and public discussions concentrating on the political dispute over nuclear issues have also created some uneasiness among politicians and the public about other security-policy issues. But essentially there has remained a broad consensus on the approach to, and direction of, defense policy. Therefore, before examining the nuclear dispute, it is important first to examine the policies for which there is general consensus.

As shown above, public support for both NATO membership and an independent defense force has grown during the 1970s and 1980s. Support of Norwegian defense exceeds support for NATO, and outright opposition to NATO is minimal. On the political elite level, strong support both for NATO membership and for continued defense spending persists. During the 1960s skepticism toward NATO increased within the Labor Party, especially from members of Parliament who were recruited directly out of the party's youth organization. Labor, however, closed its ranks behind NATO at its 1981 national convention by unanimously adopting its platform. At all previous conventions NATO had been controversial, with a minority demonstrating its misgivings.

At the 1981 convention the Labor Party determined policies on a number of other security issues, which included that of a Nordic nuclear-weapons-free zone as part of a broader international arrangement. Labor unanimity in support of NATO created a base that made critical attitudes toward different aspects of NATO policy more acceptable. By saying yes to NATO, the Labor Party demonstrated credibility for more independent assessment of different issues. Thus, solutions to policy issues had to be found on the basis of continued Norwegian NATO membership. The security debate of the 1980s, however, clearly showed a difference among the parties regarding what loyalty to NATO should mean in practical politics.

The single most important measurement of defense policies is perhaps the willingness to support a substantial defense budget. The NATO summit in London in 1978 decided that all member states ought to increase their defense budgets in real terms by 3 percent. Different Norwegian governments comprised of different political persuasions have faithfully adhered to this commitment. But since the question of a further increase in excess of 3 percent has become central to the security debate, the situation is more complex and needs further comment.

In 1974 the government established a defense review commission with representatives from most parties. The commission published its report in 1978.[34] A program for gradual strengthening of defense, with a particular emphasis on the army, was recommended. The central feature was the establishment of the so-called Brigade 90 PF, an army brigade with a stronger armor by 1990. The program of the defense commission was designed along a fifteen-year perspective. For each of the five-year periods the commission recommended a real increase in spending of 4, 3, and 2 percent, respectively. There were a number of preconditions to this policy, one of which was that the new law introduced concerning military working conditions and internal milieu should be financed by extra means.

The defense commission presented its findings at a time when there were a number of different demands for public funding of ambitious projects. Previously, largely shielded from the international recession, Norway now began to experience economic difficulties, including strong inflationary pressure. Because it had to compete with other plans for public activities, the recommendations were not implemented. Based on early 1980s price levels, the cost of the recommendations could not be met without a real defense increase of 7 percent.[35] Politically, this option was simply not possible. The defense commission, however, influenced the non-Socialist opposition to demand a real increase in defense spending of 4 percent. This set the stage for conflict over how much the defense budget should be increased above the agreed 3 percent. Labor recommended no increase above 3 percent, while the Conservative government of 1981 stuck to its request for a 4 percent increase. The succeeding three-party non-Socialist government since 1983 has offered a 3.5 percent real increase in Norwegian defense budgets.

The figures 3, 3.5, and 4 percent have become symbolic. On top of a defense budget of about 14 billion kroner, one-half percent amounts to 70 million. Although the Defense Department would undoubtedly welcome the 70 million, the disagreement should not be given too much importance. While the question of the half percent regularly places the parties against each other, they basically agree on the broad approach to defense spending. The one-half of one percent represents a "luxury problem," given the fact that what is being discussed is not cuts, but different levels of real increases in the defense budget. Compared to other NATO countries, Norway's recent spending profile is among the highest. Essentially, there is a broad consensus on defense spending, although the Conservatives remain more eager to spend than Labor. The Conservatives fear spending too little on defense, while Labor fears spending too much.

A good example of this general consensus can be found in the issue of prepositioning of heavy American military materiel. The changes in the military environment (with the growth of the Soviet navy and the big increase in speed of modern warfare) made it mandatory for Norway to arrange for such prepositioning. In 1981 this was done for the equipment of an American Marine Amphibious Brigade (MAB). A Storting vote decided the issue in favor of the Norwegian-American agreement. It was largely discussed in terms of whether it was compatible with Norwegian nonstorage and nonbasing policy to enter into such an agreement with the United States, which, apart from being a nuclear power, also had different stategic interests and pursuits than those of Norway.

In the end, the Storting concluded that prepositioning was not only a policy to ensure deterrence by making reinforcement more credible, but it was also a policy to ensure protection against an early change of the nonbasing position. With heavy equipment stored on Norwegian territory, the need for maritime transport decreased and the time frame for certain decisions changed, since personnel could be air-transported to Norway on short notice. After some internal debate between the Conservative and Labor parties as to where to locate the materiel, the Labor government finally chose to place the equipment in the mid-Norwegian counties of Trondelag. Conservatives, usually preferring a slightly stonger defense approach, advocated locating it in the exposed northern county of Troms. But the Labor government was not convinced of this wisdom. Endeavoring not to provoke the Soviet Union unnecessarily, it chose to position the materiel in the middle of Norway. The implementation of the decision had to take place after the change of government in 1981. The new government was free to raise the issue of location for prepositioning, but the Conservatives refrained from stirring up a new debate on the issue.

Similar to the debate on the Norwegian defense budget, the prepositioning incident demonstrates that there exists basic agreement in Norway on defense-policy issues. The reason for this is straightforward: There has remained a broad consensus on the basic principles that should guide Norwegian security-policy choices. What the parties do disagree on, however, is the manner or extent to which these policies should be implemented.

Nuclear Issues in Norwegian Politics

The only real challenge to the Norwegian consensus on security and foreign policy has come from nuclear strategy and arms-control matters. The challenge has focused above all on the INF issue, and it has highlighted the various differences in approach to security policy held by the various parties. The INF question lucidly illustrates the preconditions for security-policy consensus in Norway.

THE INF DEBATE. The debate first began with the neutron bomb episode in 1978, an issue brought into Norwegian politics as an Alliance question. A broad majority in the Storting rejected the deployment of the neutron weapon in Europe at that time. Little political controversy resulted. The INF issue emerged eighteen months later, introduced unexpectedly in late October 1979 with the semiannual foreign policy report of the Foreign Minister. Up to this point the government had played an active part in formulating the double-track NATO strategy of deployment and arms control. But opposition was soon to mobilize.[36]

The Foreign Minister's report clearly outlined the common NATO concern over Soviet theater nuclear modernization in a period of essential parity between the superpowers. It supported the NATO approach that combined NATO INF deployment with offers to the Soviet Union of arms control. At the same time, it stressed a threefold basis for Norwegian participation in the forthcoming NATO decision. First, there should be no deployment on Norwegian soil. Second, in accordance with its desire that the Alliance respect its nonbasing and nonstoring policies, Norway should show particular respect for the positions of other NATO countries more directly involved in eventual deployment. Third, Norway should work for a clear commitment to arms control as part of the decision.

The INF issue immediately elicited controversy within the Labor Party, governing at this time with a majority of one but which could rely on broad support on this issue from the non-Socialist opposition. In the party's parliamentary group the opposition to the double-track decision was between 20 and 30 percent. The government obtained sufficient support from the majority only after having made special pledges to stress the arms-control part of the decision. In demonstrating this commitment, the Prime Minister made a special visit to Washington to obtain assurances from President Carter, while the party chairman went to

Moscow to investigate the possibilities for arms control. The Defense Minister and the party's deputy chairman attended the special congress of the German Social Democratic Party (SPD) in Berlin in an effort to understand better the SPD viewpoint. The Norwegian Government desired to stay as close to the SPD as possible.

The Prime Minister and party chairman had resolved not to test the attitudes of the party national board, which had its semiannual meeting in November. A vote on the issue was avoided out of fear of a majority opposing government policy. Spontaneous resolutions were submitted by individual county boards of the party during November and early December. The overwhelming majority of these opposed Norwegian participation in the double-track decision. In the face of substantial opposition, the Norwegian Labor Party was able to avoid blocking Norwegian participation only by insisting on the need for a common NATO strategy.

The Labor Party soon established a special group to follow the development of the double-track decision and, in particular, to see that the arms-control part of the agreement was stressed sufficiently. The party also emphasized that the aim of the negotiations was to obviate, through Soviet reductions, the need for deployment by the West. In effect, Labor support for the double-track decision was conditional on arms reductions.

Skepticism was not confined to the Labor Party. The Left Socialists protested and the old grass-roots organization "No to Nuclear Weapons" resurrected itself. Among the non-Socialists the situation was also mixed. The Conservative Party had no problem in accepting the double-track decision and gave it clear support. But the two center parties took a more cautious approach. The Center Party leader stated that Norway should not vote against the double-track decision. The Christian Peoples Party experienced more serious internal difficulties, with seven of its twenty members of Parliament voting against the decision in the party caucus. Thus, the Conservatives were the only party that did not evoke a major discord within its ranks by endorsing the double-track decision.

The conditions stipulated by the Labor Party coincided with traditional Norwegian political attitudes with regard to nuclear weapons. The new challenge came from the NATO decision that there should be collective responsibility for the double-track decision. Adjustment to this "new" requirement produced the breakdown in Norwegian political consensus previously existing on these issues.

The Storting never voted on the double-track decision. Despite the opposition in the Labor Party, in the Christian Peoples Party, and in the Center Party, there still remained in 1979 a clear majority in the Storting for accepting the "new" responsibility. But if acceptance of the Alliance decision was politically difficult, the implementation of the decision, in the absence of progress in arms control, was even more difficult.

The elections of September 1981 were won by the non-Socialists, and the first Conservative cabinet in fifty years was established in October.

The Christian Peoples Party and the Center Party refrained from joining the cabinet but promised general support in accordance with their preelection pledges. The new cabinet had no second thoughts about supporting the double-track decision, and it made a point of the fact that the new Defense Minister had worked hard during his first NATO ministerial meeting to help persuade the American Secretary of Defense to start INF negotiations on the basis of the "Zero Option." The Labor Party again stressed the need to arrive at a conclusion that would make deployment in the West unnecessary. The party also made public its request that there be a separate evaluation of the results of the Geneva negotiations and that, regardless of the results, no automatic deployment should be undertaken.

During 1982 interest sharpened in the Geneva negotiations with regard to possible outcomes, different negotiation strategies, and the role of Norway. Spokesmen for the government indicated that negotiation could proceed beyond December 1983 even with partial deployment in order to make sure that the Soviets understood that deployment would occur and therefore that sufficient incentives for serious negotiation did exist. In this regard, the debate in Norway differed little from the international debate. The chief concern was whether preparation for deployment would provoke failure in the negotiations or force the Soviets to offer reductions.

While differences over this debate were not emphasized during 1982, the deployment conflict surfaced twice in that year. In June the Storting discussed Norway's contribution to NATO's infrastructure and learned that 49 million kroner were earmarked for deployment preparations. During the examination of the infrastructure report the Labor Party divided on the question of support for this contribution. The allocation was also opposed by the Left Socialist Party, the Liberal Party's two representatives, two members of the Central Party, and three members of the Christian Peoples Party. The Labor leader, representing majority opinion in the party, supported the infrastructure program, but he nevertheless asserted that preparations should not make deployment inevitable and he asked the government for assurances and a report on the situation. This request signaled a shift of emphasis, making the support for the NATO infrastructure contribution contingent on site preparation having no negative effect on arms-control prospects.

During the following three months no report or evaluation was forthcoming. Labor thus made its own investigation, the result of which was a party decision to vote "now" against appropriations for preparation in order not to become "a spearhead" in relation to the other nations. This new position, adopted unanimously by the national board and the parliamentary groups, created quite a controversy, particularly since it stood a real chance of gaining a majority.

The dispute held public attention for about seven weeks. Labor was charged with having changed course and was branded as disloyal to NATO and to the policies it had supported, and even led, while in office.

The Labor Party retorted that it knew best the basis of its support for the double-track decision and that it was solidly backing traditional Norwegian security preferences. Essentially, the question concerned whether the Norwegian contribution to the relevant part of the infrastructure program (11 million kroner for 1983) should be appropriated according to normal procedures in November or whether the allocation should be postponed to the end of the next year, when the position and policy of other NATO countries on this issue would be clearer. The government insisted on immediate appropriation. When the vote on contributions to NATO infrastructure was taken in November 1982, the government won by one vote.

The next phase of the INF question emerged in March 1983 when the Storting discussed the report on Norway's activities in NATO during 1982. Throughout the fall and winter the Labor Party had hammered out a more distinct platform for nuclear-weapons arms control, which paralleled the viewpoints of sister parties in Denmark, Holland, Belgium, the Federal Republic of Germany, and Britain. Its "missile group" presented a set of recommendations, which gradually obtained the support of the party's county organizations. The new Labor platform presented a general program for arms control, which included the acceptance of a nuclear freeze. With regard to INF, the platform stated:

- The INF discussions should be joined with the START negotiations so that the British and the French strategic forces would be taken into account.
- The aim of the INF negotiations should be sufficient reductions by the Soviet Union to warrant no deployment in the West.
- Preparations for deployment should be stopped.
- Negotiations should, if necessary, be continued beyond December 1983 and should not be accompanied by any deployment.

During the March debate in the Storting, the Labor Party tabled a freeze recommendation in accordance with the findings of its missile group. The recommendation was defeated by one vote. The alignments for the November infrastructure vote were repeated. In response to Labor criticism, the government argued that it was only carrying out the policies laid down by Labor when in office. It argued that its interpretation of the double-track decision was the same as other NATO governments, and that deployment was not only necessary in lieu of progress in arms control but was also critical to its future. Moreover, it maintained that Norwegian security policy should be to implement loyally NATO agreements that had been made with Norwegian participation.

Disagreement on INF arose on a number of other occasions during 1983 and peaked in the November parliamentary debate just prior to the Pershing II deployment in the Federal Republic of Germany. The arguments had changed little, although supporters of deployment increasingly described it as a means for arms control and not as something necessitated by military strategy. By the end of the year, when deployment had commenced and arms-control negotiations had collapsed, the issue no longer dominated political attention. The political parties gradually placed more emphasis on issues on which they possessed more influence; for example, rising unemployment.

It is important to complete this picture with some brief references to the positions of the two middle parties—the Center and the Christians. Both parties undertook their own examination of the INF issue as well as of the other pressing nuclear issues. The parties had experienced internal opposition within their parliamentary groups, but members who had earlier voiced opposition refrained from doing so later in order to avoid bringing down the government. Moreover, when the government was enlarged in June 1983, the Conservatives insisted that the governmental platform should demonstrate loyalty to the double-track decision, which meant no wavering from the deployment plan.

The Center Party favored adhering to the double-track NATO decision on INF. While indicating that negotiations should continue after December 1983, there was no willingness to stop physical preparation. At the same time, the recommendation contained a number of positive references to a freeze, but it stipulated that this proposal should not be discussed at the INF table in Geneva. The Center Party also indicated a positive attitude toward other propositions by Labor. The Christian Peoples Party also had problems with the double-track decision. One-third of its parliamentary group had advised against it in 1979. The party felt its support of the decision had been politically costly. Consequently, they gradually demonstrated positive dispositions toward the ideas of the "No to Nuclear Weapons" group and the Labor Party.

Thus, the same attacks levied against the Labor Party—vacillation and misdirected policy—could also to a certain degree be directed at the Christian Peoples Party and the Center Party. This fact was not lost on the Labor Party, since it lost no time in pointing out the disparity between Conservative policy and the profiles of the two middle parties. Labor wanted to demonstrate that the middle parties' attitudes were in fact closer to its own and that they were restrained only by Prime Minister Kari Willoch's implicit threats to resign.

OTHER NUCLEAR ISSUES. During the four years of INF discussions, attitudes changed in Norwegian politics on other important nuclear matters. These included the question of "freeze" as a strategy for nuclear arms control; the problem of revising "flexible response" in order to examine the possibilities for a move toward a no-first-use strategy; and the issue of the Nordic nuclear-weapons-free zone. All three problems were raised by the Labor Party and later received support from the non-Socialists. Each helps to illustrate the delicate political nature of nuclear questions in Norway.

The changes in positions on these questions were the political price that had to be paid for an unusually high profile on nuclear weapons incurred by participating in the double-track decision. While the fight on the implementation of the double-track decision continued, and while the government managed to keep a majority in support of its position, the pressures mounted on the other issues. The Labor Party first formulated its point of view, which was then gradually accepted by the Christians and eventually by the Center. By the spring of 1984 the Conservatives had also modified their positions on these issues, thus helping to reduce political conflict on nuclear questions.

The first of the three problems involved an immediate halt to the production and deployment of nuclear weapons. The "freeze" idea developed in conjunction with the INF debate, and it gained support rapidly during 1982 and 1983. The main inspiration came from the positive reaction the idea received in America. In December 1982 the Storting discussed the government's decision to vote against the United Nations' freeze resolution introduced by Sweden and Mexico. The debate revealed that there might by a majority opposed to the government's decision, a position that had been taken without prior consultation of Parliament. The Labor Party suggested that abstention, with a reasonable explanation, might be a better solution for Norway. The government argued that the freeze idea ran counter to Alliance policies in Geneva, and that it should not be criticized for having voted with the vast majority of NATO countries.

The Center and the Christian Peoples parties did not openly criticize the government at that time; but the parliamentary leader of the Christians indicated that his party would have supported a Norwegian decision to abstain from voting. These "reservations," occurring at the same time as the controversy on INF, had their effect. When the Swedish-Mexican freeze resolution was reintroduced in the U.N. in the fall of 1983, the government, now enlarged by the two parties, abstained from voting.

The idea of reexamining NATO's flexible-response doctrine was introduced into Norwegian politics during the foreign-affairs debate in late spring 1982. Two factors were primarily responsible for inducing this reexamination. The first was the Palme Commission report, which introduced to the public the issue of NATO's battlefield weapons by its proposal to eliminate such weapons within a 150-kilometer belt on each side of the "iron curtain."[37] The second was the desire to create conditions in which one could safely, and with NATO protection, create a Nordic nuclear-weapons-free zone.

In the spring of 1982 the Labor Party suggested a Norwegian initiative in NATO for a reexamination of official doctrine. The government rejected the idea, arguing that the demonstration of less reliance on nuclear weapons could undermine deterrence and lower the threshold of war. The Labor Party did not agree. It contended that a viable alternative was to increase conventional defense. The matter became the subject of a parliamentary debate in December 1982. The Christian Peoples Party supported reexamining flexible response. Again, therefore, a possible parliamentary majority in support of the idea seemed to exist. But the Conservatives maintained their skepticism. They did not come around to accepting the notion that a need to reexamine the doctrine existed before the spring of 1984.

Finally, the Norwegian nuclear-weapons debate is not complete without discussing the Nordic nuclear-weapons-free zone issue. Until 1980 Norwegian politicians had refused to participate in different schemes for making Northern Europe a nuclear-weapons-free zone by treaty. The existence of Soviet nuclear weapons near the Nordic area was an important stumbling block. Norwegian thinking about a nuclear-weapons-free zone, however, suddenly changed during the fall of 1980 and the spring of 1981.

The catalyst for this redirection was a suggestion made by former Law of the Sea Minister Jens Evensen in October 1980 for Norwegian participation in such a zone. Prior to this statement, no party with the exception of the smaller parties of the extreme left had ever mentioned the idea in its program. Evensen struck a cord in public opinion, and although his proposal originally drew criticism from leaders of the Labor Party, after some reflection they decided to capture the initiative. Thus, Prime Minister Odvar Nordli, in his New Year's speech, advocated the idea of a Nordic zone, provided that it could be part of a broader European framework. The Labor Party then adopted the idea of this broader setting in its platform for the 1981 national elections.

The other main political parties likewise formulated their views on the matter. The Center Party was the first, followed by the Christians. The zone, however, never became a major issue at the Conservative Party's national convention in the spring of 1981. But in June 1983 the three non-Socialist parties agreed upon a formula during the parliamentary debate on the long-term national program of the government. They stressed that a possible zone would have to be part of a larger international agreement and arrived at by joint NATO negotiations. The difference between the Labor point of view and the three non-Socialist points of view was the degree to which one verbally stressed the attachment to NATO on this matter.

The most important aspect of the zone clarification was clearly that it was introduced into Norwegian politics after the acceptance of the double-track decision. All parties, even the Conservatives, used positive references to the idea. This may be perceived as a means of checking the Norwegian nuclear profile, which had grown too high as a result of Norwegian participation in the 1979 NATO decision.

A number of difficult problems are associated with the zone idea, and there has been a multitude of suggested approaches and solutions. The role of non-Nordic states presents a number of complications. The Soviet Union has indicated that it is ready to offer some concessions in order to help create such a zone, but it has failed to delineate them specifically. Among the most difficult problems, as seen from the NATO perspective, is whether Norwegian and Danish participation in a nuclear-free arrangement is compatible with continuing the policy of flexible response. Initial reactions from the United States and the United Kingdom were negative. Former Secretary of State Alexander Haig is reported to have told Foreign Minister Frydenlund, in a meeting in New York in July 1981, that Norway would have to choose between NATO protection and a Nordic nuclear-weapons-free zone. Former British Foreign Minister, Lord Carrington, also offered a negative response.

The American ultimatum helped terminate public discussion on the issue, and politicians directed their attention to other issues during the remainder of the Storting election campaign. But it is important to note that the harsh Haig remark also provoked public statements emphasizing that Norway was no satellite of the United States. The episode undoubtedly stimulated antinuclear attitudes and perhaps also anti-American feelings. Public-opinion polls showed a clear majority in favor of a nuclear-weapons-free zone despite American opposition. Even a majority of Conservative Party members supported this proposal.

Thus, on all three subsidiary nuclear issues, each of the major parties used its stance to compensate for its position on the INF debate. Labor pushed its approach on these issues to rebut criticism that it had been the ruling party that approved the 1979 NATO decision. The Center and Christian parties maintained moderate support for the Labor position on these three issues to balance their cautious endorsements of the INF decision. The Conservative Party modified its approach in order to demonstrate that its strong support of the INF decision did not reflect complete subservience to Alliance policy.

THE NUCLEAR FALLOUT. The INF issue has been the most controversial issue in recent Norwegian politics. The handling of the issue has led to a breakdown of the broad political consensus that characterized most of the postwar period. The INF controversy has revealed above all a disagreement about the interpretation of the double-track decision regarding the relative importance of negotiations and deployment. It has also shown differences in attitudes concerning arms-control negotiations regarding how, and how much, pressure should be brought to bear on the Soviets. A delicate compromise like the double-track decision has proven difficult to sustain over time with the strains of coalition politics and East-West controversies.

Moreover, it has highlighted diverging attitudes toward the interaction of democracy and diplomacy. Conservative government spokesmen, fearing that the Soviet Union would exploit Western division, argued for cohesion and discipline. Public protest in the streets of Western Europe, they contended, could undermine the Western negotiators and strengthen Soviet opposition. Russian negotiators could then wait for public opinion in the West to block deployment. The government believed that opinion differences among NATO members should be handled quietly, thus denying the Soviets the opportunity to exploit Western dissent. By presenting a position of Allied cohesion to the world, they believed they would have a better opportunity to influence Alliance partners in private councils, and, they argued, the precondition for this approach was domestic agreement on the main lines of policy.

Yet it was precisely this basic agreement that proved elusive, as Conservative and Labor party leaders struggled with the INF issue and the traditional problem of balancing the Norwegian priorities of deterrence and nonprovocation. The rank and file Conservative supporters showed little apprehension about eventually having to deploy new nuclear missiles in Western Europe. Members of the Labor Party were much more uncomfortable, even frightened by the prospect of a new round in the nuclear-arms race. The Conservatives feared that security needs had not received strong enough military buttressing, while the Labor Party worried that military preparations would become unnecessarily strong. Following Norwegian political tradition, the Conservatives wanted deterrence to be adequately reinforced, while Labor feared that reassurance would suffer.

The Conservative Party has sought to minimize Norwegian reservations toward general NATO policies, arguing that Norwegian security is better served this way. Norway is viewed as a small, geographically exposed country and in great need of Allied support. The Labor Party has been concerned that the traditional Norwegian security profile, originally hammered out by a Labor Party in power during twenty-nine out of thirty-seven post–World War II years, will now emphasize military deterrence at the expense of political reassurance. The Conservatives have focused primarily on whether NATO policies provided necessary defense preparations; Labor has focused primarily on whether NATO policies, with regard to Norway, had the broadest possible support. These differences in security policy reflect the Conservative view that Norwegian independence is best served by the highest possible integration with NATO policy. Conversely, Labor stresses a stronger independence on different issues vis à vis other NATO member states. In form, Labor's line may appear more nationalistic than the Conservative approach.

The INF controversy brought these conditions and preferences into the open in a new manner, and it demonstrated that at least for this security issue the conditions for implementing policy have changed. The struggle between the different preferences of the two bigger political parties is played out using the two parties of the middle—the Center Party and the Christian Peoples Party—as their political arena. Expressions of preferences by members of these two smaller parties indicate that in some questions they may be even further left than Labor.

By mid-1984 the Norwegian security debate had returned to the era of broad public agreement. Apart from the INF issue, a broad understanding on Norwegian policy had been created. The new consensus was established more in line with the premises of the Labor Party than with those of the Conservatives. Labor's assertive approach to arms control, to the nuclear freeze, to flexible response and its reexamination, and to the Nordic nuclear-free zone had established the foundation for this consensus. The Conservative Party reinforced this foundation in the spring of 1984 by choosing to support the Labor position on these issues. But the security debate will undoubtedly continue, and this new consensus may prove fragile over time.

The Future

This study has sought to demonstrate that there has been and still remains a broad national consensus in Norway on national-security policy. NATO membership is not called into question. Proposals by the extreme left for its termination are immediately rejected. Support for membership has in fact been growing over the years. The same is true with regard to support for national defense, which can be witnessed in the increase in defense spending over the past few years. National strategy likewise enjoys broad support, even in a period of increased public awareness of the issues involved. A case in point is the decision to support the policy of prepositioning of heavy military materiel for Allied forces on Norwegian territory in peacetime. The challenge to Norwegian security-policy consensus over the last few years has emerged in the field of nuclear strategy and East-West arms control.

If the Norwegian public is the object of the security-policy controversy between left and right over nuclear issues, it is not the cause. Nor is a breakdown of political consensus, in the true sense of the word, at the origin of current difficulties; significant differences are confined primarily to one area of policy. Rather, it has been a specific set of changes in the international environment that have forced Norwegian political leaders to reinterpret the broad lines of the traditional Norwegian security profile in the face of new conditions. The dispute represents the reassertion of a problem that has frequently plagued political leaders throughout the postwar period. The problem of managing consensus has always been one of finding the balance between deterrence and reassurance that is acceptable both within and between government and opposition. There can be little doubt, however, that this balance has been more difficult to maintain than in times past.

Norway's NATO membership is not contested by contemporary controversies, but the more ready and easy acceptance of Alliance priorities by an overwhelming number of right-of-center governments stimulates Labor Party warnings against NATO becoming an organization that can flourish only when Conservative governments reign. The changes in American policies, introduced by the Reagan Administration, set the stage for lively discussions in most member states. In Norway the differences between the Conservative Party and the Labor Party seem smaller than in many other countries. Security profiles, however, are important for party identification. Security issues have been used to attract political supporters and to foment internal strain within other parties. With regard to the latter, the most prominent example has been the Conservative attempt to strengthen the moderate leadership in the Labor Party by taking issue with the "left wing." Such "help" has been viewed more as an attempt to sow dissent than to stimulate broad national consensus.

At present, it seems that Labor's new line has helped consolidate party activists, but, not surprisingly, at the expense of grass-roots support. Different polls indicate that Labor has lost approximately 2 percent of its supporters because of its altered approach to security issues. This development may already have inspired the Conservatives to make harsher criticisms. If this trend continues, security affairs could loom even larger as an election variable. At the same time, however, the Conservatives face difficulties with the political center; namely, the Center Party and the Christian Peoples Party. In both parties there is considerable sympathy for the more extreme policies advocated by the "No to Nuclear Weapons" movement and the Labor Party. Any major Conservative attempt to sharpen distinctions between itself and Labor—hence to exploit Labor losses—runs the risk of undermining its relationship with the other two government parties. Thus, there exists a moderating mechanism among the government parties.

Despite the existence of these factors, it has taken considerable time to establish a new equilibrium. The initial deployment of American INF weapons in accordance with the double-track decision has had to be cleared first, the controversy over INF has been the hardest to settle. It was not resolved in the new consensus that emerged in the spring of 1984. The new consensus does not suggest abandonment of the security-policy debate; rather, it creates a basis from which new proposals can be initiated. It will allow Norway to work within NATO for a no-first-use policy, a freeze, and a nuclear-weapons-free zone for the Nordic area and Europe.

Moreover, the level of debate may not be as calm as that enjoyed since the early 1960s. The outside world is likely to continue to force Norway to reexamine its security profile. The main challenges will not come from the domestic political setting, but rather from the international environment. This is likely to produce a continuous debate regarding alternative preferences for either a higher or lower profile. To the right-of-center the disposition for a higher profile both with regard to national defense and to NATO membership is likely to continue. To the left-of-center the inclination toward a lower profile seems more likely. Again, it must be stressed that this debate will occur against a general background of consensus on the basic need for a policy that embraces both deterrence and nonprovocation. Many issues will not be controversial.

Four areas serve to illustrate both the profile continuities and conflicts that will dominate Norwegian policy debates in the coming period.

Relations with the Soviet Union

The concern at the core of all Norwegian security considerations is how to ensure against the Soviet threat with sufficient military deterrence while maintaining an adequate nonprovocating posture. Norway differs from all of its allies, except Turkey, in that it has a common border with the Soviets, and is unique in that this border is very close to the largest Soviet naval base. Thus, Norway has a dual problem: It must work within the Alliance to develop an Allied profile toward the Soviet Union, and it must work within the confines of Norwegian national choice and bilateral relations with the Soviet Union to deal with specifically Norwegian security problems. One cannot be separated from the other. Norwegian policy makers must seek to keep the two compatible. Their aim is stability at the lowest possible level of tension. Stability in Norwegian-Soviet relations is also in the interest of the Atlantic Alliance.

There is not likely to be much controversy in Norway about which aspects of Alliance policy should be given priority. Norway will emphasize détente, arms control, and cooperation with the East. She will seek to guarantee that any absence of progress in the field of détente stems mainly from the behavior and objectives of the East and not from the West. Political bridge building has emerged periodically and will likely continue to do so. In this field Norwegian policy makers will continue to use three Allied countries as main reference points: the United States, Great Britain, and the Federal Republic of Germany. If there is any new emphasis in this area, it will be that of directing more attention to Germany. Norway will also continue its alertness to the Nordic situation, especially the policies emanating from Stockholm and Helsinki. Sharper Swedish reaction to Soviet policies could be lived with more comfortably in Oslo than in Helsinki, but a less-stable relationship between the Nordic neutrals and the Soviet Union could also cast an ominous shadow over the Nordic NATO member states.

More interesting in terms of the internal debate will be the problem of defining the response to the direct challenge in the North. It will continue to be a Norwegian preoccupation; Norwegians will remain convinced that no other government can do the job on their behalf. The necessity of having a national appreciation of Soviet policy toward Norway, and toward the other Nordic countries, will be felt as much in the future as it has in the past. Because the Soviet Union is likely to continue to place major importance on its naval policies, the challenge for Norway will increase rather than diminish.

The sensitivity to Soviet behavior by the Alliance's naval powers will greatly influence the choices confronting Norway. Of particular importance will be American naval policy toward the Norwegian Sea, both the height of the posture chosen and the consistency of the policy. Part of the problem will be to resolve the areas where Norway can retain an influence and what others will be exclusively the province of American decision makers. Few will deny that there is, and will continue to be, a close relationship between the security of "metropolitan" Norway and the security of the Norwegian Sea. But the final disposition of the Norwegian profile could be a matter of considerable debate.

Spending for Defense

The Norwegian defense-spending problem is a luxury compared to other NATO members, although even in Norway spending takes place under increasingly more difficult economic conditions. Unemployment is rising and the rate of economic growth is declining. But the need to concentrate more resources on defense is not the subject of significant political controversy. As described earlier, all parties, except the extreme left, support at least a 3-percent real increase in the defense budget, and the debate is only on how much more should be spent.

There are difficulties on the horizon, however, that will make the question of how to spend defense money an increasingly important problem for Norwegian governments of all stripes. Along with most of its partners, Norway faces the problem of spiraling costs of modern military equipment; the same money buys less quantity. An air force of about 125 F-5s and 104s has been reduced to seventy-two of the new F-16s and will further be reduced when planes are put out of service as funds cease to be made available for maintenance and spare parts. There is also a great lack of pilots. A fleet of fourteen submarines is being modernized, but the number of vessels is being reduced to six. Frigates are inactivated because of lack of funds. Army units are not sent on refresher courses, and the average number of days of field training has dropped from forty-three in 1979 to twenty-eight in 1983. There is even difficulty for all conscripts to serve their military service immediately at the age of nineteen because funds are not available. This problem may soon change because of diminishing birthrates, which will raise the question of military service for women in the 1990s.

The Norwegian defense situation has to be viewed against the background of the steady modernization of the Soviet armed forces, including those deployed in the vicinity of Norway. Chief of Defense General Sven Hauge argued in early February 1984 that defense needed 2 billion kroner in addition to the 3.5-percent increase already allocated at that time. The general's request would have meant a 15-percent real increase. This example illustrates the disparity between what the military believes necessary and what the economic and political factors allow.

Norway, thus, must confront the same problems as other military establishments in the Alliance. If greater specialization of equipment and roles were to be the chosen path to help alleviate the economic woes, there may be difficulty in reconciling this decision with the Norwegian desire to keep a certain independence from strategies chosen by its allies. This independence appears to be a precondition for maintaining the basic consensus on defense that still exists in Norwegian society.

The problems are not going to be easy to resolve. Should Norway concentrate on land forces and increasingly leave other roles to Alliance partners? If Norway would never have opted for seventy-two F-16s had it not been financially solvent, will it be correct to continue an independent Norwegian air force? If not, who would provide air support? Similar problems affect the Norwegian royal navy. Inshore-oriented, it operates in waters that no one else knows so well. But is it really feasible to maintain such a large navy? A sharply reduced Norwegian navy might raise the question of a reallocation of regions of responsibility of the NATO military commanders. SACLANT might be given responsiblilities closer to Norway than the present fifty nautical miles.

Problems of adequate resources and optimal force structures thus conflict with specific preferences about the way to structure alignment. It may yet become an even more important issue in Norwegian politics. A relative decrease in the strength of the Norwegian military, along with further development in the policy of prepositioning of materiel from other NATO countries, might question the feasibility of the nonbasing policy. Any serious debate on this question is bound to be politically disruptive because it will shake deeply rooted preferences and beliefs.

Military Strategy

Regardless of whether political leaders attempt to enhance consensus or whether they will choose to sharpen differences, it is likely that nuclear-weapon strategies will remain politically problematic. The Norwegian profile will certainly be lower than the postures of states possessing nuclear weapons. It is difficult to imagine that a small democratic country without any real influence on Allied (that is American) nuclear policy would be able to maintain active support for a high-profile strategy. But the development of new weapons, new strategies, and the concurrent need to react to all these changes will not disappear. The best one could hope for would be tolerance of others' policies, provided that too much pressure is not exerted by other Alliance partners in these matters. This arrangement would amount to a form of second-class membership status for the country, and although this would be difficult to accept, it might, in real terms, be preferable to the continuation of a permanent dispute over nuclear policies.

A more cautious nuclear profile would not eliminate the possibility of expressing concern in such matters, but it might help mute the expressions. Some argue that willingly accepting second-class membership would lead to less responsibility and hence less influence; coresponsibility to some is the twin brother of moderation. Conversely, others reason that genuine responsibility in nuclear matters is unattainable for most small nonnuclear Alliance members, not just Norway.

The future of this controversial subject will depend on whether or not a need arises for the Storting to vote on a policy decision. In the absence of such a need, it is likely that frustration stemming from the lack of real influence will turn into weariness rather than greater activism. Initially, it is easy to criticize American policy makers for not paying sufficient attention to European political sensitivities, but in the long run Norwegians face problems that are difficult, costly, and even politically painful to alter. If a Storting debate does not provide a new stimulus, public interest and even political interest will turn elsewhere.

Out-of-Area Questions

Out-of-area questions are not politically controversial in Norway. The country has always resisted attempts at extending Alliance involvement beyond NATO's geographic area of responsibility. In the past, calls for support by larger Alliance members have often been viewed as requests for solidarity with colonial traditions and in later years with American policeman-of-the-world inclinations. For Europeans the American role in Vietnam was not a pursuit of broader Western interests, and the United States never presented the war as a Western problem, although the American administrations of Johnson and Nixon felt the need for greater understanding from the NATO countries for the Vietnam effort. The fact that Vietnam never became a divisive issue for NATO helped stabilize the situation in Western Europe and preserve NATO's foundations.

Norway generally prefers, in the nuclear age, the geographical limitation of conflicts rather than an all-embracing alliance that may be good for deterrence but perilous if it fails. Global perspectives may be a natural predilection for the Alliance's superpower, but for a small country like Norway the means for forming an independent view are so limited that political activism may either look amateurish or dependent. The idea, however, that small Alliance partners are obliged to follow the political lead of the United States on questions outside NATO in gratitude for the protection of NATO has never been entertained in Norwegian politics.

The security of oil supplies and deliveries has been seen as a very different problem from that of Vietnam or from what has recently been transpiring in Central America. The Soviet invasion of Afghanistan heightened this concern. The necessity for a steady stream of oil to the industrialized countries and the problems of the Middle East and the Persian Gulf are particularly significant to Europe because of its resource vulnerability and proximity to the problem areas. Although, during the 1970s, Norway produced five to seven times the quantity of oil it consumed (the merchant marine excluded), Norwegian policy makers still do not treat the problem of energy supply lightly. Even if Norway is not directly vulnerable to discontinuity of oil deliveries, its main trading partners and protectors are. If economic strength and security are threatened, Norway's security is endangered as well.

This understanding, however, has never made Norway willing to see any widening of responsibilities outside the narrow geographic confines of NATO. Conservative Foreign Minister Svenn Stray suggested a compromise formula to the effect that any question might be discussed in NATO whether it originated from problems inside or outside the NATO area, but that this discussion should not necessarily be aimed at any formal agreement. Such a formula is designed to protect NATO as a security organization with a geographically restricted responsibility. The argument reads: One should not throw the baby out with the bath water when it comes to requests for a more global orientation. Providing regional security in Europe should be possible in times of greater Western security requirements.

Norway's view is that out-of-area problems must be left to the NATO members that have the capability to handle such conflicts. Norway's capacity for involvement is marginal. This does not, however, present a barrier to the Norwegian tendency to take moral stances against, and criticize the behavior of, any state or group anywhere in the world. Recently, the protection of human rights has become a particularly important question in Norwegian politics. Pinochet's Chile and Botha's South Africa provide prime examples of problem areas, as does Soviet behavior in Afghanistan and in Poland.

Public support for the notion that NATO countries defend democratic values and human rights also places certain demands on other NATO countries. In the 1960s it was important for Norwegian leaders to demonstrate support for democratic values and to protest the absence of democracy in NATO member states. Norway protested against the policies of the Greek colonels and the Portuguese regime under Salazar. Today, Turkey is the object of much criticism, in particular for putting labor leaders in prison without due process of law. Most often, protests are directed toward the United States because of the putative influence it has over these countries. These efforts have never been particularly successful, and Norway has clearly avoided pushing the issues to a point where American officials might indicate that the security of NATO's southern flank could be more important than that of the northern flank.

The issues are nevertheless potent. In 1982, for instance, human-rights violations in Turkey and El Salvador surfaced in Norwegian politics on the local level. The Nordland branch of the Labor Party voted with a small majority not to welcome Americans on NATO exercises on Norwegian territory as long as the United States was interested in human rights only in Poland and not in other countries. Although there was little support in other branches of the party for linking the two issues, incidents like this one reveal the difficulty of strictly observing the traditional rule that problems outside NATO's geographical scope should not be allowed to contaminate cooperation within NATO.

Widespread feeling persists that right-wing governments in Central America would have greater difficulty in their suppression of human rights if the United States showed a stronger will to help put an end to these violations. Needless to say, the American Government is perhaps credited with greater influence than it may actually have. Yet no matter how cumbersome moral and ideological dedication may be in an imperfect and complex world, the absence of a genuine commitment to human values risks undermining support for policies designed to produce security, no matter how indispensable.

In conclusion, it is likely that future Norwegian security strategy will resemble past policies. The milieu of course has changed. Increased public awareness of the role of nuclear weapons, the complexities of great-power politics, and the increased politicization of security issues will constitute new challenges to the leadership. These challenges will not lead to sharp changes in the direction of traditional Norwegian preferences, however. Norway's geostrategic position will continue to lead her to adopt policies of moderation, realism, and avoidance of abrupt change, at least in the absence of major external shocks to the Norwegian system.

Less predictable, however, is the external environment. A number of factors could test the willingness of the main political parties to moderate their position in order to maintain the broad national consensus. Among the key factors will be Soviet security policy in Europe, the development of Soviet naval profiles in neighboring waters, American-Soviet relations, and the attitudes expressed by the Conservative governments in leading European countries of NATO. A particular problem could arise with sudden fluctuations in American policy. Possible changes in the security policies of other Nordic states will also be important. Most central of all will be the extent to which nuclear strategy remains a dominant focus of public attention. In reacting to all these considerations, Norway will strive for continuity and moderation whenever possible. Thus, it will adhere to its traditional approach to defense: adequate deterrence and effective reassurance. Its objective will be to protect and maintain its security posture, and to do so at the lowest possible level of armaments and international tension.

Notes

1. For a brief overview of the period and a comprehensive bibliography, see Nils Oervik, *Norwegian Foreign Policy: A Bibliography 1905–1965* (Oslo: UP, 1968).

2. The early parliamentary history of Norway is described in detail by a Swede. See Arne Bjoernberg, *Parlamentarismens utveckling i Norge efter 1905 (Upsala and Stockholm: Almqvist & Wiksells Boktryckeri, 1939).*

3. Olav Riste, *The Neutral Ally: Norway's Relations with Belligerent Powers in World War I* (Oslo: Scan Books, 1965).

4. The standard work on Norwegian security policy during the interwar period is still Nils Oervik, *Sikkerhetspolitikken 1920–1939,* vol. 1: Solidaritet eller nøytralitet (Solidarity or Neutrality), and vol. 2: Vern eller vakt (Defense or Guard) (Oslo: Johan Grundt Tanum, 1960 [vol. 1] and 1961 [vol. 2]).

5. See Olav Riste, *"Functional Ties—A Semi-Alliance? Military Cooperation in North West Europe 1944–1947,* Notat, no. 6 (Oslo: Forsvarshistorisk Forskningssenter, 1981).

6. The standard work on the development of Norway from bridge building to Alliance membership is Magne Skodvin, *Norden eller NATO? Utenriksdepartementet og alliansespørsmålet 1947–1949* (Oslo: Oslo University Press, 1971).

7. Two books on Finnish postwar security policy are especially valuable. See J. O. Søderhielm, *Tre resor till Moskva* (Three Visits to Moscow) (Helsingfors: Schildts, 1970), and Max Jacobson, *Finnish Neutrality: A Study of Finnish Foreign Policy Since the Second World War* (London: Hugh Evelyn, 1968). See also George Maude, *The Finnish Dilemma: Neutrality in the Shadow of Power* (London: Oxford University Press, 1976). Finnish policy from the view of the President is explained in Urho K. Kekkonen, *Neutrality: The Finnish Position. Speeches by Urho Kekkonen, the President of Finland* (London: Heineman, 1970).

8. This point is stressed by historian Helge Pharo while summing up a long discussion between Norwegian historians about 1948–49, "Den kalde krigen i Norsk og internasjonal historieforskning" (The Cold War in Norwegian and International History Research), in *Den Truede Freden* (The Threatened Peace), ed. Øyvind Østerud (Oslo: Oslo University Press, 1984).

9. Among works on the problems of Scandinavian cooperation, see Barbara G. Haskel, *The Scandinavian Option: Opportunities and Opportunity Costs in Postwar Scandinavian Foreign Policies* (Oslo: Oslo University Press, 1976).

10. The most careful study of the policies of the Norwegian government-in-exile is done by Olav Riste, *London-regjeringa: Norge i krigsalliansen* (The London Government:

Norway in the Wartime Alliance), vol. 1: 1940–42 *Prøvetid* (Trial), vol. 2: 1942–45 *Vegen heim* (The Way Home) (Oslo: Det norske samleget, vol. 1, 1973; vol. 2, 1979).

11. Another valuable work from the same period is Nils Morten Udgaard, *Great Power Politics and Norwegian Foreign Policy: A Study of Norway's Foreign Relations November 1940–February 1948* (Oslo: Oslo University Press, 1973).

12. The most comprehensive documentation of Norwegian security policy is found in Johan Jørgen Holst, *Norsk sikkerhetspolitikk i strategisk perspektiv* (Norwegian Security Policy in a Strategic Perspective), vol. 1: *Analyse,* and vol. 2: *Dokumentasjon* (Oslo: Norwegian Institute of International Affairs, 1967); hereafter cited as Holst I and Holst II.

13. For a more extended discussion of the Nordic balance, see Arne Olav Brundtland, "The Nordic Balance and Its Possible Relevance for Europe," in *Sicherheit Durch Gleichwicht?* ed. Daniel Frei (Zürich: Schulthess, 1982). A detailed examination of the arguments used in the Storting against a Scandinavian defense arrangement in found in Arne Olav Brundtland, "Hvorfor ikke et skandinavisk forsvarsforbund? Argumentene slik de ble presentert i Stortinget," in *Internasjonal Politikk* (special issue on Nordic security questions) 2–3 (1964): 179–98.

14. Former Secretary General of the Labor Party, Mr. Haakon Lie, has discussed these matters in his work . . . *slik jeg ser det* (The Way I See It) (Oslo: Tiden, 1975) and further examined the problems of security policy for Labor in . . .*slik jeg ser det 2* (The Way I See It 2) (Oslo: Tiden, 1983). A recent political/personal biography of the former Labor Prime Minister, Mr. Trygve Bratteli, also examines these years from the point of view of security. See Giske Anderson, *Trygve Bratteli* (Oslo: Gyldendahl, 1984).

15. Point stressed by Francis Sejersted in *Høyres Historie,* vol. 3: *Opposisjon og posisjon 1945–1981* (Oslo: Cappelen, 1984), 85–97.

16. This created a public debate in which this author sharply criticized the Foreign Minister for his lack of enthusiasm for joining. *Aftenposten,* 25 October 1965.

17. Holst II, 234ff. This observation is borne out by the author's readings of Mr. Lange's foreign-policy statements in the Storting. It is a matter of some controversy among Norwegian foreign-policy commentators as to how much more flexible Lyng was compared to Lange. Lange is often seen as having a fixation on Cold War policies. It should not be overlooked, however, that the international conditions during Lyng's period of office were more suited to flexible initiatives.

18. Figures made available by the Royal Ministry of Defense.

19. Text in Norwegian from Holst II, 71–72 (my translation). Note that I use "nonbasing policy" throughout in keeping with terminology in the article, while the official term is the "basing policy."

20. Among typical Soviet contributions to this debate, see P. Krymov, "The Soviet Union and the North European Countries," *International Affairs,* 9 (September 1979): 18.

21. Holst II, 159.

22. Quotations from text of communiqué after the meeting. Holst II, 169–71 (my translation). Text also in the *New York Times,* 26 November 1961.

23. Acceptance noted in the text of the communiqué. Other factors than respect for the Norwegian warnings of a change in policy should also be observed. Among these were the fact that the Soviets were about to change their attitude toward the West away from direct confrontation, and the fact that the Finnish political milieu closed ranks behind Mr. Kekkonen's candidacy for president. Mr. Kekkonen also took upon himself the "new role" of following more carefully political developments in the north and the Baltic areas, thereby giving him a diplomatic card to play against requests from Soviet hard-liners.

24. Mr. Frydenlund's statement is hard to trace in written form. It is here taken from the memory of the author. The whole question naturally consumed much public attention in Norwegian politics during the first half of 1977, with numerous public statements both by the Prime Minister and the Foreign Minister inside and outside the Storting. See, for example *Norsk Utenrikspolitisk Årbok 1977* (Norwegian Yearbook of

Foreign Policy 1977) (Oslo: Norwegian Institute of International Affairs, 1978), 298–306; hereafter cited as NUPÅ.

25. Among numerous contributions, see Nils Oervik, *Europe's Northern Cap and the Soviet Union*, Occasional Paper no. 6 (Cambridge, Mass.: Harvard University Center for International Affairs, 1963); and a Finnish response by Jan Klenberg, *The Cap and the Straits—Problems of Nordic Security*, Occasional Paper no. 18 (Cambridge, Mass.: Harvard University Center for International Affairs, 1968). Reviewed by Arne Olav Brundtland in *Cooperation and Conflict*, no. 4 (Oslo: Oslo University Press, 1968). For a more recent and comprehensive discussion, see Johan Jørgen Holst, "Norway's Search for a Nordpolitik," *Foreign Affairs* (Fall 1981): 63–86.

26. This model was underlined in different statements by Foreign Minister Knut Frydenlund. See, for example, Knut Frydenlund's lecture to the Oslo branch of the Labor Party, 12 September 1978, in NUPÅ 1978, 446–48. Emphasis on the avoidance of raising tensions naturally sets strict limits for policy and makes Norway vulnerable to Soviet pressures. If some impatience could be detected in Norwegian northern policy during the late 1970s, the tone has since gradually changed. If the Soviets can wait, the Norwegians also demonstrate that they can wait. There may be a particular price to be paid by the "demandeur" in the north.

27. The performance of Prime Minister Gerhardsen has been the object of much discussion. Among the more recent ones, see Jostein Nyhamar, *Einar Gerhardsen 1945–1983*, vol. 2 (Oslo: Tiden, 1983), 193–211. Mr. Nyhamar sees the problem from a left-wing point of view and is particularly pleased by Mr. Gerhardsen's role.

28. Defense White Paper 1960–61 (Storting Melding no. 28, 1960–61) (Oslo: Royal Ministry of Defense, 1961).

29. Outlined in *Hovedretningslinjer for Forsvarets organisasjon og virksomhet i tiden 1964–1968* (Main Guidelines for the Development and Activities of Defense 1964–68), Storting Melding no. 84, 1962–63 (Oslo: Royal Ministry of Defense, 1963).

30. Point made by Foreign Minister Halvard Lange in the Storting, 27 February 1962. Holst II, 176.

31. *Om sikkerhet og nedrustning: Rustningskontroll- og nedrustningsarbeidets plass i sikkerhetspolitikken* (On Security and Disarmament: The Role of Arms Control and Disarmament in Security Policy) Storting Melding no. 101, 1981–82 (Oslo: Royal Ministry of Defense, 1982), 28.

32. Mr. Frydenlund has collected his reflections in *Lille Land—hva nå? Refleksjoner om Norges utenrikspolitiske situasjon* (Little Country—What Now? Reflections upon Norway's Foreign Policy Situation) (Oslo: Oslo University Press, 1983).

33. Point further developed by Mr. Knut Frydenlund, "Utenrikspolitikk i et mediasamfunn" (Foreign Policy in a Media Society), *Internasjonal Politikk*, special issue on the media and foreign policy, 3 (1983).

34. Forsvarskommisjonen av 1974. Norges Offentlige Utredninger no. 9, 1978.

35. Figures taken from *Hovedretninglinjer for Forsvarets virksomhet i tiden 1984–88* (Main Guidelines for Defense Activities 1984–88), Storting Melding no. 74, 1982–83 (Oslo: Royal Ministry of Defense, 1983), 8.

36. See A. O. Brundtland, "INF og sammengruddet av den sikkerhetspolitiske enighet" (The INF and the Collapse of the Broad Agreement in Security), *Internasjonal Politikk*, 3 (1983). The article concentrates on the different phases in the treatment of the INF issue on parliamentary debates. The amount of details may be felt as a burden by the reader, but it seems warranted in order to understand the forces at work in this particular context in Norwegian politics.

37. *Common Security: A Program for Disarmament*. The Report of the Independent Commission on Disarmament and Security Issues (London and Sidney: Pan Books, 1982).

5

The "Scandilux" Connection: Belgium, Denmark, the Netherlands, and Norway in Comparative Perspective

JOSEF JOFFE

Introduction: Allies Alike?

At first, even at second blush, the four countries in this study have little in common—with the exception of that deceptive label "Scandilux," which is a recent invention of the Socialist International.* The four countries are not even all small. In terms of population, they are of course outranked by the classic middle powers like France, Britain, and West Germany. Yet among the four, there are impressive variations in size and population. Dutch (14.4 million) outnumber Norwegians by a ratio of 3.5 to one, and there are also three times as many Dutch as there are Danes. In terms of sheer geographical extension, Norway looms as a colossus among the drawfs. Its territory (324,000 square kilometers) could accommodate almost ten Hollands and more than ten Belgiums; it is seven and a half times the size of Denmark and slightly larger than Italy.

There are also large disparities in economic weight. In terms of gross

---

*The "Scandilux" appellation does, however, echo a precedent known as the Oslo Group, which brought together the Benelux and Scandinavian countries in a loose association during the 1930s. After the Italian invasion of Abyssinia, the Oslo Group countries pledged themselves to a kind of collective neutrality by repudiating their obligation to assist in League of Nations sanctions.

domestic product (GDP), Norway and Denmark are roughly equivalent. Yet Belgium's GDP of $81 billion is roughly 60 percent larger than that of either Denmark or Norway, and the Dutch domestic product ($130 billion) is more than twice as large as that of the two Nordic countries.

In terms of military strength, as measured by the number of armed forces, there is a similar gap between the "Scandi" and the "Lux" countries. Belgium (with 93,000 troops) and the Netherlands (with 103,000 troops) are again roughly comparable, but they each dwarf Denmark and Norway, with their armed forces of 31,000 and 37,000, respectively.

Adding the dimension of history provides even more diversity. There is only one historical experience all four share, and that is the occupation by Nazi Germany during World War II. In all other respects, geographical separation has also made for stark historical differences. The two Nordic countries have not sought a global role; they have never colonized others, with the exception of the brief interlude of the Danish West Indies and Greenland, which are insignificant in terms of population. Nor have they been ruled by a foreign empire as were the Low Countries by Spain in the 16th and 17th centuries. Certainly, Norway's existence as a separate state is short. The country was under Danish rule from 1380 to 1814, and thereafter it was forced into union with Sweden. Yet subjection was tempered by a large degree of autonomy, and then it was *en famille,* as it were, which stands in marked contrast to the domination of the Low Countries by the far-flung, alien, far-reaching Spanish Empire.

The historical experience of Holland and Belgium was dramatically different. Belgium's existence athwart the crossroads of Western Europe has made it an inviting target for each and all: for Romans, Celts, and Franks, and for Spaniards, French, Austrians, and Germans. Nor did the Dutch enjoy the blessings of natural borders (apart from the sea) or geographic remoteness that might have given pause to would-be conquerors. For almost a century, the Dutch fought for independence against Spain. They finally attained it with the Peace of Münster in 1648.

In terms of its international role, Holland is historically the odd man out. For about a century after the Peace of Münster, the "United Provinces" joined the ranks of the great powers of Europe, an evolution that sets the Netherlands distinctly apart from the other three countries in this study. In the process, the Dutch not only fought the British intermittently for commercial and maritime advantage, but they also acquired an overseas empire of remarkable size and diversity. Colonies added a worldwide dimension to Dutch foreign policy, shared only partially by the Belgians (because of their Congolese possessions) and not at all by the Danes and Norwegians. (Denmark ceded its symbolic "empire" in the Caribbean—the Virgin Islands—to the United States in 1916.) As a result, the two Nordic countries were spared the painful process of decolonization that embroiled Dutch forces in Indonesia during the late 1940s and which kept Belgium entangled in Africa until the independence of the Congo in 1959.

Finally, there is the differing impact of geography. Located in the

Table 5.1 Economic, Defense, and Population Statistics

I. Belgium

Area: 30,519 sq km
Population: 9,900,000
Defenses:

Total:	93,607 (31,908 conscripts)
Army:	65,102 (26,163 conscripts)
Navy:	4,557 (1,227 conscripts)
Air Force:	20,948 (4,518 conscripts)

Defense Spending: $1.847 bn. (1983)
Gross Domestic Product (GDP): $81.143 bn. (1983)
Defense Spending/GDP: 2.27%
Military Manpower/Population: 0.94%

II. Denmark

Area: 43,033 sq km
Population: 5,150,000
Defenses:

Total:	31,400 (9,500 conscripts)
Army:	18,100 (6,800 conscripts)
Navy:	5,900 (1,200 conscripts)
Air Force:	7,400 (1,500 conscripts)

Defense Spending: $1.128 bn. (1983)
Gross Domestic Product (GDP): $56.380 bn. (1983)
Defense Spending/GDP: 2.0%
Military Manpower/Population: 0.6%

III. Netherlands

Area: 36,175 sq km
Population: 14,400,000
Defenses:

Total:	103,267 (46,368 conscripts)
Army:	64,664 (40,785 conscripts)
Navy:	16,867 (1,437 conscripts)
Air Force:	16,810 (3,565 conscripts)

Defense Spending: $4.431 bn. (1983)
Gross Domestic Product (GDP): $129.83 bn. (1983)
Defense Spending/GDP: 3.4%
Military Manpower/Population: 0.71%

IV. Norway

Area: 324,219 sq km
Population: 4,146,000
Defenses:

Total:	36,785 (22,500 conscripts)
Army:	19,500 (12,000 conscripts)
Navy:	7,500 (5,500 conscripts)
Air Force:	16,810 (5,000 conscripts)

Defense Spending: $1.740 bn. (1983)
Gross Domestic Product (GDP): $54.997 bn. (1983)
Defense Spending/GDP: 3.1%
Military Manpower/Population: 0.8%

Note: The defense-spending-to-GDP ratios in this table may differ from other comparisons because the denominator is GDP rather than GNP, while the numerator derives from national budget figures rather than from the so-called NATO definition of defense spending.

Source: International Institute for Strategic Studies, *The Military Balance, 1984–1985* (London: IISS, 1984).

European periphery, the two Nordic countries were, throughout their history, more shielded from the pulls and pushes of the European system than Belgium and Holland. The Low Countries, on the other hand, could never escape from a geographical fate that had placed them at the center of Western European conflicts. Since the beginning of the European state system, they were destined to be the stake and the arena of every major European war. Neutrality was thus but an aspiration that foundered regularly on the hegemonial ambitions of the Valois and Hapsburgs, of the French under Napoleon, and of the Germans under Wilhelm II and Adolf Hitler.

The destruction and simultaneous enlargement of the European system that resulted from World War II marks a crucial watershed as well as an inversion of the traditional state of affairs for the Nordic and Benelux countries. With the integration of Europe's great flanking powers, the United States and the Soviet Union, the dominant line of conflict shifted eastward. In contrast to centuries past, Belgium and the Netherlands were now no longer caught in the immediate focus of Europe's quarrels but were relatively safely ensconced behind a massive barrier of West German and American military power to the East.

On the other hand, the Nordic countries were now much closer to the scene of potential devastation. Norway suddenly found itself in a far more exposed geographical position than ever before. After 1945 the country no longer enjoyed the benefits of relative quiescence on the Continent's periphery. Apart from Turkey, Norway is the only NATO country that shares a border, although short, with the Soviet Union. And like Turkey, Norway's value as a strategic asset (and stake) is compounded by its key role in the naval strategies of both blocs. A similar change in geostrategic position has impinged upon Denmark. Isolated from nearby great powers until the rise of Prussia in the second half of the 19th century, Denmark found itself almost on the frontline at the beginning of the Cold War. Soviet troops in East Germany were but tank-hours away from its southern border, and Denmark's position astride the Baltic Straits made it an inviting target for a Warsaw Pact thrust toward the Skagerrak. In short, the label "small" is as deceptive as the "Scandilux" designation. Differences loom larger than similarities, and yet there is an understandable tendency to plumb for commonalities.

First, these four countries are obviously "small" by comparison with Britain, France, West Germany, or Italy. The strategic value of some of them notwithstanding, all four countries play a less influential role in the affairs of the Alliance than the middle powers. Second, the four present a large degree of internal homogeneity when compared to their allies on NATO's southeastern and southwestern periphery. In contrast to Spain, Portugal, Greece, and Turkey, they are blessed with highly developed economies marked by an elaborate division of labor and an efficient apparatus of administration. Their societies function at a high level of prosperity and egalitarianism. Their political systems, while not universally blessed by a sturdy national consensus, as in the case of Belgium, are solidly beholden to democracy and the rule of law. Third, they are "civilian powers" *par excellence*: pacific in outlook and aspiration, prone to take a moral view of international affairs, and loath to employ force as a tool of statecraft—which sets them apart from middle powers like France and England, as well as from the more violent lesser members of the Alliance like Greece and Turkey.

Finally, they all shared a common fate during World War II. During World War I, only Belgium's neutrality was violated (by the German Reich). The others just managed to maintain theirs—the Danes by mining their waters in prudent response to German pressures, the Norwegians by rendering valuable shipping services to the British, and the Dutch by putting their army on a war footing for four years (although, in 1917, all Dutch ships in Allied ports were peremptorily requisitioned by the entente powers).

During World War II all four suffered Belgium's fate of 1914—perhaps because all of them had woefully neglected their defenses in the interwar period. Neutrality, eagerly proclaimed in 1939, became the prelude to conquest as Denmark fell, with nary a shot, to Hitler's armies in April 1940. Norway fell immediately thereafter, while Belgium and Holland were invaded one month later, and organized resistance in the latter two countries had collapsed by June.

These memories were largely responsible for the abandonment of neutrality in favor of NATO. Yet the older aspirations have not disappeared; nor should this be a surprise. All small countries *tend* to seek security in the escape from the quarrels of the strong, and they do so for three reasons. One is resignation—the sense that their power counts for little in the world of the mighty, that it will neither deter nor repel a superior aggressor. The second reason is safety-through-weakness, the calculation that their very insignificance in the larger scheme of power will spare them the hostility of the strong. The third reason is hope tempered by cynicism—the bet that they might enjoy the benefits of protection without the cost of alignment by courtesy of those great powers who will shelter them against rivals out of sheer self-interest. On the other hand, small powers, such as the four under consideration, *do* align sometimes, and thus the instinct for neutrality can only define a residual dream. Whether or not that dream is translated into actual policy must be decided by causes other than the presumed penchant for neutralism on the part of the weak; that is, by domestic circumstances and external constellations. Since these powers did align, it would suggest that there are other elements of similarity amidst diversity, and this is precisely why comparative analyses are undertaken.

The Road to Alignment: Continuity in a New Guise?

Generalizing on the basis of size, geography, or history is a tricky business, as the four countries under consideration are apt to show. Taking geography as a guide, one might have surmised that the two Nordic countries, suddenly thrust toward the focus of potential confrontation, would have been quite eager to break with their tradition of noninvolvement and to huddle under the new shelter, NATO. Conversely, one might have predicted that Holland and Belgium, now no longer on the front line and surrounded by the armed might of others, would toy with a "free rider" policy, trying to enjoy *gratis* the security provided by the greater powers, notably by American and West German forces to the east. In fact, the contrary was to happen. The Low Countries were among the first to look for formal alliance with the United States, while the two Nordic countries were at first hesitant and then joined the Alliance but with significant qualifications.

While all four had thoroughly realized the perils of neutrality in the 20th century, the two Nordic countries were a good deal slower than Belgium and Holland in accepting the implications of that lesson. At least until the dramatic escalation of the Soviet-American confrontation in 1948, the two Nordic countries placed a good many hopes on *noncommital* versions of collective security, such as those universal security concepts embodied in the U.N. Charter. "Although the League of Nations had not proved effective as an international mechanism for the enhancement of small states' security," writes Martin Heisler in the Danish chapter, "the leaders of most Danish parties looked once more to such a collective security regime—this time to the United Nations, which appeared to have 'more teeth' than its predecessors."

In Norway, hope buttressed by *Realpolitik* initially produced a similar policy of noninvolvement. Hope centered on the United Nations and great-power cooperation in the Security Council, and the tenets of *Realpolitik* shaped the belief that "there would be military assistance from nonattacking great powers whose strategic interests would be jeopardized by aggression against Norway." In both countries, then, the initial instinct was to avoid association with a Western power bloc. In both Nordic countries the more recent memory of German aggression was tempered by earlier impulses (and memories) that saw security in relative geographic insulation, a nonprovocative stance vis-à-vis their great-power neighbors and a kind of "minimal deterrent" posture just about commensurate with their presumed low strategic value in the overall balance.

The road toward alliance was slow at best. Both nations moved only reluctantly toward NATO, and then only after a thorough review of the "Scandinavian option," a defense pact less closely aligned with the West than NATO. "The major objective of the Danish government was to find a solution which kept the Scandinavian countries together, either independent of or in association with the Western powers; only when in February 1949 it became crystal clear that Norway and Sweden would not be able to agree on the character of an SDU (Scandinavian Defense Union), did the Danish Government turn toward its reserve option, membership in the Atlantic Pact."[1]

The events of 1948, presenting a functional equivalent to the declaration of the Cold War, tipped the scale. The Prague coup, the Berlin blockade, the Soviet-Finnish Friendship Treaty, and mounting Soviet pressure on Norway (to which Denmark looked for leadership) imposed the logic of NATO as a sort of *faute de mieux*. Or, as Martin Heisler puts it in the case of Denmark: Since an independent defense could not be mustered, since the SDU did not materialize, and since a globalist security framework à la U.N. had become increasingly unrealistic, "alliance was the only remaining alternative." In other words, while an adequate supply of security was not forthcoming, demand for it suddenly soared as a result of Soviet pressures. The Norwegians, in particular, interpreted the Friendship Treaty between Helsinki and Moscow (6 April 1948) as a prelude to similar pressure on Oslo, and here too the breakdown of the SDU negotiations in early 1949 "cleared the path for Norway to join the Atlantic Alliance." The alternative of alliance was still not eagerly grasped, and in the process of alignment the two Nordic countries displayed a calculated ambivalence that mirrors classic small-state behavior.

When security-dependent states contemplate commitment to an alliance, they must steer a careful course between the Scylla of "abandonment" and the Charybdis of "entrapment."[2] Both extremes of this dilemma are but two sides of the same coin: how to maintain control over a more powerful ally who may either choose to deny support in the moment of truth (abandonment) or, conversely, drag his partner into a conflict in which the latter would rather not participate (entrapment). In other words, nations-in-alliance want iron chains when *their* security is at stake, yet these should dwindle into gossamer strings when their partners demand loyalty in a confrontation that does not impinge on each and all alike. To avoid entrapment, allies typically take a dim view of the "indivisibility of conflict," trying instead to loosen the tie that binds and to compartmentalize the security market by constructing a low security demand function for themselves. Characteristically, this takes the form of partial propitiation by which an ally seeks to reduce the common adversary's incentives to attack. To reinforce the insurance taken out from a patron power (for example, Washington), allies are perennially disposed to buy reinsurance from the would-be aggressor (for example, Moscow) through a posture of *limited* assurance and conciliation. (It could not be total because that would be tantamount to defection and the end of alliance.) The instinct for partial propitiation grows when the protector is far away and the adversary is near at hand, as in the case of Denmark and Norway. Such an attitude is not exclusively restricted to small powers, as exemplified by West Germany's *Ostpolitik*. On the front line of the potential battle, the Federal Republic has for the past fifteen years (since the onset of strategic parity, which has cut into the mainstays of "extended deterrence") conducted a policy toward the Soviet Union that has sought to diminish Soviet hostility through political cooperation and economic rewards.

In the case of Denmark and Norway, the penchant for propitiation—reducing the Soviet Union's reasons for aggression through reassurance—boiled down to a policy, to use Heisler's expression, that worked "the two sides of the security equation—increasing military capability through alliance while simultaneously seeking to decrease the threat confronted" from the outset through "confidence-building policies vis-à-vis the Soviet Union." Upon its accession to NATO, Norway added to the insurance taken out from the West a crucial element of reassurance toward the Soviets: Norway would not "join in any agreement . . . involving obligations to open bases for the military forces of foreign powers on Norwegian soil as long as Norway is not attacked or exposed to threats of attack."[3] Denmark pursued a similar policy from the very beginning. Although it did not duplicate the formal commitments issued by Norway, Copenhagen imposed in 1957 stringent limitations on the stationing of nuclear weapons on Danish soil. The limits of alliance embodied in the Nordic choice in the early days are still starkly visible today. Both countries have remained staunchly opposed to the basing of nuclear weapons within their frontiers and in their waters. During the Theater Nuclear Forces (TNF) deliberations of NATO's High Level Group in 1978 and 1979, Oslo opposed sea-based long-range TNF because it feared having these weapons located too close to Norwegian shores and harbors.

In the case of the Dutch and Belgians, the road toward alliance was taken with far more speed and less ambivalence—which adds an interesting facet to the rich variety of small-power behavior. As early as the winter of 1947, The Hague and Brussels reacted speedily to British proposals for what, in March 1948, became the Treaty of Brussels, establishing the Western Union. Indeed, as Jan Siccama points out, Eelco N. van Kleffens, the Foreign Minister of the London-based Dutch government-in-exile, had already sketched out a postwar Euro-American alliance in 1943. Explicitly directed against Germany, the automatic mutual defense commitment contained in the Brussels Treaty provided a comfortable stepping stone toward the North Atlantic Pact of 1949. Both treaties were passed by large majorities in Brussels and The Hague.

Why was there this rapid move toward alignment that set the Low Countries apart from the two Nordic countries? On purely conceptual grounds, the road taken by Holland and Belgium exemplifies another basic option of small powers. Instead of maintaining their distance from a leading power, they may choose the opposite strategy—influence-through-intimacy—on the assumption that closeness to the bloc leader yields leverage through loyalty. This logic was buttressed by more specific and tangible reasons, which grew out of historical habit as well as fear of the future. Since the Dutch withdrew from their great-power rivalry with Britain in the 18th century, there emerged the tradition of the extra-continental balancer whereby British strength would check French and, later, Prusso-German ambitions in the Rhine delta. After World War II the United States was Britain writ large—the appropriate counterweight against the old contender for European hegemony; that is, a resurgent Germany, and against the new challenger, Soviet Russia.

Having achieved relative insulation against the vagaries of great-power politics in centuries past, Norway and Denmark were both more hesitant and ambivalent in their commitment to NATO. (The fuzzy concept of a "Nordic balance," acting both as a buffer and excuse, was later to reinforce that attitude.) Too close a bond with the Western superpower appeared as a mixed blessing. For the Benelux countries the situation pointed in the opposite direction: The remote and rich patron across the sea served as a welcome counter against the continental great power, both past and potential.

That distinct regional logic was aptly adumbrated by J. J. C. Voorhoeve: "The Netherlands . . . preferred the gentle hegemony of a remote Atlantic superpower over what would be a less credible leadership, but a more immediate domination by Britain, Germany, France, or any combination of them in a militarily independent Europe."[4] That principle explains why the Dutch strained to block any attempts—for example, de Gaulle's efforts in the early 1960s—to harness the Western European states to a purely continental (and by no means pro-American) venture. It may also explain why the Dutch (in 1957) and the Belgians (in the early 1960s) decided to host American nuclear weapons on their soil— as an alternative to purely national nuclear forces, like those of the French, which these two countries strongly opposed.

Nor were the habits of close cooperation with the Anglo-Americans merely imposed by postwar necessity. Unlike the Danes, the Dutch and the Belgians had established governments-in-exile in London after the German invasion, and the ties established then were extended after the liberation. They were evidently enhanced by the prospect of large-scale economic aid from the United States. Between 1948 and 1952, as Jan Siccama points out, the Netherlands "received one billion dollars from the United States which was considered a crucial contribution to the recovery of the war-stricken economy. Furthermore, U.S. military aid accounted for half the military equipment that the Dutch acquired during the 1950s." Similar "side-payments" reinforced the alliance-mindedness of the Belgians. "It was frequently argued," notes Luc Reychler in his chapter, "that Belgium, as a member of the Atlantic Alliance, would receive more aid to rekindle its economy."

Yet these "side-payments" do not explain the convergent roads taken by the "Scandi' and "Lux" countries in the aftermath of World War II, since the United States from 1949 to 1969 invested heavily in the military infrastructure as well as the major weapons systems of the Norwegian armed forces. The Danes, too, were long-term beneficiaries of American military largesse. In sum, the comparison between the Nordic and Benelux countries serves as a reminder that neither size nor side-payments adumbrate adequately the "logic of collective action." Smallness, to borrow from Sigmund Freud, is not necessarily destiny.*

---

*Mancur Olson in his pathbreaking book *The Logic of Collective Action: Public Goals and the Theory of Groups* (Cambridge: Harvard University Press, 1965, 1981) seeks to explain why smaller members of an organization, such as an alliance, regularly "pay less" than the larger ones for the production of collective goods like security. In general, it is true that the powerful contribute more to the common purpose than lesser allies, and that all smaller powers are inherently "Gaullist," meaning that they will try to exploit the common structure as "free riders." Yet as the preceding analysis tried to show, the behavioral diversity *among* small powers cannot be explained by the "logic of collective action" alone. Additional factors must be adduced to explain why the Low Countries committed themselves to the Alliance more rapidly than the Nordic countries.

Nor are history or geography by themselves adequate explanations of countries' international choices. Those all-encompassing variables of international analysis tend to explain too much and, thus, too little. Which part of history does a nation remember as it faces its choices for the future? The Danes and Norwegians were, at least initially, less impressed by the very recent experience of conquest than by centuries of relative safety-through-insulation. How determinate is geography? Again, the "Scandi" countries might have obeyed the new geography of conflict that had suddenly thrust them toward the front line of potential confrontation. But instead of moving toward rapid alignment with the United States, their first instinct was to seek security in geographically more limited ventures like the Scandinavian Defense Union. Thereafter, and until this day, Norway and Denmark have refused to base their security on unconditional alignment with NATO. Instead, they have tempered insurance in the West with a strong dose of reinsurance in the East; hence their refusal to host nuclear weapons on their soil and their well-developed penchant for détente and nonprovocative policies. Yet *between* the two "Scandi" countries, geography still makes for interesting differentiations. Norway, presenting a key strategic target to the Soviet Union, has been most stalwart in maintaining its conventional strength. Denmark, on the other hand, is both smaller and more sheltered (by German power astride its land approaches), and these facts may explain why its defense efforts declined along with easing of the Cold War, while a burgeoning welfare state came to claim an ever-increasing share of the national product.

Geography and history offered similarly ambiguous lessons to the "Lux" countries. Belgium and Holland, suddenly one step removed from the main locus of war, might have harkened to the Olsonian imperative and opted for a "free rider" approach. Yet, in fact, they remembered an older part of their history, which bade them to seek out an extracontinental balancer, and then not so much against the new enemy in the East as against their great-power neighbors, France and Germany. Moreover, rather than obeying Olson, they opted not for "free-riding," but for the opposite choice open to smaller powers—namely, influence maximization through intimacy with the alliance leader. In short, while history and geography do matter, it is never obvious *ex ante* which "chunks" of these large-scale variables actually tip the scales.

Atlantis Lost? The Nature of the Domestic Consensus

If the postwar alignment of the four countries represented a sharp break with past policy, it turned out to be neither capricious nor fleeting. Indeed, in many respects these four countries, although small by comparison with the middle powers, became model allies, with the two Low Countries assuming a vanguard role in the pursuit of Atlanticism. *Mutatis mutandi*, Luc Reychler's portrayal of Belgium holds also true for the other three: "For nearly 30 years, the Belgian role in the Atlantic Alliance enjoyed a broad national consensus." Or as Arne Brundtland puts it with respect to Norway: "The framework of debate and disagreement during the first thirty years of alignment was well-defined and carefully circumscribed. Differences over the balance between defense and nonprovocation . . . were seldom a matter of major political import." Popular support for the Alliance remained remarkably high.[5] Nor did defense spending decline during the first three decades. On the contrary, there was a sturdy upward movement, which, in dollar terms, peaked everywhere only as late as 1980.[6] Levels of military manpower also held steady everywhere but in Denmark. During the "decade of détente," the 1970s, and beyond, Danish manpower totals dropped from 40,000 in 1971 to 30,000 in 1983—by 25 percent. In the other countries there were only minor changes in the same period. In Belgium there was a slight drop from 96,000 to 94,700. In the Netherlands the armed forces declined from 116,000 to 103,000. In Norway troop levels actually rose from 36,000 to 43,000.[7]

Yet these statistics cannot dispel the sense that at the end of the 1970s the old verities and signposts of the Alliance had begun to crumble. Among the four countries, two were even singled out to lend their names to two new dread diseases. "Hollanditis" came to denote nuclear pacifism; "Denmarkization" was to signify creeping abandonment—the neglect of the common defense effort in favor of drift, lassitude, and free-riding. Yet with the exception of Denmark, the four countries did not noticeably reduce their physical or financial contributions to the Alliance. Thus, there are four questions that call for an answer.

The first concerns the distinction *between* countries: If the transition from the 1970s to the 1980s does mark a break in continuity, is this primarily a small-state affliction or a trait shared by all or most of the European members of the Alliance? The second distinction we must plumb concerns the *nature of the issues:* Does the insistently decried malaise derive from a general disaffection with alliance and defense, or does it have more limited origins that must be sought in the specific issue area of nuclear weapons, in particular the deployment of cruise and Pershing II missiles? Third, there is the *problem of actors:* Are we confronted with a genuine societal revolt against the mainstays of Alliance strategy or with a more limited political phenomenon that has pitted elites (or counterelites) against elites? The fourth problem is the nature of the *transformation:* If there is discontent and rebellion—most dramatically manifested in the surge of a European-wide peace movement—does this signify a *secular* break or merely a *cyclical* burst?

Countries Great and Small

Table 5.2 seeks to compare small and middle/great powers in terms of some key ratios: defense spending as share of government expenditure and defense spending as percentage of gross national/gross domestic product. There are some significant but not consistently dramatic differ-

Table 5.2 Sharing the Burden: Defense, Budgets, and the Economy

Small Countries

Defense as % of Government Spending

	1972	1982	% Change 1972/82
Belgium	10.1	8.3	− 18
Denmark	8.1	6.6	− 18.5
Netherlands	12.9	9.0	− 30
Norway	9.9	9.9	0
		Average Change:	− 16.5

Small countries

Defense as % of GDP/GNP

	1972	1982	% Change 1972/82
Belgium	2.8	3.4	+ 21.0
Denmark	2.4	2.5	+ 4.0
Netherlands	3.4	3.3	− 3.0
Norway	3.4	3.0	− 12.0
		Average Change:	+ 2.5
Average Share:	3.0		

Middle/Large Powers

Defense as % of Government Spending

	1972	1982	% Change 1972/82
Britain	13.1	11.4	− 13.0
France	19.0	18.1	− 5.0
FRG	25.9	28.2	+ 8.0
USA	31.5	27.0	− 14.0
		Average Change:	− 6.0

Middle/Large Powers

Defense as % of GDP/GNP

	1972	1982	% Change 1972/82
Britain	5.2	5.3	+ 2.0
France	3.7	4.2	+ 13.0
FRG	3.4	4.1	+ 20.0
USA	6.7	6.5	− 3.0
		Average Change:	+ 8.0
Average Share:	5.25		

Source: International Institute for Strategic Studies, *The Military Balance,* 1975-76 and 1984-85 (London: IISS), 76 and 140.

ences between the small and the large, and these differences are wrapped up in an apparent paradox.

Grosso modo, defense spending throughout the West went up in real terms during the decade of 1972–82, with the significant exception of the United States, which, after 1972, came down from a Vietnam-related peak and resumed rapid growth in fiscal year 1981. Yet with the exception of the Federal Republic of Germany and Norway, the ratio of defense/government outlays declined throughout the West. This is the apparent paradox, which, however, is easy to unravel, and which, again, reflects a general Western pattern. In the halcyon days of the welfare state (and détente), government spending on nondefense items—on the social safety net, education, entitlements and so on—rose faster than defense outlays. It was not that guns were sacrificed for butter; guns just received a smaller share of the growing collective wealth. The 1970s, one might surmise, was a "Social Democratic decade" everywhere, marked by the rapid expansion of the state's role in the national economy and inspired by the attempt to redistribute income in an evolutionary manner "from above." If the time series are extended, the shift is even more dramatic. Table 3.8 in Jan Siccama's chapter tells the dramatic tale of twenty years. Defense spending, while on the rise in absolute terms, plummeted from 19 percent in 1962 to 9 percent of the national budget in 1984.

While that trend was more or less a general one, some rather significant differences emerge from the comparison of small and big powers, as shown by Table 5.2. On the whole (the odd man out is Norway), the defense/government spending ratios fell more rapidly in the four small countries, almost three times faster than among the big four—Britain, West Germany, France, and the United States. Conversely, the defense/national product ratios rose faster among the large countries—almost three times faster. Together, these ratios yield some suggestive evidence for the "Olsonian imperative," which postulates that small members of an organization tend to contribute less to the production of collective goods than the larger ones. On the average, in 1982 the large countries contributed 5.25 percent of their national product to defense; on the average, the four small countries yielded only 3.05 percent. During the 1970s the Scandilux countries spent more rapidly on nondefense items in their national budgets than the four largest members of the Alliance. However, none of these figures allows the conclusion to be drawn that the small members have either reduced their burdens (as measured in terms of the defense/GNP-GDP ratio, the burden rose slightly) or flung themselves wantonly into "welfare-statism" (defense outlays rose in absolute terms while declining only as a share of the budget.) Finally, these statistics reveal something that intuition would not expect. As the economies contracted everywhere in the West in the early 1980s, defense spending as a portion of a diminishing or flattening GNP was not being sacrificed to bad times. This is the significance of the rising defense/GNP ratios of 1982 as compared to during the full-employment period of the early 1970s. Together, the four collectively show at least a small rise (average change 1972–82: plus 2.5 percent), although the Netherlands and Norway have allowed that share to diminish slightly.

In short, the differences between small and large powers are visible but not breathtaking. *Both* groups allocated a growing portion of their budget to nondefense pursuits, but the small countries did so a bit more thoroughly. Both protected their defense spending against the 1980s recession, as evidenced by rising defense/GNP shares all round, but the large countries did so with more vigor than the small ones. Yet neither set of data proves that the small had fallen prey to the heinous curse of "Denmarkization."

Nor has the dread disease of "Hollanditis" gripped the small more forcefully than some of the large, at least not in terms of public opinion. In March 1981, as the West European peace movement was approaching its zenith, the United States International Communications Agency (USICA) tried to plumb the depth of "Euroneutralism" by posing the following question in various countries: "All things considered, do you think it is better for our country to belong to NATO . . . or would it be better for us to get out . . . and become a neutral country?" Interestingly, neutralist sentiments (as presumably measured by this query) were not widespread, except in France. In Britain and West Germany, 67 percent opted for NATO; in Italy, 60 percent; in the Netherlands, 62 percent; and in Norway, 74 percent. The biggest "neutralist" was France, where pro-NATO and proneutrality responses were almost evenly divided (45 to 40 percent). By this yardstick, then, the Netherlands was less "neutralist" than Italy, and Norway was more Alliance-minded than any other country in the survey.[8]

When it comes to "nuclear neutralism"—that is the unconditional aversion to nuclear weapons—the country with a strong Atlanticist bent and the least impressive peace movement, Italy, scores higher than the "Hollanditis-infected" Dutch. Also, the aversion to nuclear weapons seems higher in France, Germany, and Britain than in Norway. When respondents in these countries were asked to choose among various statements about nuclear weapons, the most radical antinuclear alternative, "Give up all nuclear weapons regardless of whether the Soviet Union does," was selected by 16 percent in France, 23 percent in the Federal Republic, 17 percent in Britain, 35 percent in Italy, 25 percent in Holland, and only 15 percent in Norway—which, by this particular measure, makes the Norwegians the least antinuclear population in Western Europe.[9]

The evidence changes, however, when the neutralist syndrome is measured along a "better-red-than-dead" scale. As Table 5.3 shows, there are significant distinctions between the small and the large, although the table also reveals an unexpected twist.

Among those who prefer to fight rather than avoid war, there is a clear gap between Denmark and Belgium, on one hand, where only 51 and 45 percent are willing to fight, and West Germany, Britain, Switzerland, and the United States, on the other, where between seven and eight out of ten would choose war rather than domination. In a related poll, as shown in Table 5.4, the Netherlands appears just as defense-minded as Britain and West Germany, with 73 percent of the respondents choosing resistance over submission. Even when the use of nuclear weapons in a possible war was added, more than half of the Dutch declared themselves willing to fight.

Table 5.3 Better Red than Dead?

Question: "Some people say that war is now so horrible that it is better to accept Russian dominance than the risk of war. Others say that it would be better to fight in defense of (country) than to accept Russian domination. Which opinion is closer to your own?"

	Better to fight %	Better to be dominated %	Don't know %
United States	83	6	11
Switzerland	77	8	15
Great Britain	75	12	13
West Germany	74	19	7
France	57	13	30
Denmark	51	17	32
Belgium	45	14	41

Source: Gallup Political Index, no. 259, March 1982.

Table 5.4 Better Red than Dead? The Case of the Netherlands

How to react if the Netherlands were attacked by the Soviet Union?

	With conventional weapons %	With nuclear weapons %
We should:		
resist	73	56
not resist	18	33
don't know/no answer	9	12

Source: USICA Poll, October 1981, as cited in Phillip P. Everts, "Public Opinion on Nuclear Weapons, Defense, and Security: The Case of the Netherlands," in *The Public and Atlantic Defense,* Gregory Flynn and Hans Rattinger, eds. (Totowa, N.J.: Rowman & Allanheld, 1985), 234.

With the usual caution reserved for all public-opinion data, these polls suggest a threefold conclusion. First, if there is small-power lassitude, it seems to be concentrated in Belgium and Denmark. Second, the Dutch seem to be no more afflicted by "Hollanditis" than the British, Germans, Swiss, and Americans. Third, these polls suggest once more that "size" is not the best predictor of attitudes and behavior: Switzerland, one of the smallest European countries, where almost eight out of ten would take to arms, turns out to be more defense-minded than anybody but the United States. Indeed, there is a great deal of variety among the four; weakness measured on one scale is generally compensated by strength on another. Belgium, for instance, is more "nuclear-neutralist" than others, but it has excelled in defense-mindedness as measured by a rising defense/national product ratio between 1972 and 1982. The Netherlands has been weak on "Hollanditis," but the defense/government spending ratio has slipped more rapidly than anywhere else. Norway shows the most pronounced decline on the defense/GNP scale, yet in terms of total government outlays, the defense-spending effort has remained constant.

The Targets of Discontent: The Ends or the Means?

In assessing the malaise that befell the Alliance at the turn of the 1980s, we cannot dispense with the distinction between the purposes of NATO and its nuclear means. As we assay the nature of the "crumbling consensus," we may find that there is less than meets the eye and the headlines. The consensus has undoubtedly weakened, but the domestic fabric of Western European defense has been rent most dramatically in specific places rather than throughout the entire web. More concretely, the available evidence shows a crucial distinction between stable popular support for the *Alliance* and vociferous opposition to its *nuclear components*—"neutron bombs" in the late 1970s and Pershing II and cruise missiles in the early 1980s.

Throughout the four countries, no political force of any import questions, let alone attacks, membership in NATO. In Belgium "the majority . . . are still convinced that NATO represents the best framework for the country's defense." Similarly, the Soviet Union is still regarded as the supreme threat to the country's military security. In the Netherlands support for NATO membership has held steady around 70 percent, and in 1982, almost seven out of ten people agreed with the proposition that "Western Europe needs a military counterweight to Russia and the other countries of Eastern Europe."[10] In Norway, also in 1982, 68 percent believed that NATO was either "very" or "quite" important, and 72 percent stated that Norway ought to remain in NATO.[11] Among the more ambivalent Danes, at least twice as many people favored membership in NATO as those who opposed it, and 53 percent believed that the Soviet Union presented a greater threat to the security of Western Europe than the United States (August 1980). While this was not an overwhelming measure of sentimental attachment, it was consoling to know that only 5 that only 5 percent targeted the United States as the greater threat.[12] In other words, anti-NATO, pacifist, or pro-Soviet attitudes were not the correlates, let alone the causes, of an Alliance crisis.

The significant indexes of trouble lay elsewhere, and they were more specific, yet not unique, to the four countries. If there was a crisis, it was a crisis of confidence between Western Europe and the United States and an aversion not against the Alliance but rather its nuclear weapons. (As usual, the French were the exception, having begun to scale new heights of affection for their old allies d'outre-mer after having come down from the peaks of anti-Americanism, which set them apart in the 1950s and 1960s. Similarly, the French antinuclear movement was the least significant of them all.)

The possible reasons for this twin disaffection will be analyzed further below. Suffice it to say at this point that the most interesting shifts in public opinion were linked not to NATO but to nuclear weapons, not to the United States as such (that is "anti-Americanism") but to trust in Washington's wisdom and leadership. Moreover, with respect to these two sets of attitudes, the four were but a part of the larger Western European pattern. Indeed, the most drastic drop in confidence vis-à-vis the United States occurred not among the four but among America's British cousins. If British expressions of confidence in American "ability to deal wisely with present world problems" ("very great" or "considerable") and the opposite ("little/very little/no confidence") were about evenly balanced in 1977, the gap had grown to an astounding 46 percentage points by 1983.[13] While comparable time series are not available for the four "Scandilux" countries, there is evidence that points in the same direction. Dutch surveys registered a sharp decline in the overall image of the United States, from 65 percent "favorable" in 1978 to 46 percent in 1981.[14] In Belgium only 45 percent admitted in 1982 that they had a "great deal" or "fair amount" of confidence in the United States to deal "wisely with world problems"[15] After a massive survey of the available Western European data, a recent Atlantic Institute study concludes: "There exists a profound concern about the United States and levels of trust seem to have dropped to the lowest point since the Second World War."[16]

The second key source of disaffection was nuclear weapons. To put it in the simplest terms, no one, not even the staunchly conservative citizens of Utah and Nevada when they were confronted with having to host MX missiles on their soil, likes new nuclear weapons and least of all when they are to grace one's own backyard. No one likes to be reminded of the fact that his country's security depends on the existence of weapons that, if ever used, might obliterate his society and his person in a matter of hours or days. In normal times, when nuclear weapons are safely tucked away in the innermost recesses of the collective unconscious, these fears are solidly repressed. There is an economists' saying that old taxes are good taxes. The same is probably true of nuclear weapons. Once nuclear weapons are psychologically absorbed, once they are hidden in remote silos or isolated bases, they become "good"—that is, nonoppressive—weapons. Yet, when the abstractions of deterrence literally come down to earth, when Pershing and cruise missiles are about to be stationed on one's own soil, repression ceases to function and the murderous implications of defense policy are swept to the surface of the collective psyche. This was true in the late 1950s, when the arrival of the first generation of intermediate-range nuclear weapons (Thor and Jupiter) and especially their tactical counterparts galvanized a European-wide peace movement. It was also true a generation later, when neutron bombs and cruise and Pershing II missiles intruded on the mind.

Electorates throughout Western Europe did not take kindly to the information that they were sitting on 6,000 tactical nuclear weapons, and that this arsenal was about to be reinforced by yet another generation of land-based systems in the form of cruise and Pershing II missiles. On the other hand, Western European publics were realistic enough not to question the need for a military counterweight against a Soviet Union whose military muscle they perceived as having grown in the 1970s and as continuing to grow in the 1980s. This may well explain the puzzling bifurcation of popular attitudes: yes to NATO, no to new nuclear weapons. It reflects the congenital ambivalence of dependence on the United States as security "lender of last resort." All European allies would like the best of all possible worlds. They want full protection but minimal risks; they will the end, which is the credibility of American power, but not necessarily the means, which entail the reassertion of American power—be it in the form of a confrontationist course vis-à-vis the Soviet Union or new nuclear weapons like INF. Confrontation and Cold War increase tension and the risk of actual conflict; they disturb the tranquillity that Western Europe learned to take for granted during the 1970s. They remind allies of the costs of protection and compress margins of diplomatic maneuver; and, hence, they do not increase sympathies for a remote patron power that controls the existential fate of its clients.

Nuclear weapons, whether tactical, as in the 1950s, or intermediate-range, as in the 1980s, have always dramatized the basic dilemma between the ends and means of defense. Nuclear weapons not only buttress deterrence, they also drive home the fatal consequences of its failure. Precisely because nuclear weapons tighten the link to the United States, they also drive home the choice the Allies made in the late 1940s: for alignment and against the putative freedom of action evoked by noncommitment. Nuclear weapons evoke both dependence and danger, and instinctively people react by wishing away both the weapons and their provider—which has the additional advantage of propitiating the mighty adversary to the East.

While time-series data are virtually nonexistent, some evidence reinforces what is intuitively plausible. In 1972, 36 percent of a Dutch sample agreed completely with the statement, "The use of nuclear weapons is not acceptable under any circumstances, not even if we are attacked with nuclear weapons ourselves." By 1983 that group had grown to 45 percent.[17] In a December 1980 survey, 90 percent of Norwegians answered that Norway should not resort to nuclear weapons under any circumstances;[18] 69 percent were against the deployment of "new missiles," even though the question specifically listed Britain, Germany, Holland, and Belgium as the locus of deployment.[19] In a cross-national survey of 1983, Dutch and Norwegians ranked nuclear weapons as their second most important concern after unemployment.[20] In Belgium almost six out of ten were against INF deployment on their country's soil.[21]

The "Crumbling Consensus": A Problem of Party or Populace?

The events of the early 1980s, variously described as "breakdown of the defense consensus" or the "democratization of foreign policy," are said to mark a break with the routines of the postwar era when the collisions of democratic politics would end "at the water's edge," and when the "masses" were apparently content to leave national security policy in the hands of the "elites." Without doubt, there is some truth in this perception. The rise of the 1980s peace movement throughout most of Western Europe, which mustered hundreds of thousands for the cause of fundamentalist opposition, is but the most vivid symbol of revolt. The mass media, previously content to treat security and Alliance issues as compulsory exercise in reporting, have taken to military matters with a vengeance.

Politically most significant, however, has been the passionate polarization within and between parties. At the threshold of the 1980s, the parties of the democratic left, for decades seemingly sturdy guardians of the NATO and nuclear consensus, were suddenly to stake their electoral fate on antinuclearism, arms control, and détente *über alles*. With the exception of France and Italy, whose Socialist parties in government turned out to be the staunchest defenders of NATO orthodoxy, that was the general trend in Western Europe. By the early 1980s an (inverted) "Arc of Angst" stretched from Britain via the Low Countries and Germany into Scandinavia. The Social Democratic parties of these countries stood virtually ready to outflank Greens, the churches, and the peace movement in their quest for East-West amity and nuclear abstentionism.

Yet one should not draw the wrong lessons from this sudden polarization, even though the trend has captured political parties that are neither new nor of the fringe but among the pillars of governance in Western Europe. For the time being, at least, *vox partitii* is not *vox populi*. As these parties drifted leftward, the electorate throughout the "Arc of Angst" either moved to the right or huddled closer to the center. Between 1979 and 1983 all those Social Democratic parties that had shifted toward the fringes of the ideological spectrum in matters of foreign and defense policy ended up by moving straight into an opposition role. In Britain, Labour lost tenure to the Conservatives in 1979, and Margaret Thatcher was reelected triumphantly in 1983. In West Germany, Helmut Schmidt fell in 1982, and his Christian Democratic rivals were reconfirmed in power in 1983. In Norway, the Conservatives captured power in 1981. In the Netherlands and Denmark, left-of-center governments were replaced by right-of-center coalitions in 1982. In Belgium, the Socialists lost votes in the 1981 elections and were excluded from the government coalitions formed at the end of the year.

Clearly, the left lost ground everywhere either because they had presided over the onset of recession or because the electorate throughout Western Europe (except in Italy and France) felt more comfortable with centrist or conservative parties in times of economic stringency. Presumably, the various electorates were also not reassured by parties who professed fealty to the Atlantic Alliance but then proceeded to unleash a rising barrage of antinuclear rhetoric, anti-American code words, and policy pronouncements that did not echo but resembled Soviet preferences. While the link between foreign policy and electoral punishment is at best loose, there is still a fascinating relationship between these two variables: The peace issue did not help those who, like the established left, sought to capitalize on the presumed antinuclear and anti-American sentiments of the populace. The attack against the nuclear strategy of the Alliance was not a winning issue. In Britain it even proved to be a losing issue, since almost half of Labour's defectors pointed to the party's unpalatable defense position as the cause for their switch.[22]

Widely seen as the fountainhead of "Hollanditis," the Netherlands provides the most vivid explanation for this unexpected turn of events. Asked in 1982 to list the factors that influenced their electoral choice, Dutch respondents relegated "new nuclear weapons in the Netherlands" to fourth place. Unemployment was mentioned by 24 percent, protection of lowest incomes and social security by 16 percent, security in the streets by 13 percent, new nuclear weapons by 11 percent, and the protection of the environment by 10 percent.[23] In all of Western Europe, unemployment ranked as the uppermost concern for populations, mentioned by six to seven out of ten respondents; in most cases nuclear weapons ended up in fourth or fifth place. Where the nuclear issue ranked second—as it did in West Germany, Holland, and Norway—it was separated by 20 to 35 percentage points from the number-one concern, unemployment.[24]

These figures correlate nicely with the most frequently posed question of the early 1980s—that concerning attitudes on NATO's "two-track" decision and the deployment of INF. Apart from a welter of contradictory and confusing detail, these polls yield one basic pattern. Opposition is strongest when the question is bald and bereft of policy alternatives (such as "Do you favor new missiles on your soil?"); there are large proportions of "I don't know" and "Have not made up my mind yet"; and support takes a quantum jump when the question is enveloped in a number of positive cues. As an example of the latter approach, *Time Magazine* polled with the formulation: "The countries of Western Europe and NATO are generally on the right course now, trying to negotiate arms reduction in Geneva, but also planning to deploy Pershing IIs and cruise missiles if the USSR does not reduce its own nuclear threat."

Predictably, agreement was very high. In the Netherlands, 62 percent agreed, and in Belgium 66 percent agreed. Elsewhere in Western Europe, agreement ranged from 52 percent in France to 67 percent in Germany—the country that was slated to host the bulk of the new weapons.[25]

These numbers were predictable because the question cued not only on such "bad" things as Pershing and cruise missiles but also on such "good" things as "NATO," "Western Europe," and "arms control" while relating all of them to the perhaps most powerful cue of them all—the "Soviet threat."[26] Together, the low-issue salience of nuclear weapons and the ambivalence about them help to explain why the Western European left could not ride to electoral victory on the vehicle of antinuclearism, which leads to one conclusion and one query. The conclusion is that the politics of antinuclear resentment, far from signaling a wholesale breakdown of the postwar security consensus, was and remains a *minority quest*, no matter how vociferously pursued and how strongly amplified by key segments of the print and electronic media. The question is: Why did the parties of the left jump onto that listing ship?

The answer probably is *faute de mieux*. First, none of the Social Democratic parties that had been in power at the onset of the economic decline could run on its economic record, let alone against it. Previously the guarantors of an expanding economy that had seemingly resolved the ancient conflict between private prosperity and public welfare, the democratic left could no longer present itself as keeper of the flame that would warm Peter without freezing out Paul. As Martin Heisler puts it in the Danish context, "a government left-of-center, or based on the Social Democrats, is seen as less able to deal with the cardinal issue of the 'economic crisis' (since it is less likely to curb public expenditures)."

Second, the left had previously hitched its fortunes to détente, East-West amity, and arms control, and it had not forgotten the lessons of the Cold War—that Conservative, defense, and Alliance-minded parties tend to profit from a chilly climate in international affairs. Hence, the left fastened on to the peace issue not only from lack of powerful domestic alternatives but also for reasons of self-legitimization. To have sailed with the prevailing wind that, by 1980, blew cold from Washington as well as from Moscow would have meant competing on the "wrong" platform; that is, on military strength and anti-Sovietism. These issues were triply unpromising: They would have required slicing into an already shrinking social and welfare budget; they were the natural and more credible preserve of the right; and they would have amounted to an *ex post facto* admission that a decade of Social Democratic détente policy had failed to deliver on its lofty promise.

Third, there was the catalytic factor of generational change among those politically active. The problem was not the fabled "successor generation" *per se*, since opinion data tend to reveal that "age" is not a good predictor of attitudes on Alliance, nuclear weapons, neutralism, and such things, but was rather more complex. The parties of the left had absorbed most of the sixties generation, those who a dozen years earlier had come to political consciousness in the battle for the universities and against Vietnam. The demonstrators of the 1960s had become the precinct captains and convention delegates of the late 1970s. They had fought an establishment that was pro-American, pro-NATO, and prodefense. Throughout Western Europe the heirs of 1968 would thus turn against the icons of their elders. They saw the West, and especially the United States, as an instigator of international tension and the Soviet Union as a hapless victim of Western encirclement. They saw alliances and nuclear weapons not as inhibitors of armed conflict but as its most likely causes. To wrest power from the postwar generation of leaders meant appealing to those of the New Left who had moved from radical university circles into the local organizations of the Social Democratic left and from there into the convention halls.

Competing for advancement in parties whose subinstitutions control the nominating process for parliament has thus forced aspiring candidates into a more radical stance. In the Dutch case, which may well be paradigmatic, "PvdA voters are more 'conservative' than PvdA members, . . . PvdA delegates, who decide the rank order of candidates for the Second Chamber, want to express the more leftish view of the party's members, . . . elected PvdA parliamentarians are more to the right than PvdA Council members and PvdA ministers are further to the right than PvdA parliamentarians." The peace issue, meaning, the increased fear of conflict triggered by the post-Afghanistan chill, the Soviet buildup, and the impending advent of new nuclear weapons, thus interacted with the ongoing passage of power from the postwar leadership to the generation of the forty-year-olds.

To these factors should be added another—the pseudo-populist flavor of the television age, which tempts aspiring politicians to travel outside the institutional channels of advancement and to appeal directly to the populace at large. "Populism," notes Siccama, "has thus become an alternative means of enhancing the career prospects of politicians." This was the route that Michael Foot traveled to beat the Callaghan forces for the leadership of Labour in Britain, that Oscar Lafontaine (the radical mayor of Saarbrücken) took against the Social Democratic Chancellor Helmut Schmidt; and which might explain the "success of the New Left within the [Dutch] Labor Party (PvdA)." It might also explain why "the older leadership of the SP [The Flemish Socialist Party] was replaced by a younger generation, made up of such people as Van Miert, Tobback and van den Bossche" who had "opted for a more populist and New Left look." They gave "special attention to foreign policy issues such as . . . defense, and to the growing peace movement. When in opposition, the pursuit of policies linked to this new identity became more vigorous."

The dynamics of recruitment and intraparty advancement may thus help to explain the radicalization of the Western European democratic left. It is not clear, however, what is cause and effect. Has the shift in popular sentiment, energized by the peace issue, imposed a leftward shift on the parties or vice versa? Who leads and who follows? We can measure only one thing: a strong correlation between opposition to established national security policy and party preference for the left. Do parties react to shifting demand for political goods, or do they in fact *create* their own demand by mobilizing their partisans? Intuitively, one would not expect the populace to take to the vanguard when it comes to defining new demands on the complicated arcana of nuclear strategy, especially since these issues, as opinion research shows, have a low-issue salience to begin with. Nor would one expect popular protest to emerge fully developed from the depths of an *Angst-ridden* subconscious. What looks like a spontaneous clash between leaders and led, between old and young, is more often than not an *intraelite* struggle played out on a populist stage—where one part seeks to outmaneuver the other. Underlying everything, there is always politics, and its protagonists are neither the naive uniniti-ated nor grass-roots supporters, but ambitious politicians who seek to rouse and ride forces that promise victory in the battle for intraparty or domestic power. That, in fact, is the name of the democratic game.

In the end, covariation does not elucidate causation, but there are at least two pieces of indirect evidence that support this "from-the-top down" view of politics. First, the peace issue remained a distinct minority concern throughout Western Europe, insufficiently strong to affect elec-tions or to galvanize a sustained mass movement, and hence it is not easy to see how irresistible demands from "below" forced the parties to change course. The second piece of evidence emerges, *cum grano salis*, from comparison with countries outside this study. In Germany and Holland, where the PvdA and SPD took an early lead on the peace issue (circa 1977), partisan polarization has been high. By contrast, in the United States and in France, where nuclear fears and neutralist instincts are by no means low, the Democrats and Socialists tried, only haphazardly at best, to mobilize protest, and party polarization has been relatively low.

This "polarization gap" between Germany, Britain, and Holland on the one hand, and France and Italy on the other, casts a glaring light on the role of political parties in the populist drama of antinuclear revolt. The connection between party radicalization and popular resentment may well be a chicken-and-egg problem, but in terms of sheer sequence the (party) chicken came before the (populist) egg. Nuclear weapons became a potent issue *within* the democratic left of Northern Europe long before the huge peace marches of 1981 and 1983 would converge on the capitals of Western Europe. The nuclear issue was shaped and exploited in the internal power struggles of the northern left (such as Brandt against Schmidt and Foot against Callaghan) years before anybody had even conceived of the "double-track" approach to INF modernization, which is widely, but incorrectly, perceived as the source of all trouble. Conversely, in France and Italy, nuclear weapons remained a peripheral issue at best within the respective Socialist parties, even though antinuclear and neutralist sentiments were measurably higher in France and Italy than elsewhere. To express it differently, where the established parties of the democratic left seized on the peace issue, polarization followed; where they did not, polarization remained weak. This suggests that, in the grand antinuclear drama of the 1980s, party was more important than populism, the "top" more important than the "bottom." In France and Italy the democratic left refused to ride the forces of antinuclear populism, and in these countries the peace movement remained weak, if not impotent.

In Northern Europe, by contrast, many Social Democrats and Laborites at first consciously exploited the peace issue in the quest for intraparty power; then they tried to embrace and absorb the forces they had helped to rouse with their campaign against "neutron bombs" and INF. As a result, they legitimized and amplified the voices of protest, endowing their cause with a strength they could not have acquired on their own and did *not* acquire where the democratic left, as in France and Italy, pursued a very different defense and Alliance-minded course. Which leads to a subsidiary question: Why did the French and Italian Socialist parties behave differently from their brethren in the north? The answer flows from the existence of powerful but marginalized Communist parties on their left. To gain and keep power, Mitterrand and Craxi *had* to move toward the center, and they *could* do so because their left flanks were well protected by Communist parties that were also trying to push into the "majority zone" and hence loath to lose their hard-fought but shaky respectability by mobilizing the streets against nuclear weapons. Conversely, the northern Socialists faced no such enemy on *their* left. They could move into that political space and try to absorb the Greens and the peace-minded, because it was not contaminated by the presence of large Communist parties that posed the risk of taint-by-association with parties that still shared ties to Moscow.

As a trend, the radicalization of the democratic left held substantially true for all of Western Europe (except Italy and France), but the longer-term consequences may be different in the four "Scandilux" countries. In Britain and West Germany the defeat of Labour and the SPD in 1983 translated directly into the acceptance of cruise and Pershing II missiles. One reason for their defeat may stem from the electoral system in these two countries that makes for a small number of parties and (normally) for clear governing majorities. Given the fragmentation of the party system in the Scandilux countries, described by all four authors, elections deliver not decisive verdicts but shifting coalitions, if not minority governments. Fragile coalitions make for limited departures, and they tend to strengthen the veto power of the small. Thus, not even the right-of-center coalitions that have ruled the Low and Nordic countries since the early 1980s have been able to commit themselves on the INF issue. Nor has the pressure to do so increased since 1984, when the three large participants in the INF scheme—Germany, Britain, and Italy—initiated deployment on their soil. Because as a result of the three larger countries' actions, Belgium and Holland no longer risk torpedoing the deployment program as such, and thus they may be relatively free to enjoy the benefits of deployment without having to carry its costs. Perhaps, then, it is no accident that the four have decided in favor of nondecision and the status quo. By 1985 the Belgian and Dutch governments were still caught between commitment and refusal, between prudence at home and loyalty abroad.

The "Democratization of Defense": Cyclical Burst or Secular Break?

Confronted with a seemingly unprecedented surge in popular disaffection with NATO, nuclear weapons, and national security policy, many thoughtful observers were quick to surmise that the antinuclear movement of the 1980s presaged something more fundamental than yet another cycle of nuclear anxieties (as in the late 1950s). Or, as one British commentator put it: "Pandora's Box has been opened. For good or ill, nuclear strategy in Europe has been a 'leadership decision' taken by an informed few—a tiny nuclear elite—on behalf of an only intermittently-interested many. . . . That no longer applies in Western Europe. The Pandora's Box of the nuclear age is public participation in nuclear policy making; and the true message of the protest movement . . . is that the lid has opened."[27]

In other words, Western Europe was apparently caught in a true sea change, and the new nuclear politics betrayed a secular transformation that was there to stay. According to this widespread view, Western elites had finally lost their authority over national security. Like all the other bastions of power that jealously guarded preserve of a disembodied *raison d'état* had finally also fallen to the forces of universal suffrage and mass participation. The ramparts of the last stronghold had crumbled, and the people—spearheaded by a militant protest movement—were about to outflank the institutional routine of representative government and to wield a permanent veto over national security policy.

Yet we know that the protest movement remained a distinct minority force that, in the large countries at least, could not back the government into a corner; that the unwillingness of the two Nordic countries to seek shelter behind foreign nuclear weapons merely reaffirmed continuity with three-and-a-half decades of foreign policy; that nuclear weapons were not a winning election issue in *any* West European country; and that representative government was not swept away by the onslaught of populist revolt. Far from transforming the nature of domestic politics, the nuclear issue can be related to only two incontrovertible facts: the radicalization of Western Europe's democratic left and the immobilization of the government's deployment policy in the Netherlands and Belgium.

Moreover, Western Europe has been in the grip of an antinuclear movement before, which has later disappeared. Certainly, its 1980s heir has endured longer, it has cast a wider spell, and, at least in the smaller countries, has had a stronger impact on governmental policy. These facts may well be explained in terms of various domestic factors that have amplified dissent: generational change within the left that, in government, was never comfortable with the classic issues of the right, such as anticommunism, defense spending, and pro-Americanism; the breakdown of traditional authority patterns (what Siccama calls the "depillarization of Dutch society"), which has yielded a competitive advantage to single-issue and protest groups; or the pseudo-populist promise of television-*cum*-instant polling that seems to have short-circuited the institutions of representative democracy.

However, these factors have not transformed the nature of Western European politics, nor have they *caused* the malaise of the early 1980s. Nor is it the "successor generation" as such that has brought hard times on the Alliance, even though there is a distinct generational flavor to the antinuclear revolt.[28] In Western Europe the rise of the 1950s and 1980s peace movements is separated by about a quarter of a century, and perhaps it is no accident that this period spans the normal generational cycle of twenty-five years. Each generation must come to grips with nuclear weapons on its own. In each case, then, as in the immediate past, a new generation had to learn to live with "the bomb" that could not be banished from the earth and might one day incinerate it. To accept the horrifying paradoxes of deterrence—that more is never enough, that we must threaten to destroy the world in order to save it—goes against the very grain of a post-Enlightenment teleology that sees all problems as temporary and all evils as mere stepping stones on the path to ultimate salvation. It should come as no surprise, therefore, that the young— whose very life experience used to be progress incarnate in the first postwar decades—will revolt against so powerful a symbol of doom as nuclear weapons.

Yet moods alone do not for movements make, and they did so neither in 1958 nor in 1982, when hundreds of thousands thronged through the streets and squares of Western Europe's capitals. There have to be triggering concrete events that convert a vaguely felt malaise into the push and pull of personal revolt. A sense of crisis must intrude before people start voting with their feet. There were three common crisis factors present at the creation of both antinuclear protest waves, and they were external rather than internal to the various body politics, cyclical rather than secular.

First, the rise of the 1950s and 1980s peace movements was paralleled in each case by momentous shifts in the nuclear balance. Khrushchev's rocket threats against Paris and London during the Suez Crisis of 1956 were the early harbingers of a new age; one year later, the West was shocked to learn that the Russians had launched an intercontinental ballistic missile ahead of the Americans. Before 1957, "assured destruction" had been a one-way threat—the comfortable monopoly of the United States. Now Western societies were suddenly brought face to face with their own vulnerability to the nuclear firestorm.

What Suez and Sputnik did for the first peace movement, the relentless Soviet buildup during the 1970s did for the second. Matched by the

breathtaking expansion of the Soviet strategic arsenal, the three-genera-
tion jump from the half-forgotten SS-4 and SS-5 to the SS-20 missile in
the European "theater" drove home the fearsome realization that all of
Western Europe, although a serene island of seemingly permanent
détente, was an immovable target and hostage to Soviet nuclear might.

Rapid technological change—the shift from older to newer and more
powerful weapons systems—yielded a *second* trigger event. We live most
comfortably with "the bomb" when we are allowed to forget its existence.
Forgetfulness and repression cease to function, however, when the existence of new weapons intrude on the mind. In the late 1950s the
deployment of American medium-range systems like Thor and Jupiter
and of thousands of tactical nuclear weapons suddenly brought the
abstractions of deterrence back to earth. The bulk of these weapons was
short-range, destined to explode not in the faraway reaches of the enemy,
but on densely populated home ground.

Similarly, at the threshold of the 1980s, yet another generation of
nuclear weapons punctured the veil of repression that we normally
spread over death, taxes, and the accoutrements of "mutual assured
destruction." Many of the new weapons entering the arsenals of the 1980s
were smaller, more precise, and hence ostensibly more "useable"; "war-
fighting" suddenly seemed to edge out "deterrence" as the doctrine of the
day. "Neutron bombs" and cruise and Pershing II missiles abruptly
reminded the Europeans that nuclear terror was the price of an unprecedented peace *cum* prosperity, that survival, in Churchill's legendary
words, was indeed the "twin brother of annihilation." From there it was
but a short step to sheer hysteria, which resulted in the claim that the
United States was no longer Europe's loyal guardian but in fact a
coconspirator bent on turning the Continent into the "shooting gallery of
the superpowers."[29]

The *third* factor was more properly political and perhaps the most
important of them all: the breakdown of détente. New generations of
nuclear weapons are frightening because they suddenly cast a glaring
light on the murderous premises of our security policies. A surge in
Soviet power awakens us to our ever-present vulnerability. But sharply
deteriorating East-West relations add urgency to the *angst*. Rightly or
wrongly, democratic societies, especially those who cannot underwrite
their security alone, instinctively recoil from the sound and fury of
international tension because they habitually equate the noise with the
real war.

In 1958, right after the famous post-Stalin thaw and the arrival of huge
numbers of battlefield nuclear weapons, there came the long ice age of
Khrushchev's Berlin Ultimatum, which would continue to send shivers of
a third world war through Western Europe until the resolution of the
Cuban missile crisis in 1962. In the end, Khrushchev pulled back from
the brink; but those were very good years for proclaiming the moral
superiority of "redness" over "deadness," for Easter marches and "ban the
bomb" movements.

A similar atmosphere prevailed at the threshold of the present decade, which was ushered in by such unnerving events as the Iran hostage crisis, America's apparent loss of will, the Soviet invasion of Afghanistan, and the war of nerves over Poland. The new Euromissiles thus forced themselves on the collective unconscious of Western Europe precisely at a time when détente gave way to neocontainment in the wake of Afghanistan and sundry Soviet adventures elsewhere. Together, these events seemed to make war more likely, inexorably turning attention away from the obvious sturdiness of the "balance of terror" and toward the unthinkable consequences of its collapse.

Twice in the postwar period, peace movements were spawned by strikingly similar events—the thudding arrival of new weapons systems, the darkening shadow of Soviet power, and the deepening chill in East-West relations. History then suggests why peace movements are born, but the question remains as to why and when they disappear. Peace movements do not presage the transformation of democratic politics. They are hardy perennials because they depend on very narrow soil and climate conditions. By 1962–63 the first antinuclear wave in Europe had vanished virtually without a trace, which at first glance is puzzling, for the West—the United States in particular, but also Britain and France—was then in the midst of a resolute strategic buildup, and the Soviet Union was soon to follow suit. This would suggest that it is not the weapons as such, but rather the large turbulences in the global political climate that provide the clarion call for revolt.

What did change, about 1962, and what did sap the *élan* of the first antinuclear movement, was the psychological prism—the way in which the West looked at the world and the growing nuclear stockpiles. The Cuban missile crisis was an obvious watershed. To the rattled Western mind, the happy ending at the brink was doubly reassuring. It revealed that statesmen laboring in the shadow of the apocalypse do not behave as recklessly as did their forebears in 1914. To those who would have yielded to Khrushchev's bluff in Cuba and Berlin for survival's sake, it demonstrated that it helps to be strong when moving toward the edge of the nuclear unknown.

With the global balance so palpably restored (leading to yet another period of Soviet retrenchment and recuperation), the fear of nuclear weapons rapidly disappeared into the innermost recesses of the Western mind. But there was another factor, just as weighty, which helped to pacify the global détente that followed the reassertion of Western strength in Cuba and Berlin. In the wake of deadly confrontation, the United States and the USSR took their first steps toward controlling the nuclear menace by linking Washington and Moscow through the vaunted "hotline" in 1962 and by concluding the Limited Test-Ban Treaty of 1963.

Modest as they were, these steps would alleviate nuclear despair. If the weapons could not be abolished, they might at least be rendered impotent. The lesson transcends the events of yesteryear. Precisely because nuclear weapons cannot be exorcised, they require a doctrine of salvation. Arms control and détente, no matter how sterile by the standards of true believers on the left and the right, have provided that doctrine—a vital myth that elevates hopes over an intractable reality. The peace movement of the early 1980s could not have flourished without the apparent denigration of arms control and détente that accompanied the frightening upsurge in the quantity and quality of nuclear weapons. Nor would the movement have receded as quickly without the calming moderation in the tone and language of international discourse, which reflects another parallel to the early 1960s: a sense of the military balance restored. Having turned away the great Soviet Euromissile challenge, the West could approach Détente II with a renewed sense of confidence. Having failed to shake NATO's resolve, the Soviet Union implicitly admitted failure when, in late 1984, it decided to return to the Geneva bargaining table in 1985. Given these first timid steps away from cold war, the fear of war in Western Europe would palpably decline by the mid-1980s, and with it the chances of the remnants of the peace movement to mobilize the populace for the cause of yesterday's battles.

Peace movements fail because they fail. Behind this tautology lurks a simple insight into the nature of populist politics. Extraparliamentary movements try to mobilize maximum numbers at maximum speed; by necessity they become a motley crowd. Yet pastors and pacifists, "Greens" and "Reds," Leninists and idealists, ecologists and feminists, are factions; they do not make a coalition. For a time, they manage to submerge their ideological differences for the sake of the great single issue—such as the battle against cruise and Pershing II missiles. Yet what happens when that banner becomes tattered, as it did in December 1983, when the first missiles arrived on schedule in Britain and Germany?

The first response is the communal huddle and the collective soul-searching: Where did all of us go wrong? Then comes the intramural reckoning, the not-so-comradely squaring of accounts: Who "lost" the battle? The third stage brings the beginning of breakup as the diverse factions either retract into the cosiness of their own fold or, conversely, strike out to impose uniformity by capturing the entire organization. Unlike political parties, populist movements have a hard time surviving the cold. Established parties are *geared* for survival in opposition. They have organizations that have existed since time immemorial. They have a base, and they dispense patronage and positions. Even after defeat in a national contest, they can seek cover in local and regional power bastions, where they can regroup for a counterattack several years later. For entrenched political parties, defeat does not spell the end, but a new beginning. Not so for ad hoc groupings like the peace movements. If the call to stop the missiles did not rouse the masses yesterday, will the call to stop the next batch prove more persuasive tomorrow? The worst enemy of grass-roots movements is not the "establishment," but boredom.

By 1985 much of this had already come to pass in Britain and West Germany. In the Netherlands and Belgium, where the deployment decision was in limbo, the movement continued to have an overriding *raison d'être* that had begun to elude its brethren in Britain and Germany. The question, however, remains: How well can the movement in the Low Countries flourish while its powerful allies to the north and the east are moving toward disintegration? In the Netherlands there certainly seems to exist a strong current against unilateralism. Asked whether the Netherlands should unilaterally remove all nuclear weapons from Dutch soil, only 13 percent of the respondents opted for "yes," while 73 percent were willing to do so only in consultation and agreement with other NATO countries. This trend is matched by a strong sense of realism. Even among the two most antinuclear parties, the PvdA and the D'66, 70 and 82 percent, respectively, surmised in late 1982 that the deployment would eventually take place.[30]

Moreover, there is the crucial distinction between populism and politics (qua representative government). The cyclical factors analyzed above may explain moods, perhaps even movements, yet in functioning democracies (such as the four countries in this study), moods by themselves do not spawn majorities. The key intervening variable, frequently underestimated by those who would conclude from disaffection the democratization of defense policy, is the role of political parties. Parties may rouse moods and try to ride them to victory, but in the end, even Socialist parties are in the business of politics for power, not for principle. Throughout Western Europe, every Social Democratic or Labor party that tried to ride the antinuclear vehicle from 1979 to 1983 ended up not in power but on the opposition benches. The German SPD tried to do so in the late 1950s; in Britain, Labour followed suit around 1960/61, and both failed to convert moods into majorities—then as in the early 1980s. As a result, they dropped the antinuclear banner, moving toward the center and ultimately into government. Concomitantly, the once-impressive peace movements in those two countries dwindled into political sects. It is not at all foreordained that this pattern shall come unhinged in the 1980s. While the radicalization of the democratic left in the Arc of Angst was by no means halted by the mid-1980s, it was at least faced with the powerful necessity of choice in favor of a more centrist ideology. Nor was there much electoral profit in the embrace of a peace movement whose disintegration began along with the initial deployment of INF in Western Europe. Power, as the electoral history of the early 1980s was apt to show, continued to reside in what Italians call the "majority zone," that vast, sluggish, and—at bottom—conservative center that has dominated West European politics since the end of World War II. Even after the great upheavals of the 1980s, that center continued to hold. If this continues, then, the "politicization" or "democratization" of defense policy, anxiously eyed by some and enthusiastically celebrated by others, will have been not a secular break, but yet another cyclical burst in the political history of a half-continent that can dispense neither with the atom nor with its American protector.

Conclusions

The four countries in this study were part and parcel of a general disaffection with nuclear weapons, with the United States, and with the demands of the Alliance. Yet they were also part and parcel of the countertrend: the attempt to balance Alliance obligations with national needs, the enduring faith in the necessity of Alliance, and most important, the inability to perceive any real alternatives to the commitments made in the late 1940s. To offer this assessment is another way of stressing the obvious: that the bipolar system, which in 1945 replaced the European state system that had been swept away by Europe's second Thirty Years War, has endured beyond the most pessimistic expectations. That system, as Stanley Hoffman pointed out almost two decades ago, is a "stalemate system" and "dreams are [its] victims."[31]

As small powers, the four found it perhaps easier than, for instance, Britain, Germany, and Italy to resist the harsher claims of alliance in the early 1980s—as evidenced most vividly in their ability to evade a clear commitment on the INF deployment. As "small" countries, which have nothing to gain from the confrontation of the great but a reduced margin of maneuverability and costly demands on their highly developed welfare-state order, they have been more avid in the pursuit of neodétente, confidence building, and arms control than some of the big. Yet they have not been more so than, say, the Federal Republic of Germany, which is as big as France or Italy but as small as Norway or Denmark in terms of its unique security exposure vis-à-vis the East. Thus, differences between the small and the large ought not to be overemphasized. Indeed, merely a brief glance at two highly similar and neighboring countries like Denmark and Norway reveals an astounding variety in small-power behavior. During the 1970s, the decade of détente, both deviated dramatically from the norm. Denmark's armed forces decreased by 30 percent; in Norway they rose by 11 percent.

As "new" nuclear weapons become "old" and thus "good" nuclear weapons, they will presumably pale as the focus of popular attention and discontent. If by mid-decade, Détente II, cautiously eyed by the superpowers, follows on Cold War II (*circa* 1979–84), dwindling fears of war and confrontation will further blunt the edge of resentment that has cut into Alliance cohesion during the early 1980s. Whether the decline of societal antagonism within the West will make the four "Scandilux" countries less neglected or neglectful is a different question.

Given its unique exposure and tradition, Norway can be expected to pursue the continuity of foreign policy with a sharp eye on the balance of power: between alignment that ensures rapid reinforcement in times of real crisis and war, and a posture of reassurance to avoid provoking the Soviet Union. The decision on prepositioning heavy American equipment in 1981, coupled with a slight rise in the number of Norwegian forces, may be an emblematic case in point. While the Norwegian-

American agreement took due note of the growth of Soviet power at NATO's nothern flank, the actual location of the storage site—at a symbolic distance from the Kola Peninsula—sent a powerful message of reassurance to the Soviet Union.

In the case of Denmark, as Heisler points out, "neither the political nor economic means will exist for Denmark to break out of its current impasse. [T]he outlook is only for marginal improvements in a far less than optimal situation during the balance of this decade." He surmises that there are no "solutions," apart from the prospect that "the Alliance—and the United States in particular—[might] become inured to the Danish way of alignment."

Nor should any significant departure be expected from Belgium, the country that is more fragmented and politically stalemated than the other three because of barely contained nationality conflicts that compound traditional cleavages of political faith. Jan Siccama's conclusion for the Netherlands, the least "small" of the small countries, is cautiously balanced. On the one hand, there is the fear that "a negative deployment decision would give the country the role of an outsider in the Alliance." On the other hand, an evident trend to the right in matters economic and social is unlikely to find its parallel "in nuclear policies."

While tensions between Western Europe and the United States will undoubtedly diminish if arms control and a semblance of détente are restored (or perhaps emerge elsewhere as a result of two much "big twoism"), a triple hallmark of the 1950s and 1960s has probably vanished for good. One was the existence of an "American" party within the various politics of Western Europe, notably in the two Low Countries. Even on the right, intimacy with Washington no longer defines an outstanding asset in the contest for domestic power; there is now a good deal of benefit in friendly distance and even occasional critique. Forty years after World War II, the United States simply no longer disposes of that unique cornucopia of resources and authority by which it could shape the evolution of Western European policy in the 1950s and 1960s.

Second, even an increased perception of Soviet military power, which occurred in all of Western Europe in the first half of the 1980s, no longer translates into an increased sense of fear that would legitimize dramatic defense efforts, strengthen Alliance-mindedness, and delegitimize those political forces that emphasize a benign and cooperative approach toward the East. Anticommunism or anti-Sovietism, the fixtures of the 1940s, 1950s, and part of the 1960s, are no longer key determinants of Western European politics.

Third, the insistence on arms control, bloc-transcending cooperation, and détente will, in the absence of any truly cataclysmic upheavals—and Afghanistan and Poland were not—remain an essential part of European foreign policy, which implies future drastic limits on the power of the big two to recentralize their blocs at will. As the events of Cold War II have shown, the two superpowers are still mighty in a negative sense—when it comes to limiting the freedom of the small. But their positive power has visibly diminished, cutting into their ability to harness their clients to their own preferences.

These are the new parameters of West European politics. For the four "Scandilux" countries, there may be a fourth one. Least able to influence the global course of events, they may be most prone to opt out when confronted with demands that threaten to unhinge their sheltered role as the foremost "civilian" powers of the Atlantic Alliance. Because they matter less, they can do less—in both senses of the term. They cannot inflict their wishes on the strong, but they can get away with resisting the claims of their larger partners. Thus, neglect by the strong may indeed lead to the neglectfulness of the weak.

Notes

1. Nikolaj Petersen, "Danish and Norwegian Alliance Policies 1948–1949: A Comparative Analysis," *Cooperation and Conflict*, 14, no. 4 (1979): 196.

2. I have borrowed this distinction from Michael Mandelbaum, *The Nuclear Revolution: International Politics Before and After Hiroshima* (Cambridge: Cambridge University Press, 1981). For a stimulating elaboration, see Glenn H. Snyder, "Alliance Politics and the Security Dilemma," *Working Papers*, no. 45 (Washington: Wilson Center, October 1982).

3. Norwegian note to the Soviet Union of 1 February 1949, as cited in Robert K. German, "Norway and the Bear: Soviet Coercive Diplomacy and Norwegian Security Policy," *International Security*, 7, no. 2 (Fall 1982): 60.

4. J. J. C. Voorhoeve, *Peace, Profits and Principles: A Study of Dutch Foreign Policy* (The Hague: Nyhoff, 1979), 115.

5. See, for instance, Siccama, 72, Table 3.1. which shows an average of 70 percent of Dutch respondents favoring NATO membership during the period from 1967 to 1983.

6. International Institute for Strategic Studies, *The Military Balance, 1984–1985* (London: IISS), 138–39. In the Norwegian case, defense expenditures resumed growth in 1982.

7. Figures taken from *The Military Balance, 1975–1976*, 78; and *The Military Balance, 1984–1985*, 140.

8. Poll cited in Kenneth Adler and Douglas Wertman, "Is NATO in Trouble? A Survey of European Attitudes," *Public Opinion* (August/September 1981): 10.

9. Atlantic Institute/Louis Harris Poll, *Security and the Industrial Democracies* (Paris, 1983).

10. See Siccama, Tables 3.1 and 3.2.

11. Ragnar Waldahl, "Norwegian Attitudes Toward Defense and Foreign Policy Issues," in *The Public and Atlantic Defense*, ed. Gregory Flynn and Hans Rattinger (Totowa, N.J.: Rowman and Allanheld, 1985), 292, 309.

12. David Capitanchik and Richard C. Eichenberg, *Defense and Public Opinion* (London: Routledge and Kegan Paul, 1983), 47, 41.

13. Of those polled, 24 percent expressed confidence, whereas 70 percent did not. Norman L. Webb and Robert J. Wybrow, "Friendly Persuasion: Advice from Britain," *Public Opinion* (February/March 1983): 13, fig. 1.

14. Capitanchik and Eichenberg, *Defense and Public Opinion*, 33.

15. "The U.S. and Europe: A Poll," *Newsweek* (Europe), 15 March 1982.

16. As a cautionary note, it adds: "Unfortunately, this is another case in which earlier data are sparse, and it is impossible to know whether the figures are really more dramatic, or whether it just seems as if they must be. What one can say, however, is that this time it is less U.S. reliability and more U.S. political judgment that is being called into question." Flynn and Rattinger, *The Public and Atlantic Defense*, 376.

17. Philip P. Everts, "Public Opinion on Nuclear Weapons, Defense, and Security: The Case of the Netherlands," in *The Public and Atlantic Defense,* ed. Flynn and Rattinger, 235, Table 6.15.

18. Ragnar Waldahl, in Flynn and Rattinger, eds., *The Public and Atlantic Defense,* 299.

19. *Ibid.,* 305.

20. Atlantic Institute/Louis Harris Poll, "Security and the Industrial Democracies."

21. As cited by Alfred van Staden, "Pays-Bas et Belgique; la tentation neutraliste," in *Pacifisme et Dissuasion* ed. P. Lellouche and N. Gnesotto (Paris: IFRI, 1983), 93.

22. Ivor Crewe, "Britain: Two and a Half Cheers for the Atlantic Alliance," in Flynn and Rattinger, eds., *The Public and Atlantic Defense,* 25.

23. Philip P. Everts, in Flynn and Rattinger, eds., *The Public and Atlantic Defense,* 234, Table 6.10.

24. Atlantic Institute/Louis Harris Poll, "Security and the Industrial Democracies."

25. *Time,* 1 October 1983, 49.

26. See Flynn and Rattinger, eds., *The Public and Atlantic Defense* 374.

27. John Barry, "Just Who Is Deterred by the Deterrent?," *The Times* (London), 18 August 1981, 12.

28. The following analysis of the cyclical nature of populist protest is borrowed from the authors, "Squaring Many Circles; West Germany Security Policy between Deterrence, Détente and Alliance," in *The Federal Republic of Germany and the United States* (Boulder and London: Westview Press/Woodrow Wilson International Center for Scholars, 1984), 194–97.

29. This is the memorable expression of Pastor Heinrich Albertz, one of the early celebrities of the West German peace movement that produced important cues for its counterparts in the four "Scandilux" countries.

30. Philip P. Everts, in Flynn and Rattinger, eds., *The Public and Atlantic Defense,* 249, Table 6.24, 259, and Table 6.37.

31. Stanley Hoffmann, *Gulliver's Troubles* (New York: McGraw-Hill, 1968), 55.

6

Lilliputs and Gulliver: Small States in a Great-Power Alliance

JOHAN JØRGEN HOLST

Small May Be Beautiful, but What Is Small?

While small states share the international quest for security, their means and options are more constrained than those of the major powers. Their limited influence on the pattern of international politics and on the code of behavior of the trend-setting nations often leads to an ambivalence toward and an alienation from the realities of an international order to a large extent structured by balance-of-power imperatives. Even in small states that have chosen alignment perhaps more out of necessity than passion, the search for security is often troubled by a certain neutralist nostalgia for a freer choice, or just a desire to be let alone by a turbulent world. They are sometimes reluctant allies; although their reluctance stems not from a lack of concern or commitment to the purposes of their alliances, but rather from a feeling of impotence. Thus, while alliances provide protection, they also imply involvement and complicity and constitute barriers on the high road of moral rectitude in an immoral world.

General statements about small states and their behavioral characteristics are, of course, dangerous. Size is hardly the most important determinant of state behavior, and it is not easy to determine size in relevant terms. Norway, for example, is the fifth largest country in Europe, exceeded only by the Soviet Union, France, Spain, and Sweden. But Norway also has the smallest population of these four countries, and eleven of the thirty-five countries in Europe have even smaller populations. The Netherlands, a fraction of the geographic size of Norway, is the tenth largest country in Europe in terms of population. Norway's

Gross National Product is the smallest of our four countries, but it is number seventeen in Europe, and only twenty-one countries outside Europe have a larger GNP. Only six countries in the world have a larger GNP than the total GNPs of the four countries in this study. Smallness is indeed a relative term.

Nevertheless, the four countries have the self-image of being small. They most certainly are small in comparison with the superpowers that dominate the security environment, but so are almost all the other countries that make up the international system. These four smaller Northern European Allies sometimes seem to espouse a cult of smallness, a presumption that small is beautiful in the sense of being virtuous, although both the Netherlands and Belgium were colonial powers even after World War II. The two most puritan of our four countries, the Netherlands and Norway, tend to couple this presumption of virtue with a propensity to express a feeling of guilt associated with success.

History, geography, technology, and international constellations are stronger determinants of state behavior than size, however measured. The four countries whose policies are examined here nevertheless seem to share certain propensities and characteristics. It is the purpose of this chapter to explore the implications of these propensities and characteristics for policy making within the Alliance.

How can the Western Alliance remain relevant and responsive to the interests and sentiments that inspire political support in its smaller members? The option of alignment—that is, membership in the Alliance—is not a matter of major controversy in any of these four countries. What does create controversy is the position taken by the Alliance on specific issues and sometimes the Alliance's strategic guidelines that incorporate the major thrust of its policy. It is as relevant, of course, also to pose the question of what the smaller members can do for the Alliance. In actuality, they have performed rather well and have, on the whole, been loyal allies. The manner in which issues relating to foreign policy and security are discussed within the Alliance, however, often makes the Alliance appear to be an unwelcome constraint to the pursuit of more idealistic visions, particularly in distant regions of the world. This dichotomous attitude is present in all four countries, but it warrants emphasis that both views are held simultaneously and are not necessarily at the expense of the other.

Implications of Alignment

The traditional purpose of alignment is to obtain security. In the words of George Liska, an alliance "associates likeminded actors in the hope of overcoming their rivals."[1] Smaller states tend to view alignment in terms of net security benefits because they obtain "drawing rights" on the military capability of great powers. They tend to do their sums only in the calculus of military power; so long as they do, they view themselves as importers or consumers of security. They tend to ignore or overlook the degree to which they contribute to the provision of security in a broader context through engagement in the shaping of a pattern of security, by rendering specific services, playing special roles, and contributing to the cohesion and cohersion of a particular order. They sometimes tend toward narrow or minimalist views of the purposes of consequences of alignment.

Although smaller countries tend to perceive themselves as net consumers of security, their alignment may contribute significantly to the construction of viable regional order and of credible security arrangements. They contribute not only capabilities but also access, position, and space, which enable the larger powers to organize their defense and deploy their forces in an efficient manner. Belgium and the Netherlands provide essential entry points and logistic nodes for the defense of the central front in Europe, and they contribute key links in the chain of defense arrangements that tie North American to Western Europe. Norway and Denmark provide essential flank protection for the central front and for the transatlantic sea lines of communication.

Nations choose alignment in order to contain a threat or to achieve aggrandizement. The threat need not be imminent; it need not present a clear and present danger to survival for a state to take out insurance against aggression. Alignment is a means of dissuasion, of convincing a would-be adversary that the risks and costs associated with aggression would exceed expected benefits.

Such calculations are never exact, and the valuations and assessments involved depend on specific circumstances, not the least of which is the matrix of alternatives and opportunities. If states seek to increase the stakes associated with aggression through alignment, other factors enter into play. The gravity of a challenge to the territorial integrity of a member of an alliance would no longer be determined by an assessment of the intrinsic value of the real estate involved. The credibility of a whole system of guarantees, linking the fate of more countries and larger territories, would then be at stake in the event of aggression. Nations in alliance want to create the expectation that a fight for control of their country will not be confined to a fight with that country alone.

States have other goals, however, than maximizing the deterrence of war. They want to protect their independence vis-à-vis their chosen protectors as well as their would-be adversaries. Alignment is not synonymous with submission, nor does it amount to an abdication of independent judgment. A commonality of interest in respect of the broad pattern of power relationships does not imply an identity of interest in specific circumstances or in areas beyond those comprised by alignment. Nor do shared interests translate easily into shared assessments concerning behavior and actions in specific situations. The smaller countries are likely to adopt minimalist views on alignment in the sense of wanting to confine the discipline of joint positions to the narrow fields of defense and negotiation while resisting attempts to globalize common positions. In part this is the result of the lack of means and ambitions to structure events in distant areas, and in part it may reflect a tacit bargain for national consensus: The discipline of alignment is accepted as long as the state can demonstrate independence and project idealist visions in contexts that do not directly involve matters of national security. Such tacit bargains probably operate in Denmark and Norway and to a smaller extent in the Netherlands; Belgian politics tend to revolve almost exclusively around domestic issues. Tensions arise whenever the imperatives of the Alliance collide with the propensities for independent posturing or involvement against the commitments and policies of their primary allies outside the formal scope covered by the NATO treaty. Such tensions bite at the core of the Alliance if they involved disagreement about policies toward the Soviet Union, the Alliance's primary adversary.

The smaller states in an alliance may at times view themselves as protégés of their major allies, but they do not want to become instruments in the latter's contest with other powers. Alignment may amount to entanglement, which increases risks and reduces freedom of action. Moreover, states must correlate policies of deterrence and reassurance vis-à-vis neighboring countries that do not belong to their chosen system of alignment.

Countries that occupy exposed positions or border on major potential adversaries must pay particular attention to fine-tuning this equilibrium. These are exactly the areas where deterrence can verge on provocation, just as reassurance can verge on appeasement. The constraints of position may require a *Realpolitik* approach that can be at odds with the idealistic propensities of small states policies. All four countries in this study have found themselves in such positions in the postwar years.

Alignment influences the foreign-policy perspectives of the smaller states in other important ways: They obtain access to deliberations from which they would be excluded in the absence of alignment, and they assume responsibility for the management of interests and relationships that otherwise would prove elusive or beyond their influence. Alignment may increase the political clout that smaller countries can bring to bear in bilateral negotiations with adversaries or third parties, and it can help stiffen the back against political intimidation, a perspective probably more relevant to Norway in its exposed position on the Northern flank than to the "better-cushioned" continental countries in this study.

To the extent that alignment impels involvement, however, the degree of involvement and the roles that states may assume are circumscribed by their domestic societies and by the images that these societies hold about their commitments and undertakings. Tensions between state and society clearly arise when alignment requires a role to be played by the state that is not sustainable by the society as a whole. The controversies about burden sharing in general and the INF disposition in particular bear witness to the reality of such tensions and the difficulty of attenuating them.

NATO, however, is something more than an alliance with a narrow security aim. It was established in the wake of the collapse of the high hopes and expectations for an international order based on the continued cooperation of victorious Allied powers in World War II. It became in many ways the centerpiece of an alternative and more limited world order with Washington as the radiating nucleus. NATO became an element, indeed the key element, in a novel experiment in the international organization of nations that cooperate in order to preserve the security, vitality, and prosperity of a civilization based on Western democracy. Hence, the smaller states not only assumed the traditional benefits and obligations of alignment; they also became partners in the construction and management of a new cooperative international order.

All four countries were "present at the creation" of a new political experiment that gave direction and purpose to the reconstruction of Western Europe. Commitment to the construction of a viable political order in Western Europe was probably stronger and certainly more pronounced in Belgium and the Netherlands than in the three Nordic countries that decided to join NATO. The former were inextricably and inevitably involved in the construction of a political order that could put an end to Franco-German rivalry and hence protect the Low Countries against the destruction and turmoil of war. Norway was looking more for continued cooperation with the maritime Anglo-Saxon powers with whom she had cooperated so closely through her government-in-exile in London during World War II. Denmark was probably between the two. The Scandinavian membership in the Western Alliance was thus more a result of security calculations than of a commitment to community building. In terms of association with a political community, the "Scandinavian option" represented a perfectly valid alternative, although Norway and Denmark finally opted for linkage with the Western powers.

These broader conceptions of alliance were strengthened by the accession of the Federal Republic of Germany to NATO. Membership in the Alliance was also viewed by Bonn as a means of stabilizing the German political system. Later, similar perspectives prevailed in post-Salazar Portugal and post-Franco Spain. NATO can thus be viewed as having provided for some of its larger members a framework for the preservation of regime stability by serving as an obstacle to the growth of extremist political forces. The political cultures of the four smaller countries in this study, however, were less vulnerable to domestic extremism and instability, and they largely tended to view NATO's stabilizing functions as more relevant and more applicable to the larger member states: Italy, France, and, most particularly, West Germany.

The broad political conceptions that inspired the foundation and construction of NATO incorporated idealist visions and a broader sense of community that seem to have been lost through the decades of détente policies, the Vietnam War, and American oscillation. They surface intermittently in calls for "burden sharing," "a two-way street" in the procurement of arms, and in the American notion that Washington should provide the transmission belt for Western interests beyond the treaty area. The latter has always conflicted with the Scandinavian world view, and over time the Low Countries have come to resist the concept as well. The passage of time has transformed the frames of reference, as well as the nature and the perceptions of the challenges that confront the Alliance. NATO has become part of the established realities, an accomplished fact rather than a vision of the future.

The postwar era has come to an end. New generations, with another frame of reference and with a different set of formative experiences from those of the generation that participated in "the creation," have moved into positions of power in the member nations of NATO. Détente and Ostpolitik served the political purpose of helping the West Germans break out of bondage, thereby giving the Federal Republic a role as a major actor in the international arena.

Détente and Ostpolitik also created expectations of a different kind in the Federal Republic and in the smaller North European NATO countries as well. Exponents of a "new creation" believed that the process of détente might involve the construction of a united Europe in which the division between East and West would be overcome. In this optic, of course, NATO was viewed as a part of the system maintaining the division. The Europe of the Brussels Treaty and the North Atlantic Treaty Organization over time would be superseded by the Europe of the Helsinki agreement. The accent is not so dissimilar from the Gaullist notion of a Europe stretching from the Atlantic to the Urals.

In this process of changing generational perspectives, the role of NATO as a political community may have faded somewhat. It is still referred to, however, as the cornerstone for the foreign and defense policies of these four smaller North European NATO member states. But, in Norway, for instance, one hears increasingly that NATO is not an end in itself, but rather a temporary expedient on the road to a more encompassing international order. The assertion of American globalism and demands for proper European burden sharing appear to conflict with a more limited view of the Alliance, certainly a view prevalent within these four smaller NATO members. The issue is not the Alliance as such, or even membership in the Alliance, but rather the strategies and undertakings that the Alliance should properly embrace and pursue.

All four smaller NATO allies encompassed in this study made the pursuit of détente a major purpose and even a justification of their continued commitment to the Western Alliance as the Cold War receded into the background. Poland became a major symbol of the West's developing dialogue with the East. The clampdown on Solidarnosč, the imposition of martial law, and the inward turn of governmental attention in Warsaw, dried up a major channel for the foreign affairs activity of these smaller NATO allies. The fading of détente caused major frustration to all of them. Their ability to act as faithful allies had, to some extent, become hostage to their continued ability to build bridges to the East.

The Burden-Sharing Syndrome

An alliance constitutes a chosen instrument to enhance the collective good of security for the contracting parties. Security is not a "perfect" collective good in the sense that what is good for the security of one ally is equally good for the other allies. Positions and requirements differ. But how much should each state contribute? How much should each state be allowed to consume? To each according to need and from each according to ability? Equity has proved to be as elusive a concept as the concept of fair shares. The U.S. Secretary of Defense, Caspar Weinberger, has accurately observed that "NATO has been unable to agree on an acceptable definition of the burden or how to measure it."[2]

Even if the Allies were to agree on definitions and measurements, the problem of setting targets and negotiating the distribution of effort would remain. There is no detailed agreement on requirements—on how much is enough. Again, to quote Secretary Weinberger: "Unfortunately, one of the basic disagreements in the Alliance today is the diverging view among the Allies of the threat and the resulting differences in opinion about how much defense is enough."[3]

The perception of free riders in the chariot of collective defense has taken hold in the United States. There is talk of the twin dangers of "Denmarkization" and "Hollanditis." Allegedly, the Europeans, particularly the smaller European countries, are not carrying their proper burden. But, as Mancur Olson has pointed out, there is a normal tendency toward inequity and suboptimality in groups.[4] He observes perceptively that "in groups of members of unequal 'size' or extent of interest in the collective good, there is the greatest likelihood that a collective good will be provided; for the greater the interest in the collective good of any single member, the greater the likelihood that that member will get such a significant proportion of the total benefit from the collective good that he will gain from seeing that the good is provided, even if he has to pay all of the cost himself."[5] And furthermore, "the largest member, the member who would on his own provide the largest amount of the collective good, bears a disproportionate share of the burden of providing the collective good. The smaller member by definition gets a smaller fraction of the benefit of the amount of any collective good he provides than a larger member, and therefore has less incentive to provide additional amounts of the collective good."[6] He concludes that "in small groups with common interests there is accordingly a surprising tendency for the 'exploitation' of the great by the small."[7]

Ideally, the costs of providing security should be shared in the same proportion as the benefits derived from the security that is produced by an alliance. The Atlantic Alliance, however, is based on a division of labor, particularly with respect to nuclear deterrence. Moreover, the very concept of burden sharing generates political pressures and perspectives that tend to increase tensions within the Alliance. In addition to insoluble definitional and measurement problems, there is a problem of motivation and objective. Countries should be motivated to contribute to the common defense in order to contain specific dangers and reduce particular threats. Defense, of course, should be concerned with constraining the options of would-be adversaries rather than with satisfying the demands of one's allies. The whole burden-sharing debate runs the danger of projecting the Alliance as a team with a coach external to Europe who is constantly cajoling the European Allies into doing things they would prefer not to do. Public support for the Alliance could erode in member countries if it were to be viewed as the embodiment of undesirable obligations rather than beneficial commitments.

From the point of view of the smaller states, however, the issue is broader than simply one of public presentation. The opportunity costs and social costs of defense cannot be tabulated solely in terms of budgetary expenditure, even the latter is difficult to compare because of differences in budgetary rules and procedures. All four of the countries, for example, maintain a system of national conscription. Moreover, arms industries are not significant in any of them. Hence, defense expenditures are plowed back into their national economies at a significantly lower rate than defense expenditures in the United States. In fact, however, calculations done by the U.S. Department of Defense indicate that the four countries' shares of defense expenditures correlate quite well with the GNP share of each. The burden appears to be shared quite equitably (see Table 6.1).

Most of the criteria used to measure contributions focus on inputs rather than on outputs. They do not in fact encompass considerations of defense for a given input if the input is used more efficiently, or if the factor cost of inputs is significantly less expensive. A case can be made for both elements in many European countries. But the habit of defining objectives and challenges for the Alliance in terms of expenditures rather than in terms of capabilities in fact runs counter to the real objective of alignment—the production of security.

The NATO pattern of establishing force goals that everyone knows will not be met—the force goals are called a "challenge" in the discussions—tends to make the joint-force planning exercise rather irrelevant in terms of national behavior; it generates irritation and cynicism about the implications of alignment and may well tend to strengthen the minimalist tendencies of the smaller members. In a word, its nuisance value may exceed the guidance value. The military credibility of the Alliance is not only a matter of popular attitudes and perceptions but also a function of the professional attitudes of those charged with force planning and security policy at national levels. The bureaucratization of the Alliance is a serious problem for the smaller countries. Too few people have to go to too many meetings dealing with too much detail. Their lack of capacity to do so breeds a sense of impotence and even estrangement. The simplification of the force-planning machinery and procedures in the Alliance might well facilitate better coordination of national efforts.

The notion of burden sharing carries moral connotations of justice and

Table 6.1 Burden Sharing in NATO (and Japan), 1980: Selected indicators

	GDP Share	Population Share	Defense-Spending Share	Active plus Reserve Defense Manpower Share	Per Capita Defense Spending % of U.S.	Ground Forces ADE's[a] Share	Ratio Active plus Reserve Defense Manpower/ Population Share	Ratio Aircraft Share/ Prosperity Index Share	Official Development Assistance as Percentage of GDP
Belgium	01.76% (9)	01.42% (11)	01.52% (9)	02.00% (11)	66.20% (6)	01.81% (12)	01.41 (5)	01.49 (4)	00.49 (5)
Denmark	00.98% (10)	00.74% (13)	00.62% (13)	01.11% (14)	51.70% (8)	02.25% (10)	01.50 (4)	01.13 (7)	00.72 (3)
Netherlands	02.48% (8)	02.03% (9)	02.02% (7)	02.45% (10)	61.04% (7)	03.03% (9)	01.21 (8)	00.89 (10)	00.99 (1)
Norway	00.85% (11)	00.59% (14)	00.64% (12)	02.47% (9)	67.30% (5)	02.22% (11)	04.19 (1)	01.11 (8/9)	00.82 (2)
West Germany	12.11% (3)	08.86% (3)	10.23% (3)	11.67% (3)	71.40% (4)	10.74% (3)	01.32 (6)	00.59 (13)	00.43 (6)
United States	38.19% (1)	32.75% (1)	52.97% (1)	35.13% (1)	100.00% (1)	38.62% (1)	01.07 (9)	01.11 (8/9)	00.27 (10)

[a] ADE = Armored Division Equivalent.

Source: U.S. Congress Report on Allied Contributions to the Common Defense, by Caspar W. Weinberger, Secretary of Defense (March 1982), 17, 21, 22, 23, 75.

equity. It tends to focus on matching the contributions of the other Allies rather than on complementing them. In this perspective the benefits of an efficient division of labor unfortunately fade into the background. Ideally, each ally should concentrate on those tasks that could produce the largest increment to the common defense. Comparative advantage— that is, reaping the benefits of the highest marginal productivity—would appear to be a major task of Alliance defense, and each of the Allies could then concentrate on the task it can do best, or that it can do only because of its location or prevailing political constraints.

These issues are particularly acute for smaller states, which probably have to pay even more attention to the trade-offs between quantity and quality in their procurement policies than others. The exploding costs of advanced military systems make it difficult for many countries to maintain balanced forces in meaningful numbers. They have to exceed a minimum number of units, to cross a threshold, in order to justify at all procurement of a given capability. The dilemma is compounded by force-to-space requirements, which constitute a particularly vexing challenge for a country like Norway with a large area to defend, or by a requirement uniquely derived from membership in the Alliance, such as Canada's need to buy tanks because of its European mission and for which there would be no requirement in Canada itself.

Hence, economic necessity may force nations of the Atlantic Alliance toward specialization based on comparative advantage and a division of labor. The rising costs and complexity of military equipment create greater interdependence among allies. The ability of political structures and decision-making systems to keep pace with technological change is, however, far from perfect. The pressures for integration and specialization tend to collide with the tradition of providing balanced forces for national defense. Certain peacetime functions of the armed forces, such as the policing of territories and boundaries, will be ceded only with great reluctance to allies. While such concerns are likely to prove more relevant in a country with a large area like Norway than in the compact sovereign space of Belgium, Denmark, or Holland, it should be recalled that Denmark has responsibilities for defense of the Faeroe Islands and of the distant and largest island in the world, Greenland; the Netherlands continues to be responsible for the defense of the Dutch Antilles. Norway's reluctance to give up peacetime police functions results also from its being the youngest nation of the four, jealously guarding a sovereignty obtained only in 1905.

Smaller states must concentrate on numbers and eschew the complexity that could prevent "graceful degradation," or gradual rather than precipitous reduction in capability, in the event of war. However, small states that are integrated into a larger structure of defense arrangements in a given theater, like the Low Countires in relation to the defense of the Federal Republic, are able to pursue a different path than countries like Denmark and Norway, which must plan for the eventuality of direct attack and must thus be able to hold their own for some period. Indeed, a

major criterion for the assessment of alternative force postures in Norway is that of "holding time." Norway, in addition, faces the challenge of
developing and procuring the means appropriate to defense in an area
that is topographically and climatically very different from that of the
primary focus for military planning of the major powers within the
Alliance. During the 1950s and 1960s the Norwegian armed forces were
equipped to a large extent by the American Military Assistance Program.
However, the equipment tended to drive both organization and doctrine
in directions that were not always suitable for Norwegian conditions.
Because Norway later had to procure equipment from her own defense
budget, she developed a strong defense-research establishment in order
to generate responses to unique requirements.

One final consideration concerning burden sharing. Major powers with
global interests tend to define their efforts to defend national interests
worldwide as an expression of their burden of allied defense. The smaller
NATO Allies have tended to define alignment more narrowly and to
eschew suggestions of a leadership role for their protectors in defining
and defending objectives beyond the treaty area; they have quite consistently objected to any enlargement of the treaty area or of the commitments that flow from alignment.[8] They may be accused of adopting a
narrow outlook and of violating principles of strategy and inherent
linkage, but they nevertheless have no aspiration or inclination to shape
the pattern of politics in distant areas. The major powers should not want
to be constrained by the political reluctance of the smaller states; nor
should the smaller states be committed in the Third World by the political
judgment and interests of the major powers within the Alliance. There
are practical limits to the notion of community.

In an alliance of democratic states the defense effort must clearly
appear to be shared reasonably equitably among the members. The
precise definition of equity and even the identification of criteria for such
definition, however, have proved controversial and elusive. The very
concept of burden sharing implies role definition in terms of justice and
equity rather than maximum security, effectivenesss, and comparative
advantage. Concentration on maximizing the overall capacity for deterrence and defense, rather than the statistics of various input categories,
would emphasize the productivity of national efforts and reduce the
cajoling role of Alliance institutions.

At the same time, a system of military cooperation based on some
agreed formula for a division of labor would work only if it did not give
rise to the practice (or suspicion) of beggar-thy-neighbor policies, picking
the rewarding and "cheap" parts while leaving the exacting roles and
functions to other allies. Furthermore, nations are aware that influence,
to a large extent, is a function of the roles that nations play. Hence, the
smaller Allies are reluctant to go too far down the road of specialization
for fear of losing influence in the deliberative and decision-making
processes within the Alliance.

Efforts to distribute Alliance burdens according to some ill-defined and elusive principle of equity have thus created problems and will continue to create problems for the smaller Allies. Evoking collaboration in areas where the smaller states have some comparative expertise to meet the external threat would probably tend to achieve positive results if limited experience is any guide.

The INF Controversy

The social costs associated with contributions to the common defense are not necessarily proportional to the amount of resources committed. The controversy over the deployment of Intermediate-Range Nuclear Forces (INF) is a case where the nature of the contributions weighed more heavily than the financial cost.

It is not the task here to analyze the complex background for NATO's double-track decision of 12 December 1979 regarding INF. However, some of the political considerations involved should be recalled in order to assess the controversy it engendered, particularly in the smaller countries of the Alliance.

The major challenge posed by the Soviet deployment of the SS-20 missile was to the balance of the political order in Europe rather than to the balance of military capabilities. The new intermediate-range missile was deployed at a time when approximate parity at the level of strategic nuclear forces had been achieved as a result of the Soviet missile buildup during the 1970s. This strategic parity was reflected in the SALT II agreement, which was being negotiated as SS-20 deployment was initiated.

Hence, the politico-strategic context of the deployment of intermediate-range nuclear missiles differed from the context that prevailed when SS-4/5 missiles were deployed in the early 1960s. The SS-20 deployment represented a buildup that exceeded the framework of a negotiated balance between the United States and the Soviet Union. It thus inevitably raised issues about long-term Soviet objectives in Europe. The challenge was not directed primarily at the nuclear-weapon states, such as Britain, France, or the United States, but rather at the major nonnuclear-weapon states in Western Europe. The SS-20 missile loomed as an instrument whose political purpose could be to focus pressure during crises on particular countries in Western Europe with a view to cutting the links between those countries and the American nuclear guarantee. American central systems would be independently countered by Soviet strategic forces. Such fears were compounded by the special characteristics of the SS-20 missile, particularly its accuracy and high and steady state of readiness, which made it into a potential first-strike weapon against key NATO defense installations. The strategic unity of the Western Alliance was challenged.

The Federal Republic understandably did not want to be the only continental nonnuclear-weapon state in Europe to house NATO's new intermediate-range missiles. Bonn wanted to avoid a position where the territory of the Federal Republic could make the sole regional nuclear riposte to Moscow within NATO's defense arrangements in Europe. Such a position could lead to a concentration of pressure on it during crises of the kind that the NATO decision on the deployment of intermediate-range missiles was designed to prevent or contain in the first place. There was a strategic reason as well: Deployment over a broader area would compel the Russians to consider preemption on a scale that would be incompatible with limited-war objectives and hence contribute to deterrence.

The "nonsingularity" requirement could have been satisfied with only Italian and British participation, or the principle could have been established that deployments would take place only in countries that had housed previous deployments of missiles capable of hitting targets in the Soviet Union. Beginning in 1958, for example, sixty Thor IRBMs were deployed in Britain; starting in 1959, thirty Jupiter IRBMs were deployed in Italy, and starting in 1960, fifteen were deployed in Turkey. They were all withdrawn by 1964. Between 1963 and 1968 six squadrons (ninety missiles) of MACE-B long-range cruise missiles capable of reaching targets in the Soviet Union were deployed in the Federal Republic.[9] Criteria of this kind were not adopted, however.

The burden-sharing perspective contributed to the emphasis that was put on adding some of the smaller NATO countries to the list of deployment states. Norway and Denmark both had established policies, dating from 1960, of not permitting the deployment or storage of nuclear weapons on their territory, and both countries stood by that position. The other Allies accepted the fact that the nonnuclear status of Scandinavian territory had become an important element in the equilibrium prevailing in Northern Europe and, by extension, in the political order in Europe more generally. The two Nordic countries for their part agreed to accept the assessment of their Allies regarding the requirements for deployment in other areas of Western Europe. In the name of an equitable sharing of burdens and risks, the decision on INF deployments was processed as a collective decision in NATO, in consonance with the frequently expressed wishes of the smaller states to participate in decision making. The Netherlands, in particular, had sought influence in the discussions about nuclear sharing in the early 1960s, while Norway, on the contrary, played a low-key role, staying out of the Nuclear Defense Affairs Committee established in 1965.

The Scandinavian nonnuclear option made it harder to argue in favor of deployment in Belgium and the Netherlands. The decision to deploy long-range cruise missiles in the Netherlands and Belgium may have produced a major clash between the role they were asked to play as a consequence of alignment on the one hand, and their perception of the role they should play in the European security order on the other. Threatening the Soviet Union with nuclear retaliation clearly exceeded Dutch and Belgian conceptions of their security roles, giving rise to tensions between state commitments and society's perception of state purposes. But for the INF case, the roles and options were not shaped in a manner capable of commanding broad social support. The Dutch and Belgian roles in the NATO response to the deployment of Soviet SS-20 missiles are fairly marginal, but they contribute rather significantly to the political vulnerability of the decision by the Alliance to deploy new missiles.

The issues involved are difficult to resolve, and the attitudes of the smaller Allies are certainly ambiguous. On the one hand, the Alliance will be stronger if a basic harmony prevails between what a member state does and what its society wants. However, the acceptability of roles and missions may change over time. A certain "socialization" may take place as a consequence of involvement and identification with the goals and purposes of the larger collectivity of the Alliance. There is considerable evidence that membership in NATO enjoys more widespread acceptance now than it did when NATO was formed, even if certain NATO policies are contentious. Such "socialization" seems more likely if the Alliance is viewed as the core of an international order rather than as a traditional alliance confined to the military protection of its members. Those who have traditionally opposed Norway's membership in NATO, for example, now concentrate on circumscribing and narrowing Norway's involvement in Alliance cooperation rather than attacking the membership as such.

Governments may be more prone to accept and strive for "socialization" than society at large. They are concerned about maintaining influence through access and participation, recognizing that self-exclusion from key activities in the Alliance will reduce their influence in key sectors of Alliance policy making. The governments of the smaller countries sometimes view themselves as mediators and bridge builders between competing views. The Netherlands, which sometimes refers to itself as a middle power, is particularly concerned about preserving influence and avoiding the connotation of second-class membership. In nuclear matters a fine line separates consultation and planning on the one hand, and actual decision on the other, since ultimately the power of decision rests with the nuclear-weapon states.

The decision to include several countries in the deployment of NATO's new missiles also tended to raise the number of missiles. The High Level Group, which studied the requirements for deployment in NATO, concluded by suggesting a range of 200 to 600 missiles.[10] The actual number of 572 was in reality decided by Washington and pegged at the high end of the scale by the Joint Chiefs of Staff with the support of the National Security Adviser, Zbigniew Brzezinski, who was concerned that the figure would be scaled down by NATO or as a result of negotiations with Moscow.[11] It is important, however, to observe that the number was not chosen with a view to matching numerically the Soviet deployment of SS-20s (by launchers, missiles, or warheads).

Deployment under the INF decision has proved controversial in the four countires of this study. These countries, together with the Federal Republic of Germany, represented the bulk of the opposition, which suggests that size and/or military vulnerability may be a particular factor. It is arguable that much of the opposition has been lopsided in the sense that it focused on the Western response rather than on the Eastern challenge, and that it applies a double standard by belittling or even justifying Soviet SS-20 deployment, which is much larger than that decided by the West. Furthermore, arguments are frequently presented as if deployments in the West would be less easy to reverse through negotiation than deployments in the East, and that modernization in the Soviet Union is somehow more acceptable than modernization in the West. Rather than build any theories on this point, it seems better to recognize a typical phenomenon of the political process in Western society focusing primarily on decision making in Western states—on the decisions within reach—rather than on those that result from the tightly protected deliberations in the Kremlin.

Western governments have thus far largely failed to acknowledge that nuclear weapons pose existential issues, and they have failed to come up with policies that incorporate and project that fact. The scale of destruction associated with nuclear warfare tends to saturate the consciousness of small polities, since extinction of the communities and nation with which the individual identifies appears to constitute a more direct and concrete danger than in mass societies; the sense of vulnerability is larger and more immediate. At the same time, and paradoxically, vulnerability in the face of the military might of the major powers is accepted as a fact of life. The addition of extra missiles in the armory of the Soviet Union is not widely believed to alter the condition of the small nations.

The NATO decision about the intermediate-range missiles became a "double-track" decision because Western societies demanded an alternative to open-ended arms competition. That construction made eminent sense insofar as the primary concern was focused on the need to preserve balance within the political order in Europe. Such balance was to be established and maintained at the lowest possible level of forces. The zero option was hailed as a generous and enlightened identification of an ideal outcome of the negotiations. However, it was hardly expected that the actual outcome would coincide with the ideal one. Compromises would have to be made in order to reach agreement. Hence, the dissatisfaction that developed in the four countries with the long-held unwillingness of Washington to move away from the zero option did not reflect disagreement with the ideal projection, but rather disappointment with the apparent inability of the Americans to use that projection as a means to identify other acceptable outcomes that would be substantially preferable to a situation of no agreement. It seemed like the old story of letting the best become an enemy of the good.

In this context, of course, impatience and frustration again tended to focus on accessible decisions and authorities; that is, those of the West. The perception of American intransigence was nourished also by Washington's insistence that the zero option was not only a negotiating position but also a moral position that assumed the quality of being nonnegotiable spite of reiterations to the effect that any Soviet counterproposal would receive serious consideration. The zero-zero formula established an object of juridical equality that would not result from implementation of the decision on deployment, but which nevertheless was flagged in the NATO communiqué as a negotiating principle, primarily on German insistence.

The smaller states in NATO are likely to continue pressing for solutions through the INF negotiations in Geneva. Reports and repeated evidence of internal disputes and battles over arms-control policy in Washington strengthen the perception that major obstacles to agreement are found on the shores of the Potomac as well as in Moscow. Hence, a measure designed to preserve and protect Alliance cohesion and coupling between the defense of Europe and American power risks becoming a major source of a transatlantic crisis of confidence.

If a primary purpose of the double-track decision was to bring the nuclear challenge in Europe into the framework of a negotiated balance between the two major custodians of peace, bringing Moscow's intermediate-range missiles down to zero is much less important than bringing them under a negotiated ceiling. It was deemed important to avoid the suggestion of a separate Euro-strategic balance sustained by intermediate-range nuclear forces in Europe in order to preserve the strategic unity of the Alliance and the credibility of the American guarantee to Western Europe. This perspective was embodied in the explicit presumption that Soviet-American negotiations about INF should take place in the context of negotiations on strategic arms limitation (and reduction). If the two sets of negotiations were to be merged, preferably under a single negotiator on both sides, a single-ceiling-force agreement based on the principle of a freedom to mix—that is, either side determines the distribution of assets among intercontinental ballistic missiles, submarine-launched missiles, bombers, and intermediate-range nuclear forces— could combine a situation of overall juridical equality with *de facto* differentials in each of the force components contained under the agreed ceiling. Partial or interim agreements regarding INF, as well as subceilings on particular weapon systems or classes of weapon systems, could be encompassed by such a formula.

Having been brought into the process of decision making and coresponsibility for decisions concerning the possible deployment of intermediate-range nuclear forces by NATO, the four countries are likely to insist on being heard in the internal deliberations in the Alliance concerning the progress of negotiations and implementation of the decision on deployment. The Special Consultative Group (SCG) developed into a rather successful mechanism for political consultations concerning the followup of the double-track decision. It is noteworhy, however, that apparently neither the "walk-in-the-woods" nor the "walk-in-the-park" formulas and initiatives were discussed in that consultative body prior to Washington's announcement of its position. The governments of NATO countries appear to have developed a certain ideological consensus concerning attitudes to Moscow in general and the INF negotiations in particular. That consensus does not totally reflect broad political consensus in all of the member countries, although the intensiveness and scale of concern and perceived saliency of the INF issue varies from country to country, and hence it tends to add to the frustration and alienation that developed in several NATO countries, particularly in the Protestant north.

Opposition and concern appears to focus on nuclear matters rather than on defense policy or the conduct of East-West relations in general. Expectations concerning codetermination that were nurtured by the SCG process will constrain management options in future. Demands for a merger of INF and START involve also a European claim for influence over negotiations concerning strategic nuclear weapons. American resistance may increase European fears and expectations for American unilateralism, particularly in view of the American failure to ratify the SALT II treaty, which had been strongly endorsed by NATO in the communiqué announcing the double-track decision in December 1979.[12]

Public opinion in the smaller states in the Alliance has not been moved by the complex reasons of state relating to the structure of the political order in Europe, and governments have failed to explain them. Instead, the issues have been reduced on both sides to simple tabulations of missiles colliding head-on with the popular perception that the number of nuclear weapons is already too large. There is no doubt an element of escapism in the attitudes that are particularly prevalent in the smaller nations—a presumption that the nuclear genie can be brought back into the bottle, that nuclear weapons are both too powerful and irrelevant, that it is possible to escape from the ugly world where nuclear weapons exist by declaration and announcement, and that the world can be stopped so that the virtuous countries may get off—but this does not change the reality of the concern that does exist.

Nuclear Weapons and Conventional Defense

The role of nuclear weapons in Alliance policy has proved a particularly vexing problem for the smaller states of the Alliance. The Netherlands and Belgium have been heavily involved in the implementation of Alliance arrangements for defense with nuclear weapons and appear to be engaged in a gradual process of extrication. Norway and Denmark have pursued a policy of distance and near virginity and are now engaged in asserting and delineating their special position and role.

The arrival of approximate parity at the level of battlefield nuclear weapons in Europe has called into question some of the basic tenets and trade-offs upon which the NATO posture and strategy have been predicated. A new consensus is in the making about the need to reduce reliance on nuclear weapons in general and to remove a substantial portion of the short-range battlefield nuclear weapons in particular. There is a problem of vulnerability and preemption, particularly of political decision making being imprisoned by the need to use the weapons before they were lost to a preemptive strike of the adversary. Views differ, however, with regard to how the change is to be effected. The Independent Commission on Disarmament and Security Issues (The Palma Commission) has put the matter on the political agenda through its proposal for a battlefield nuclear-weapon-free zone in Europe.[13] Others have argued that NATO should proceed to carry out the necessary changes and not let needed reform become hostage to the uncertain fortunes of negotiations about arms control.

The emerging consensus also appears to encompass a convergence around the need to move away from reliance on early use of nuclear weapons toward a posture based on the presumption of no early use. Some would move all the way toward an explicit no-first-use pledge, while others emphasize the need to impose operational constraints on the adversary and to impel him to disperse his forces by maintaining the deliberate ambiguity of the present presumption that the Alliance would employ nuclear weapons if necessary, but not necessarily *use* nuclear weapons. Reduced reliance on nuclear weapons is likely to be viewed as a desirable change by the smaller states in NATO. The major powers in the Alliance, however, may hesitate about heralding and implementing a major reform for fear of stimulating and legitimating propensities in the smaller Alliance states to disassociate themselves from the nuclear portion of the common defense, and thereby making more difficult the construction of a new balance. Norway and Denmark, on the other hand, would welcome changes that would reduce the distance between their defense posture and that of the Alliance as a whole, making their position less unique than in the past.

Creating viable conventional defense options for NATO will require careful attention to the interrelationship between strategy and politics, between the need for flexible options and military effectiveness. The conventional defense option must be considered in the context of the overarching task of reconstructing an operational concept for deterrence in Europe. A capability must exist for negating limited-war options for the Soviet Union. Credibility requires persuasiveness in the eyes of the would-be adversary and acceptability in the view of Western society. Deterrence and reassurance coexist like Siamese twins in the formulation of defense policy.

It is difficult to combine the prevailing notion about the likely uncontrollability of war in Europe with a strategy that relies on deliberate escalation, particularly since NATO could hardly expect to establish escalation dominance at every rung of the ladder. The key task for NATO strategy may instead be to block Soviet options rather than to rely on escalating a conflict to more extensive or intensive levels. The configuration of Soviet military posture in Europe and the military planning associated with that posture have led to a heavy Warsaw Pact reliance on speedy and tightly scheduled offensive operations. In addition to an ability to blunt the first echelon of an attack, NATO must maintain the ability to disrupt second-echelon forces, thereby blocking the primary-attack option of the Red Army. Yet, the Air-Land Battle Concept[14] currently under discussion and the various high-technology approaches to the delivery of dispensers with special submunitions, including terminally guided submunitions, raise fundamental issues of political purpose.[15]

Perceptions of NATO military strategy clearly have an impact on relations between Western Europe and Eastern Europe during peacetime. The prospects and scope for political relationships will be influenced by the perceived consequences of implementing the strategies for war. Eastern Europe may be locked into the unenviable position of constituting a "transit zone"[16] for the Red Army as well as a "firing zone" for SACEUR. In addition, NATO wartime strategies would, of course, also influence the behavior and incentives of the Soviet Union and the states of Eastern Europe in the event of crisis or war. In this connection one must consider the structural impact of a Western strategy that would threaten to increase the velocity and intensity of warfare beyond the point where political decision making would be able to cope with the conduct of war in decisive terms. A strategy of rapid and extensive preemption strikes against airfields and interdiction targets associated with the thrust of second-echelon forces toward the front could provide the adversary with strong incentives for equally extensive preemption, although the need to preempt extensively would tend to foreclose options for limited military action. The problem then becomes one of guarding against military posture driving decisions over the precipice under the pressure of an intense crisis.

There is a need for a broad consideration of alternatives with respect to conventional defense in Europe, including low-technology options, expanded reserves and reserve stocks, improved deployments, and obstacles. The smaller states have a stronger interest in options that permit them to participate effectively in the political decision making and military preparations of the Alliance, rather than being enveloped by the inexorable pressures of a war machine primed for rapid and extensive engagement in the event of war. Commitment to a conventional war of high velocity and intensity could produce social opposition reminiscent of the opposition to nuclear warfare, particularly in densely populated countries like the Netherlands and Belgium.

In view of the topography, demography, and territorial size of Norway, protracted defense—the trading of space for time—makes a conventional option more attainable than in the Danish, Belgian, and Dutch perspectives. The nuclear option involves a series of complex strategic evaluations. Under conditions of nuclear parity, maintaining the saliency of the nuclear threshold may be considered more important than imposing uncertainty concerning the risks of escalation for purposes of deterrence. The dangers of inadvertent escalation may outweigh the possible benefits to deterrence from uncertainty, particularly in view of the intricate comingling of theater and nuclear systems due east of the Norwegian border. The strategic calculations are affected by the contiguity of Soviet territory and initial deployment of weapons. A threat to use nuclear weapons as a means of deliberate escalation in consonance with NATO strategy could tax the credibility of extended deterrence unduly during crises, and it could produce uncomfortable pressures for preemption. Confidence could erode, moreover, in peacetime as a result of the subliminal questioning of American willingness to risk New York and Chicago for Finnmark. The Low Countries, and Denmark to a somewhat lesser degree, find protection against limited war threats in their integration into the defense arrangements for the central front; Norway finds such protection in its proximity to a vital strategic-base complex of the Soviet Union and in a posture that can deny the Soviet forces the imposition of a rapid *fait accompli* in northern Norway. For the deterrence of a major war they are all dependent on the military capacity—nuclear as well as conventional—of their major allies, but they bite into the conventional/nuclear dilemma from different angles.

Perspectives on Political Order

The smaller states live off the balance of power that is configured and maintained by the major powers. They tend to view alliances as a means of obtaining protection through solidarity and political commitments rather than as mechanisms for joint management of the balance of power. Smaller states are used to a condition of permanent vulnerability and power differentiation. Hence, they may be more prone to accept inequality in certain dimensions of military capability than the major powers, whose rivalry and position are determined by perceptions of relative capacity to attack and defend. For similar reasons they are more prone to believe in extended deterrence, to trust guarantees, even in circumstances where uncertainties and doubts arise in the calculations of countries with a larger impact on the calibration of the overall balance of military force and pattern of political influence.

Denmark and Norway have adopted an explicit policy of not permitting the stationing of foreign troops on their territories in peacetime. Dutch and Belgian security is not made dependent on the presence of Allied troops as protection. Hence, their relationship with the major protector, the United States, does not revolve around a given level of physical presence, and so it creates greater immunity against American vacillation and a firmer basis for formal equality in their cooperation. The psychological and social tensions produced by the presence of foreign troops in a country are particularly strong in small states, which jealously guard their independence and identity. The issue is particularly clear in Norway, where the defense effort is concentrated in some of the smallest communities in a sparsely populated country. Nevertheless, all four countries live off the American commitment to Europe, manifested in the physical presence of American troops in the Federal Republic.

Norway has constructed a system of unilateral restraints. Some are made explicitly conditional on the good behavior of would-be adversaries; others are confidence-building measures with fewer qualifications.[17] The restraints have been adopted in order to reassure neighboring states, to maintain broad public support for the main lines of Norwegian security policy and to contain and deflect potential pressures from her great-power allies. Because of its strategic position and contiguity with the Soviet Union, Norway has been concerned about maintaining national control over activities that have a direct impact on Soviet-Norwegian relations in the high north in order to reduce the danger of the latter becoming hostage to American-Soviet confrontations. Norway's self-denying ordinances do not constitute reservations about the basic political purposes of the Western Alliance; they refer to specific arrangements for the organization of military security. Circumstances have forced Norway to focus more on the detailed configuration of such arrangements than they have the other smaller NATO countries in Northern Europe. Hence, Norway does not permit the stationing of foreign troops as long as it is not attacked or threatened with attack, no nuclear weapons are stored or deployed in Norway, and no Allied maneuvers take place east of the 24 degrees east meridian. Denmark has followed the Norwegian lead by not permitting the stationing of foreign troops or nuclear weapons, initially "under the existing circumstances"; now the formulation is "in peacetime." In addition, Denmark does not participate in NATO maneuvers east of the 17 degrees east meridian.

The geographical circumstances of the Netherlands and Belgium are different. However, domestic constraints are growing with regard to their involvement in nuclear-weapon arrangements. The Netherlands accepted six nuclear missions but is now in the process of cutting back, possibly to two. In Belgium the nuclear issue did not achieve real political saliency until the end of the 1970s, with the controversies surrounding the ERW or "neutron bomb" and NATO's decision on INF modernization. However, Dutch and Belgium constraints with regard to nuclear deployments reflect the domestic politicization of the issues rather than an explicit policy of confidence building, aiming for national rather than international reassurance.

The smaller states are likely to view the issues of political order in rather general and formal terms, focusing on the value of agreement and constraint rather than on the detailed configuration of the pattern of political influence. Hence, there has been a certain propensity in the four countries to accept the apparent equity and simplicity of the Soviet contention that their intermediate-range missile force should be equated with the level of British and French nuclear forces. The real issues of political order in this connection seldom emerge in the discussion. The Soviet contention would amount to a construction of a Eurostrategic balance based on Soviet, French, and British forces, excluding the only nuclear forces in NATO with the announced purpose of protecting nonnuclear-weapon states; namely, those of the United States. It would tend to equate nuclear protection with nuclear possession. Furthermore, the formula would seem to institute the principle of a Soviet right to match every potential adversary in a manner that would result in a right to maintain numerical superiority in nuclear weapons vis-á-vis each potential adversary.

In addition, a construction whereunder the level of Soviet INF deployments were made dependent on the total level of British and French *strategic* forces as a result of Soviet-American agreement would imply a *droit de regard* for the Soviet Union vis-à-vis allies of the United States who have chosen to take out extra insurance for the protection of national interests in extremis. The implications for the whole structure of the Western Alliance could be substantial. Acceptance of the formula would mean falling into line with the preferred Soviet conception of security in Europe. This is not to argue that arrangements for taking into account the existence of British and French systems—which in nature and purpose are strategic forces rather than theater forces—could not be found in the context of a comprehensive U.S.-Soviet agreement encompassing both strategic and intermediate-range nuclear forces. That point, however, is rarely focused on in the four countries.

The role of the smaller states in the construction and management of the security arrangements that sustain the political order in Europe is better defined and accepted in terms of specific tasks, where the participation and contribution of the smaller states are indispensable to the common defense of the Alliance. Forward defense on the northern flank, denial of limited-attack options against the flanks of the Alliance, support functions for the American strategic deterrent, and protection of NATO's sea lines of communication and of the lines of supply to the central front constitute discrete and essential tasks toward the solution of which these smaller states have played a critical role.

Smaller and medium powers have played an active role in the construction of confidence-building measures within the CSCE (Conference on Security and Cooperation in Europe) process. Of the four countries, Norway has played the most active role, while the Netherlands has concentrated on human rights. Confidence- and security-building measures constitute possible elements in comprehensive strategies for shaping and structuring political relations, means that may protect the political processes against the danger of being enveloped and dominated by military considerations. Reducing the shadows thrown by military forces is a primary concern of the front-line countries. They will want to expand the system of notification and observation to encompass constraints on military activities, including special restrictions in national border areas, and to extend the system of notification to comprise also amphibious, air, and naval forces. The latter is likely to also constitute a Danish concern.

The Challenge of Arms Control

In general, the politics of the four countries have sustained a substantial defense effort, a much higher effort than small states have normally sustained in the past. Participation in an alliance lends credence to the proposition that it is possible to establish a plausible defense. A certain amount of implicit parasitism is inherent in an alliance among countries of unequal strength and resources. However, the very ability to borrow power from the strong sustains the credibility of the weak in a world where armaments are maintained at high levels. Alignment for many weak states constitutes the alternative to appeasement or subservience. And even those states that, because of opportunity or necessity, have adopted a posture of nonalignment in Europe enjoy drawing rights on the balance of power that is maintained by the two alliances.

However, the steady and sustained effort needed to maintain the balance of power requires social support that will crumble unless visible and credible efforts are made to stake out an alternative to an indefinite extension of the arms competition. The vision of a more rational and humane order where weapons are hobbled rather than released and where the arsenals dwindle rather than grow must be preserved and pursued if democratic societies are to make the sacrifices needed to maintain military security. Weariness and desperation will coalesce in the absence of a credible approach to arms control. The notions that war cannot happen (because peace has come to be taken for granted) and that war is imminent (because of an escalation of the arms race) coexist and interact in ways that produce widespread protest against the apparent incapacity or unwillingness of governments to assert political control over the forces of destruction.

Smaller countries are prone to place high hopes on arms control. However, as arms control has come to occupy a key position in their foreign policies, and as present burdens are wrapped in promises of future delivery from danger, it can breed frustration and estrangement. The institutionalization of arms control that took place during the 1960s and 1970s tended to obscure the purposes of arms control and the obstacles to its achievement. Most important, the interrelationships between political order, military balance, and stability in various dimensions and contexts were quickly forgotten as experts set out to deal with the engineering of arms-control arrangements.[18] In fact, a "dual hostage-relationship" has emerged: Defense policy has been made a hostage to the uncertain fortunes of arms control in order to broaden social acceptability, and at the same time arms control itself has become hostage to world insecurity and tensions arising from East-West competition outside the European arena. Increasingly, therefore, frustrations about the failure of arms control to deliver on promises tend to feed back into the discussion of NATO strategy and defense posture. The pursuit of negotiated arms control can indeed become an obstacle to the pursuit of arms-control objectives by other means.

It is not only a question, then, of not asking arms control to do too much, but also of being able to pursue the objectives that arms control presumably can achieve. The new emphasis on reduction rather than just stabilization of nuclear forces at high levels would appear to be in consonance with the social requirements in the smaller states—and in the larger ones too. However, the parameters for reduction should be chosen so as to generate increased stability rather than new instabilities. Formulas that would structure incentives to reverse undesirable trends—for example, by encouraging the nuclear-weapon states to eschew large missiles with multiple independently targetable reentry vehicles (MIRV) and eventually to choose small single-warhead missiles rather than MIRV'ed systems—illustrate a possible approach to meaningful arms control.[19] However, Soviet vested interests and investments may militate against transformations that are driven by technological choices made by the Americans.

The deliberate construction of linkage between the general foreign-policy behavior of the Soviet Union and the Western approach to negotiations about arms control is likely to increase tensions within the Western Alliance. To begin with, the assessments of issues, interests, and alternatives in connection with conflicts arising outside the NATO treaty area are likely to differ. Differences are likely to widen, moreover, to the extent that threats to disengage from arms-control negotiations and agreements are used as means for exerting pressure on the parties involved in such conflicts. The smaller states in the Alliance are likely to object to arms control being converted into a reward for the good behavior of would-be adversaries rather than a mechanism for the pursuit of shared interests with respect to the threat of military instabilities. Linkage policies are likely to reduce the commitment of the smaller Allies to the broader political purposes of the Alliance, for they contain the danger that the policies of the great powers of the Alliance, particularly the United States, outside of NATO, will come to be viewed as incompatible with their essential interests in stability within the treaty area and in relations with the East.

The smaller states cannot produce arms-control agreements against the will of the major powers. They do not possess insights into the intricacies of modern weapons and their interrelationships with political objectives and structures that have escaped the more powerful actors in the international arena. They can obtain influence by acquiring competence and insight into special aspects of the arms-control problem (as Norway has done with respect to the verification of a nuclear test ban or a chemical-weapons agreement), or by posting particularly skillful and persistent diplomats to negotiating arenas where they participate (as the Netherlands has done to the MBFR negotiations in Vienna). In any case, they will continue to attach great importance to the pursuit of arms control at the level of Alliance objectives. Such emphasis is in consonance with the pressures emanating from their societies, and in objective terms smaller states stand to gain from movements to reduce the impact of arms in the pattern of international politics. Arms tend to differentiate the role and influence of nations, to create hierarchies, pressures, and dependencies. The smaller states inevitably prefer a pattern where the legal notion of the equality of states has a larger impact on the conduct of international relations.

From the point of view of social acceptability and legitimacy, it is important to the smaller countries that NATO appears to be committed to a vigorous pursuit of arms control. The complementary objectives of deterrence and defense on the one hand, and détente and arms control on the other, constitute the only viable basis for an active commitment on behalf of the smaller states to the Western Alliance. In view of the zigzag nature of the thrust of policy in recent times, it could prove useful for NATO to undertake another study of the overall political purposes and strategy of the Alliance for the 1980s, a kind of up-date of the Harmel Report of 1967. There is a need to redefine and reaffirm the nature and purposes of an alliance that was born under political conditions very different form those of the 1980s. In the absence of each reexamination, the essence of the Alliance may wither away by default and stability in Europe and the viability of democracies could suffer serious strains.

The Role of the Smaller States

The four countries occupy different strategic positions in the NATO defense arrangements for Europe. Belgium and the Netherlands provide key access points to the central front. Denmark links the central front to Northern Europe, and Norway holds the key position in a rather elongated northern flank. NATO's defense priorities and efforts are often discussed in terms of choices between the flanks and the center, a false dichotomy that overlooks the interrelationship between the northern flank and the central front. A stable central front, where stability rests on a credible NATO posture for blocking Soviet-attack options, constitutes a *conditio sine qua non* for the Alliance's ability to extend credible protection and guarantees to the northern flank. Similarly, a credible ability to deny the Russians a limited-war option against the key strategic areas of northern Norway is a necessary precondition for the ability of the Alliance to extend protection to the sea lines of communication necessary to bring reinforcements to the central front from North America. Hence, the security of each of the four countries is dependent on the ability of the Alliance to maintain and protect the strategic unity of the area to which it applies.

The smaller states expect the major powers in the Alliance to have a major say, but they expect to be heard as well. The Alliance constitutes an important framework for political consultation, involvement, and co-determination. Hence, they have consistently objected to schemes for select groups or directorates in the Alliance, fearing exclusion from the councils of political decision making. Such exclusion would inevitably raise domestic issues about their alleged influence, which has always been a major argument for alignment in the public position taken by the governments of the smaller members of NATO. Nuclear matters may constitute a special case, although the Netherlands in particular has objected to exclusive arrangements even in this realm. The Nuclear

Planning Group has been reconstructed to include all of the members of the military organization of the Alliance on a permanent basis.

Does "small-state unionism" have a role to play in the future of the Alliance? The issue assumed renewed attention after the Social Democratic parties of Belgium, the Netherlands, Norway, and Denmark started to meet regularly to discuss security issues, most particularly the INF problem. However, as the West German Social Democratic Party and even the British Labour Party have participated, it is apparent that "Scandilux" is primarily an example of transnational party caucusing. In fact, it is rather difficult to see how size could become a criterion for subgrouping within the Alliance. In security terms the smaller members have stronger and more "natural" interests in intensifying their cooperation with some of the major powers in the Alliance—in the case of Norway, for instance, with the United States, Canada, and the United Kingdom—the countries that provide the major sources of reinforcement.

However, small-power unionism could develop in response to selective caucusing of the major powers within the Alliance. The tendency of the Western economic summits to discuss general political issues has been viewed with apprehension by the small states of NATO that are excluded from that council. Similarly, Norway remains concerned lest the European Political Cooperation of the European Community countries develop into a European caucus on security issues preempting the discussions in the North Atlantic Council. The primary interest of the smaller states of NATO is that NATO remain a multinational alliance where the procedures for consultation and force planning continue to be based on the presumption of the equality of the member states with respect to participation and rights.

Selective small-state consultation on the basis of like-minded approaches to, for example, arms control and disarmament could, however, prove both feasible and beneficial. A precedent exists in the successful cooperation with the developing countries by a group of like-minded industrialized countries. However, like-mindedness is unlikely to prove a function of size but rather to reflect political values, geographical circumstances, acquired competence, and assigned priories. In the wake of the INF controversy, arms control is likely to be accorded a higher political priority and saliency in the four countries.

Participation in a multinational alliance enables the small states to pursue their idealistic visions of equity and world order rather than succumb to the ignoble "realism" or escapism of adherence to the principles of *sauve qui peut*. At the same time, the Alliance must remain truly ecumenical with respect to its ideological orientation. The Alliance would weaken if it were reconstructed on a more narrow party-ideological basis. It should remain sufficiently flexible to enable member states to pursue foreign-policy objectives and roles that are consistent with their national ethos and the outcome of their electoral processes.

Neglectful or Neglected?

Are the four smaller Northern European states behaving like neglectful allies? The available evidence hardly supports such a conclusion. According to most indexes of burden sharing, they appear to perform in consonance with their relative capacities. The concept of burden sharing is, however, misleading and inadequate. The defense tasks are substantial, and some of the four states are being more neglectful than the others. Norway and the Netherlands probably exhibit the more substantial efforts. Norway has been engaged in a major effort in cooperation with some of her principal allies to improve the arrangements for external reinforcements. The adoption of SACEUR's RRP (Rapid Reinforcement Plan) and the conclusion of COB (Colocated Operating Bases) agreements for the major military airfields in Norway produce the option of tripling the number of modern fighter aircraft that could be committed quickly in an emergency to a battle for the control of Norwegian airspace.[20] Belgium and the Netherlands contribute significantly to the defense of the central front, each with an army corps of six brigades. All four countries maintain a system of conscription: in the Netherlands it is fourteen to sixteen months in the army or fourteen to seventeen months in the navy or the air force; in Norway, twelve months in the army or fifteen months in the navy or air force; in Belgium, eight to nine months; and in Denmark, nine months for all services.

Public opinion in all of the four countries supports continued membership in the Alliance by overwhelming majorities and membership in NATO is not an issue of active political contention. Views on the nature and purpose of the Alliance, however, may be changing, with more minimalist views prevailing in Scandinavia. An alliance must prove relevant to the concerns and interests of the member states to remain viable and pertinent. Since the concerns and assessments that affect the choice of policy and strategy rather than basic interests have been changing over time, the Alliance must prove able to adapt accordingly. Management is difficult, however, since the shifting concerns and assessments are not synchronized among the Allies. Obviously, changing perspectives and priorities of the major powers in the Alliance have a stronger impact on the direction of Alliance policy than changes taking place in the outlooks of the minor states. Systematic divergences between the major and the minor states could, however, breed attitudes of disillusion and estrangement toward alignment in the polities of the latter.

In a comparative opinion poll conducted in September 1982, 33 percent of the Norwegian and 32 percent of the Dutch respondents considered the U.S. role in defending Western interests as "essential," which were the highest scores after those of the Federal Republic, with 46 percent.[21] In a similar comparative poll in February 1982, 49 percent of the Danish respondents thought that Denmark should remain in NATO as it is presently constituted, while 10 percent favored the establishment of a unified West European command, but allied to the United States. For

Belgium the corresponding figures were 25 percent and 18 percent (the "don't know" portion was high: 21 percent and 35 percent, respectively).[22]

But there was substantial opposition to the deployment of new intermediate-range missiles to Western Europe in all of the four countries. Interestingly enough, a Norwegian poll showed that the propensity to support NATO's double-track decision was somewhat stronger among those who had experienced and remember the occupation during World War II—58 percent versus an average 53 percent.[23] The results of the polls on public support for the NATO position on new missiles are in part contradictory, sometimes because of the formulation of the questions, the context, and sequence in which the questions occur and the lack of familiarity with the issues. (Norwegian data indicate that the propensity to support the double-track decision is considerably higher among those who profess to know the contents of the NATO double-track decision than among those who do not.) Polls, of course, do not measure the intensity with which the respondents hold the views that are recorded. But the political cultures of the four smaller NATO Allies in Northern Europe comprise the tradition of governments that do not fight against strong minorities in the security-policy area for fear of shattering the basic consensus.

The four smaller states live off the balance of power, but they tend to view the arms competition as an external phenomenon beyond their influence. In the comparative opinion poll in September 1982, 57 percent of the Norwegian respondents and 38 percent of the Dutch (the highest and third-highest score) considered the Soviet military buildup most responsible for the current international tension, but at the same time 28 percent of the Norwegian respondents and 24 percent of the Dutch held that the more recent U.S. military buildup was also responsible.[24] The vicissitudes of the arms race cause frustrations, bewilderment, and ambiguity, particularly with regard to their major protector. The United States should be strong enough to deter the Soviet Union, but not so strong as to appear menacing for her small allies.

Have the small Allies been neglected by their great-power friends? Hardly in terms of strategic involvement and attention to the organization of the common defense; however, in terms of understanding of the particular nature and functioning of their political cultures and systems, there has been some benign neglect, which harbors the seeds of malign consequences for NATO.

Notes

1. George Liska, *Nations in Alliance: The Limits of Interdependence* (Baltimore: The John Hopkins Press, 1982), 3.

2. Caspar W. Weinberger, *Report on Allied Contributions to the Common Defense.* Department of Defense report by the Secretary of Defense to Congress (March 1982), 6.

3. Ibid.

4. Mancur Olson, *The Logic of Collective Action: Public Goals and the Theory of Groups* (Cambridge, Mass.: Harvard University Press, 1981), chap. 1.

5. Ibid., 34.

6. Ibid., 35.

7. Ibid., 35.

8. For further discussion, see Johan Jørgen Holst, "Bedrohungen Ausserhalb des NATO-Gebiets: Strategische Interessen und innenpolitische Zwänge," *Europa Archiv*, 37, no. 21 (1982): 629–38.

9. For a good analysis of NATO's first INF controversy, see Michael H. Armacost, *The Politics of Weapons Innovation: The Thor-Jupiter Controversy* (New York: Columbia University Press, 1969).

10. The best account of the process that produced the double-track decision of 12 December 1979 is David C. Elliot, *Decision at Brussels: The Politics of Nuclear Forces* (Santa Monica, Calif.: California Seminar on International Security and Foreign Policy, 1981). See also Hans-Henrik Holm and Nikolai Pedersen, eds., *The European Missiles Crisis: Nuclear Weapons and Security Policy* (London: Frances Pinter, 1983).

11. Zbigniew Brzezinski, *Power and Principle* (New York: Farrar, Strauss, Giroux, 1983), 308.

12. For a further analysis of the issues and exploration of possible outcomes for the INF negotiations, see Johan Jørgen Holst, *Kjernevapen og forhandlinger: Hva ma gjøres?* (Oslo: Den Norske Atlanterhavskomite, 1983).

13. *Common Security: A Programme for Disarmament*, Report of the Independent Commission on Disarmament and Security Issues (London: Pan Books, 1982).

14. See Report FM-100-5 *Operations* (Washington, D.C.: Headquarters of the Department of the Army, 1982).

15. An informed presentation of the technological options may be found in N. F. Wikner, "Interdicting Fixed Targets with Conventional Weapons," *Armed Forces Journal International* (March 1983): 77–95.

16. See the interesting discussion of the Polish predicament by Ryszard Frelek, "Nuclear Weapons and European Security: A Polish Perspective," in *Security, Order, and the Bomb: Nuclear Weapons in the Politics and Defense Planning of Nonnuclear Weapon States*, ed. Johan Jørgen Holst (Oslo: Universitetsforlaget, 1982), 93–99.

17. For a general discussion of the functions and categories of confidence-building measures, see Johan Jørgen Holst, "Confidence-Building Measures: A Conceptual Framework," *Survival*, 25, no. 1 (1983): 2–15.

18. See the chapters by Hedley Bull, Johan J. Holst, Uwe Nerlich, Henry S. Rowen, and Philip Windsor in *Soviet Power and Western Negotiating Policies*, ed. Uwe Nerlich, vol. 2 (Cambridge, Mass.: Ballinger, 1983).

19. See, for example, Henry A. Kissinger, "A New Approach to Arms Control," *Time*, 21 March 1983: 24–26; and Jan M. Lodal, "Finishing START," *Foreign Policy*, 48 (Fall 1982): 66–81.

20. See Johan Jørgen Holst, "Norwegian Security Policy for the 1980's," *Cooperation and Conflict*, 17, no. 4 (1982): 207–96.

21. The Atlantic Institute for International Affairs—International Herald Tribune-Louis Harris Poll, *Europe and the U.S.: Diverging Perceptions? A Comparative Opinion Poll in 8 Western Countries* (20 October 1982), 7.

22. Comparative Gallup Poll in Great Britain, France, Germany, Belgium, Switzerland, Denmark, and the United States, February 1982, commissioned by and published in the *Daily Telegraph*, 8 and 9 March 1982.

23. "NOI-undersøkelse," *Aftenposten*, 26 (March 1983).

24. The Atlantic Institute Poll, *Europe and the U.S.*, 11.

Index

The Authors

Arne Olav Brundtland is a senior research fellow in strategic studies at the Norwegian Institute of International Affairs, Oslo and is editor-in-chief of the Institute's journal *Internasjonal Politikk*. He writes a weekly syndicated commentary in the Norwegian press and is the author of *Sikkerhetspolitisk Omproving?* (Reappraisal of Security?) Oslo, 1968. He was educated at Oslo University and has studied at Harvard, Helsinki, and Moscow universities.

Dr. Gregory Flynn is Deputy Director of the Atlantic Institute for International Affairs and Director of the Institute's International Studies Program. Among his publications are *The Public and Atlantic Defense* (Rowman & Allanheld, 1985), *The Internal Fabric of Western Security* (Allanheld, Osmun, 1981), and "Opinions publiques et mouvements pacifistes," in *Pacifisme et Dissuasion*, ed. Pierre Lellouche, (IFRI, 1983).

Dr. Martin Heisler is Associate Professor of Government and Politics, University of Maryland and a former member of the Political Science faculties of the University of Illinois (Urbana-Champaign) and Aarhus University (Denmark). He has published widely in the fields of European politics, comparative public policy, and international relations and is currently writing a book on the security-related problems of Western European states.

Dr. Johan Jørgen Holst is Director of the Norwegian Institute of International Affairs. From 1976 to 1981 he was Secretary of State in the Norwegian Ministries of Foreign Affairs and Defense. He is coeditor of *Beyond Nuclear Deterrence* and has written widely on arms control and defense issues, contributing articles to numerous books, journals, and newspapers.

Dr. Josef Joffe is columnist and foreign editor of the *Süddeutsche Zeitung*. Prior to that he was professorial lecturer at the Johns Hopkins School of Advanced International Studies and Senior Associate of the Carnegie Endowment for International Peace. He has written numerous articles on the subject of international affairs and strategic issues.

Dr. Luc Reychler is Professor of International Relations and Strategic Studies at the Catholic University of Leuven and Director of the University's Center for Strategic Studies. He is the author of *The Patterns of Diplomatic Thinking* (1979) and *Directory Guide of European Security and*

Defense Research (1985) as well as many articles on European security and arms control.

Jan Siccama is a member of the research staff of the Netherlands Institute of International Relations "Clingendael". He is author of *Call Sign: Air-Land Battle* and numerous articles on arms control, strategy, and European security. He is currently doing quantitative research into the causes of war.